Religions of a Single God

Religions of a Single God

A Critical Introduction to Monotheisms from Judaism to Baha'i

Zeba Crook

SHEFFIELD UK   BRISTOL CT

Published by Equinox Publishing Ltd.

UK: Office 415, The Workstation, 15 Paternoster Row, Sheffield, South Yorkshire S1 2BX

USA: ISD, 70 Enterprise Drive, Bristol, CT 06010

www.equinoxpub.com

First published 2019

British Library Cataloguing-in-Publication Data

A catalogue record for this book is available from the British Library.

ISBN-13   978 1 78179 805 8   (hardback)
ISBN-13   978 1 78179 806 5   (paperback)
ISBN-13   978 1 78179 807 2   (ePDF)

Library of Congress Cataloging-in-Publication Data

Names: Crook, Zeba A., author.
Title: Religions of a Single God : A Critical Introduction to Monotheisms from Judaism to Baha'i / Zeba Crook.
Description: Bristol : Equinox Publishing Ltd., 2019. | Includes bibliographical references and index.
Identifiers: LCCN 2018025072 (print) | LCCN 2018045576 (ebook) | ISBN 9781781798072 (ePDF) | ISBN 9781781798058 (hb) | ISBN 9781781798065 (pb)
Subjects: LCSH: Monotheism. | Religions.
Classification: LCC BL221 (ebook) | LCC BL221 .C76 2019 (print) | DDC 211/.34–dc23
LC record available at https://lccn.loc.gov/2018025072

Designed and produced by Queenston Publishing, Hamilton, Ontario, Canada and Witchwood Production House, Sheffield, UK

Printed and bound by Ashford Colour Press, UK

Contents

List of Figures

-

List of Figures

List of Figures

List of Text Boxes

Theory	Interactions	Primary Texts
People	Concepts	Places

Sources and Acknowledgments

Original Maps

The maps (Figures 9, 20, 24, 25, 29, 32, 40, 45) are courtesy of Don Shewan.

Wikimedia Commons

Figure 2. Portrait of Sigmund Freud. Photographer: Ludwig Grillich. Public domain. https://commons.wikimedia.org/wiki/File:Sigmund_freud_um_1905.jpg

Figure 3. Portrait of Karl Marx. Photographer: John Jabez Edwin Mayall. Public domain. https://commons.wikimedia.org/wiki/File:Karl_Marx_001.jpg

Figure 4. An illustrated page from the Sarajevo Haggadah. Public domain. https://en.wikipedia.org/wiki/Sarajevo_Haggadah#/media/File:Sarejevohagadah.gif

Figure 5. "The Resurrection" by Piero della Francesca. Public domain. https://commons.wikimedia.org/wiki/File:Resurrection.JPG

Figure 16. Aerial view of Masada. Photograph: Andrew Shiva. Creative Commons Attribution-Share Alike 4.0 International (https://creativecommons.org/licenses/by-sa/4.0/deed.en). https://az.wikipedia.org/wiki/Masada#/media/File:Israel-2013-Aerial_21-Masada.jpg

Figure 22. Illuminated manuscript of Jewish moneylenders in France. Public domain. https://commons.wikimedia.org/wiki/File:Medieval-Jewish-moneylenders.jpg

Figure 23. The Game of the Goose. Musée du Barreau de Paris. Public domain. https://commons.wikimedia.org/wiki/File:Jeu_de_l%27oie_-_l%27Affaire_Dreyfus_et_de_la_V%C3%A9rit%C3%A9_1898.png

Figure 26. The Catacombe di San Gaudioso. Photograph: Fabien Bièvre-Perrin. Creative Commons Attribution-Share Alike 4.0 International (https://creativecommons.org/licenses/by-sa/4.0/deed.en). https://commons.wikimedia.org/wiki/File:Catacombe_di_San_Gaudioso_(Napoli)_03.jpg

Figure 27. Mosaic of Constantine in Hagia Sophia, Istanbul. Photograph: Myrabella. Creative Commons CC0 1.0 Universal Public Domain Dedication (https://creativecommons.org/publicdomain/zero/1.0/deed.en). https://commons.wikimedia.org/wiki/File:Constantine_I_Hagia_Sophia.jpg

Figure 31. "Our Lady of the Sign." Public domain. https://commons.wikimedia.org/wiki/File:Mother_of_God_-Znameniye.jpg

Figure 35. An etching by Jacques Callot depicting a hanging. Public domain. https://commons.wikimedia.org/wiki/File:The_Hanging_by_Jacques_Callot.jpg

Figure 36. Sermon delivered by Rev. Jonathan Edwards. Library of Congress. Public domain. https://commons.wikimedia.org/wiki/File:Sinners_in_the_Hands_of_an_Angry_God_by_Jonathan_Edwards_1741.jpg

Figure 39. The Investiture of Ali at Ghadir Khumm by Ibn al-Kutbi. Public domain. https://commons.wikimedia.org/wiki/File:Investiture_of_Ali_Edinburgh_codex.jpg

Figure 43. The Umayyad Mosque as depicted in the Book of Wonders. Creative Commons Attribution 4.0 International (https://creativecommons.org/licenses/by/4.0/deed.en). https://commons.wikimedia.org/wiki/File:Book_of_Wonders_folio_36b_cropped.jpg

Figure 48. Portuguese discoveries and explorations (1415–1543). Creative Commons Attribution-Share Alike 3.0 Unported (https://creativecommons.org/licenses/by-sa/3.0/deed.en). https://commons.wikimedia.org/wiki/File:Portuguese_discoveries_and_explorationsV2en.png

Figure 50. The 1978 Iranian revolution. Public domain. https://commons.wikimedia.org/wiki/File:1978_Iranian_revolution_-_row_of_men_holding_khomeini%27s_photos.jpg

Figure 53. Shofar, a Jewish ritual horn. Photograph: Zachi Evenor. Creative Commons Attribution 3.0 Unported (https://creativecommons.org/licenses/by/3.0/deed.en). https://commons.wikimedia.org/wiki/File:Shofar-16-Zachi-Evenor.jpg

Figure 54. "Helping a Dying Impenitent" Francisco Goya. Public domain. https://commons.wikimedia.org/wiki/File:St._Francis_Borgia_Helping_a_Dying_Impenitent_by_Goya.jpg

Figure 55. A representation of a demon in Islamic mythology from the fifteenth century by Mehmed Siyah Kalem. Public domain. https://en.wikipedia.org/wiki/File:Depiction_of_a_demon_in_Islamic_mythology.jpg

Figure 58. Hasidic Jews in Stamford Hill. Photograph: dcaseyphoto. Creative Commons Attribution 2.0 Generic (https://creativecommons.org/licenses/by/2.0/deed.en). https://commons.wikimedia.org/wiki/File:Stamford_hill.jpg

Figure 59. Torah scroll. Photograph: Willy Horsch. Creative Commons Attribution-Share Alike 4.0 International (https://creativecommons.org/licenses/by-sa/4.0/deed.en). https://commons.wikimedia.org/wiki/File:K%C3%B6ln-Tora-und-Innenansicht-Synagoge-Glockengasse-040.JPG

Figure 60. Lindisfarne Gospels. Public domain. https://commons.wikimedia.org/wiki/File:Meister_des_Book_of_Lindisfarne_001.jpg

Figure 65. "The Rapture: One at the Mill" by Jan Luyken. Public domain. https://commons.wikimedia.org/wiki/File:Teachings_of_Jesus_39_of_40._the_rapture._one_at_the_mill._Jan_Luyken_etching._Bowyer_Bible.gif

Figure 66. Teresa of Avila by Peter Paul Rubens. Public domain. https://commons.wikimedia.org/wiki/File:Peter_Paul_Rubens_138.jpg

Figure 67. Whirling Dervishes. Photograph: Kemal.kubbe. Creative Commons Attribution-Share Alike 4.0 International (https://creativecommons.org/licenses/by-sa/4.0/deed.en). https://commons.wikimedia.org/wiki/File:Whirling_Dervishes_at_Hodjapasha.jpg

Figure 68. 20 Somoni banknote. Photograph: Steve Burke. Creative Commons Attribution-Share Alike 4.0 International, 3.0 Unported, 2.5 Generic, 2.0 Generic and 1.0 Generic. https://commons.wikimedia.org/wiki/File:TajikistanP17-20Somoni-1999(2000)-donatedsb_b.jpg

Figure 72. "Talmud Readers." Public domain. https://commons.wikimedia.org/wiki/File:Adolf_Behrman_-_Talmudysci.jpg

Figure 73. "The Adoration of the Magi," by Edward Burne-Jones. Public domain. https://commons.wikimedia.org/wiki/File:Edward_Burne-Jones_-_The_Adoration_of_the_Magi_-_Google_Art_Project.jpg

Figure 75. Napoleon Bonaparte emancipating the Jews. Public domain. https://commons.wikimedia.org/wiki/File:Napoleon_stellt_den_israelitischen_Kult_wieder_her,_30._Mai_1806.jpg

Figure 76. Mikveh, Boskovice, Czech Republic. Photograph: Filo cz. Creative Commons Attribution-Share Alike 3.0 Unported (https://creativecommons.org/licenses/by-sa/3.0). https://commons.wikimedia.org/wiki/File:Mikveh_inside_house_-_Boskovice.jpg

Figure 77. "The Feast of the Rejoicing of the Law at the Synagogue in Leghorn, Italy," by Solomon Alexander Hart. Public domain. https://commons.wikimedia.org/wiki/File:Solomon_Alexander_Hart_-_The_Feast_of_the_Rejoicing_of_the_Law_at_the_Synagogue_in_Leghorn,_Italy_-_Google_Art_Project.jpg

Figure 81. Russian Orthodox Church in Düsseldorf. Photograph: Velopilger. Public domain. https://commons.wikimedia.org/wiki/File:Liturgy_St_James_1.jpg

Figure 82. Fresco on the catacomb of Saints Marcellinius and Peter. Public domain. https://commons.wikimedia.org/wiki/File:Baptism_-_Marcellinus_and_Peter.jpg

Figure 84. A Venetian doctor during the time of the plague. Public domain. https://commons.wikimedia.org/wiki/File:Jan_van_Grevenbroeck,_Venetian_doctor_during_the_time_of_the_plague._Museo_Correr,_Venice.jpg

Figure 85. Diego Velázquez's "Christ Crucified." Public domain. https://commons.wikimedia.org/wiki/File:Cristo_crucificado.jpg

Figure 87. U2 performing. Photograph: Remy. Creative Commons Attribution 4.0 International (https://creativecommons.org/licenses/by/4.0/deed.en). https://commons.wikimedia.org/wiki/File:U2_on_Joshua_Tree_Tour_2017_Brussels_8-1-17.jpg

Figure 92. Shi'a Muslims commemorate the martyrdom of Husayn. Photograph: Gabby Canonizado. Creative Commons Attribution 2.0 Generic (https://creativecommons.org/licenses/by/2.0/deed.en). https://commons.wikimedia.org/wiki/File:A_day_of_mourning,_annual_celebration_of_Muharram_in_Bahrain.jpg

Figure 97. Ceiling of Shamsuddin Hafez's tomb in Shiraz, Iran. Photograph: Roozbeh Taassob. Public domain. https://commons.wikimedia.org/wiki/File:Hafez-8.JPG

Figure 99. "Martyrdom of Joseph and Hiram Smith in Carthage Jail, June 27th, 1844," by G.W. Fasel. Public domain. https://commons.wikimedia.org/wiki/File:G._W._Fasel_-_Charles_G._Crehen_-_Nagel_%26_Weingaertner_-_Martyrdom_of_Joseph_and_Hiram_Smith_in_Carthage_jail,_June_27th,_1844.jpg

Figure 100. An anti-Mormon political cartoon from the late nineteenth century. Public domain. https://upload.wikimedia.org/wikipedia/commons/6/66/Anti-MormonCartoon.jpg

Figure 102. The Salt Lake Temple in Utah. Photograph: Diliff. Creative Commons Attribution 2.5 Generic (https://creativecommons.org/licenses/by/2.5/deed.en). https://commons.wikimedia.org/wiki/File:Salt_Lake_Temple,_Utah_-_Sept_2004-2.jpg

Figure 103. Celestial room of the Salt Lake Temple. Photograph: NewNameNoah. Creative Commons Attribution 4.0 International (https://creativecommons.org/licenses/by/4.0/deed.en). https://commons.wikimedia.org/wiki/File:Salt_Lake_Temple_Garb_In_Sealing_Room.jpg

Figure 104. Baha'i symbol. Public domain. https://commons.wikimedia.org/wiki/File:Ringstone.svg

Figure 106. Students of Tarbiyat School for Girls. Public domain. https://commons.wikimedia.org/wiki/File:Tarbiyat_School,_Tehran,_ca_1911.jpg

Text box – "Competing Modern Reformers": Syed Ahmad Khan. Public domain. https://commons.wikimedia.org/wiki/File:Sir_Syed1.jpg

Text box – "What is in the Talmud?": A page of the Talmud. Creative Commons Attribution-Share Alike 3.0 Unported (https://creativecommons.org/licenses/by-sa/3.0/deed.en). https://commons.wikimedia.org/wiki/File:Gemara-rosh-hashana-2a.jpg

Text box – "The Christian Fish": Funerary stele of Licinia Amias. Photograph: Marie-Lan Nguyen. Former Kircherian Collection. Public domain. https://commons.wikimedia.org/wiki/File:Stele_Licinia_Amias_Terme_67646.jpg

Sources and Acknowledgments

Text box – "Figurative Art": "Jahangir Preferring Sufi Shaykh to Kings." Public domain. https://commons.wikimedia.org/wiki/File:Bichitr_-_Jahangir_Preferring_a_Sufi_Shaikh_to_Kings,_from_the_St._Petersburg_album_-_Google_Art_Project.jpg

Published Sources

Figure 1. Zoroastrian procession, Iran. Photograph by Jassem Ghazbanpour. From Michael Stausberg, *Zarathustra and Zoroastrianism*. Translated by Margret Preisler-Weller. Equinox Publishing, 2008.

Figure 7. Israelite scriptural history. Taken from Philip R. Davies, *The Bible for the Curious: A Brief Encounter*. Equinox Publishing, 2018.

Figure 34. Sale of indulgences. Infovaticana. https://infovaticana.com/2015/03/28/que-son-las-indulgencias

Figure 37. Mural depicting Óscar Romero. Public domain. https://www.nycreligion.info/javis-story-troubled-el-salvador

Figure 46. The mosque at Bole. © Denis Genequand/Gonja Project. *Journal of Islamic Archaeology*, 4(2) (December 2017), p. 156.

Figure 61. A medieval woodblock. Philip R. Davies, *The Bible for the Curious: A Brief Encounter*. Equinox Publishing, 2018.

Figure 74. Nowruz in Toop Aghaj. Qantara.de. https://en.qantara.de/content/nowruz-the-iranian-new-year

Figure 80. Dukla Synagogue. *Journal of Contemporary Archaeology* 4(10) (2017). © 2015 Peter Cvijović. http://www.petercvijovic.com

Text box – "Dinar": An example of a dinar. Courtesy of Salvador Peña. From Avelino Gutiérrez and Magdalena Valor, *The Archaeology of Medieval Spain*, 1100–1500. Equinox Publishing, 2014.

Text box – "Rumi". A depiction of Rumi. The Threshold Society. https://sufism.org/origins/rumi/rumi-excerpts/rumi-daylight-tr-by-kabir-camille-helminski-excerpts-2

Photographers and Private Collections

Figure 6. "Conflict of the Knotted Heart" by Ian Garrett. A piece of digital art by Ian Garrett uploaded on June 28, 2013. Courtesy Ian Garrett Designs. http://www.iangarrettdesigns.com

Figure 8. Wall detail showing the mythical snake-headed *mushushshu*. Photograph courtesy of Michael Weigl.

Figure 12. The Dead Sea Scroll of the book of Isaiah. Photograph by Zev Radovan.

Figure 14. A tetradracham. Courtesy of Dr. David M. Jacobson.

Figure 17. A denarius. Courtesy of Dr. David M. Jacobson.

Figure 18. Basalt "Seat of Moses." Photograph by J. Garstang. Courtesy of the Palestinian Exploration Fund.

Figure 21. Palau Reial, the former palace of the Inquisition in Barcelona. Photograph by Ana M. Gómez-Bravo.

Figure 78. Passover sacrifice on Mount Gerizim. Photograph generously provided by Dr. Ori Orhof.

Figure 79. Zodiac mosaic floor. Photograph by Zev Radovan.

Figure 83. Mpho, daughter of Desmond Tutu. Photo by Ian Berry. Magnum Photos.

Text box – "Competing Modern Reformers": Jamal al-Din al-Afghani. 1883, by Yacquub 'Abd al-cAziiz Abul Ala Maududi

Text box – "Fortune Telling Parrots": Fortune-telling parrots. Photograph: © David Pinault.

Text box – "Sufism in America": Sufi Sam. Adapted from William Rory Dickson and Meena Sharify-Funk, *Unveiling Sufism: From Manhattan to Mecca*. Sheffield: Equinox Publishing, 2017.

Archives and Collections

Figure 10. Group of Samaritans assembled on Mount Gerizim for Passover. Courtesy of the Palestinian Exploration Fund.

Figure 11. Cliff face surrounding the grotto of Pan at Banias. Photograph by J. Garstang, 1928. Courtesy of the Palestinian Exploration Fund.

Figure 15. The Arch of Titus in the city of Rome. Courtesy of Alfred Molon Photo Galleries. http://www.molon.de

Figure 30. A fifteenth-century plan of Constantinople. Constantinople. Plan view. Vat. Urb. Lat. 277, fol. 131v. Courtesy of Biblioteca Apostolica Vaticana.

Figure 38. Seal of Vatican II. Courtesy of The Vatican Council. http://www.vatican.va/archive/hist_councils/ii_vatican_council/index.htm

Figure 41. Rock crystal seal. © Trustees of the British Museum.

Figure 42. "The Mosque of Omar Shewing the Site of the Temple," by David Roberts. Courtesy of the Palestinian Exploration Fund.

Figure 44. Revelers preparing a feast. Freer Gallery of Art and Arthur M. Sackler Gallery, Smithsonian Institute, Washington, DC. Purchase – Smithsonian Unrestricted Trust Funds, Smithsonian Collections Acquisition Program, and Dr. Arthur M. Sackler, S1986.255.

Figure 47. Ottoman ceramic tile. © Victoria and Albert Museum, London.

Figure 49. Earthenware plate with Islamic inscription. © Victoria and Albert Museum, London.

Figure 56. First record of the precursor of the name YHWH in the list of Shasulands of the temple of Soleb. Courtesy of Alfred Molon Photo Galleries. http://www.molon.de

Figure 64. "Last Judgment Triptych" by Hieronymous Bosch. Collection of the Academy of Fine Arts, Vienna.

Figure 69. Tree of life mosaic (Islamic art: Bathroom mosaic. Khirbat al Mafjar). Copyright Photo Scala, Florence. http://www.scalarchives.com

Figure 70. Illuminated Qur'an. BL Or.15571, fol.1v-2r. Chinese School (17th century). Credit: British Library, London, UK © British Library Board. All Rights reserved/Bridgeman Images.

Figure 94. *Al Maqamat al Hariri*. Courtesy Bibliothèque nationale de France.

iStock

Figure 13. A replica of the Second Temple in Ancient Jerusalem. Credit: tzahiV. iStock. https://www.istockphoto.com/gb/photo/second-temple-ancient-jerusalem-gm641348336-116116819

Figure 19. The western wall of the Second Temple. Credit: miljko. iStock. https://www.istockphoto.com/gb/photo/the-western-wall-in-jerusalem-israel-gm157733179-20609489

Figure 28. A view of Istanbul that shows the Hagia Sophia. Credit: prmustafa. iStock. https://www.istockphoto.com/gb/photo/high-sophia-istanbul-gm918407222-252631905

Figure 33. Crusaders besieging Damascus in 1148. Credit: sjhaytov iStock. https://www.istockphoto.com/gb/photo/church-st-cyril-and-methodius-in-center-of-village-of-ustina-plovdiv-region-bulgaria-gm889409134-246577976

Figure 86. The Sydney Mardi Gras Parade. Credit: georgeclerk. iStock https://www.istockphoto.com/gb/photo/sydney-gay-and-lesbian-mardi-gras-jesus-is-gay-banners-gm872497050-243703257

Figure 89. Muslim men doing ablution. Credit: THEPALMER. iStock. https://www.istockphoto.com/gb/photo/muslim-men-doing-ablution-gm458607477-15984064

Figure 90. Mosque interior. Credit: iboter. iStock. https://www.istockphoto.com/gb/photo/mosque-interior-gm872043368-243592776

Figure 91. Holy Mecca. Credit: ramzihachicho. iStock. https://www.istockphoto.com/gb/photo/holly-mecca-gm186094379-27522693

Figure 93. The al-Aqsa Mosque. Credit: Mattis Kaminer. iStock. https://www.istockphoto.com/in/photo/the-wailing-wall-and-dome-of-the-rock-in-jerusalem-israel-gm961580962-262588815

Figure 95. Decorated car. Credit: aquatarkus. iStock. https://www.istockphoto.com/gb/photo/haft-sin-table-on-a-car-gm916300968-252145983

Figure 96. A Muslim woman wearing a burka. Credit: Juanmonino. iStock. https://www.istockphoto.com/gb/photo/muslim-woman-wearing-a-burka-gm157561234-11957646

Figure 98. Jameh Mosque of Isfahan. Credit: javarman3. iStock. https://www.istockphoto.com/gb/photo/jameh-or-friday-mosque-of-isfahan-iran-gm511322306-86607131

Figure 101. The Book of Mormon. Credit: alacatr. iStock. https://www.istockphoto.com/gb/photo/book-of-mormon-gm155158069-15947026

Figure 105. Baha'i temple and gardens in Haifa, Israel. Credit: stellalevi. iStock. https://www.istockphoto.com/gb/photo/bahai-temple-and-gardens-in-haifa-israel-gm452092489-30568068

Shutterstock

Figure 51. Muslim refugees clamber aboard an overcrowded train near New Delhi. Shutterstock. Uncredited.

Figure 62. Stained-glass window. Photograph: Nancy Bauer. Shutterstock. Royalty-free stock photo ID: 122655007.

Figure 71. The Mausoleum of Imam al-Bukhari. Photograph: Yulia_B. Royalty-free stock photo ID: 627248510.

Figure 88. Interior of Chester Cathedral. Photograph: posztos. Shutterstock. Royalty-free stock photo ID: 77868931.

Getty

Figure 52. Elijah Muhammad addresses followers, including Muhammad Ali. Getty Images. Smith Collection/Gado. https://www.gettyimages.co.uk/detail/news-photo/nation-of-islam-religious-leader-elijah-muhammad-addresses-news-photo/538714718

From the author

It is good to be able to rely on the expertise and generosity of others, and I did that many times over the course of writing this book. The following people read substantial portions of this work, and I remain grateful to them for their support, their comments, and their corrections: Eric Stewart, Kelly Quinn, Keith Bodner, Johannes Wolfart, Deidre Butler, Shawna Dolansky, Erik Stephenson, Esther Guillen, Carmen Palmer, Jason Lamoreaux, Mohammed Rustom, Herbert Berg, Isobel Walker Khoury, Mounir Khoury, Sophie Crump, Kim Stratton, and Winnie Quinn. No book can do everything, and so I hope they will forgive me for the times I did not follow their advice and recognize the number of times that I did. I benefited from their comments, but they are not to blame for what follows.

Zeba Crook, April 2019

—1—
Towards a General Theory of Religion

Chapter Overview

This chapter surveys a portion of the history of studying religion, and introduces some of the complex issues that scholars of religion wrestle with. Scholars of religion disagree on so many things, substantial and seemingly insubstantial, but the one feature that permeates all of their work despite those differences is that the *study* of religion differs from *being* religious. It is not that they are incompatible. They're just different.

Monotheism

When Babylonians arrived in Judea in the sixth century BCE, Judeans were henotheists: they preferred one god over and against all the others, and were loyal to that one God. The vast majority of other peoples asked different gods for different benefactions: crops, personal fertility, healing, victory, safety, revenge, wisdom, protection, and so on. The idea that one god could do it all would have sounded very strange to people in the ancient world.

But the exile of Judeans into Babylonia brought them into contact with an even stranger religion. **Zoroastrians** had a theology that was even more monotheistic than the Judean religion, which, after the exile, also became more monotheistic. Today, billions of people are monotheistic, but 2500 years ago it was a radical and unpopular idea; some were even deeply offended by it.

Today, there are six major religions that are monotheistic because of this chance encounter between Judeans and Zoroastrians: Judaism, Christianity, Islam, LDS Church (also known as Mormonism), Baha'i religion, and Sikhism. Why are only the first five of these covered in this book? Because of a relic and a habit in the teaching of religion in universities: namely the separation of "eastern" and "western" religions into separate courses and textbooks. That separation is arbitrary, not to mention historically and ideologically problematic, but it does help to keep the material manageable. Sikhism has always been covered in "eastern" religion courses and textbooks.

Before we can focus in on the religions that are the subject of this book, we need to back up considerably. We need to exchange the microscope for the telescope in this chapter. In order to study "religion" we need to be clear about what it is we are studying, and how that is to be done in an academic setting.

What is Religion?

The question "What is religion?" seems, at first glance, so obvious one might wonder why academics even bother asking it. A conversation among friends on this subject might elicit a number of possible answers:

- Religion is devotion to or belief in God.
- Religion is revealed in scripture.
- Religion is a group with shared commitments.
- Religion is a world-view.

Each of these definitions is unsatisfactory. "Religion is devotion to or belief in God." Many Jews, Christians, and Muslims feel a great deal of devotion to God, so in some ways the definition works. But it does not work as a broad definition of "religion" because, even for those people who hold a deep devotion to God, it is almost certainly the case that their religiosity does not end with devotion. Maybe they also practice sacrifice, proper ways of dressing and eating, proper ways of adorning, concealing, or decorating the body, personal purity codes and household codes, prayer, pilgrimage, fasting, and the observance of holy days and calendar cycles. And they likely believe that these practices are extensions of their devotion. Devotion, or faith, even where it is paramount, then, is rarely all there is to religion. It cannot be the core of a definition.

A second problem is that, for some, the essence of religion is not devotion or faith at all but practice. For those, it might matter little what one actually believes or how deeply one feels it. For example, a ritual sacrifice in an ancient Roman or Israelite temple might emphasize the order of actions and the precise tools to be used, but "faith" on the part of the person doing the sacrificing might not be required.

And what about those who devote themselves to many gods, each god offering something different depending on the need of the practitioner (e.g., safety in travel, recovery from an illness, bountiful crops, etc.)? For these people, our opening definition – "Religion is devotion to or belief in God" – does not work at all. The religions covered in this book are monotheistic, so their members might not see the problem with this definition, but it does not work for religions that are not monotheistic. And the solution is not to change "God" to a more pluralistic-sounding "God or gods," because some religions do not have any kind of god at all!

Thus, that first definition not only eliminates too many other religions, but it does not even work well for Jews, Christians, and Muslims.

How about "Religion is revealed in scripture?" It is true that Judaism, Christianity, and Islam, the LDS Church, and Baha'i religion are "scriptural," in that they each have a core of writings they consider sacred and authoritative. But, as you will see later in the book, "scripture" does not mean the same thing to all five religions, nor does it mean the same for all members of the individual religions. By "scripture," some people mean that the writing came from God

Figure 1. Zoroastrian procession, Iran. Contemporary followers of this religion number only approximately 130,000. From Zoroastrianism comes the dualistic idea of the personified evil constantly threatening to undermine the power of good, God.

from capitalism, Buddhism from hockey? In some places, people seem to be as devoted to and ritualistic about their favorite sports teams and sporting events that they take on near-religious features. But if you feel strongly that sports are not religions, this is likely because of an implicit or intuitive definition of religion you are working with. One feature of scholarship is that scholars try to do things explicitly, not implicitly. We consciously and thoughtfully choose our definitions; we shape and develop them, criticize and challenge them. What is key here, though, is that it is always the scholars doing the defining; definitions do not just come to us.

And as with all intellectual endeavors, scholars choose where to set the boundaries, how to define their terms and their disciplines. In the case of religion, we choose to define religion in such a way that sports are eliminated. We might also choose to define religion in such a way that eliminates religions without gods (Daoism) or with too many gods (Hinduism), as some religious communities have been known to do. We might choose to define religion as faith or believing, thus eliminating religions that stress conduct, a position that is still maintained by some religious people. As you can see, so much depends on how one chooses to define religion. The complexity of this very process shall become increasingly evident in the sections that follow.

completely unchanged by human hands. Others mean that the writings were inspired by God but expressed with human words, a process that is admittedly susceptible to human error and fallibility. For others, it means that a set of writings is important and authoritative but were created by humans for humans. They are not "divine" in any way. But the real problem with this as a broad definition of "religion" is that there are too many religions over the course of human history for whom texts are not key at all. For them, oral history and oral memory is how story and identity were transmitted from generation to generation.

The last two definitions are no better. "Religion is a group with shared commitments" and "Religion is a world-view." If this is so, what distinguishes Christianity

The Modern Study of Religion

The study and definition of religion was, of course, originally the sole domain of religious groups and their institutions. So, Catholics, Protestants, and Jews in different periods, Shi'a and Sunni had their own ways of defining religion (their own and others') and determining the "proper" way to study religion. Their efforts were generally directed at defending their claims of truth over and against other claims. Not surprisingly, we find that historical rigor was more evident when these people studied other truth claims.

One feature of the modern study of religion is that it occurs outside of the synagogue, church, and mosque, and also outside the authority of the synagogue, church, and mosque. As such, it is not limited by their interests and perspectives. Generally, those who work in universities do not have to fear censure from religious authorities for asking difficult questions, and for arriving at conclusions that contradict official narratives.

Take one example, which can be applied to Judaism, Christianity, and Islam equally. Imagine that your religious authorities support the position that your scripture is inerrant: there are no contradictions and no errors of any sort in the text. If you study scripture within such a framework, you will find no contradictions and no errors. Anything that looks like a contradiction and an error is merely a failure of understanding on your part. Your job in this framework is to discover and defend the truth of the text.

But, if the framework changes, so does everything else. If you begin from the positions that the text is written by humans and susceptible to human error and experience, then you might discover, via errors and contradictions, evidence that the text has a complex compositional history. You might deduce that some parts of the text were written later than others and by different people, that this part was not written by the person it claims to be, that the writer of this part relied on that part, which was written by someone else. If your job is not to defend the truth of the text but to apply to the text the same rigorous historical questions you would apply to any other text, then a world of new questions becomes possible.

There are a number of scholars whose work established the field of religious studies: Edward Tylor, James Frazer, Émile Durkheim, Sigmund Freud, Karl Marx, Max Weber, and Mircea Eliade among them. In what follows, we will briefly consider the strengths and weaknesses of their arguments. But, despite their contradictory arguments, there is one feature that unites their work: there is a sharp distinction to be drawn between the practice or defense of a religion and the academic study of it. Scholars use all the tools at their disposal, drawn from the vast array of social scientific and humanistic disciples, but "faith" is not one of those tools. Faith is a tool of the religious study of religion, but not of the academic study of religion.

Another feature of the modern academic study of religion is that it not only takes a critical approach to the arguments of other scholars, but to the assumptions and presuppositions of the discipline itself. Time and again, scholars have questioned how to define and categorize religion, and they question the terms we use. They question all the things we take for granted as obvious (for instance, that "world religion" is a self-evident category).

Criticism

The words "criticism," "critical," and "critique" can make people nervous, especially when the context is a discussion about religion. They are not as bad as they sound, however. The root *crit-* comes from the Greek "to judge," as in to act like a judge whose job it is to weigh and assess evidence and compare arguments in a court of law. Judges are expected to be open to all evidence, consider all questions and options, and they are expected to be impartial. If a judge decides a case before considering (or despite) the evidence presented, or if a judge ignores evidence, we think of that judge as corrupt. This is the model for all academic disciplines: to weigh evidence as impartially as possible. To be critical in the study of religion, then, is not to criticize religion (religion is bad, religious people are ignorant and delusional), but to weigh all evidence, to test claims, and to dig beneath the surface of appearances. One needs to remember this, as these words are common in the academic (critical) study of religion.

E.B. Tylor and James G. Frazer

Edward Tylor (1832–1917) and James Frazer (1854–1941) studied religion in a way that combined anthropology (the study of human culture) and evolutionary science (the notion that things are constantly improving with the march of time). The result can be called "cultural evolutionism": the conviction that societies are constantly improving. We become smarter, more reasonable, more just, simply better overall.

Tylor saw in human cultures a desire to understand and to control the world around them. Humans, after all, are powerless and the natural world is often hostile. The earliest attempt to control phenomena in the world was premised on the notion that seemingly inanimate objects (like the sky, trees, rivers, and mountains) and natural events (like storms, droughts, and earthquakes) are actually made alive by the spirit world. Humans thought that if they could control the spirits that animate the world, they would make surviving in the world easier, so they devised incantations, binding spells, and rituals to do so. Tylor called this perspective on the world animism, and the attempt to control it magic.

But neither animism nor magic were satisfactory. If rain was a spirit that could be controlled by the appropriate incantation or ritual properly executed, then it should work every time. But of course it does not. The second stage then was to posit gods with personalities, open to human pleading but ultimately independent of it, and Tylor called this religion. In magic, if a request is not granted, no one knows why. It should work every time. But in religion, if a prayer or sacrifice for rain goes unanswered, many explanations are possible: the god in question had other plans or motives, the god was not persuaded by the human pleas or was unimpressed with the sacrifice, the god is unhappy with you, the god is testing you. Religion took over from magic because it did a better job of explaining why some (or more likely most) requests to the gods were not granted.

Tylor and Frazer disagreed here only about the extent of the separation between magic and religion: Tylor saw much overlap between religion and magic, whereas

Frazer stressed the difference between them. Whereas magic understood the world to be controlled by forces within the world, religion understood the world to be controlled by forces (and sometimes just one force) outside of the world. Magic used incantations to control the world; religion used prayer to control the gods.

The final stage of human evolution saw a transition from religion to science. Scientific explanations of the world were vastly superior to religious explanations, Tylor and Frazer accepted, and thus just as animism (or magic) was long ago abandoned, so too religion would be replaced by science.

Tylor and Frazer are correct in some ways. They are correct that some aspects of religion surely originate in attempts to understand the world, to explain the origin of things, and to explain natural occurrences. The main problem with their explanation is that the stages – magic to religion to science – do not actually exist as three discrete stages. Nor are they even entirely separated from one another. Put simply, magic and religion are not opposite to one another, the latter superior to the former. Magic is a form of religion, but the label "magic" tends to be used as a charge or insult by one religious group to denigrate the practices of another. In other words, the difference between magic and religion is created by groups attacking other groups. The distinction between magic and religion continues to be a fascinating area of scholarship.

Émile Durkheim

Like Tylor and Frazer, Émile Durkheim (1858–1917) focused his search for the origins of religion on so-called "primitive" societies, in his case the **Totemism** of indigenous tribes in Australia. He reasoned that if we can understand the "simpler" religions of "primitive" societies, then we will be better positioned to understand the more "evolved" religions like Christianity. Unlike Tylor and Frazer, however, Durkheim was less interested in the intellectual offerings of religion (e.g., its ability to explain the world) and more interested in its social functions: its use of ritual to build society. **Functionalism** not only explained the origin of religion for Durkheim, but also its endurance. Tylor and Frazer as well as Freud later were baffled by the survival of religion. Durkheim was not surprised, for religion he supposed would survive as long as there were social communities.

Durkheim observed a common tendency among humans to divide the things around us into **sacred** objects associated with a sacred realm (e.g., spirit world, heavens), and **profane** objects associated the profane realm (e.g., the material world around us). Every community chooses which objects to make sacred, and in so doing renders all other objects profane (that is, regular, belonging to this world). For example, if a community uses a particular blade in a religious ritual, it is unlikely that blade will be used at dinner. The first blade is sacred; the one used at dinner is profane.

Some groups do this with animals or plants rather than objects. A group may set apart a cow as sacred, while for a competing group it is a frog or a crow. Sacred animals are treated differently: either they are not eaten, or can only be eaten on specific occasions, but either way they are honored and protected. In addition, the sacred animal (or plant) comes to represent the group;

it serves as a symbol of the group, and also something around which a group rallies. Durkheim called this Totemism.

This relates to Durkheim's view of religion in two ways. First, the function of religion (the sacred object) is group cohesion and identity. The group rallies around its sacred animal. Second, as societies evolved and became more complex, they replaced their sacred animals with gods. Durkheim concluded that society and the sacred were inseparable: devotion to the sacred (god, deity, etc.) is tantamount to devotion to the group. This is so much the case for Durkheim that he would conclude that "God is Society, writ large," meaning the gods are merely a reflection of the society that creates them.

Durkheim's focus on the way religion functions as a social adhesive is still highly influential. But there are two problems with Durkheim's view of things. First, the social separation of the world into sacred and profane divisions is not universal. Some groups do not distinguish between the sacred and profane at all. This undermines the value of his work for arriving at a general theory of religion. Second, while religion does surely have positive social functions, Durkheim overlooks the problem of power, privilege, and conflict with which religion is also often associated; religion is often forced on people as a tool of oppression and social control (thus, one does not say that oppression is one of the functions of religion). Durkheim's approach to religion, therefore, while useful and ground-breaking in many ways, cannot provide the complete picture of where religion comes from, how it functions, and why it survives.

Max Weber

Max Weber (1864–1920) and Durkheim were near contemporaries, and both were interested in the sociology of religion, but Weber's approach was very different. Durkheim believed that societies and religions began simply and became more complex as they evolved. Thus, Durkheim could study Totemism and argue that it contained all the component parts of more modern and elaborate religions like Christianity, but it was easier to study because it was less evolved and less complex. Weber, in contrast to both Durkheim and Frazer, did not subscribe to cultural evolution: magicians and priests are different, he agrees with Durkheim, but magicians and magic did not disappear with the arrival of religion. Put differently, simplicity is not replaced by complexity; rather, both come to the fore and then recede into the background at different times and rates in different places. What dictates the ebb and flow is not linear evolution, but social context. And here Weber differs from Durkheim again: religion for Durkheim was a mere reflection of reality (the social world), whereas for Weber religion had real and marked effects in the social and political world.

For Weber, religion and social context influence each other in a sort of dialogue. Religion evolves out of and develops within complex constellations of local social, political, economic, and cultural facets, and in turn religion influences each of these. Freud, as we shall see shortly, claimed that religion was an illusion caused by mental distress, but for Weber even ideas held in people's imaginations have a real effect on the real world. When people hold to ideas and are motivated by them, the ideas need to be taken seriously for their ability to motivate change in the world. Ideas are real motivators of human action, but they do not exist separately from the world around them. They are produced by the world, and then they shape that world.

Weber illustrated this by arguing that certain characteristics of Protestant theology and world-view contributed to the rise of capitalism in Europe. Weber was not interested in questioning the truth of that theology, but focused on how religious views can effect profound social change. While his work can be critiqued at the level of explanatory power, when it comes to the academic study of religion, it is exemplary. Weber looks at how religion influences the real world and how the world influences religion, but he never defines what he means by religion nor attempts to explain its origin.

Sigmund Freud

Like Tylor and Frazer, Sigmund Freud (1856–1939) was confident in science's ability to explain all things, and was somewhat baffled as to why religion continued to survive. Freud explained the survival of religion in terms of psychoanalysis: humans are naturally rational, as the evolution of human societies and the rise of science illustrates, but religion is irrational. If in the face of rational scientific explanation people persist in their religious views, it must be because of psychological neuroses, obsessions, and past traumas.

Freud explained the persistence of religion as a cultural phenomenon the same way he explained irrational behavior in individual psychotherapy patients. He felt that when individuals experience trauma as children, they repress the memory of

Figure 2. Portrait of Sigmund Freud, the founder of the psychoanalytical school of psychology.

that trauma, only to have it surface later in life as obsessive or irrational behavior. The psychoanalyst's ability to pierce the surface shows the patient the deeper origin of the behavior, returning the patient to the point of repression, thereby resolving the crisis.

The source of that crisis, as it relates to religion, is where Freud's work becomes quite fanciful. In some primordial time in the very distant past, he suggested, humanity experienced a trauma, perhaps in the form of killing a patriarchal figure, the memory of which was repressed. When this cultural trauma becomes latent, it results in irrational behavior, which for Freud was religion. In keeping with his psychoanalytic analogy, Freud believed that if the root causes of these psychological neuroses could be addressed, then the need for religion (as a symptom of these psychological neuroses) would dissolve. This is because for Freud religion derived exclusively from internal psychological distress, and nothing else.

Freud was right that religion does have a deeply psychological aspect to it, and he is also right that religion can be a psychological crutch for some, a way of coping with life's suffering and distress. But the origin, existence, and persistence of religion as a whole cannot be reduced solely to this, nor can the experience of religion for all people be reduced to mere neurosis.

Karl Marx

Karl Marx (1818–1883) is a complex character in this discussion. He had surprisingly little to say about religion, as he was much more interested in economics and political philosophy. But what he did say has been extremely influential, spawning entire social and religious movements as well as resulting in visceral hatred for the man.

Marx neither offered nor even attempted a general theory of religion. Few people realize that Marx actually had a rather positive view of religion. A key feature of human existence is material – we work with our hands, we work to feed and house our families. Life is hard, but it is inherently rewarding: we are happy when we are self-sufficient, Marx claimed. But there can be suffering, poverty, and oppression, which is to say that life can be hard without reprieve. In Marx's view, capitalism had made human existence worse: people were disenfranchised from their labor, so there was no pleasure in it for the workers: only profit for the factory

Figure 3. Portrait of Karl Marx.

owners. Worse, the poor were working merely to survive, while the owners became increasingly wealthy and powerful. For these poor, then, religion was a salve, and an escape. It offered the hope of something better in the next world. This is the core meaning behind his famous phrase in which he described religion as the "opium of the masses." Opium masks pain, it takes the mind off of the crushing reality of grinding poverty and oppression. And it is self-administered, which is to say that people clamor for it. They do this to themselves, in other words. Religion, for Marx, was a pain-killer.

But Marx also recognized that this feature of religion served the interests of the ruling classes: as long as the masses were drugged on religion, they would never appreciate that this material life is all there is. There is no thing afterwards: no paradise, no heaven, no noble reincarnated existence. If people could recognize this, they would rebel against their overlords (priests, bankers, and land- and factory-owners). The biggest problem with religion for Marx, then, was that it distracted people and kept them from seeing the world as it truly was.

Of course, the ruling class and landowners recognized this, and exploited it to full effect, using religion to encourage passivity and obedience among the masses. So, religion was an opiate when the ruling classes used it to drug the masses into submission, threatening them with divine punishment if they ceased being obedient.

Marx is correct that religion and economic power go hand in hand: Temple priests conducting sacrifice in ancient Mediterranean religions rarely went hungry; the Holy Roman Empire combined the power of the Roman Catholic Church and the resurrection of the old Roman empire; the Brahmin in Hinduism sit atop a caste system that privileges and protects their interests. In many places, both present and past, criticism of religion is seen as criticism of the state, and is therefore considered political treason. There is no doubt that, in places, religion has been and still can be used to suppress dissent and oppress nations and people.

But Marx misses the fact that religion can also function to resist power. This is visible in a movement he could never have predicted, a movement the religiosity of which inspired resistance and rebellion against political and economic oppression. This is Liberation Theology, and it developed in twentieth-century Latin American countries (El Salvador, Nicaragua, Brazil, and Peru), and thus was made up primarily of Catholics,

although it spread quickly to include Protestant Christians and Muslims. Yet the ability to use religion to resist oppression is not unique to Christianity, for we see it in Mahatma Gandhi as well, whose religion played a noticeable part in his resistance to the British occupation of India; religion was also germane to the Iranian Revolution in the 1970s.

Mircea Eliade

Mircea Eliade (1907–1986) disagreed with attempts to identify social and cultural features behind the experience of religion (e.g., Weber, Durkheim, and Tyler). Eliade argued that religious ideas, feelings, and beliefs are the only factors that explain the origin of religion. Devotion to the sacred for Eliade really is devotion to the sacred; it is not a proxy for devotion to something else (such as for Durkheim). For Eliade, religion is not intertwined with other phenomena, such as politics, economics, psychology, or history, but exists independently of them. Religion is unique, and autonomous and cannot be explained as a product of other things. Religion is a cause of things; it is not a product of them.

Eliade argues that in order truly to understand religion, or people's religious ideas or experiences, one must inhabit the world of the religious person, and approach the religion as if a believer or practitioner. He rejected attempts at scientific objectivity (which all of the other figures discussed here were at least attempting, successfully or not), and the notion that comes with it, namely scientific distance. One understands religion, Eliade claimed, not by standing outside looking in (as an outsider), assuming some semblance of detachment, but by standing inside looking around, by becoming one with the locals, as it were (as an insider). Eliade called this approach "phenomenology": the study of things as they appear, on their own terms.

In *The Sacred and the Profane*, Eliade argues that religious people behave as they do because the gods have commanded it. They follow patterns of behavior set by the gods, who have the authority to set all codes of conduct. Motivation for their behavior is not to be found in deeper psychological (Freud), social (Durkheim), or economic (Marx) explanations, and to make the claim is to discount the testimony of religious people.

This perspective drove Eliade to collect vast amounts of information pertaining to religion. He wanted to know everything, it seemed, and he remains a valuable source of information. But the most recent thinking on religion has turned much of what Eliade argued on its head:

- It may not be possible to achieve perfect objectivity, but that doesn't mean scholars should not strive for objective distance;
- insider discourse is data for our collection;
- the job of the scholar of religion is to analyze insider discourse, not merely describe and accept it;
- religion is too intertwined with other aspects of the world to be imagined as some wholly separate entity.

The Study of Religion in the Twenty-first Century

The scholarly reaction to Eliade, as I have just suggested, took his terms and reversed them. Consider the difference between **insider discourse** and **outsider discourse**. Eliade argued that if you want to understand how religion works, ask a religious person. Take their testimony at face value. But contemporary scholarship argues for the opposite. Insider discourse is data; scholars collect data, and they examine and analyze it. That analysis produces arguments and explanations that might be wholly unrecognizable to religious communities. This is called outsider discourse.

The distinction between explanation (outsider discourse) and testimony (insider discourse) is an important one. Modern scholarship on culture can perhaps help us here. Culture refers to the way people in groups dress, what they eat, how they eat, how they speak to or interact with one another, their music, literature, language, recreation, and so on. When people are raised in a culture, they grow up to feel that their conduct is natural, and needs no explanation. But modern scholarship on culture now recognizes that culture is created by humans. Culture is what people do, and because of that, culture is fluid: it keeps changing as people change. What is culturally normal in one location might be looked on with distaste in another. What is culturally normal at one period might be rejected in the same place some generations later (e.g., men wearing earrings). Culture is not timeless, or stable, and it is not given to humans from something outside of them. Culture is created by each human group. To describe people as following the laws of culture given to them (from the gods, from above) is not an analysis of culture, it is a description of what it feels like to be enculturated.

It is the same with religion: part of being an insider within a religion involves feeling that your religion is inherently true, real, and external to you, which was Eliade's point. That describes the feeling or experience of religion. But true as this is, it should not be confused with an analysis or explanation of religion. Scholarship in religion needs to explain religion analytically, not promote it to a universal truth. The latter might be the goal of interfaith dialogue, a perfectly valid enterprise, but not of scholarship on the study of religion.

The experience of, and defense of, religion is part of what happens inside religions, whereas the study of, explanation of, and analysis of religion is part of what happens outside of religion. A biologist cutting open a frog does not attempt to become a frog, to take on a frog's mentality. Critical distance is key to the scientific enterprise.

In what follows, we shall look at some the ideas that characterize the academic study of religion as it currently stands.

Religion as Empty

To say that religion is empty is not to say anything pejorative about it: it does not mean that religion is a childish game of make-believe or mere delusion. To say that religion is empty is to say that religion is a category that can be "filled" with almost anything. Every human group in the history of the world has determined the contents of its own religion, and will continue to do so: this is why religions over the course of history and the geographical expanse of the world look as different as they do, but also why sometimes they look remarkably alike, as siblings often do.

Religion is empty until people fill it with content (e.g., these people pray to this god, those people dress in this way). Of course, most religious people ("insiders") will not see it this way. For them, very often religion is given to them (from above, from outside this world, from the past). Clearly then, the idea that religion is empty until people fill it with content is a scholarly way of approaching religion, an approach that attempts to imitate the methods of science, first and foremost involving classification and critical distance.

If religion is empty until it is filled with content, what is that content? That content includes prayer, which for some must happen in groups, for others alone, which for some is delivered in repeated formulas, and for others is always spontaneous. It includes sacrifice, which some groups practice, other groups reject, and yet others think of metaphorically. It includes pilgrimage, which for some groups is a key feature of how they express their devotion, for others not at all. It includes diet, which for some is established by their religion, for others not at all. Think of how many other practices and ideas provide the content for religion: marking or dressing the body, doctrine, reading or memorizing texts, learning languages, singing, volunteering, visions and ecstatic experiences, and friendships, to name but a few.

Religion is a Concept, Not a Thing

Another feature of recent scholarship on religion is the point that religion is not a thing, not an entity, but a concept. A concept is a mental representation, a way of categorizing things one thinks are related. A concept is conceptual, it is not material.

Fruit is an example of a concept. Scientists observe that, of plants we eat, some bear the ability to reproduce themselves and others do not. If a carrot, for instance, is left on the ground, it will never grow into another carrot. But an apple left on the ground could, in the right conditions, grow into an apple tree. Scientists thus create the category "fruit" to classify the parts of plants that carry their own seeds – apples and oranges, for instance. But all concepts are mental exercises; they exist only in the brain. Of course, apples and oranges really exist, but the category "fruit" is a mental construction.

Likewise with religion: people praying or sacrificing to the gods really exist, but the category "religion" is a mental construction, a concept that allows the scholar to bring a wide variety of ideas or behaviors into a single category. So it is important to recognize that "fruit," that is the category, is an invention of scientific scholarship. We eat apples, we eat oranges; we classify them as fruit. So too is religion a category, an invention of scientific scholarship.

The analogy between fruit and religion as analytical categories can be extended. There are popular, even intuitive, ways of defining fruit and there are scholarly or scientific ways. No one eating a "fruit salad" wants to bite into a piece of squash. A child who asks for a piece of fruit does not expect to be handed a slice of cucumber. If you feel the same way reading this, it is because you are reacting intuitively to what "fruit" refers to. Yet cucumber and squash (and many other things you might be surprised to learn) are, from a scholarly perspective, fruit just like

apples and oranges. Like "fruit," then, "religion" is a scholarly and analytical category, a way for scholars to define and classify sets of behavior we deem to be similar, but it is not always an intuitive or popular category. Intuitively, people might think that spells are magic while prayer is religion, but from a scholarly perspective, both are religion.

A scientific way of understanding our world requires classification and concepts. In classification, we observe features of the world around us (physical things like plants) or phenomena (how people dress or behave) and we classify them according to features we think they hold in common. We place them into categories (animals and plants), and subcategories (fruits and vegetables, and then simple fruits and aggregate fruits). Operating with concepts is what allows higher orders of thinking. So the academic study of religion is "scientific" not because it uses science to say miracles do not happen or that God does not exist, but because it recognizes that "religion" is itself a concept and a classification. To say that religion is a concept and not a thing is to say that one cannot point to religion: one can only point to religious behavior, religious objects, religious dress, and so on. But really, in each case what we are pointing to is nothing more than behavior, objects, and dress, often indistinguishable from other behavior, objects, and dress, except for the fact that an insider has designated something as having religious significance, at which point we become quite interested!

Reifying and Totalizing Religion

Because religion is a concept, a mental construct, it cannot have agency. Put differently, religion cannot do things of its own accord. Yet when people say, "Religion is responsible for crimes against humanity," they imagine that religion is a concrete entity with physical properties that behave or influence people in predictable ways. To do this with a concept or idea is to reify it, and it is a logical fallacy to do so (**reification**). Ideas or concepts cannot act or respond to stimuli in predictable ways because they are not concrete entities that exist in the natural world. Yes, religious people exist, but their religiosity does not cause them to act or respond to stimuli in predictable ways (not all religious people react to criticism or mockery the same way, or feel awe at the sound of music). If religion does not have agency, it cannot be responsible for crimes against humanity. "Religion is beautiful" or "Religion is peaceful" are other examples of reification. To give concrete attributes to something that exists only as a concept or an idea is a logical fallacy.

Totalizing religion is a related but different problem. When one reduces religion to a single feature or characteristic, or mistakes a local feature of religion for a universal feature, one totalizes religion: "the essence of religion is prayer," or "religion is violent" are totalizing statements. Religion is too complex to be reduced to a single essence or characteristic. Another common example in everyday discussion is to use "faith" and "religion" as synonyms, as in the statement "Christianity and other faiths are struggling with secularism." Faith is not a feature we can find in all religious people or in all religions through time, and therefore it cannot be used as a stand-in for "religion."

The risk of totalizing religion applies not only to religion in general, but to individual religions as well. The religion of the Jews has existed in many forms over several thousand years, and some of these forms bear little resemblance to each other. Judaism is not just one thing, and it never has been. Nor have Christianity, Islam, or Hinduism ever been just one thing.

The greatest risk in reducing a whole religion to a single feature is that it hides and denies the profound diversity that exists in every religion. The place of the scholar of religion is not to simplify religion, nor to simplify individual religions, but to complicate it all. Take, for instance, the statement that "The core of Christianity is devotion to Christ." At one level, it seems perfectly reasonable: Christians are distinguished as a group from Hindus by their devotion to Christ. But at the same time, this statement hides the fact that faith in or devotion to Jesus Christ is not merely the one thing on which all Christians agree; it is the foundation of everything about which they disagree. Christians have fought wars over how best to believe in Jesus Christ. So the above statement fails not because it is technically wrong, but because it is inadequate and it ignores too much of what distinguishes Christians from each other.

The Democratization of Religion

Individual religions cannot be reduced to a single feature or a single set of requirements. The problem is that there can sometimes be a body of people or texts from within a religion that attempt to do just that. Catholicism has a Pope and a papal curia that attempts – not always successfully – to define and control what it is to be Catholic, and when someone does something unapproved, they risk being excluded from the Catholic community. Jews and Muslims do not have anything like a Vatican; nonetheless, authority can emerge from consensus, creating the illusion that being Jewish or Islamic requires certain beliefs or practices, and the use of rebuke, censure, or abuse to correct errant behavior. These are the processes with which communities form boundaries around themselves: they establish rules and set limits on what members of the community must (or must not) do or think. Groups commonly set these boundaries: they are a way of reducing difference and developing homogeneity, consistency, and therefore coherence within a community. It is one way that communities maintain their existence, for, without boundaries, how is one group to be distinguished from another?

These boundaries, and the ways groups develop and sustain them, are part of what scholars of religion study. We do not uphold, or support, or honor those boundaries ourselves. Put differently, we do not become embroiled in the debates either within or between religions about who is right. In addition, religion is not a democracy, in which majority rules. Consensus matters only to religious insiders attempting to establish (or enforce) authentic/proper belief or practice. To the scholar of religion, however, minority practice is as interesting as majority practice. Refusal to celebrate Christmas is not less Christian because only a small percentage of Christians do so. Playing in a punk-rock band or choosing not to wear the hijab is not less Islamic merely because a large number of Muslims object. The same applies to a sentence that starts: "Judaism (or Christianity or Islam) teaches that . . ." Such a claim ignores the many different teachings that different members of the same religion promote.

The Data of Religion

Jonathan Z. Smith offered the provocative and compelling observation that there are no data for religion. What did he mean by that?

A datum (the singular of data) is a fact, something certain and known, and also something that can be seen, touched, heard, or smelled. To say that there are no data for religion means that there is no item or action that is inherently religious or that belongs uniquely to "religion." Consider this: are getting dressed, traveling, speaking, and killing an animal religious actions? No. They are mundane, common, and daily actions. They only become religious when the person doing them claims to be doing something religious. In this way, covering one's head with a piece of cloth or wearing a suit to church becomes different from wearing a suit to work and covering your head in winter, wearing a kippah becomes different from a baseball cap; traveling to a location where a god resides becomes pilgrimage, and it is held to be different from a vacation; speaking to God, speaking to an ancestor, or speaking to the sky becomes prayer, and different apparently from speaking to a sibling or friend; offering an animal to a god becomes sacrifice, a way of distinguishing it from killing an animal for one's supper. In each instance, the action (datum) does not belong to religion.

There are no data for religion because everything around us in the world is a potential datum for religion. Any item, any thought, and any action can be made part of one's religion: a stone, a bolt of lightning, an earthquake, the birth of a child, a speech, a language, fasting or feasting, a treaty, a book, a statue, a rug, a candle, a tree, water. The list is endless. There are no data for religion because all things are potential data for religion.

Because there are no data unique to religion, it means there is no unique method for studying religion. By contrast, psychologists study human behavior and economists study monetary systems, and because there are data unique to each of those disciplines, there are methods (ways of studying, models for explaining) that are unique to them. Thus, a psychologist does not normally rely on the model of "supply and demand," which comes from economics, and the economist would never explain a recession by referring to the psychological traumas of citizens. The study of religion is multi- and interdisciplinary.

Lincoln's Theses for the Study of Religion

In addition to the seminal and provocative work of Jonathan Z. Smith, this book also takes as programmatic for the contemporary study of religion a short article by Bruce Lincoln. In the manner of Martin Luther, Lincoln presented thirteen theses that seek to establish the boundaries of the academic study of religion, though he did not as far as I know nail them to anyone's door.

Lincoln begins by asserting that religion is what we study; religion does not describe *how* we study. We study religion; we do not study religiously. Religion is a subject matter of study, not a method of study. In this way, religion is no different from other subjects: English literature, psychology, history, engineering, and so on. The study of religion must be carried out according to the same rules as the study of other disciplines. Studying religion as a subject means that the activities, claims, and beliefs of religious people are data. For instance, people once believed that the Roman emperor Vespasian (he ruled 69–79 CE) cured people with his miraculous powers of healing, and there are writings that record this with witnesses present. But the scholar of religion is not required to accept those claims as true. In fact, the scholar of religion is obligated to assume the miracle did not actually happen, and to inquire instead into the story's origin and function: the story likely emerges from a sense of awe and reverence that Roman people had for their adored emperor.

Similarly, Christians often believe that the Bible was composed with the guidance of the Holy Spirit, and Muslims that the Qur'an was written by God long before it was revealed to Muhammad. In the academic study of religion, these are data, and they are claims to truth. But the scholar takes the position that every religious text was written by humans, and that the time and location in which they were written will affect the content and meaning of the writing.

It is critical to realize that Lincoln does not claim or imply that the historical way of studying religion is superior to a religious way. They are simply two different, though mutually exclusive, ways of talking about the same subject matter. They are mutually exclusive because the theological (or insider) perspective tends to assume and accept the timelessness, the inherent authority, and unique rightness of perspectives held, and the accuracy of things felt or believed, while historical (or outsider) perspectives, represented by the academic study of religion, does not make these assumptions. In fact, the academic study of religion actively resists these claims.

While it is emphatically not the role of the scholar of religion to insult religious people, it is her job to ask destabilizing and irreverent questions, questions that resist the authoritative claims made by religious texts, rules, or leaders. The scholar of religion might question the authorship of texts or sayings, might reject the authority of some person to make a claim, or might question whose power interests are served by a certain belief, claim, or position. It is the case, unfortunately, that some religious people can feel injured when such questions are asked. I stress that insult might be an unavoidable consequence of some academic work on religion, but it is not its goal. Lincoln's tersest point in this regard is that

> Reverence is a religious, and not a scholarly virtue. When good manners and good conscience cannot be reconciled, the demands of the latter ought to prevail. (Thesis Five)

When Christian Europeans conquered much of the world (1500–1900), they began a process of colonialism: enforcing Christian religion and western cultural values and practices on foreign people, while exploiting them economically. The attack on others' religions was often part of western colonialism (though it ought to be pointed out that this was also the case with "eastern colonialism," namely the expansion of Muslims into new lands that were formerly Christian, Zoroastrian, Hindu, and polytheist).

Many in the west are now, rightly, sensitive to this western past, and there is sometimes the feeling that to subject the religions of other people to probing historical inquiry is a new form of colonialism, of cultural imperialism, and of denigration. Lincoln warns that one must be careful not to confuse the attacks on religion and culture that were part of western colonialism with the critical, academic inquiry that is part of western religious studies. They are not the same. The academic study of religion does not involve value judgments: it is not the role of the scholar of religion to conclude that a religion is wrong, or false, or evil because some of its claims appear not to be historical. The scholar of religion does not assume, or conclude, that one religion is better or worse than another.

Being part of a religion is like being part of culture: it can be hard to imagine things in any other way. Often, it is easier to spot the constructed, arbitrary features of other people's cultures. Lincoln warns that scholars of religion must endeavor to submit their own religion to critical scrutiny, in addition to critically scrutinizing the religions of others, and often the former takes much greater effort to do because of the pervasive nature of enculturation.

Religion and Critical Inquiry

A key feature of the academic study of religion is "methodological atheism." Whereas "atheism" is the belief that there is no god, "methodological atheism" refers to the practice of doing one's work as if there is no god. Historians do it, biologists do it, literary critics do it, and many of them are religious. Scholars of religion, many of whom are religious, need also to do their work from this position. In other words, one can believe in God but still undertake one's study of religion as if there is no God. The same person can minister to their congregation, delivering sermons or *khutbas* that uphold doctrine and affirm the glory of God in one setting, and then perform scholarship in which they seek to explain religion (theirs or someone else's) as if there is no God. One might liken it to having a job as an accountant but coaching children's soccer on the weekends: two totally different enterprises with two completely different sets of rules expectations, dress codes, and even languages, each performed by the same person. Just not at the same time.

Religions, Religion, and Religious Studies

I would like to offer one last analogy, this time for clarifying how the terms "religions," "religion," and "religious studies" relate to one another. If you think about the relationship between three comparable terms – "languages," "language," and "linguistics" – the distinction becomes easy to visualize.

- People communicate with each other using languages. Some are dead (like Latin), many are living, most are spoken (e.g., Spanish, Zulu, Mandarin), but not always: American Sign Language (ASL) is a language too. Because actual people communicate with languages, we hear and see them in use around us all the time, and they feel real to us.

- "Language," on the other hand, is a concept. No one speaks "language"; they speak or sign a language (or several languages if they work hard enough). "Language" is a term used for classifying a human form of communication, and one that has grammatical rules and structure: whales communicate with one another, but we do not classify that as language; humans wink and shrug and make hand-gestures at each other, but we do not classify that as language because they have no grammar. Yet, to the uninitiated, ASL looks like a series of gestures. Clearly, some scholarly effort went into generating a classification of "language" and distinguishing it from other forms of communication.

- Linguistics is the academic (scientific) study of how the concept of language and particular languages developed, how sounds are formed in the mouth and how the use of sound creates meaning, how sentences are structured and words formed, how language communication has changed over time, how social and historical forces shape language, how word forms are borrowed and adapted by competing groups, and how humans acquire language. In linguistics, one does not learn how to speak German, since linguistics is the study of language, not the study of a single language. Linguistics is not about the practice of a language, nor does it promote or denigrate particular languages. And finally, because of the many different aspects of language one can study, linguistics draws from many other academic disciplines: anthropology, sociology, psychology, philosophy, biology and human anatomy, neuroscience, to list but a few.

The parallels between languages, language, and linguistics and religions, religion, and religious studies should be clear.

Defining Religion

James Leuba, a psychologist of religion, collected in 1912 more than fifty different ways that religion could be defined. That number is surely higher today. It might be natural to conclude from this that religion cannot be defined, but I draw a different conclusion: religion can be defined in many different ways and we do our best with the best tools we have. I believe that the contemporary study of religion provides the best tools currently.

For the purposes of this book, we shall work with the following definition of religion, a combination of definitions developed by Jonathan Z. Smith and Bruce Lincoln:

> religion is a concept that refers to a system of beliefs, practices, and narratives relative to superhuman beings.

Consider the following keys items and implications here:

- As a concept, religion is a mental construct, a way of classifying behaviors we argue are related to one another, though they may look nothing alike on the surface, and they may mean quite different things to the various practitioners;

- The term "system" is meant to suggest that although religion involves a complex constellation of features that can differ greatly, these features must be sufficiently integrated that they cohere (without coherence among its parts, there can be no "system");

- There will be a set of beliefs, practices, and narratives – sometimes all three, sometimes not, always in different ratios – that any community shares, invests in, and participates in;

- And the most important feature is that this system of beliefs, practices, and narratives relates to something superhuman, literally meaning "above or beyond human": spirits, gods, God, demons, or a human who is believed to have non-human healing powers or teaching abilities. It is this feature that allows us to say that hockey, baseball, and soccer are not religions: because no matter how much fans admire the prowess of an athlete, they will ultimately always recognize those players to be merely human. Equally, it is this feature that helps us to realize that the debate between Tylor and Frazer – about whether magic and religion were different – is moot. Magic is a form of religion by this definition.

The vast diversity of religions in the world over time and location share this: what they think or believe, what they eat, how they dress, whether they pray or sacrifice or both, and the stories they tell about their history, their heroes, and their community, all happen in relation to something or someone that is not human in the way the rest of us are human.

This Book

Comparative Religion, as a discipline, is outdated. Comparative Religion seeks out universals in religion, searching for themes like myth, pilgrimage, gender, rites, prayer, sacrifice, body, and so on. One of the effects of this approach is that different religions are homogenized. Differences among religions are hidden, not recognized and understood. Also, the search for themes makes it difficult to locate the development of religions in history. The result is a study of religion that is detached from historical location.

The structure of this book, with Judaism, Christianity, and Islam together in sections on History, Theology, and Practice, might look like Comparative Religion, but it is not. I want readers to think about how interrelated and intertwined these religions are, and some comparison is inevitable. But it is as important to see difference as it is to see commonalities. The structure is meant to stress the relationship among these religions. But ultimately, the reader needs to understand each religion individually. That is made more difficult by the structure of this book, but I trust the reader to do that work.

The five religions covered in this book are genealogically related. That is worth noting, and it explains why they appear together in this book. They are also all monotheistic religions, at least in their modern forms. Monotheism is a rather distinct idea in the history of religion. This is not a book on monotheism, *per se*, but on five religions that are monotheistic, a feature they owe historically to Judaism. Nonetheless, a few words on monotheism are in order here.

Monotheism is the theological position that there exists in the world only one god, and that God is sovereign, omnipotent, and demands exclusive loyalty. We are conditioned to think that monotheism is limited to Judaism, Christianity, Islam, the LDS Church and Baha'i, as well as Sikhism and Zoroastrianism. But elements of monotheism can be found in many places. For instance, ancient Israelites did not deny the existence of other gods, but they did practice loyalty to one god above all, the God of Israel. Also, it is common among polytheists to elevate one god as uniquely powerful or superior, and from there to all-powerful and omniscient. It is common among humans, in other words, to make their favorite god into the best god, and from there to the only god worth loyalty.

And though we group these five religions together as monotheistic, do not think that they agree on that monotheism. Over the course of history, Jews and Muslims did not recognize Christians as monotheistic. Mainstream Christians do not agree with the LDS Church's form of monotheism. These differences in how monotheism is expressed and maintained owes to their different historical locations and to their different experiences. Sometimes those positions defy logic. That's when things get creative and interesting.

Each chapter ends with learning resources for the student: prompts for discussion groups or thoughtful reflection, a few recommended websites and readings where students can find more information for research purposes, and two different kinds of word lists. Words are listed in the glossary when I felt that a more precise or full definition was required. The "Other Important Vocabulary" words were adequately defined in the chapter when they were used, and students are encouraged to go find them, and glean a definition by reading. It is not the case that the glossary words are more important than the other important vocabulary.

Chapter Summary

This chapter provided a brief history of the academic study of religion, and illustrated the complexity of defining and classifying religion. Of key importance is the point that humans create religion, using the stuff around them to do so – whether in the form of nature (water, mountains), or material objects (paper, pottery), phenomena (language, power), or social institutions (kinship, economics). Because of this, there is nothing around us that cannot be used religiously, leading to the proposition that there are no data for religion. This book works with the following definition of religion: "a concept that refers to a system of beliefs, practices, and narratives relative to superhuman beings," and much of this chapter was spent arriving at this point.

Glossary

Functionalism. An approach to the study of society that looks for the function of social and cultural institutions. In the case of the study of religion, this was found in Durkheim's interest in religion's ability to produce social cohesion.

Insider/outsider discourse. The theoretical approach to the study of religion that distinguishes between the way members of a religion speak about themselves and their religion (insiders) and the way scholars speak about that religion.

Profane/sacred. Things are sacred when they are set apart from everyday, or profane, objects. "Profane" is not negative, it is merely normal: things in daily use.

Reification. To take an abstract concept (like love, anger, or religion) and turn it into something more concrete, such as an entity with agency and other concrete or human characteristics.

Totemism. Refers to the religious belief that humans are connected by spirit to an animal or object, which usually also stands as a symbol of the group's kinship.

Zoroastrianism. A religion of Persia before Islam, Zoroastrian theology was highly influential on Israelite/Jewish thinking about monotheism, good and evil in the world, and eschatology. This influence naturally extends to Christianity and Islam though Judaism. Zoroastrians still exist, though they number as few as 100,000–200,000.

Other Important Vocabulary

Animism

Bruce Lincoln

Criticism

Cultural evolutionism

Edward Tylor

Émile Durkheim

James Frazer

Jonathan Z. Smith

Karl Marx

Liberation Theology

Mircea Eliade

Methodological atheism

Phenomenology

Magic

Max Weber

Sigmund Freud

Discussion Questions

1. How do you think the distinctions between languages, language, and linguistics (p. 17) provide an analogy for religions, religion, and religious studies? Are there any ways in which the analogy does not work?

2. Consider the definition of religion used in this book. Is there anything you feel should be considered as "religious" that does not fit into that definition? Would you define religion differently?

3. Religion has changed over time. People used only to worship spirits in nature, then they worshipped many gods, then monotheism emerged. Does thinking chronologically about religion imply a Darwinian evolution? Is "evolutionism" a useful way to think about religion? What would the alternative be to thinking about religion evolutionarily?

4. Allowing that social change appears always to result in changes to religion and religions, what do you think the future holds for religion or religions?

Recommended Reading

Braun, Willi, and Russell T. McCutcheon, eds. 2000. *Guide to the Study of Religion*. London: Cassell.

Durkheim, Émile. 1915. *The Elementary Forms of the Religious Life*. New York: Macmillan.

Eliade, Mircea. 1957. *The Sacred and the Profane: The Nature of Religion*. Translated by Willard R. Trask. New York: Harcourt, Brace, and World.

Frazer, J.G. 1922. *The Golden Bough: A Study in Magic and Religion*. Abridged Edition. London: Macmillan.

Lincoln, Bruce. 1996. "Theses on Method." *Method & Theory in the Study of Religion* 8: 225–227.

McCutcheon, Russell T. 2003. *Manufacturing Religion: The Discourse on Sui Generis Religion and the Politics of Nostalgia*. New York: Oxford University Press.

Marx, Karl, and Freidrich Engels. 1964. *Karl Marx and Friedrich Engels on Religion*. Introduced by Reinhold Niebuhr. New York: Schocken Books.

Smith, Jonathan Z. 2004. *Relating Religion: Essays in the Study of Religion*. Chicago, IL: University of Chicago Press.

Stausberg, Michael. 2008. *Zarathustra and Zoroastrianism*. Translated by Margret Preisler-Weller. Sheffield: Equinox Publishing.

Strachey, James, with Anna Freud, eds. 1961. *The Standard Edition of the Complete Psychological Works of Sigmund Freud*. London: Hogarth.

Tylor, E. B. 1903. *Primitive Culture: Researches into the Development of Mythology, Philosophy, Religion, Language, Art, and Customs*. London: J. Murray.

Weber, Max. 1958. *The Protestant Ethic and the Spirit of Capitalism*. Translated by Talcott Parsons. New York: Charles Scribner's Sons.

Recommended Websites

http://www.equinoxpub.com/blog

- This British and American blog offers regularly written short articles on how religion is discussed in popular media and academic scholarship.

http://www.pewforum.org

- This American site offers a wealth of data in the study of contemporary religion.

http://www.religionfactor.net

- This site, associated with Groningen University in The Netherlands, offers articles on the controversial place of religion in modern public life.

—Part One—
Histories

Many introductory textbooks on Judaism, Christianity, and Islam have chapters that claim to offer the history of Judaism, the history of Christianity, and the history of Islam, but they do not. What they offer is a history of people loyal to the God of Israel long before there was a Judaism, a history of others who were followers of Jesus the Messiah before there was Christianity, and finally a history of people who were loyal to Muhammad's view of submission to God before there was an established religion of Islam. Think about it this way. The first people one meets reading the Hebrew Bible, and thus the first people one meets reading a standard history of Judaism, are Adam and Eve, Noah, and Abraham, but these people were not Jewish. King David was not Jewish. That statement might sound particularly outlandish, but how can he have been? He wasn't even a monotheist. His form of faith in the God of Israel can be described as monolatrous or henotheistic, but not monotheistic. This book takes the position that until there is monotheism, there can be all sorts of things – the religion of Abraham, Isaac, and Jacob, or Yahwism, or the worship of the God of Israel – but there cannot be

Judaism until there is monotheism, a belief system that takes hundreds of years and a catastrophe to develop.

If the length of time it takes to arrive at monotheism is the complicated part of discussing the history of Judaism, it is different for Christianity. The first Christians were Jews, so not surprisingly Romans could not distinguish Jews from Christians for most of the first century of the Christian era. Jesus was Jewish, he was not Christian. Paul the Apostle was devoted to Jesus the Messiah, but that does not make him Christian. Paul also was Jewish. It takes a couple of hundred years for Christianity to become a stand-alone religion, apart from Judaism, and it happens not overnight but at different rates in different places around the Mediterranean.

The religion of Christianity really takes on the characteristics that will define the rest of its history in the fourth century. Two things happen, and they are related to each other. First of all, Constantine begins the process that will make Christianity into a religion of empire. Secondly, Christians complete their development of a profoundly creative and unpredictable innovation of monotheism,

Figure 4. An illustrated page from the Sarajevo Haggadah, written in fourteenth-century Spain. Top: Moses and the burning bush. Bottom: Aaron's staff swallows the magicians' rods.

loss of Israel left Jews with no state through which to exercise political power. This changes after the founding of the modern state of Israel. But unlike Christianity, Islam becomes a political religion under the guidance of it founding figure, Muhammad. This is why we start the history of Islam with the Constitution of Medina. It is an interesting statistic for students of religion that the period between the very first beginnings of a religion to its establishment in a form we can currently recognize is shortest in the case of Islam relative to the others under discussion in this book.

What do we do with all those stories that are normally treated as part of the history of these religions, but are not so treated in this book, such as creation and flood, Abraham, Moses and Exodus, David, Jesus, Paul, and the Jahiliyyah and the early life of Muhammad? These stories are treated in the theology chapters for each religion (Chapter Five for Judaism, Chapter Six for Christianity, and Chapter Seven for Islam). Why? Because these are the foundational stories for each religion, and as such they are so infused with theology, and in some cases with mythology, that reconstructing history from them is not only impossible, but beside the point.

What is the distinction between "theological" and "historical," and how does it impact our work? "Theological" and "historical" are modes of discourse, or ways of speaking. A theological narrative is one whose primary purpose is to say something about God; a historical narrative is one whose primary

known as the Trinity. And that is why we start the history of Christianity in the fourth century.

Like Christianity, Islam is a religion of empire, and both are political religions, in that they assume that religious life and political power are intertwined. For the record, Second Temple Judaism was also a political religion, but not Rabbinic Judaism. The

Figure 5. "The Resurrection," by Piero della Francesca, c. 1460, depicting the resurrected figure of Christ.

rising from the dead, they are not giving us history. And when Islamic tradition talks about Muhammad having his heart removed from his chest by angels and cleaned, it is not giving us history. What these stories do communicate is each group's beliefs about God. That God's presence in their darkest moments is why there is light in the world, that God favors and protects, that God sends prophets and messiahs because he wants what is best for people, and so on. Even when theological narratives are set in the past, it is not the past they are interested in, but God's role in the past. Readers are meant to extrapolate: as it was in the past, so it will be in the present and future. Thus, even "historical"-sounding narratives in religious writings have a thorough-going theological purpose. And this makes them very difficult to use for reconstructing history. To treat David, Jesus, and Muhammad in

purpose is to say something about the past as it actually happened (even if we know, by post-modern standards, that this is impossible). I do not mean that one is bad and the other good, or one true and the other false. Nonetheless, the differences really matter, and they should not be confused. When people mistake theological narratives for historical narratives, they are not doing religious studies. They are reading their sacred texts religiously.

When the Hebrew Bible talks about Moses parting the Red Sea, it is not giving us history. When the Gospels talk about Jesus

Figure 6. "Conflict of the Knotted Heart" by Ian Garrett. Heart images are common in contemporary Islamic popular culture and allude to the legend whereby the two archangels, Mikal and Jibril (see p. 172) are credited with having purified the Prophet's heart before his Night Journey (*Isra*) from Mecca to Jerusalem and subsequent ascension (*Miraj*) to heaven (see p. 253).

the theology chapter does not mean these people did not exist historically. It simply means that their theological value is much higher for each religion than their historical value. In perfect illustration, when defenders argue for the historical accuracy of narratives about David, Jesus, and Muhammad, the purpose is *always* a theological one.

These stories not only tell the communities that value them important things about God, but also about where they have come from, who they are, how they are different (and generally better) than others. In this way, it can be useful to think of these stories as collective memory. Collective memory refers to the memories people have for events they did not witness. Those memories are given to us all by the groups that form us, that enculturate us, and that educate us. They are thus a critical element in our formation as members of communities. This is another thing that makes treatment of that material more appropriate in a discussion of theology than in a discussion of history.

—2—

History of Judaism

Chapter Overview

That no religion has an essence is a feature of contemporary theory of religion. To say that we cannot speak of Judaism in the past until monotheism has been developed is not to say that monotheism is the essence of Judaism. But it is to suggest that monotheism is the most innovative theological development before the Common Era, and that until its development, the religion of Israel is one among many competing national religions devoted to a national god. It is monotheism that sets Israelites apart from the religions around them, and which allows us to suggest a shift from "Israelite religion" to Judaism. The development of monotheism occurs as a response to the Babylonian exile, and so we begin there. The rest of the history of Judaism is one of interaction and interchange with non-Jews, with Jews as minorities always living among Babylonians, Greeks, Romans, Syrians, Egyptians, Byzantine Christians, Muslims, and then European Christians. This is a history of diaspora and eventually nationhood.

Second Temple Judaism

Israelite Religion was henotheistic and monolatrous. The first term means that they worshipped one god, rather than many, but readily acknowledged the existence of other gods. The second term refers to practice: they served one god, not many. Neither term should be confused with monotheism. One must register just how radical **henotheism** and monotheism were in the first millennium BCE. Most people in that world believed that it took many gods to meet the needs of surviving in the world. The notion that one god could provide everything would have made little sense to most people. The idea of monotheism appears to have made its way into Judaism because of the Babylonian conquest and exile. First of all, exiled Judeans would have come into contact with Zoroastrians, who, while not monotheists strictly speaking, were the closest thing to it in the ancient world. Second, the experience of being separated from Judea may have inspired those in exile to conclude that the God of Israel was not merely one

History of the Kingdoms

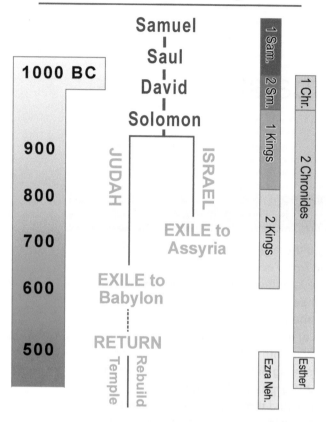

| 1000 BC | | Samuel |
| 900 | JUDAH | Saul |

Samuel
|
Saul
|
David
|
Solomon

1000 BC
900
800
700
600
500

JUDAH   ISRAEL

EXILE to Assyria

EXILE to Babylon

RETURN

Temple   Rebuild

1 Sam.
2 Sm.
1 Kings
2 Kings
Ezra Neh.

1 Chr.
2 Chronides
Esther

Figure 7. Israelite scriptural history.

Figure 8. Wall detail showing the mythical snake-headed *mushushshu* molded into the mud bricks along the main processional way, Babylon.

national god among many, but the one God of the universe.

No one quite knows how there came to be two kingdoms, one by the name of Israel (the northern kingdom) and the other Judah (the southern kingdom), with Jerusalem as the capital of Judah. The biblical account has the legendary King David (c. 1000 BCE) uniting twelve loosely confederated tribes under one king, which split into two after the death of his son Solomon. The alternative is that there never was unity, and that the northern kingdom always existed. Either way, in about 720 BCE, the Assyrians arrived

from Mesopotamia, and in taking over their corner of the world, demanded tribute from Israel. Israel apparently refused to pay and was crushed for it. Perhaps the Judahites to the south agreed to pay the tribute, and therefore survived the Assyrian assault.

The Assyrian Kingdom came to encompass what is currently Iraq, Syria, Jordan, Israel, Egypt, and much of Turkey. It was

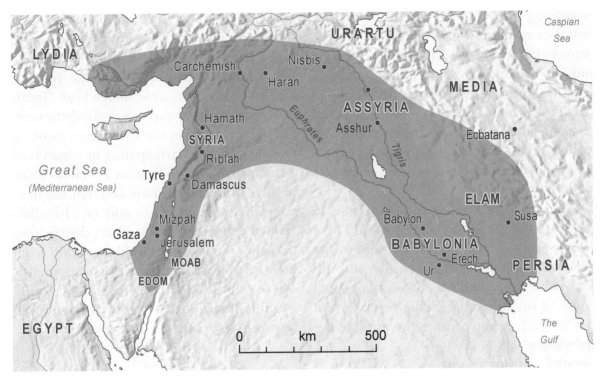

Figure 9. The Ancient Near East, showing Babylonia, as well as the Assyrians whom the Babylonians also conquered on their way to conquering Israel and destroying Jerusalem.

displaced by Babylon, a city south of Assyria in Mesopotamia, in the sixth century BCE. The Babylonian Empire moved north to take over Assyria, and then west to take over the entirety of the kingdom established by Assyria. But the Babylonians also attempted a move eastward into Persia (what is now Iran), and that would be a costly mistake for them. In 586 BCE, Babylonian King Nebuchadnezzar destroyed Jerusalem and the First Temple, and dispersed the people of Judah. The priests and any elite members of society who did not flee the land were kidnapped and removed to Babylon.

When the Babylonians attempted to push eastward from Mesopotamia into Persia, the Persians pushed back swiftly and decisively. The Persian Empire became much larger than the Babylonian Empire ever

was, extending from the Indus river well into Greece and including Egypt and what is now Libya. The result was positive for the Judahites: about fifty years after the destruction of Jerusalem, the Babylonians were defeated by the Persians (538 BCE), led by King Cyrus, and the Israelites were invited back from exile. In addition, the Judahites, were given help in rebuilding their destroyed temple. The Persians ruled Judah, they did not restore the monarchy or bequeath independence; nonetheless, they were seen as enough of a force for good that Israelite tradition would later bestow the title "Messiah" on the Persian king, so much did they feel that Cyrus was an instrument of God.

The Persian kings Cyrus (576–530 BCE) and Darius I (522–486 BCE) helped in the rebuilding of the new temple, the completion date commonly given as 515 BCE. This begins the period we call **Second Temple Judaism**, a period that would last until that temple's destruction by Rome in 70 CE. In fact, the Second Temple was not the sort of place that was ever really completed, as it was under almost constant renovation, expansion, and refurbishment over its nearly six hundred years.

Though Cyrus allowed those in exile to return to their land, not all returned. These people come to form the beginning of the Diaspora, which we shall consider shortly. Jews who remained in Babylonia would come to be influential in the formation of the Talmud. As you can see, the event of the **Babylonian exile** reverberated through this people for centuries.

Others, however, did return. The Hebrew Bible claims they found their religion in disarray: people sacrificing to other gods and abandoning, some by malice others by laziness and forgetfulness, the traditions of their fathers and the laws of Moses. The covenants that had been made with Abraham, Moses, and David appeared broken. Whether this depiction is entirely accurate is impossible to discern, but regardless, it is the depiction offered by those who returned,

particularly a Judahite figure named Ezra the Scribe, also known as Ezra the Priest.

The narratives associated with Ezra depict him taking control of an Israelite religion that had gone off-course: he read the "Torah of Moses" to the people of Jerusalem, moving them to reform their behavior, insisting that people stop participating in pagan rituals, and installing covenant renewal rituals in their place. He also insisted that any marriages between Israelites and non-Israelites (mixed marriages) be dissolved, threatening that any who refused would be cut off from their people. Ezra would also apparently oversee the start of the process of creating a canon of scripture, but that discussion will be postponed until Chapter Five.

Figure 10. A group of Samaritans assembled on Mt. Gerizim for Passover (1867). (See Figure 78 for an image of contemporary Passover celebrations.)

Where Were the Women?

Notice how male-centered (or androcentric) this narrative is. We refer to society in this period (and in most of the ancient world) as patriarchal, the etymology of which refers to the power men held. Men were overwhelmingly the leaders, conquerors, builders, and destroyers in antiquity. And, not surprisingly, the texts of these ancient cultures are androcentric, meaning they are focused on the male world and perspective. Nonetheless, it would be wrong to assume that women were entirely invisible or silent in this period (see Figure 17). Indeed, there are often female characters in the Hebrew Bible who are colorful, and narratively interesting figures. A more in-depth study of the history of Israel would allow one to see those women in action.

Another effect of Ezra's reforms is that it increased animosity between Israelites and **Samaritans**. The Samaritans descended from the Israel that was toppled by the Assyrians. In the wake of that defeat, they developed their own Jewish traditions, and used a different set of scriptures (accepting the books of Moses, but not the prophetic writings). In the same century as Ezra's return, and the rebuilding of the Jerusalem temple, the Samaritans built their own temple on **Mt. Gerizim**, claiming it to be the true home of God, and claiming themselves to be the true inheritors of the traditions of Moses. It seems that Ezra's return and his reforms exacerbated tensions with the Samaritans. These tensions grew, resulting in a few battles between the Judeans and the Samaritans. The Samaritan form of Judaism continues to exist today, though there are fewer than one thousand of them. They live on Mt. Gerizim and near Tel Aviv (see Figure 10).

Judahite tradition credits Ezra with reforming a religion nearly destroyed by military conquest and exile: the covenant with God was renewed with vigor, the temple functions were set as a locus of authority and respect, and the Torah was collected, edited, and authorized.

The Diaspora

War always displaces civilians. The Assyrian and Babylonian conquests forced many Israelites into neighboring nations: Egypt, Asia Minor (now Turkey), Greece, Italy. Both the Assyrian and Babylonian conquests had an additional feature not typical of war: the forced exile and relocation of people, particularly the elite. In these two wars, about two hundred years apart, people both left their land and were taken from their land by conquering armies.

The word "Diaspora" in this context refers to Jews who were scattered throughout the Mediterranean and the Near East, and who remained (presumably voluntarily) in foreign lands. Some Diaspora Jews tried futilely to resist being influenced by the dominant cultures around them. Others did not resist at all, but outright embraced change. The result was a growing number of Jews who did things differently, who thought differently, and who spoke languages other than Hebrew.

Such was the case with Jews living in Egypt in this period. When Egypt itself was taken over by the Greeks, the language of Jews living there became Greek. Unable to read their scriptures in Hebrew, they produced, probably in the second century BCE, a Greek version of their Bible. This translation is known as the Septuagint (and by the abbreviation: LXX). It purports to be a translation of the Hebrew Bible, but it is in fact much more than that. It is in parts a translation, though one heavily influenced by Greek philosophy, but in other parts there are additional passages and additional books.

Another indirect effect of the Diaspora experience on Judaism, seen as well in the Septuagint, was Hellenization. Hellenization resulted from the conquest of Alexander the Great over the Persians in 333 BCE. In addition to the obvious military imperialism that comes with the expansion of an empire, there was in this case a cultural imperialism. For the most part, people who lived in the Greek empire embraced Greek culture: dress, learning, art, and language. A modern analogy can be found in American culture's attractiveness to many around the world: its food and fashion trends and television shows are watched and imitated with near frenzy around the world. So the term "Hellenization" refers to the process of non-Greek cultures taking on the features of Greek culture.

Hellenization was especially controversial in Judea itself, which was the name for Israel in this period. Though some embraced Hellenistic culture, others were wary of it, and some openly hostile. But the fact remains: Hellenism was pervasive. Scholars used to think that Jews, having such an interest in purity and in separating themselves from non-Jews, would have been isolated from the effects of Hellenism in Judea itself. But when archeologists discovered Greek theaters even in the smaller cities of Judea, let alone the plethora of Greek institutions in Jerusalem, it became clear that it was no longer safe to wonder *whether* Judea had been Hellenized, but rather *how much* it had been Hellenized.

Legitimating Myths

A myth is a story designed to *do* something, very often to provide answers to pressing questions: why do our people dress the way we do? Where did language come from? Why do rainbows appear after rainstorms? Why do snakes not have legs? But myths can also be developed in order to provide legitimacy to something (a text, a practice, an idea, a community), to explain why this thing is *right, proper*, or *authoritative*. These exist in every religion, and there is one about the Septuagint (LXX). Because the original language of the Bible was Hebrew, some would have felt that translating the Bible into another language would rob it of its divine authority. So a Greek-speaking community associated in some way with the translation of the LXX developed a myth about its origins designed to address the particular question about divine authority. According to the story, the king of Egypt wished to own a translation of the law books of all the peoples of the world in his library, so he invited 72 learned men from Israel (teachers, scribes, priests) to his palace. They translated the Bible in total isolation from each other, and after 72 days all emerged with exactly the same translation. People then knew as well as we do now that 72 independent translations of something as long as the Hebrew Bible that were identical would be impossible. The story was meant to express that God had a hand in the creation of the LXX, and therefore it was good!

Figure 11. Cliff face surrounding the grotto of Pan at Banias (Panias), shown at the lower left. The rock-cut niches, with scalloped semi-domes, once contained statues dedicated to Pan, and are located in the Golan Heights. The Greek inscription beneath the niche to the right of the cave dates that dedication to 148/149 CE, although the sanctuary to Pan, known as the Paneion, was established at this site before 200 BCE.

Hellenization was not always voluntary. There are a few points at which Hellenistic rulers tried to force the replacement of Judean culture with Greek culture. One such point was in the second century BCE. The ruler of the **Seleucid** dynasty in Syria, which controlled Israel at the time, decided to force wholesale Hellenization on it. He was Antiochus IV Epiphanes, and he decreed it illegal to own or read a Torah, and to follow the Laws of Moses, and he killed many Jews found to be abiding by their religion. Finally, Antiochus IV Epiphanes entered the Jerusalem temple and dedicated it to another god by sacrificing a pig on the altar. This event came to be known in Jewish collective memory as the Abomination of Desolation, and it triggered a rebellion by the Maccabees,

which they won over Syria in 161 BCE. This is the story that serves as the backdrop for Hanukkah (see Chapter Eight). The result of the rebellion led by the Maccabees was the establishment of the Hasmonean Dynasty.

The Effects of Roman Occupation

The Hasmoneans ruled over Judea for nearly one hundred years. It was the first time Jews had political autonomy in over four hundred years, and it went badly. There was no peace and no stability. The Hasmoneans broke the long tradition of keeping the High Priesthood within the bloodline of the Levites, which Temple law required, by repeatedly selling the office to the highest bidder. The perception of impurity was worsened by

What's in a Name?

The descendants of Jacob have many names, depending sometimes on who is using the name. Sometimes they are called Israelites (being descendants of Israel and eventually residents of a nation called Israel). When they are in Egypt, they are called Israelites sometimes, but also Hebrews. The Assyrians conquer Israel, located in the north, while the Babylonians conquer Judah. After the exile, Judah is known as Judea, the north is known as Samaria, and there are half a dozen other provinces, comprising Israel. And finally, because the Romans named the whole area Palestine (originally a mispronunciation of Philistine), they will also be known as Palestinians in that period.

In the same period, in Greek they were called *Ioudaioi*, literally Judeans, and probably best transliterated that way, rather than translated as "Jews," a more distantly related term etymologically. In the same way, we reserve the term "Israeli" for citizens of the modern state of Israel, and do not use that term for antiquity. Despite this historical variety of names, the terms "Jew" and "Judaism" are often used in this book for convenience, even when it is not technically or historically accurate to do so.

the rank corruption, when the Hasmoneans would happily replace a recently installed High Priest with a new, higher bidder for the office. Many people in Judea were unhappy with the state of affairs under the Hasmoneans, but it was the Romans who changed everything.

Unwilling to tolerate what had become a civil war between Hasmonean brothers, the Roman general Pompey took over in 63 BCE. Judea, as it was called then by Rome, was once again no longer an independent Jewish state, and it would not be again until 1948. The presence of Romans on Judean soil was a problem for many Jews, for the Romans tended to be insensitive to Jewish religious practices, and their taxation burden was heavy. Therefore, the next 120 years would be increasingly tumultuous, peaking in the Jewish War against Rome in 66–72 CE.

The crisis of Roman occupation and how to respond to it appears to have resulted in the development of formal, internal divisions. Because religion and politics were wholly intertwined in the ancient Mediterranean (e.g., the Temple was as much a political institution as a religious one, and the Roman emperors were gods), these divisions were both political and religious.

- Pharisees (arose in the second century BCE). A grassroots movement, the popular Pharisees worked among the people. Though there were some elites in Jerusalem who identified with the Pharisees, the group was comprised mainly of the common people, those outside of the circles of power. Pharisees were concerned with purity and with Torah observance. But they also held some unique beliefs: they believed in the resurrection of the body in the afterlife, and that they were in possession of a special body of orally transmitted teachings from Moses. This was known as the Oral Torah, and it would eventually form the basis of the Talmud. The Pharisees lacked political or religious power until the destruction of the Second Temple. Pharisees responded to Roman presence by focusing on Torah observance and purity. It is possible that their interest in purity in the home and daily life developed because of the meddling with the office of the High Priest at the Temple. The Pharisaical movement eventually developed into the Rabbinic movement.

- Sadducees (arose in the second century BCE). In contrast to the Pharisees, the Sadducees were elite, small in number, and not very popular. Sadducees tended to serve as interim leaders on behalf of the Romans, and thus always risked being accused of collusion with the occupier. The Sadducees rejected the ideas that made the Pharisees unique: resurrection, and the Oral Torah. Since they were closely allied to Temple governance, Sadducees were more concerned with priestly purity, in contrast to the Pharisees, who sought ways to have the Torah apply to all walks of life. Sadducee response to Roman power was to work with it in order to keep the peace.

- Essenes/Qumranites (arose in the first century BCE). It is widely thought that Essenes lived in the community found at the site of Qumran, on the northeast shore of the Dead Sea. Whoever lived here, and produced the Dead Sea Scrolls, we know that the community represented a group that fled Jerusalem. Because their writings refer to their own "Teacher of Righteousness" and complain about the "Wicked Priest," scholars guess that the group originated during the period of Hasmoneans' meddling in the affairs of the Temple. This group felt they were the true, pure remnant of Israel, and that all other Jews were in the wrong. We do not know

Figure 12. The Dead Sea Scroll of the book of Isaiah.

their opinion of Rome, but we do know that Roman troops flattened Qumran on their way to besiege Jerusalem in 68 CE.

- Zealots/Sicarii (arose in the first century CE). The Zealots and Sicarii were militant groups who carried out a guerrilla war on the Romans. They enjoyed a few early victories, which pushed Rome to bring in its best legions and siege engines to surround and eventually destroy Jerusalem. They also carried out assassinations of Sadducees for colluding with the Romans, and even fought openly with one another in the streets of Jerusalem while the city was under siege. When the city was destroyed, they fled to Masada to finish out the war.

- Christians (arose in the first century CE). Followers of the Jewish figure Jesus of Nazareth came to believe he was the long-awaited Messiah of Israel. The language they used of Jesus had powerful political overtones to a Roman ear – Lord, Savior, Messiah – bordering on the treasonous. Christians appeared to resist Roman occupation by focusing on and hoping for the arrival of a new kingdom, the Kingdom of Heaven preached by Jesus. At the same time, they appear to have resisted in an entirely peaceful manner.

How to categorize these groups, or what to call them, is a tricky question in the academic discussion of this period. Some refer to them as sects. In some respects that is

Figure 13. A replica of the Second Temple in ancient Jerusalem.

Figure 14. A tetradracham (ancient Greek silver coin) showing the temple containing the Ark of the Covenant from the period of the Second Jewish Revolt.

enough with the majority that they no longer want to be members of that group. Second, the breakup tends to involve tension, anger, accusations of betrayal or illegitimacy, and sometimes violence. This does not describe the relationship of Sadducees and Pharisees to each other, nor to the larger group of Second Temple Jews. But it does describe the early experience of the followers of Jesus, many of whom were Jews and who came to think about Jesus in a way that the majority of Jews did not. Pharisees, Sadducees, and Essenes are better categorized as "schools of thought," not least because we suspect that these groups were not easy to tell apart in the first century CE. Whatever the case, they do seem to represent different ways of being Jewish in Roman-occupied Palestine.

reasonable. A sect is a smaller group of people who are to a certain degree distinct from others within the larger group. The fact that Pharisees and Sadducees, for example, are reasonably distinct from one another might suggest they can be categorized as sects. But sects have other characteristics that do not apply to Pharisees and Sadducees. First, the formation of a sect involves disassociation, wherein a group of people disagree strongly

The Jewish War

Romans governed over Judea from 63 BCE onward. They were initially interested in appointing Jews to govern over the land, including Herod the Great (who dramatically renovated and enhanced the temple). His sons governed after him, with Rome dividing up the land among the three of them. However, in Judea, the province that

Flavius Josephus

Yosef ben Matityahu (b. 37 CE) was a commander of a rebel group in the war against Rome. In 67 CE, he and his men were surrounded by Roman troops in Yodfat. Unwilling to surrender, they undertook a suicide pact, but when all his men were dead, Josephus himself surrendered to Rome. Though initially imprisoned, he became a client of the Romans, and a member of the family of the emperors Vespasian and Titus. Josephus would change his name to Flavius Josephus, because Flavius was the family name of Vespasian and Titus, his patrons. Josephus wrote extensively, under the patronage of the Flavians, about the war, about Judaism at the time, and about the history of the Jews. Considered a traitor by many Jews, and with a heavy agenda in some of his writings, he remains one of our best sources for this period of history.

Figure 15. The Arch of Titus in the city of Rome contains this relief image of Roman soldiers carrying a giant menorah as loot from the conquered Temple in Jerusalem.

combined with what could be an oppressive burden of taxation, increased tensions. Some Jews felt that only God could rule over the land (the term for this is theocracy). It did not help that the Roman emperors considered themselves to be gods. Judeans, particularly those in the north – the Galileans – chafed at taxation.

Small rebel groups formed as tensions increased, and these groups sought to disrupt Roman power and wealth by robbing Roman granaries and caravans, and ambushing small groups of Roman soldiers. Open war broke out in 66 CE between these rebel groups and Rome, but the rebels were no match for Rome in open battle, so they fled to Jerusalem, a walled city on a mountain. But over the next three years, various

included Jerusalem, Archelaus governed so badly that he was removed by Rome. After this, only Roman procurators (non-Jews) were appointed to that province. The best known of these is Pilate (who governed 26–36 CE), in part because of controversial decisions he made, and in part because it was he who authorized the crucifixion of Jesus of Nazareth. Pilate cared little about offending the religious sensibilities of the Jews, and frequently had to rely on his soldiers to quell dissent and possible rebellion.

As Roman subjects (though not citizens), Judeans were required to pay taxes to Rome. The taxes were used above all to support Roman troop presence there. The presence of Roman troops and Roman governance,

Figure 16. Aerial view of Masada in the Judean Desert with the Dead Sea in the distance.

Figure 17. A denarius (coin) struck by the Romans in 70 CE to commemorate their suppression of the First Jewish Revolt. The obverse features Vespasian, who was sent as Roman commander to Judea by the emperor Nero in 67 CE, and became emperor two years later. Of interest here is the depiction of a female Jewish prisoner with hands tied behind her back. Behind her is a palm tree, the symbol of Judea, and below is the caption "IVDAEA" (Judea).

rebel leaders arose, each claiming to be the rightful leader of the Jews. They fought each other in the city, in a civil war. In April of the year 70 CE, highly decorated Roman legions arrived to lay siege to Jerusalem, and only then did the rebels unite. But it was too late; the people were decimated, exhausted, and starving. The Romans worked quickly and methodically to breach the walls, and did so in four months. When the Romans entered the city in August of that year, there was no resistance left among the battered citizens of the city. The Romans destroyed most of the city, and burned the Second Temple (some suggest by accident) to the ground.

The temple that was rebuilt in 515 BCE with the help of Cyrus, the Persian King, and which was taken over and won back from the Syrians in the second century BCE, and which was renovated a number of times, each time becoming more grand, was now gone. Only the huge stones of the western-most wall remained, stones that remain there to this day. These stones are very significant for many Jews, for they represent the memories of a lost former glory.

A last remnant of rebels, nearly 1000 in number, escaped the burning city and holed themselves up at Masada, a seemingly impregnable fortress atop 300–1300-foot-high cliffs. But the patient Romans eventually overcame these walls too, and the rebels were massacred in 72 CE, marking the end of the Jewish War. Casualty estimates for the war as a whole range from 250,000 to 1.1 million, most of which were civilian deaths, and an additional possibly 90,000 people enslaved.

Though they lost the Jewish War badly, resistance against Rome did not stop. Bar Kokhba, which means the "son of a star," claimed to be the Messiah and led a revolt against Rome in 132–136 CE, and even managed to gain government, until Rome sent its legions to utterly crush the rebellion and re-establish Roman rule there. Ancient sources tell of half a million casualties and nearly one thousand villages razed by Rome.

Rabbinic Judaism

The effects of these two devastating wars with Rome cannot be exaggerated. The Temple was gone, and so too every activity associated with it: a High Priest and the exercise of his authority, community, sacrifice, atonement, pilgrimage, and taxation. The few people who remained in the land were not allowed to live in Jerusalem again – a Roman legion stationed there ensured that. The land would be governed by others – Romans, and then Christians, and then Muslims, and then the British – for the next 1812 years.

Figure 18. This basalt "Seat of Moses" bears an inscription in Aramaic in memory of Yudan. It was the chair used by the local Rabbi or another speaker who presided over readings from the Torah and other Hebrew scriptures.

Rome officially renamed Judea as Palestine, and Jerusalem as Aelia Capitolina.

It is difficult to know precisely what happened in the years immediately following the destruction of the Temple because the sources we have all come from the Rabbis, those who redefine and reinvigorate Judaism in the absence of the Priesthood and the Temple. Not surprisingly, these sources present the Rabbis as centrally important, powerfully present, and sometimes miracle-working heroes. There is no question that the Rabbis did succeed in redefining post-Temple Judaism, but they likely did so over a much longer, and in some instances more contested, process than these sources claim (see "Rabbis" text box, p. 200).

Eventually, the Rabbis became central to this process. We know that the center of Judaism shifted to – and was shared by – the **Galilee** and Babylonia. And we know that Rabbis came to replace High Priests as those who defined proper Jewish practice. It is likely that the influence of the Rabbis, their centrality to post-Temple Judaism, developed quite slowly, perhaps taking six hundred years to solidify their authority, but regardless, they did eventually come to form the center of this new development in the history of Judaism.

Only two Jewish groups survived the destruction of the Second Temple: Pharisees and Christians. Zealots and Sicarii were all killed in the war, the Essenes at Qumran were killed or scattered in 68 CE, and the Sadducees were rendered obsolete, since the Romans no longer needed a governing class in Judea. By 66 CE, the Pharisees and Christians were both well-established grassroots movements with broad and popular bases, and it is this characteristic that allowed them to survive the war. Both groups would respond to the destruction of the Temple in different ways: Christians by opening up Judaism to Gentiles (as we shall see in Chapter Three), and the Pharisees by shifting religious observance from the Temple to the home and to the synagogue, by shifting from sacrifice to prayer and education, and finally, by shifting authority from priests to Rabbis. The result was Rabbinic Judaism.

Rabbi is a Hebrew word meaning, "my teacher." Since the Phari-

Figure 19. The western wall was the only part of the Second Temple left by the Romans. Today it is a site of Jewish prayer and pilgrimage.

sees focused on the interpretation of Israelite writings in order to derive examples of proper daily conduct, they considered themselves teachers of the text, and thus liked, evidently, to be addressed as "my teacher." The Priesthood was (ideally) a bloodline, an office only certain families were allowed to hold, but Rabbis were simply educated and charismatic men. Since they considered themselves teachers, schools developed around them, called a *bet midrash*, "house of learning."

Rabbinic sources tell of Yohanan ben Zakkai leaving Jerusalem in dramatic fashion during the Jewish War and resettling in the coastal city of Yavneh. From there, Rabbinical schools moved to Tiberias, a city in the Galilee, safely away from Jerusalem. But Roman troop presence all over the land and their continuing distrust of the Jews made life there difficult, and many Jews joined

communities in Babylonia that had not left after the exile. Jews had a good relationship with the authorities there, and they were allowed some degree of autonomy and a life free from persecution. As a result, the Rabbinic Judaism of today owes much more to its development in Babylonia than in Palestine.

The key to Judaism's survival was in developing religious practices that could adapt to the destruction of the Temple. The challenge of this is not to be underestimated, as Judaism had been a temple religion, with sacrifice its main liturgical activity, for nearly nine hundred years. A new Judaism required a fundamentally different way of thinking about almost everything. The accomplishment of Rabbinic Judaism was to show Jews how Judaism could go on without the Temple, and their texts illustrate how the Rabbis imagined that happening. Had their vision

The Temple and Synagogues

The Second Temple in Jerusalem was not merely the heart of religious life. It was also the heart of economic, political, and cultural life. The Temple was the site of sacrifice, the central ritual of ancient Israelite religion. This ritual was what allowed the Israelites to commune with a God who lived among them – *in* the Temple. In the Holy of Holies, the High Priest would win the atonement of his people before God. Jews came from around the known world – from Rome, Greece, Asia Minor, Egypt, and Babylonia, possibly from even further – to perform the sacrifice. They came three times a year, for the festivals of Pesach, Shavuot, and Sukkot (see Chapter Eight).

Pilgrimage, not unlike tourism, always generates revenue, for pilgrims need places to eat and sleep, and they need animals to sacrifice. But Jews around the world also paid a tax to support the Temple and its operations. Doubtless, many were happy to pay the tax, seeing it as an act of loyalty to God, but it is known that at certain periods this tax was resisted and resented. Those who resisted, and others who deviated from elite expectations (those who transgress the Torah, or who cause trouble), might feel the political power wielded by the Temple. And the Temple, by the time the last renovations were completed, was a cultural center as well: people met there, and education happened there. Indeed, the entire Temple complex took up one-third of the city, and sat higher than any other building. Visually, the Temple would have been quite imposing.

The word "synagogue" comes from a Greek word meaning "gathered together." In its earliest use, the word referred to the act of gathering, not to the building dedicated specifically to the activity, a later development. Nonetheless, synagogues did exist (sometimes as buildings for that purpose, sometimes as meetings in people's homes) long before the destruction of the Second Temple. This was made necessary by the Diaspora experience: though some Jews traveled to Jerusalem three times a year, this would not be economically feasible for everyone, and even those who did go when required would want a community with other Jews more than thrice yearly. The synagogue offered Diaspora Jews an alternative between pilgrimages. But the synagogue was not initially a replacement for the Temple, and the two did not compete with one another. Sacrifice and atonement, for instance, could not happen at a synagogue, nor taxation. Synagogues were merely meeting places among Jews who were far from the Temple (though, by the time of the Temple's destruction, there were actually synagogues in Jerusalem too). The lower status of the synagogue relative to the Temple would change, of course, with the destruction of the Temple. At the same time, the home became a key location of Jewish religiosity: the dining room table and the kitchen are, for instance, where purity is exercised, through the rules of kashrut.

not taken hold, Judaism might not have survived past the second century.

Temple Judaism and Rabbinic Judaism are fundamentally different entities. Rabbis would argue for temple sacrifice to be replaced by a different kind of sacrifice: the sacrifice of the self that occurs in selfless acts of loving kindness. Sacrifice could no longer be the primary way to interact with God, so prayer would take over that role. Temple Judaism required temple purity, but with the Temple gone, concern for ritual purity shifted from the Temple to the home: Jews were to eat in a kosher way, avoid contact with blood, avoid sexual misconduct, and maintain a ritually pure household. In a way,

Rabbi Hillel vs. Rabbi Shammai

We should not be surprised to discover there is as much diversity in Rabbinic Judaism as in earlier forms of Judaism. The Rabbis appeared to have cherished dissenting opinions, for they are frequently preserved. Nonetheless, they did have favorites, and Hillel was one of them. There is a well-known story contrasting the styles of Hillel and a competing Rabbi, Shammai, both of whom apparently lived long before the destruction of the Temple. It is, however, challenging to discern how much later Rabbinic material, which comes to final form in the seventh century, can tell us about life and conversations that occurred in the first century. Anachronism – the assumption that later ideas were present or dominant also in earlier periods – is always a

risk. Nonetheless, this story reflects the fact that Hillel was held in great esteem by Jews. The story is recorded like this:

It happened that a certain heathen came before Shammai and said to him, "Convert me, on the condition that you teach me the whole Torah while I stand on one foot." But Shammai chased him away with the builder's tool that was in his hand. When the same man came before Hillel, and also asked Hillel to teach him the entire Torah while standing on one foot, Hillel replied, "What is hateful to you, do not do to your neighbor: that is the whole Torah; the rest is commentary. Go and learn it."

(from tractate *Shabbat* 31a in the Talmud)

the dining room table replaces the altar, not as a location for sacrifice, but as the place where one shows loyalty to God's laws. What is more, energy is no longer expended on pilgrimage or sacrifice, but on study. Finally, Rabbinic Judaism differs from Temple Judaism in one more, extremely important, way: it obtained a new scripture, namely the Talmud.

Recall that the Pharisees claimed to be in possession of a collection of sayings passed down orally from Moses. This collection of sayings was written down around 200 CE (forming the Mishnah) and then interpreted between 200 and 650 CE (called the Gemarah). Together, they comprise the Talmud (650 CE). The Mishnah is not sacred writing in precisely the same way that the Hebrew Bible is, but the energy the Rabbis put into learning it, developing it, and interpreting it shows that the Mishnah was approached with much the same attention as the Hebrew Bible. The Talmud is one of

the key texts Jews use to live in the world as Jews (see Chapter Five), and the Mishnah is considered to have come from God, since what came to Moses came from God.

The key result here is that in Temple Judaism, religion was controlled and defined by the Priesthood, which ran in a family blood-line. Proximity to that bloodline (or distance from it) determined the authority individuals had. By contrast, authority in the Rabbinic period had the potential to be somewhat more democratic and individualistic: sometimes, authority was determined less by family line and more by the intellectual and charismatic abilities of individual teachers. On average, learning counted for more than family name or bloodline under Rabbinic Judaism.

Living with Muslims and Christians

The arrival of Islam in the seventh century CE cemented the authority of the Rabbis and their tradition of learning in the Abbasid Dynasty (750–1258 CE). Educated Jews held prominent positions at all levels of Islamic society. The Rabbis would never exert absolute control over Jews, but they would have considerable authority and were accorded considerable respect by Jews from Europe to Persia. For example, in this period, Judaism had not yet developed a standardized system for training Rabbis, so many locations lacked experienced leadership. When a local inexperienced Rabbi had a question about Jewish practice or law – marriage or divorce, liability – he might write a letter to a far-away Rabbi. These Rabbis, known as the *geonim*, had authority because the Islamic authorities in Babylonia gave it to them, and from there this authority, reputation, and respect spread throughout Jewish communities around the world.

Rabbinic responses to these letters asking for advice were kept, and so we know a little about this period. These writings are called *responsa*. These responsa were treated like legal precedent, and in this way the *geonim* in Babylonia came to shape and define Rabbinic Judaism. The old responsa remain available in published volumes, and new ones are still being created, for many Jewish communities have continued the practice of seeking the legal advice of a distant respected teacher.

Judaism's most revered sage would come from this period of strong Jewish–Islamic relations: Moses Maimonides (1135–1204) (see text box, p. 130). Rabbi Moses Ben Maimon (known by his Latin name as Maimonides, and to Jewish tradition as Rambam) was born in Spain in 1135, but was exiled in his early teens when life

Jewish–Islamic Relations

The Constitution of Medina (see Chapter Four) imposed a vision of a unified community on the city, but not everyone in the city was happy with it. On the one hand, this was good news for the Jews of the city, because it both included them and acknowledged their religion. On the other hand, it also demanded loyalty to a central leader, Muhammad, and since Muhammad was still at war with Mecca, loyalty was paramount. But the Jewish tribes in Medina, who like the Muslims were Arab, could not accept Muhammad's prophetic claims. They, therefore, rejected and opposed the Muslims, and even cooperated with Muhammad's enemies during times of war. Two of the smaller tribes were expelled from Medina early on, and the largest tribe was massacred in 627 for treason during the Battle of the Trench.

Despite this rocky start, Jewish–Islamic relations were generally peaceful, until the modern period. Jews and Muslims were theological, intellectual, and political allies against Christianity in the time between ancient Medina and modern Palestine. Jews were frequently found in very high political offices in Islamic government. This does not mean that Jews and Muslims got along in every place all the time, but that violence between them was occasional and not inevitable. Indeed, the Qur'an reveals a similarly inconsistent view of Jews: Sura 5.51 has been read to mean that Muslims are not to take Jews (or Christians) as friends or allies; on the other hand, Sura 2.62 has been read to suggest that Jews (and Christians) will be rewarded for their belief in God. (A sura is a chapter or section of the Qur'an.)

Jewish-Islamic Philosophy

In the ninth century CE, Greek philosophy, particularly the philosophy of Aristotle and his school, became influential and prominent in Islamic theology. This is seen most ably in the writings of Islamic theologians such as al-Kindi (801–873 CE) and Ibn Sina (980–1037 CE). Ibn Sina (known more commonly by his Christianized name, Avicenna) wrote on medicine, physics, psychology, and theology. He is clearly not only a template for a Jewish figure like Maimonides, but an intellectual predecessor.

Ibn Sina's strong reliance on Aristotle showed thinkers like Maimonides what was possible. Maimonides receives credit, because of this, for being the theologian who makes Aristotle widely accepted in Jewish theology.

What is more, Maimonides' work, the *Guide for the Perplexed* was originally written and published in Arabic because Islamic philosophers and readers were his primary conversation partners. The *Guide* was not translated into Hebrew until the year Maimonides died (1204). Maimonides' influence on Christian theology is apparent in the work of Thomas Aquinas (1225–1274 CE).

---

under Islamic Almohad rule became intolerable. Maimonides eventually ended up in Cairo, where he served as doctor to the Grand Vizier of Egypt and as a leader of the Jewish community there. Maimonides wrote on medical, astronomical, philosophical, and theological topics. His most famous work was entitled *Guide for the Perplexed.*

Maimonides attempted to reconcile the tension between reason and revelation. He rejected both Jewish and Islamic positions (both known as *kalam*) that demand a starting assumption that reason and scripture must by necessity agree. Maimonides was comfortable with sometimes contradictory scripture. He also argued strenuously against the notion that God had materiality, and because of this claimed that knowledge about God could only be acquired negatively. Called Negative Theology, this position maintains that God can only be known by what he is not: God is not ignorant, not impotent, not multiple, not temporal. Because of these claims, Maimonides made opponents among both Islamic and Jewish theologians, but also had many supporters.

Life for Jews during the Middle Ages (see "Jewish–Islamic Relations" text box, p. 44) varied between extremes. The most common experience was peaceful co-existence with Islamic and Christian rulers, and in many cases cooperative relationships with their Christian and Islamic neighbors. Some of the high points of Jewish culture and learning also happen in this period, in intellectually rich Islamic environments. On the other extreme, Jews suffered from mob and state-sponsored violence, forced conversions, and wholesale expulsions from cities and nations, all of these from both Muslims and Christians. As a rule, however, Islamic persecution of Jews was less extreme than persecution from Christians: Jews were occasionally forced to convert and expelled from Islamic lands, but the Islamic versions of these tended to look mild in comparison to Christian counterparts. Jews experienced forms and levels of persecution in Christians lands never seen before.

The Crusades (eleventh century and onwards), which were supposed to be about Christians saving other Christians from Islamic persecution, also targeted Jews (see more in Chapter Three). Thousands of Jews were killed, or forcibly baptized, and sometimes their children were kidnapped as Christian armies passed through English and German cities on their way to Jerusalem. Jews were forcibly converted to Christianity, and then later subjected to torture (the **Inquisition**) to test the sincerity of these forced conversions! European Christians created the "Blood Libel" against the Jews, accusing them of killing Christians in order to use their blood for magic healing rituals, and bathing in the blood of Christian children. It was widely claimed among medieval Christians that Jewish men menstruated, and that only Christian

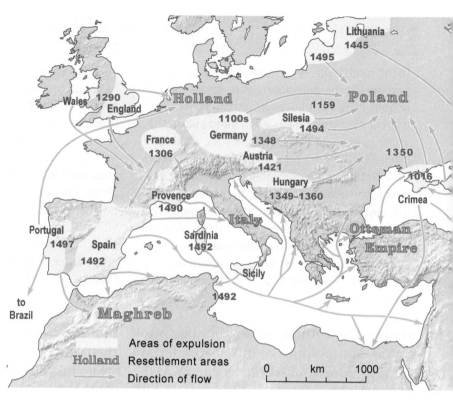

Figure 20. The Jewish expulsions and resettlement: from 1290 onwards, Jews were subject to national expulsions, which pushed them increasingly into Eastern Europe.

Jewish Middle Ages

The term Jewish Middle Ages can be used to describe the period between the completion of the Babylonian Talmud (c. 650 CE) and the expulsion of the Jews from Spain (1492). This is an interesting period for Judaism, because there is possibly no period in which the Jewish experience was as diverse. There are Jews living in every country of Europe, North and West Africa, the northern shore of the Mediterranean, the Near and Middle East as far as Persia (the Sasanian Empire in this period) and India. Some lived under Islamic rule, others under Christian rule. They spoke Aramaic, Arabic, Greek, early forms of Romance languages (e.g., French, Italian, Spanish), and Germanic languages (primarily German). Despite this diversity, Jews were quite unified by the characteristics of Rabbinic Judaism: non-Temple religiosity, reverence for the learned sages, an interest in the ongoing interpretation of the Torah and Talmud, a reverence (if not always a mastery) of Hebrew as the language of their religion, and a pining for the land of Israel.

Jewish Cities

One tends to think of Jerusalem as *the* Jewish city, but in fact, Judaism has had a number of "capital" cities: not as in "state capitals," but as in cities that hold considerable authority in the eyes of a global community and which exert profound and long-lasting influence. Before the destruction of Jerusalem, Alexandria was a very important city, producing intellectual advances in Hellenistic Judaism. After its destruction, Jerusalem was not a Jewish city at all, and in its place Baghdad became the home of the most prominent Rabbinic schools (those responsible for the Babylonian Talmud), though Tiberias in the Galilee challenged it (with their Palestinian Talmud). By the tenth century CE, Cairo was a key city in the Islamicate, and so too for Jews. And Cordoba in the twelfth and thirteenth centuries eclipsed all its predecessors for intellectual productivity and Muslim–Jewish integration. In light of the influence certain locations come to have, it is difficult to settle on only one "Jewish" city.

blood could cure Jewish men of this affliction. Therefore, many Christians believed that Jews were in constant search for the blood of Christians.

The Blood Libel appeared first in England in 1144, then in France in 1171, and Germany in the 1280s. Because Western Christians believed that the wafer eaten during the Eucharist was the body of Christ (see Chapter Nine), they were able to extend the Blood Libel to the wafer as well, accusing Jews of kidnapping the wafer and torturing it (an extension of the Christian accusation that the Jews were "Christ killers"). Finally, Jews were blamed for the plague (the Black Death) which killed millions of Europeans between 1347 and 1350, failing to notice that as many Jews as anyone died during the plague (this very point was made by Pope Clement VI in 1348, but it had little effect on popular prejudices against the Jews).

Religious intolerance, the Blood Libel, and blame for the plague resulted in the complete expulsion of Jews from England in 1290 and from Spain in 1492, as well the extermination of Jews in German cities such as Mainz and Cologne (both in 1349). By 1500, it was dangerous (and thus uncommon) to be openly Jewish in Western Europe.

Jews fled Western Europe for Germany, Poland, Hungary, North Africa, and Palestine, as Israel was known at that point. North Africa and Palestine were governed by the **Ottoman Empire** (1299–1923). The experience of Jews in this period is mixed.

Figure 21. Palau Reial, the former palace of the Inquisition in Barcelona. The Jewish areas of many Spanish cities are today marked with the plaque of Sepharad in an attempt to make their history visible.

Figure 22. Illuminated manuscript of Jewish moneylenders in France at the time of Louis XI.

On the one hand, they were courted by and free in the Ottoman Empire of the sixteenth and seventeenth centuries, which resembles the generally positive experience of Jews living under previous Islamic empires. Jews may have been second-class citizens (as were all non-Muslims), but much evidence suggests they succeeded despite this. Jews were allowed to enter guilds and become trades-people, and they began to excel in cloth making.

Meanwhile, in Christian territories (Italy, Austria, Germany, Poland), Jews were still restricted from the trades and from owning land, forcing them into moneylending and commerce as two of their few career options. Christian lands in this period were shifting from rural to urban economies, a shift that privileges merchants and money handlers over farmers and tradespeople. Jews, who had been forced into these careers, suddenly

found themselves quite wealthy. What is more, every emerging economy needs capital with which to operate, and it needs a middle class, and Jewish society was able to offer both. Many Christians therefore argued for the importance of Jews in their communities on account of their ability to lend money to the poor.

Jews found themselves in an awkward position. Christians were forbidden from lending money for interest, so as a result, no Christian wanted to lend money. Yet these emerging Christian market economies needed moneylending (credit is the backbone of capitalism), so the Jews were asked, invited, and even sometimes compelled to do it, and then were demonized for it, creating a stereotype that persists today.

At the same time, other Christians resented the presence (and the wealth) of Jews in Christian lands, and worried about their influence. For many Christians in this period, the persecution of the Jews and the supremacy of Christianity proved to them God's favor of Christians and his displeasure at Jews. In 1516, Vienna established the first ghetto: a walled quarter of the city with locked gates outside of which Jews were not allowed to live, and surrounded by water on all sides. This phenomenon spread quickly to other European cities, and appears even in Ottoman Morocco. While clearly the ghettoization of Jews was a form of persecution, ironically it also afforded Jews some degree of protection from daily persecution, and appears to have helped ensure the continuity of Jewish culture. In 1555, Pope Paul IV revived the spirit of the Inquisition, seeking out Jews who had faked their forced conversions to Christianity.

Figure 23. The Dreyfus Affair even inspired board games such as the Game of the Goose (France, 1898).

From Enlightenment to Holocaust

The upheavals of the Protestant Reformation and the writings of Martin Luther (see Chapter Three) began a new wave of Christian **anti-Semitism** in Europe. And while, over the next two hundred years, some Jews experienced ever-increasing freedoms within Christian society, serious occurrences of violence against Jews flared up regularly. Yet the Enlightenment in Western Europe (seventeenth and eighteenth centuries) displaced tradition, institutional authority, and irrational prejudice with reason, equality, and rationality. Many European nations began treating all citizens, including Jews, as equals, developing laws based not on religious values but on secular values of universal equality.

In every European nation, the Jews were slowly, eventually, emancipated. By 1900, most European nations allowed Jewish people to live where they liked and to choose their own professions, and no longer levied heavy and punitive taxes on them merely for being Jewish. Jews began participating in Christian culture, and began debating amongst themselves the risks and virtues of assimilation and acculturation (see Chapter Eight). They might be forgiven for feeling that past centuries of inhumanity – anti-Semitism, Blood Libels, expulsions, **pogroms**, forced conversions, and ghettos – were a thing of the barbaric past. Society was improving.

Nonetheless, things were not perfect. In 1894, a Jewish captain in the French military named Alfred Dreyfus was accused and convicted of betraying state secrets to Germany, with whom France was at war. The trial was a sham, and though originally found guilty, humiliated and stripped of rank, imprisoned, re-tried, and imprisoned again, Dreyfus was pardoned twelve years later and his rank restored. But the ordeal revealed that anti-Semitism in France had not retreated in the face of modernity.

Theodor Herzl (1860–1904), a journalist writing about the trial, seemed particularly troubled. It struck him that Jewish emancipation in Europe was a façade behind which hid a deep and latent anti-Semitism. Convinced that the Jews would never be safe as long as they were living as guests in others' lands, he started a movement that sought a homeland for the Jews, namely biblical Israel. This movement became known as **Zionism**.

Zionism initially had a mixed reception among global Jews. Many were suspicious of it, and worried that non-Jews around them would see support for Zionism as disloyal to their hosts. Some felt it was unnecessary, for they were certain that humanity was advancing in justice and equality. But many immediately embraced Zionism, emigrating from European nations to British-run Palestine. There were always Jewish people in Palestine (known by the epithet the Yishuv), but always comprising a small percentage of the population. By 1920, recently arrived Jews, many of whom were fleeing increasing persecution in Europe and some of whom came in the spirit of Zionism, comprised around 10% of the population, rising to around 30%

by 1933. Both Islamic and Christian Arabs were unhappy with the Jewish arrivals, and in 1933 they successfully agitated for a quota (of 15,000 per year) to be placed by Britain on the number of Jewish immigrants to Palestine. By 1939, the British had cut off all Jewish immigration into Palestine, though Jews fleeing the Holocaust still found a way in.

In the same year as the initial quota, Adolf Hitler was made Chancellor of Germany, marking the start of his Nazi dictatorship. Like fourteenth-century Christians who blamed the Jews for the Black Death plague, Hitler and his many supporters blamed the Jews for Germany's humiliation in and after World War I and for Germany's depressed economy (which of course was suffering along with the rest of the world in the Great Depression). Hitler's anti-Semitic activities progressed in stages from reinstituting ghettos and public labeling of Jews, to limiting

Holocaust Denial

After World War II, anti-Semitism among Christians waned to record lows, but it is still visible in the modern phenomenon of Holocaust denial. Given the vast amount of material evidence (graves, official records, photos, buildings) and first-person testimony (both German and Jewish), Holocaust deniers must rely on multiple levels of independent but inter-related conspiracy theories operating on a massive scale in order to deny the Holocaust. They claim the whole event was a hoax perpetrated by Jews to advance their economic interests. Some try to distinguish between Holocaust deniers and Holocaust revisionists – those who do not deny the Holocaust happened but argue that the number of casualties has been grossly exaggerated. However,

revisionists too often show themselves to be engaged not in open-minded scholarship on a difficult topic (which is a fair enterprise), but in latent anti-Semitism. This is seen in how they too must rely on an international conspiracy of Jews controlling the world through education, politics, Hollywood, newspapers, and banks in order to perpetuate such exaggerated numbers. Holocaust denial is illegal in most of Europe, and in other countries is found primarily among fringe neo-Nazi groups, though it is increasingly common in Islamic circles. For instance, in 2007, the General Assembly of the United Nations adopted by consensus a condemnation of Holocaust denial, while Iran was the only member nation to refuse.

their career options, to expulsions, and then to labor camps where they were worked to death. In 1941, at the same time that Hitler was moving his armies eastward, he devised the "Final Solution" to the "Jewish Question" (*Judenfrage*) as he saw it: extermination camps, the most well-known of which were in Auschwitz-Birkenau and Treblinka. Over the period of World War II, ghetto diseases, firing squads, labor camps, and extermination camps resulted in the deaths of just under six million Jews, approximately two-thirds of Jews living in Europe.

It is important to understand the staggering ramifications of the Holocaust on Judaism. The damage in terms of casualties is easy to quantify, but the damage in other ways can never be known: the Holocaust gutted whole Jewish communities, Rabbinic learning and scholarship, and culture, music, learning, and art. The Holocaust has shaped modern Judaism ethically and theologically. That event lurks in the background of much Jewish thought, art, theology, and politics. Judaism is not dead, by any means, but one cannot say that it has recovered from the Holocaust. Without the Holocaust, Judaism today would be extremely different.

Israel

The Holocaust changed everything for everyone: few Jewish people were untouched, but also western Christians, and both Muslims and Christians living in Palestine felt the reverberations of the Holocaust. Jews who had previously ignored Herzl's plea were persuaded that he was correct: as long as they were living in Christian countries, Jews would be prey to the whims and moods of Christian rulers and mobs. Because of the

horrors of the Holocaust, Christians re-evaluated and rejected centuries of anti-Jewish opinions and anti-Semitic actions. Suddenly, Christians were the closest allies of Jews. These two things – increased Jewish desire for the safety of a homeland, and a Christian desire to do something right after the Holocaust – resulted in the founding of the modern state of Israel.

Before the Holocaust, Palestine was governed by Britain, who limited Jewish immigration there. Attempts to restrict immigration even further during and after the Holocaust proved both incendiary and fruitless. Jews in Israel turned to violence against British rule and a hundred thousand Jews were successfully smuggled into Palestine in 1945–1948. Britain responded violently to the variety of extremist acts, but this only resulted in the proliferation of violence. In 1946, a Jewish extremist group placed a large bomb in the basement of the King David Hotel, which served as the administrative headquarters for the British. A portion of the hotel was destroyed and ninety-one people were killed, most of whom were British civilians. The British pulled out of Palestine in 1947 and turned governance over to the United Nations, who devised a compromise plan to partition Palestine. Jewish Palestinians did not get the land they were hoping for from this partition, but they accepted the compromise; Arab Palestinians did not accept the partition compromise.

Fighting erupted between Jewish and Arab militias in Palestine. Militia groups on both sides were causing casualties in the hundreds, but by 1948 Jewish militias had the upper hand. Hundreds of thousands of Palestinians were made into refugees by the fighting and by Jewish expansion into

Figure 24. The current State of Israel, the Palestinian Gaza Strip, West Bank, and the Golan Heights.

On May 14, 1948, David Ben-Gurion, Executive Head of the World Zionist Organization, declared the formation of the State of Israel, and the next day several Arab nations attacked. This was the Arab–Israeli War. Israel defeated them, and expanded its borders again, growing by approximately 20%. Another attack from the same Arab neighbors, the Six Day War in 1967, resulted in the expansion of Israel's borders again, and the creation of more displaced and refugee Palestinians.

This is the origin of the so-called "Occupied Territories," and it remains the most significant issue for Israel and Palestinians as they, at some times more successfully than at others, attempt to find peace. In other words, both sides seek justice, security, and peace, yet this remains the longest unresolved military crisis in the modern world.

The number of Jews in Europe is not remotely what it was in 1933. The global number of Jews in the world took seventy years to reach its pre-World War II level of 15 million. Of today's 15 million Jews, the vast majority live in Israel and the United States (6 million and 5.5 million respectively), with some also in Europe (just less than 1 million), and the rest scattered around the world.

Judaism is as diverse now as it ever was. There are still **Sephardic** Jews, from Spain, Portugal, and North Africa, and the Middle East, and **Ashkenazi** Jews, from Eastern Europe. On the one hand, these categories still exist, but on the other hand, they are made more complicated by the flight of Iberian Jews into Eastern Europe, and Eastern European and Russian Jews dominating politically and culturally in modern-day Israel. No less, there are Ethiopian

territory not part of the original UN compromise partition. Most of these refugees fled into the Gaza Strip and the West Bank.

Jews, who claim their traditions and community date back to King Solomon's time. North American Judaism is also different, and diverse in and of itself. North American Judaism for the most part developed from the devastation of the Holocaust. The United States became a haven for Jews around the world when Christian anti-Semitism waned after World War II and the Holocaust.

These various cultural forms of Judaism have their own forms of diet, dress, and prayer. Then we can add to this more diversity of opinion based on responses to science and the enlightenment (reform, conservative, orthodox) and politics (liberal vs. conservative). Jewish cultures clash regularly, in Israel and in North America, with Sephardic and Ashkenazi Jews disliking each other for cultural differences, with reform and orthodox Jews distrusting each other for religious or political reasons.

There is no single "Jewish" opinion on any matter, and this historical survey reveals that there never has been.

Chapter Summary

Worshippers of God have lived in what is currently called Israel for several thousand years. Even when the Babylonians conquered and scattered the people there, they had been there for maybe a thousand years. Nonetheless, it took the catastrophe of being removed from their land that resulted in the innovation of monotheism. That, to my mind, marks the start of Judaism as a religion. This history of Judaism is one of conquest and migration: without this history, Judaism today would look very different than it does. A history of migration, forced by war and persecution, has resulted in rich diversity in different ways of being religiously and culturally Jewish.

Glossary

Anti-Semitism. A hostility against Jewish people that is rooted in racist assumptions, namely that ostensibly "Jewish" characteristics are genetic, and that these genetic features render Jews inferior, in addition to a variety of other negative characteristics.

Ashkenazi Judaism. Ashkenazi Judaism refers to the host of Jewish cultural and religious practices that developed in Germany, Eastern Europe, and Russia.

Babylonian exile. When the Babylonians conquered Judea and destroyed the First Jerusalem Temple, they forced into exile priests, governors, and other elites, in some instances taking them back to Babylon with them. The exile ended only when the Persian king Cyrus defeated the Babylonians a generation later.

Galilee. A region of northern Israel. Its remoteness and mountainous terrain made it a hotbed of rebels and messianic claimants.

Henotheism. Henotheism is devotion to one god in exclusion of all others. Thus, like monotheism, there is exclusive devotion to one god, but unlike monotheism, the existence of other gods is maintained.

Inquisition. Refers to many attempts of the Catholic church to root out heresy, but it is the Spanish Inquisition that most affected Jews. After Muslims were pushed from Spain by Christians (1492), Jews who remained were forcibly converted, but when Catholics came to distrust the authenticity of those conversions, they turned to the cruel tools of the Inquisition to test former Jews.

Judenfrage. A German word meaning "Jewish question" or "Jewish problem." *Judenfrage* was part of the Nazi justification for undertaking the Holocaust, in that European Jews were a "problem" that could only be resolved by extermination.

Mt. Gerizim. A mountain in Samaria that came to hold the same symbolic significance for Samaritan Jews as Mt. Zion in Jerusalem held for biblical Jews. Samaritan Jews even built their own temple there.

Ottoman Empire. One of the Islamic empires that grew up out of the Mongol invasion. At its largest in the seventeenth century, it included much of what is now Eastern Europe, Turkey, North Africa, and the Middle East to the Persian Gulf.

Pogrom. Refers to the violent persecution of Jews by local non-Jewish populations. The riots that brutalized Jewish communities in Russia, Ukraine, Poland, and Germany before the Holocaust were sometimes spontaneous and popular, but more commonly they were instigated when government, police, and Christian clergy whipped up anti-Jewish resentment among the people.

Samaritans. During the Babylonian exile, some Jews developed new practices and theological perspectives. When Ezra returned, he criticized these changes, but rather than reform, these Jews moved into Samaria in order to maintain their own identity. Samaritanism continues to be a living religion.

Second Temple Judaism. The long period from 515 BCE to 70 CE during which the Second Temple stood in Jerusalem. This was a period of profound social, cultural, and theological change in Judaism.

Seleucid. The Seleucids were the family that reigned over what is now Syria after the death of Alexander the Great.

Sephardic Judaism. Sephardic Judaism refers to the host of Jewish cultural and religious practices that developed in Spain, Portugal, and North Africa.

Zionism. The political ideology concerning the establishment and maintenance of a Jewish homeland in Israel. It was first theorized by Theodore Herzl.

Other Important Vocabulary

Aelia Capitolina	Essenes	Patriarchal	Sicarii
Antiochus IV	Ezra	Persia	Six-Day War
Epiphanes	Ghetto	Pharisees	Theocracy
Arab–Israeli War	Hellenization	Qumranites	Torah
Babylon	Jewish War	Rabbis	Yishuv
Bar Kokhba	Masada	Responsa	Zealot
Cyrus	Messiah	Sadducees	
Diaspora	Monolatry	Septuagint	

Discussion Questions

1. Where would you have started a chapter on the history of Judaism: Adam and Eve, the call of Abraham, Egypt and the Exodus, the Davidic Monarchy, Rabbinic Judaism? Can you imagine how each of these decisions could be justified and critiqued? How would you justify your own decision?

2. Most historical narratives, including the one given here, focus on elite history: the leaders, the High Priests, and prophets. Imagine how different a people's history of ancient Israel might look. For example, when Ezra arrives from exile and demands that Israelites in mixed marriages leave their foreign husbands and wives, how do you think these people felt about Ezra?

3. Some caricatures of Judaism have imagined Judaism as a monolithic entity: Jews are one people, with one blood, of one mind. How does an understanding of the history of Jews in the world problematize this perspective?

4. In the opening chapter on the theory of religion, I made the case that "religion" is what people make it. How is that evident when looking over the history of Jews in the world?

5. How would you describe the role of the land of Israel in Jewish history?

Recommended Reading

Efron, John, Steven Weitzman, Matthias Lehmann, and Joshua Halo. *The Jews: A History*. Upper Saddle River, NJ: Pearson Education, 2009.

Johnson, Paul. *A History of the Jews*. San Francisco, CA: Harper & Row, 1987.

Schiffman, Lawrence H. *From Text to Tradition: A History of Second Temple and Rabbinic Judaism*. Hoboken, NJ: Ktav, 1991.

Recommended Websites

http://www.cjh.org

- Center for Jewish History brings together a number of museums and research bodies on the topic of Jewish history. Includes searchable collections.

http://www.templemount.org/videos.html

- Offers a virtual tour of the Second Temple.

http://www.yadvashem.org

- The website of the Jerusalem's Israel Holocaust Museum, which offers extensive digital collections of historical material.

—3—

History of Christianity

Chapter Overview

Christianity has been the largest religion in the world for over 1500 years, currently accounting for 31.5% of the global population, or 2.2 billion people, compared with 1.6 billion Muslims and 14 million Jews. This chapter attempts to explain how a movement of fourth century Christ-followers scattered around the Mediterranean went on to become the largest of all religions in the world. First, we must establish how these groups of Christ-followers become Christianity, and from there we can discuss how the twists and turns of history, politics, geography, and piety combined to establish the wealth, power, and unprecedented and unpredictable global presence of Christianity.

Establishing a Religion and an Empire

Christ-followers First, Christianity Later

As strange as it sounds, there were Christ-followers before there was Christianity. We know there were Christ-followers in Egypt and North Africa, from Israel to Spain along the north shore of the Mediterranean (including lands now known as Syria, Jordan, Turkey, Greece, and Italy), north from the Mediterranean into what are now Britain and Germany, and even as far east as India. Specific numbers are harder to generate, since our ability to count people in the first to third centuries of the Common Era is very limited. It is possible that there were several thousand Christ-followers by the year 100 CE, and six million by 300 CE. There were Christ-followers everywhere, yet there was no Christianity until the fourth century.

The defensibility of a statement like this clearly depends on how one defines Christ-followers and Christianity. A Christ-follower is a follower of Jesus the Christ, that is the Messiah of Israel. Christianity is an orthodoxic and creedal imperial religion. Christ-followers chose martyrdom rather than be assimilated into the Roman empire, and were hated for their unwillingness to join the

Roman army. Christianity became and then replaced the Roman empire, with its own emperor and imperial army, which it used to enforce its creeds. There is therefore a direct and necessary relationship between creed and empire: there was no Christianity until there was an army to define it and defend a creedal definition that revolved around a single, unpredictable innovation to the Jewish idea of monotheism: Trinitarianism.

Before Christianity, there were Christ-followers who bickered about Jesus. When there were enough of them who thought the same way about Jesus, they formed groups. Some held the position that Jesus was truly human, and only human; God had adopted Jesus as a son when he was an adult. Others claimed that Jesus was not human in any way; he merely appeared to be human, but was really the divine spirit in the form of a human. The key to following Jesus for these people was the "knowledge" that Jesus was not truly human. Yet other Christians argued that Jesus was truly human (not the illusion

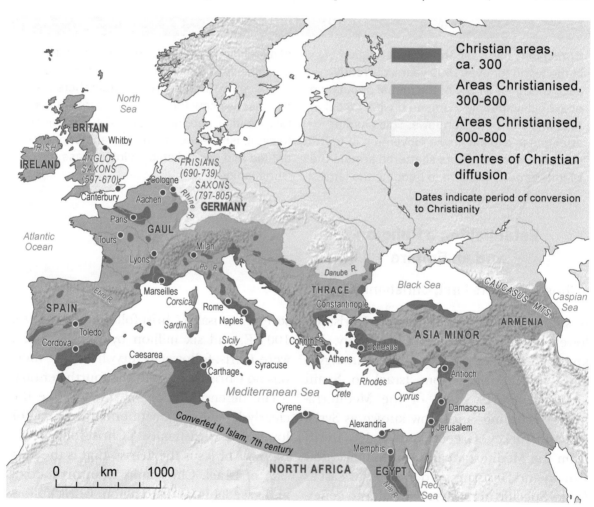

Figure 25. Before Constantine (who ruled as Roman emperor 306–337 CE), Christ-followers were found around the Mediterranean in pockets that were clustered generally around cities. After, and because of, Constantine, Christianity spread everywhere throughout the Mediterranean Basin.

of a human), and that he was born (not adopted) the son of God. These Christians stressed not knowledge about Jesus but faith in Jesus as key to following him. Faith would come to be that aspect of religion that most Christians stressed in their separation from Judaism, sometimes polemically (see Chapter Five). As such, it was that third group above, stressing faith in Jesus rather than knowledge, who gained an emperor and an army. They were the ones to define orthodox (e.g., correct/proper) Christianity, and define its opposite group – heretics. One cannot have **orthodoxy** and **heresy** without an army to enforce the difference.

The experience of Christ-followers before there was Christianity was not only one of theological diversity. It was also one of persecution. Being a follower of Jesus the Messiah was illegal in the Roman empire. Christians were viewed as misanthropic and antisocial because they refused to sacrifice to the gods

for the health of the Roman emperor, and as said above, refused to serve in the defense of the Empire. Such people naturally invited suspicion and persecution.

Roman persecution of Christ-followers was severe in places, but it was not constant over the early centuries. The most intense period of persecution was roughly between 284 and 305 CE, but it is not representative. This was during the shared emperorship of Diocletian and Galerius. Though Diocletian had a Christian wife and daughter, Galerius was hostile to Christ-followers and managed to persuade Diocletian to begin a program of persecution. Their places of gathering were destroyed, Christ-followers were tortured and killed, they were put to work in stone quarries, and their books were destroyed. When Galerius became seriously ill in 311 CE, he concluded that their God must have been punishing him, so he repented and issued the Edict of Toleration. The edict

Figure 26. The Catacombe di San Gaudioso in Naples. Catacombs were subterranean passageways usually associated with burials in the Roman period. They were used by Christ-followers for clandestine meetings and pilgrimages to tombs of their martyrs.

Pliny and Origen

Pliny the Younger was governor of part of what is now Turkey in 112 CE. He wrote to his boss, the Roman emperor Trajan, asking for advice on what to do about Christians who were arrested and brought before him for trial (Letters 10.96). Pliny wondered: are there age limits on the Christians he can try? What punishments are typical? If one ceases to be Christian, can that person be pardoned, or is being Christian, even in the past, unforgivable? And lastly, though Pliny had dutifully executed a few Christians, he is doubtful about whether it was necessary to do so. He says that they meet at odd hours and are stubborn and superstitious, but are otherwise rarely guilty of actual crimes, such as fraud, theft, and adultery. Two things are interesting about Pliny's letter. First, his real concern is that if he is rigorously to pursue Christians and execute them all, then a lot of people of all ages and social ranks are going to die. Second, Pliny finds that people are being publicly accused of being Christians who clearly were not. So the accusation of being Christian was used to get at one's enemies.

Clearly, Pliny's concern about executing Christians was not shared by many Romans. This is illustrated in the life of the Church Father named Origen (185–c. 254 CE), who was raised in a Christian household. A wave of persecution occurred in 202 CE, during which Origen's father was executed. Reverential writings about Origen himself, written a nearly a century later, claim that he wanted to follow in his father's footsteps, but was persuaded not to by his mother. Instead, he became a learned and widely respected defender of Christian claims. Origen himself was apparently arrested and tortured in another wave of persecutions, this one initiated by emperor Decius in the middle of the third century. Though Origen was eventually released, he died shortly after, likely as a result of injuries sustained during the torture (though it is not entirely certain when he died). His most famous work is one in which he set out to refute each of the objections of a well-known Roman opponent of Christian claims named Celsus (*Against Celsus*, 248 CE).

admitted that persecuting Christ-followers had failed to stop their spread, and declared freedom of religion for all.

Galerius died a short time later, and control of Rome passed to Maxentius, but a year later, his control was challenged by Constantine, a popular military commander whose troops had declared him emperor as early as 306 CE. Constantine marched on Rome in 312, and Maxentius met him in battle at the Milvian Bridge (which still exists, near the Olympic Stadium in Rome).

Constantine won this battle to become the sole emperor of the Roman empire, and with that the fate of Christians improved again. The result was the emergence of Christianity.

A year after becoming sole emperor, Constantine issued the Edict of Milan (313 CE), which extended the Edict of Toleration by making Christianity officially legal in the Roman empire. When, in 380 CE, emperor Theodosius made Christianity the official religion of the Roman empire, it sealed Christianity's fate as an imperial religion, a religion with an army and hungry to exercise its new-found power. This is why one can argue that while Christ-followers existed already for the better part of three centuries, Christianity did not exist until the fourth century, with the support of Constantine primarily and Theodosius secondarily. Christianity as we know it emerges therefore when

Figure 27. Mosaic of Constantine at Hagia Sophia, Istanbul. The prominence of Hagia Sophia is evident in Figure 28.

Trinitarianism is formally accepted, when creeds are formulated to support it, both of which happen with the participation, direction, and guidance of the emperor. Christianity is a creedal and imperial religion, different in almost every way from the different ways of following Christ that preceded it.

Roman Christianity

There is an irony in the heading of this section. Constantine may have been emperor of the Roman Empire, and he may have conquered the city of Rome, but Rome was not his city. Constantine chose Byzantium, which he renamed, after himself: Constantinople. Latin was not the primary language of the most influential Christians of this period, therefore, but Greek. The culture of Constantine's Christianity was **Byzantine**, not Roman, and it was eastern Mediterranean,

not western; it was not, ironically, Roman and Latin at all. And yet Constantine wanted his city to become the new Rome, and Roman culture and history were pervasive. Constantine may have wanted to distance himself from Rome in some ways, but he failed.

Two features of Constantine's reign as sole Roman emperor shape Christianity forever: the first was the favor he showed to Christ-followers. The second was his apparently deep

Figure 28. A view of Istanbul that shows the Hagia Sophia and its strategic positioning on the Bosphorus – the strait connecting the Black Sea to the Sea of Marmara separating Europe from Asia.

desire for peace. How does this shape Christianity? Because when Christ-followers argued with one another, Constantine demanded a quick resolution.

Here is an example. While Constantine was emperor, an argument broke out among Christians in Alexandria. One side of the argument is associated with Arius, who argued that Jesus the Son of God descended from God as a son descends from his biological father. Therefore, God was first and Jesus was second, and like a father and son, there was a time when the son never existed. As you might expect, this implies logically that God is greater than Jesus, is more authoritative, is primary, and is the creator of the world and of Jesus, while Jesus is lesser and later, secondary and created. Jesus was still, for Arius, Messiah, Lord, Savior, and Son of God. Arius' position is expressed with the Greek term *homoiousion*, which says that Jesus was of a similar (*homoi*) substance (*ousia*) to God, which is related but separate (like father and son).

Representing an opposing position was Athanasius. For him, Jesus was inseparable from God. Jesus was, in fact, God. Therefore, Jesus was there at creation with God, had existed as long as God had, and was not created by God like the rest of God's creation. This position was expressed with the term *homoousion*, meaning that Jesus and God were of the same (*homo*) substance (*ousia*). Their natures were indistinguishable.

When this Alexandrian argument started to spread to other Christians in the Empire, Constantine stepped in. He called the Empire's approximately 318 bishops to Nicaea, a city in what is now north-western Turkey. Constantine was not merely host to this meeting, he was a participant. This of course made the process quite political, in that the side that could win the support of the emperor would win the debate. That

Nicene Creed

The Nicene Creed was originally written in Greek in 325 CE and has been edited several times since then. The underlined portions reflect the historical context of the debate between Arius and Athanasius.

We believe in one God, the Father, the Almighty, maker of heaven and earth, of all that is, seen and unseen.

We believe in one Lord, Jesus Christ, the only Son of God, eternally begotten of the Father, God from God, Light from Light, true God from true God, begotten, not made, of one Being [*homoousion*] with the Father. Through him all things were made. For us and for our salvation he came down from heaven: by the power of the Holy Spirit he became incarnate from the Virgin Mary, and was made man. For our sake

he was crucified under Pontius Pilate; he suffered death and was buried. On the third day he rose again in accordance with the Scriptures; he ascended into heaven and is seated at the right hand of the Father. He will come again in glory to judge the living and the dead, and his kingdom will have no end.

We believe in the Holy Spirit, the Lord, the giver of life, who proceeds from the Father and the Son. With the Father and the Son he is worshiped and glorified. He has spoken through the Prophets. We believe in one holy catholic and apostolic Church. We acknowledge one baptism for the forgiveness of sins. We look for the resurrection of the dead, and the life of the world to come. Amen.

(from the 1979 *Book of Common Prayer*)

God and Political Rule

Because of the Roman persecution of Christians for several centuries, Christianity's close relationship with political authority had to be justified and promoted among its members. This was achieved by Eusebius of Caesarea (c. 260–340 CE), an historian and fierce defender of Christianity. In the following passage, he defends political authority by relating it to God, and in so doing, establishes a pattern that prevails in Christianity for a thousand years: namely, if God is responsible for people being emperors, then resisting an emperor is tantamount to resisting God. This would come to be called the Divine Right of Kings, and it had to be overcome before democracy would replace monarchy.

Lastly, invested as he [Constantine] is with a semblance of heavenly sovereignty, he directs his gaze above, and frames his earthly government according to the pattern of that Divine original, feeling strength in its conformity to the monarchy of God . . . And surely monarchy far transcends every other constitution and form of government: for that democratic equality of power, which is its opposite, may rather be described as anarchy and disorder. Hence there is one God, and not two, or three, or more: for to assert a plurality of gods is plainly to deny the being of God at all. There is one Sovereign . . .

(Eusebius, *Oration in Praise of Constantine* 3.5–6)

side was represented by Athanasius, and it was decided that Jesus was *homoousion*, the same substance as God, or consubstantial. He also had existed for as long as God had; that is, he was co-eternal. This position was written immediately into the Nicene **Creed** (though the Nicene Creed was altered by later councils on three separate occasions). This creed is still spoken in many Christian churches every week.

The creation of the Nicene Creed established the Trinity as the only acceptable way of thinking about the relationship between Jesus and God. Trinitarian belief holds that God has three elements: Father, Son, and Holy Spirit (see Chapter Six). This is evidenced in the threefold structure of the Creed itself (see text box on p. 62), with one section of faith for each component.

With the creed, a group of heretics were created essentially overnight. One day, there were faithful and devoted followers of Jesus who believed he was created by and

subordinate to God, and the next day, these Christians were deemed no longer properly Christian, but were labeled as heretics, their position not only wrong but dangerous. And with the support of an imperial army, adherence to this creed could be enforced, along with all subsequent edits of it. That is, Christians had to keep up to the changing theology of Christian councils lest they fall behind.

The participation of Constantine established a pattern of imperial, or political, involvement in the inner workings of the Christian church: that is, in the development and enforcement of theological debates. All subsequent councils and church schisms were as politically motivated as they were theologically motivated. The separation of church and state is a purely modern concern (debates on this did not start seriously until the seventeenth century). For 1700 years, Christianity was a political religion, and church and state were deeply intertwined.

If the Council at Nicaea marks the start of political Christianity, the decline and fall of the Roman empire seals that aspect of Christianity for the next 1200 years. In 476 CE, the Roman empire can be officially declared finished, having been defeated by a number of groups over the course of a century.

Christian Missions

Christians and Muslims have a long history of actively, purposely, and at times aggressively, seeking to convert individuals and countries. We call the practice of seeking out the conversion of others proselytization, and for the most part it explains how Christianity and Islam came to be so geographically spread out and numbering in the billions. In contrast, there is little evidence that Jews of any period were interested in proselytizing others.

The seat of power for Christianity was located in Constantinople for the fourth and fifth centuries CE. The fall of Rome created a power vacuum that Christianity filled. By the end of the sixth century, Christians were powerfully present in Rome, and Rome was once again exercising power. In part, the empowering of Rome occurred because of the missions that Roman Christians conducted into Western Europe. Pope Gregory I (also known as Gregory the Great) instructed his missionaries to demand loyalty to Rome of any leaders in the new Christian communities.

Roman Christian missions were not merely a way of spreading "the good news" but also a way of extending and then solidifying Rome's power in the western half of the Empire. Rome came therefore to hold greater wealth and power than Constantinople, and therefore to assume a greater theological authority than that held by other locations of Christianity (Edessa, Alexandria, Ephesus, etc.). Roman assumptions of authority over other Christian locations created resentment, and interaction between the Bishop of Rome and other bishops were often tense.

Jews and Muslims at this time

When being Christian was illegal in the Roman empire, Jews had a reasonable amount of freedom. Jerusalem was still off limits (by order of Rome), but Jewish centers of learning and culture existed throughout the Near East and Western Europe. But once Christians attained imperial power, persecution of Jews followed. This change in fortunes was also commonly interpreted theologically: Christians were powerful because God favored them over the Jews.

By 640 CE, Islamic armies were emerging from the Arabian Peninsula, and from there sweeping westward into Christian lands: Jordan, Palestine, Syria, Egypt, all of North Africa, and Turkey were all taken over by Muslims, and Christianity retreated into Western Europe. The Umayyad Dynasty (661–750 CE) presented a formidable opponent to Christianity. Muslims controlled Spain, but were stopped from taking over France by Charles Martel at the Battle of Poitiers (732 CE). Martel is credited with laying the foundations for what became the Carolingian Empire. So it appears that the Islamic push from the south and east is what drove the Christian missionaries north and west, into France, Germany, and England. Christians did not win back Spain for another 700 years, and when they did, Jewish suffering increased catastrophically.

Monasticism

In about 270 CE, a Christian named Anthony of Egypt (c. 251–355 CE) adapted the Jewish practice of withdrawing from the world to live in the desert. But Anthony did something different: he went alone. For thirteen years he sat alone in a tomb, praying and relying on local villagers to bring him small amounts of food. This style of monasticism is called eremitic, because it involves living well away from society, pledges of total silence, wholesale devotion to prayer, and asceticism (eating little, wearing uncomfortable clothing, and living very simply). When Christianity became legal and popular a few decades later, many others followed Anthony's example. This group is known as the Desert Fathers.

Eremitic monasticism was extremely arduous and lonely. Others preferred to live in monastic communities, which we call cenobitic monasticism. Sometimes these communities were close to villages, in which case the monks might interact with lay people quite frequently. In other instances, the communal monasteries were located far from civilization, retaining some of the eremitic experience of seclusion from society but living in a sociable community together. Benedict of Nursia (c. 480–547 CE) developed the model for cenobitic monasticism. Living in these conditions involved strict discipline, and mild forms of asceticism, but was not overly harsh. That is, monks wore simple, rough clothing and slept on thin mats, but they were encouraged to eat enough that hunger would not distract them from their prayers. Benedict's "Rules" for monastic life touched on every detail of daily and nightly routines and they still form the basis for monastic living.

Monastic living became a prominent feature of medieval Christianity, as did a further extension of it, known as mendicancy. Mendicant monastics lived and worked in urban areas, focusing on preaching Jesus Christ and helping the poor, while themselves surviving solely by begging for their food. Several mendicant orders arose in this period, which are still well known and active in the world: Francis of Assisi (c. 1181–1226) established the Franciscans; Dominic of Guzmán (1172–1221) established the Dominicans. There are dozens of other monastic and mendicant orders in Catholicism. Orthodox Christians also have a rich practice of monasticism, but do not have monastic orders.

This style of mission is best exemplified in the Carolingian Empire (800–888 CE). The Carolingian Empire was based in what is now France, and its first emperor – Charlemagne – was made emperor by Pope Leo III in Rome in 800 CE. It goes without saying that a pope who can make an emperor can also unmake an emperor, and so the church in Rome had become the ultimate political *and* theological authority: it had power over heaven *and* earth. This could happen because the Christian Church in Rome had long since taken the position that the authority of the church was greater than even the authority of kings and emperors.

Christians eventually used the phrase **Holy Roman Empire** to describe this entity. The Holy Roman Empire at this time included most of mainland Europe, but not Spain, which was under the control of Muslims. Clearly, "Holy Roman Empire" was a deeply politico-theological title. To jump briefly into the twentieth century, when John F. Kennedy became the first Roman Catholic President of the United States of America (1961), opponents wondered whether

he had the advantage of being able to claim to follow in the line of Peter. By 800 CE, Rome was the center of power for Christianity, and Constantinople, the only other real contender for that title, was long eclipsed. This forms the foundation of the impending split between the Byzantine and Roman spheres of the Christian empire.

Christianity's close relationship with political authority, while responsible for much of Christianity's rise to the largest and most powerful religion in the world, was also the cause of much strife within. On the one hand, the papacy came to embody all the characteristics of politics at its worst: influence, intrigue, extortion, bribery, and violence. Popes were elected under pressure, attempts by European kings and princes to bribe them and depose them were common (though not always successful), and they were killed off.

Figure 29. Allegiances during the Avignon Papacy (1305–1377).

America's political autonomy had just been given over to the Vatican in Rome. This concern, unfounded as it turned out, was based on the once great political reach of the church in Rome.

Because Christian collective memories thought of Rome as the place where the great apostles, Paul and Peter, were martyred, Rome carried great symbolic power. Whoever held Rome could tap into that power. Though the Bishop of Rome was, in theory, no different from the other bishops,

The episode of greatest intrigue concerns the Avignon Papacy (1305–1377). After several decades of open fighting between the King of France and the Pope in Rome, the French succeeded (likely through subterfuge) in having a Frenchman chosen as Pope: Clement V (Pope from 1305–1314). Yet the King of France never allowed Clement V even to visit Rome, keeping him instead in Avignon, France, where he could be controlled. This was the case for all the Avignon popes, seven in all. Finally, in 1377 the last Avignon pope (Gregory XI) returned to Rome, in large measure because of the advocacy of the mystic Catherine of Sienna. He died the next year, and while political intrigue continued to characterize the papacy, it remained in Rome after that.

The East–West Schism

Rome's rise in power, and the assumptions of privilege that came with it, resulted in tensions with the other locations of Christian authority. For instance, when the Bishop of Rome (the Pope) came to assume a higher status than the other bishops around the Mediterranean, the Bishop of Constantinople was annoyed.

The first serious signs of separation came in the ninth century when Rome became involved in a controversy over who should lead the Eastern church. The office of the **Patriarch** (the head of the Eastern church, but in no way comparable to the office of the Pope) had changed hands by rebellion, from Ignatius to Photius. Both men appealed to Rome's Pope Nicholas to settle the dispute. When Nicholas sided with Ignatius, Photius refused to leave the office, wholly rejecting the authority of Rome and challenging the legitimacy of all of Western Christianity. Photius attached his political opposition to a theological controversy, known as the *Filioque* Clause (see text box below). On this premise, in 867 CE Photius condemned Pope Nicholas as a heretic.

Fewer than two hundred years later, Rome again assumed the right to declare universal Christian policy, this time in the form of priestly celibacy. Eastern priests and bishops (who embraced marriage and family) again rebelled. Rome sent a delegate to mediate, but mediation failed due to the long-standing animosity that had festered between Rome and Constantinople. In 1054 CE, Rome announced the formal excommunication of the Patriarch of Constantinople, Michael I Cerularius.

This turn of events is commonly referred to as the Great Schism, referring to the formal split of Eastern and Western Christianity. The result was the division we see today in Orthodox and Roman Catholic churches. Prior to the split, there was (in theory) one

---

Filioque Clause

Above we read the Nicene Creed as it currently stands, but observed that it had undergone several changes after it was first written in 325 CE. The third paragraph relates to the Holy Spirit, and begins like this: "We believe in the Holy Spirit, the Lord, the giver of life, who proceeds from the Father and the Son." The final phrase "and the Son" is a translation of the Latin word *Filioque*. It was not part of the original creed, but was added later by Western Christians, seemingly though popular use, not by official decree, sometime in the ninth century.

Eastern Christianity's objections were theological and political. On theological grounds, they objected that adding "and the Son" changes the structure of the Trinity, which they considered very radical: the addition of *Filioque* elevates Jesus above the Spirit, so that the Spirit descends from the Father *and* the Son. It struck Eastern Christians as intolerably illogical. But they also objected for political reasons: a substantial change to a 500-year-old creed was made without the consultation of non-Western Christians.

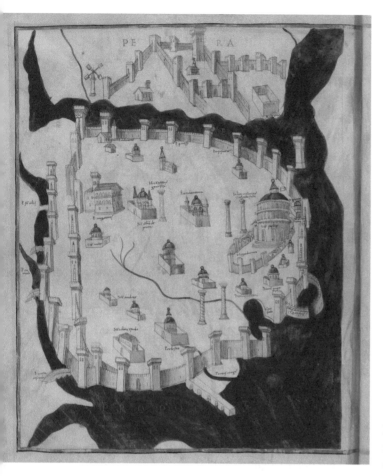

Figure 30. A fifteenth-century plan of Constantinople. The city fell to Muslim rule in 1453. Note the prominence of Hagia Sophia, the largest building on the map (see "Fall of Constantinople" text box, p. 72).

catholic (meaning "universal") Christianity. After this division, we end up with Roman Catholic Christianity, which by taking over the term "catholic" claims to represent universal Christianity, and many Orthodox Christianities in the East.

Greek-speaking Christian missionaries had been establishing churches in Eastern Europe (particularly the Czech Republic, Serbia, and Bulgaria) and Russia since the early ninth century. The result was an extensive network of Byzantine churches loyal to Constantinople, and a new language called Cyrillic: a combination of Russian vernacular language and the Greek of the Christian missionary Cyril (827–869 CE). Language is a telling feature of Eastern Orthodox missions: because they were willing to preach in local languages (either in whole, as with Slavonic for the Slavic peoples, or in part with Cyrillic), they were more successful than Western missionaries in the same territories, who insisted on preaching in Latin, requiring converts to learn it.

Orthodoxy was no more successful than Roman Catholicism, however, at maintaining cohesion among its many parts. This is evident in two ways: the Iconoclastic controversy and the fracturing of Orthodox communions. Western Christians were not the only ones who felt uncomfortable with the proliferation of images and icons used in Eastern worship. Supporters of the use of images argued that the earliest Christians were surrounded by paintings and images, and that these enhanced devotion to God by offering an image of the goal of worship.

Opponents argued that the use of icons was dangerously close to idolatry, and thus ordinary worshippers might miss the distinction between the worship of God through images and the worship of images themselves. Opponents in this debate were called Iconoclasts (smashers of images) and supporters were called Iconodules (servants of images). No doubt, the close proximity of Muslims influenced the Iconodules, as Islamic theology strictly forbids the creation of images, let alone their use in worship settings.

The debate raged in the eighth–ninth centuries, with the Iconodules eventually

Figure 31. This classic Eastern Orthodox icon, called "Our Lady of the Sign," shows Mary in a prayerful pose with the infant Jesus inside her. It is commonly found in Orthodox churches and monasteries.

controversies than intra-regional coherence. Today, Eastern Orthodox Christians account for the second-largest body of Christians (as many as 300,000,000), but there is little unity among them. By the fifteenth century, Eastern Orthodox Christians in Russia declared their independence from Constantinople, creating the Russian Orthodox Church. Other locations followed suit eventually: Serbia, Ukraine, Bulgaria, Romania, and Greece. These Eastern Orthodox churches are independent, but they nonetheless operate in communion with each other.

Of course, the Eastern Orthodox churches are also as international as their Western counterparts. The Greek Orthodox Church, for instance, represents most Eastern Orthodox Christians in Jerusalem, and there are Greek, Ukrainian, and Russian Orthodox churches in every North American and Western European city today.

We must also distinguish between Oriental Orthodox and Eastern Orthodox churches. Churches in Egypt, Armenia, Syria, Eritrea, and India comprise the Oriental Orthodox churches, and they are in communion with one another, but not with Eastern Orthodox churches. To say that Eastern and Oriental Orthodox churches are in communion within each division is to say that they share theological principles, but not that there is a centralized structure of authority. Finally, there is the Assyrian Orthodox Church, representing a small number of Orthodox Christians mostly in Iraq, Iran, Syria, and Turkey. These Christians have been badly mistreated by Muslims as a result of political turmoil in the early twenty-first century.

winning out. This resolution even influenced Roman Catholics; though they do not use images quite the way Orthodox Christians do, nor in the same distinctive artistic style, Catholic churches came to be filled with paintings, statues, and graven images too.

It did not take long for Eastern Orthodox Christians to split apart along national and cultural boundaries. Just as theological debates among Western Christians were always equal parts theological and political, so too were Eastern Christians more interested in local political (and nationalistic)

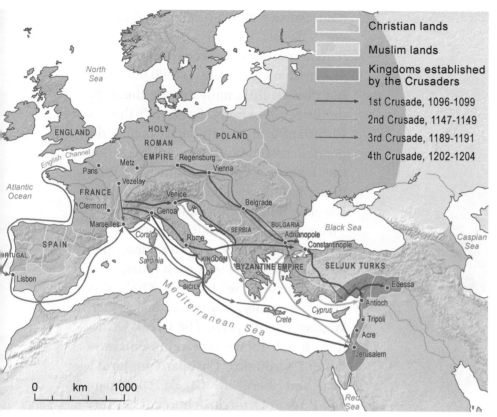

Figure 32. The Crusades (see text box on the Catholic Crusades against Muslims and Orthodox Christians, p. 100).

Medieval Catholicism

The influence of the Catholic Church in the Middle Ages (c. 800–1500) succeeded in making Christianity part of the very fabric of European culture. The church was the center of daily life; it shaped people's daily activities, their learning, their morality, and in addition the art, music, and architecture that they encountered.

The Holy Roman Empire, begun in 800 CE, did not end officially until 1806, but it ceased long before then to have the same power that allowed it to make and unmake emperors. This is not to say that the Roman Catholic Church became politically neutral. It did not. In the second millennium, it continued to exert profound political influence, which accrued mostly from being the sole representative of Christianity in the West. Between 950 and 1200 CE, the authority structure of the Catholic Church became increasingly centralized in Rome and in particular in the office of the Pope.

Towards the end of the eleventh century, the Roman Catholic Church, led at the time by Pope Urban II (1042–1099), extended its political authority in an entirely new way: with a holy war against Muslims, which soon spilled over to become a holy war against other Christians. The goal of freeing Jerusalem from Islamic persecution would have been a more obviously noble cause had the information available to the Pope been more up to date. It is true that Islamic Turks had killed some Christians (and Jews) and had destroyed the Church of the Holy Sepulcher in Jerusalem, but that had happened under one particularly (and uncommonly) irrational sultan in 1009, quite a long time prior to the First Crusade. What is more, the subsequent sultan had assisted in rebuilding the destroyed church. So the real motivation for the crusades is obscure.

Figure 33. Illuminated manuscript from the late fifteenth century showing Crusaders besieging Damascus in 1148.

Promising the forgiveness of all the sins of any who died in battle, Urban II called Christian men of all classes to assemble in an army that would march to Jerusalem. That army left in 1096, taking prominent cities from Islamic control, including Jerusalem in 1099 after a six-week siege. Crusader soldiers rampaged the city, killing men, women, and children, Muslim, Jew, and Orthodox Christian indiscriminately. None of the captured cities were returned to Byzantine control, but were established as loyal-to-Rome city-states, contributing to the extension of Roman Catholic power again. The Crusades provide further illustration of Western Christianity's politico-religious nature.

Prester John

In twelfth-century Christian sources, we find an already well-developed collection of curious and contradictory legends: together they more or less tell of a lost Christian nation in the heart of the Islamic "East." This nation was led by Prester John (a shortened form of Presbyter John, or John the Elder), a descendant of the Three Magi referred to in the Gospel of Matthew, and European Christians believed he would lead a battle against Muslims, who would then be hemmed in by Christians in the east and west.

This legend had reached even the highest levels of the Christian world. When rumors of the Mongol attacks at the east flank of the Islamicate arrived in Europe (see Chapter Four), many people thought it was Prester John coming to save them from the Islamic threat. Thus, when Islamic leaders and caliphs appealed to Europe for help against the Mongols, the Pope dismissed them. Christian proposals of an alliance with the Mongols against the Muslims were premised on widespread acceptance of the legend of Prester John. Misunderstanding the identity and intentions of the Mongols had graver consequences for Muslims than for Christians, but nonetheless, Mongols were a threat to Christian Europe too. Yet even that fact was not enough to dispel the legend that Genghis Khan was a Christian savior named Prester John.

Eight other crusades followed, with the last one ending unsuccessfully in 1272. The Crusades all followed the same pattern set by the first one: they were ostensibly about freeing Christian territories from Islamic control, but non-Catholic Christians and Jews suffered nearly as much as Muslims, and Crusader soldiers were ruthless in their conquering.

Protest and Reform

The fifteenth–sixteenth centuries in Western Europe were a period of significant social and technological change, and this led to significant religious change. We separate these for the ease of discussion, but they were, as you will see, very closely intertwined. The foremost technological change was the invention of the printing press. In 1450, Johannes Gutenberg (c. 1400–1468) added his finishing touches to a mechanical machine with movable type. This machine allowed books and pamphlets to be mass-produced, which allowed ideas (including radical ones) to move around much faster. This was also a period of increased urbanization, which is to say, more people than ever before were living in cities. Living in close proximity also aided the faster transmission of ideas. In addition, literacy was on the rise, so as more people were interested in reading, demand rose for material to read. So the printing press promoted literacy, and literacy increased the demands on the printing press.

People were reading classical texts, histories, political tractates, and, most importantly, they were reading the Bible, Gutenberg's first major printing project, the **Gutenberg Bible** (completed in 1456). And this is where technology (printing press), social change (urbanization, increased literacy), and "religion" intersect in this period: ordinary people were reading the Bible! This is more radical than it sounds. Up to

The Fall of Constantinople

By the time Ottoman Turks set their sights on Constantinople, the city had already been weakened by the Crusades (see pp. 70–71). Because of the excommunication of the Patriarch and expulsion of Eastern Christianity from Catholic Christendom, Crusader (Roman Catholic) armies frequently stopped to pillage Constantinople on their way to Jerusalem to fight Muslims. In the early fifteenth century, the Turkish Sultan Mehmed II, a young man barely out of his teens, besieged Constantinople, intent on making it the capital of his land. Though Byzantine Christians appealed to the West for assistance, none was given. Constantinople fell in 1453 CE. Though it never really came to pass, the fall of Constantinople triggered European fears of being overrun by Muslims, as the city was thought of as the gate keeping Muslims out of Europe.

The siege engines, called trebuchets, which ironically had been designed and developed for the Islamic armies by entrepreneurial Christian engineers, easily worked through the ancient city walls. The great Basilica, Hagia Sophia, was immediately turned into an Islamic place of worship. This place remained a Mosque until 1935, was closed for a short period, and then eventually reopened as a museum, called the Hagia Sophia, by the Republic of Turkey. Muslims had referred to the city as Istanbul even before the conquest, but that name did not become official until 1930.

this point, the Bible was read only by Catholic priests who told people what it said and how to understand it. The Catholic Church controlled the dissemination and interpretation of the Bible. The printing press and literacy turned this upside down. As ordinary people read the Bible, they arrived at interpretations that differed from those provided by the Church. And they talked to each other about these interpretations.

At the same time as literate people were arriving at interpretations that set them at odds with the official interpretations of the Catholic Church, they were also starting to question some of its recent practices and long-standing traditions. This was happening at the same time as European princes were beginning to form national identities independent of Rome. Europe was beginning to chafe under the control of the Catholic Church, and some elites wanted their own political autonomy, power, land, language, and wealth.

Figure 34. The sale of indulgences by the Church continued into the eighteenth century: this one dates from the Pontificate of Innocent XIII (1721–1724).

Martin Luther

It is within this tumultuous context that Martin Luther (1483–1546), a Catholic priest in Germany, emerged. Luther protested against a number of features and practices of his own church, which is obviously about religion, but his voice would not have been heard as widely without the technological and social changes, nor would it have been heard as loudly without the help of German political leaders who were eager to break away from Rome's power. This explains why the Catholic Church responded to Luther in 1521 in both a religious framework, by excommunicating him, and a political framework, by trying him for political subversion. This occurred in a council called a *diet* in a German city called Worms (pronounced *vurms*).

In 1517, Luther posted 95 Theses to the door of the church in Wittenberg, Germany. His primary target was the sale of **indulgences**, though the rationale had such broad implications that they touched on many other

Luther, Calvin, and Grebel

One of Luther's ideas likely had implications far beyond what he imagined. In rejecting the hierarchical authority structure of the Catholic Church, Luther's movement was more democratic. He described this with the phrase "the priesthood of all believers." One did not need a priest to read the Bible on one's behalf nor to mediate a relationship with God or Jesus Christ. Anyone could do these things; anyone could have the authority of a priest. This would ensure that any Protestant with a new idea could bring in a new Protestant church. The result was, eventually, hundreds of different Protestant denominations (e.g., Lutherans, Calvinists, Anabaptists, Presbyterians, Southern Baptists, Puritans, Pentecostals, Mennonites, Quakers, and on and on). Put differently, the Catholic Church may have controlled the interpretation of the Bible, but by doing so, they maintained a unity that was impossible for Protestants.

So, for example, John Calvin (1509–1564), a French-born theologian who spent his most influential years in Geneva, Switzerland, agreed with Luther on just about everything, but

disagreed on some small issues. One was free will: Luther believed that humans had free will to choose right and wrong, and that the choice to believe had a positive effect on God. In contrast, Calvin felt that giving humans free will limited the omnipotence of God. A few minor differences like this were enough to create Calvinism, a branch of Protestant Christianity different from Lutheranism. Conrad Grebel (c. 1498–1526), another Swiss theologian, felt that baptizing infants was pointless, whereas other Protestant theologians felt it reaffirmed the covenant made between God and Abraham. So Grebel broke away, forming a group of Protestants who only practice adult Baptism, including re-baptizing those who had been baptized as infants. They became known as Anabaptists.

Even more radical changes were possible too among Protestants. Italian theologian Fausto Sozzini (1539–1604) broke with the Anabaptist movement and returned to the thinking of Arius. Sozzini believed that Jesus was not co-eternal with God and was not divine, and therefore he rejected the Trinity. Non-Trinitarian Christians still exist.

Catholic ideas and practices. Indulgences were certificates one could purchase from the Catholic Church that would wipe away some of one's sins. To some, this appeared as fundraising at best, and a crass theological ploy that benefited the rich at worst.

There were three underlying theological positions that fueled Luther's objection. They are known by their Latin formulations: *sola scriptura*, *sola fides*, and *sola gratia*. *Sola scriptura* is the position that all Christian practices, doctrines, and beliefs should derive from the Bible alone. If they do not, they are mere human innovations, and have

no real authority over people. *Sola fides* is the position that people are justified (their relationship with God is repaired) only by faith in Jesus, not by works or actions. *Sola gratia*, which is closely related, is the position that God alone, by his grace, elects whom to save. That is, one cannot earn salvation, nor purchase it.

These three positions undermined Catholic practice well beyond the sale of indulgences; they also undermined the Catholic notion that revelation from God did not end with the revealed Bible, but continued through each of the popes. For Catholics,

ces Voleurs infames et perdus ,
fruits malheureux a cet arbre pendus
Monstrent bien que le crime (horrible et noire engeance)
Est luy mesme instrument de honte et de vengeance ,
Et que cest le Destin des hommes vicieux
Desprouuer tost ou tard la iustice des Cieux .

Figure 35. An etching by Jacques Callot, published in 1633, depicts the brutality of the French army during the Thirty Years' War.

tradition is as authoritative as scripture. In short, nearly the entire authority structure of the Catholic Church was undermined by Luther's Theses.

German princes rallied in support of Luther, eager to antagonize Rome, and Rome responded violently. The result was the fracturing of Western Christianity. Christianity was now split among Roman Catholics, several brands of Orthodoxy, and eventually, hundreds of Protestant denominations. What is more, the formation of several European nations and many European wars between Catholics and Protestants originates here. The reverberations of Luther's protest were broad, deep, and lasting.

Protestantism

Luther's many followers, some of whom supported him for theological reasons and some of whom supported him for political reasons, came to be called Protestants, and the rupturing event that ensued is called the Protestant Reformation. The spirit of the reformation swept through Europe. Though the Catholic Church tried to slow its spread through persecution and peace treaties, Protestantism spread quickly from Germany into Switzerland, The Netherlands, France, England, and Scotland.

The sixteenth and seventeenth centuries were a particularly bloody period among Christians. Protestants and Catholics fought long and violent wars, but some Protestants were murdering other Protestants, and Catholics fought with each other too. For instance, in England in the 1500s, rule alternated between Protestant and Catholic monarchs, each of whom reversed the policies of the former and killed as many enemies as possible while in power. In France in the 1600s, a Catholic cardinal secretly supported the Protestants in the Thirty Years' War (1618–1648) because he felt the Habsburgs, a Catholic dynasty centralized in Austria, was more of a threat to him than Protestants.

In England, Henry VIII (1491–1547) broke from Rome, thereby creating space for Protestants to exist in England. In fact, Henry VIII was originally a staunch defender of Catholic doctrine against Protestants, but when he wished to divorce his first wife, the Pope refused. This refusal came in part because divorce is forbidden in Catholicism, but also because Henry's marriage to a Spanish princess was good for the papacy. In 1534, Henry declared himself independent of the Pope's authority (thus, he remarried many times after that). Henry appears to have been more inspired by the political implications of the Protestant resistance to the Catholic Church than its theology. He broke from the authority of the Pope, but he maintained a good deal of Catholic tradition afterwards. After Henry, however, the Church of England (also commonly known as Anglicanism) became thoroughly Protestant in its theological outlook.

Accusations of Witchcraft

Because the pilgrims who came to the United States were fleeing persecution for their religious affiliation, they were among the first in the Christian world to see the value of freedom of religion and the separation of church and state. The Christian colony at Rhode Island was the first to end discrimination on the basis of religion, extending religious freedom to other Christians and even Jews (1642). Religious tolerance spread from Providence to other states, particularly Maryland and Pennsylvania, and eventually to Massachusetts. In fact, there were enough places where religious tolerance was either practiced or was the law that when persecution happened in other places (e.g., in Virginia in the 1640s), these places tended to suffer mass migrations as people fled towards tolerant states. States learned their lesson from this, and soon freedom of religion was the norm, not the exception.

Nonetheless, there were outbursts of violence. One of the more notable and strange examples concerns the witch trials that occurred in and around Salem, Massachusetts in 1692–1693. What is clear in retrospect is that the accusations of sorcery and witchcraft are about social deviance and not about actual evidence of demonic forces being unleashed at pious Christians. The women who were accused of being witches were commonly ethnically different (neither white nor Puritan), never attended church, or were homeless beggars. Trust in the system of naming witches finally fell apart when even the wife of the governor was accused of being a witch. It then became clear that other factors were at play in these accusations, but not before twenty people (including six men) and two dogs were executed either as witches or as accomplices.

Scholars of religion recognize that accusations of this nature are always rhetorical and social. They are motivated by fear of the other, and are closely related to xenophobia, racism, and misogyny. Witchcraft accusations frequently reflect concerns over diversity within a community: how different, strange, or anti-social are people allowed to be before they need to be brought into line with communal expectations? Accusations of deviance are one way that groups establish and enforce those expectations.

Council of Trent

Before we leave the tumultuous sixteenth century, we must consider one final event: the Catholic Church's **Council of Trent**, a series of meetings that took place from 1545 to 1563. Catholics learned an important lesson from Luther and his followers: the importance of the printing press and pamphlets. Now it was Catholics who were using pamphlets to argue for their position and to attack Protestant ideas and leaders. Their primary argument in favor of their own position was the consistency of Catholic teaching, which Protestantism lacked, as every year seemed to produce another Protestant denomination rejecting the teachings of other Protestant denominations. At the Council, the bishops defended traditional Catholic doctrine, relenting only on the issue of indulgences, the use of which was altered but not eliminated.

The Globalization of Christianity

Colonialism, the practice of Christian nations establishing Christian colonies that would bring in resources and create wealth, happened because of politico-religious persecution, economic opportunity, and theological fervor. Protestant Christians fleeing persecution crossed oceans and continents, arriving in North America and South Africa; Christians left Europe in search of economic opportunities and wealth. They also left to establish new churches, make new converts, and worship according to their own consciences.

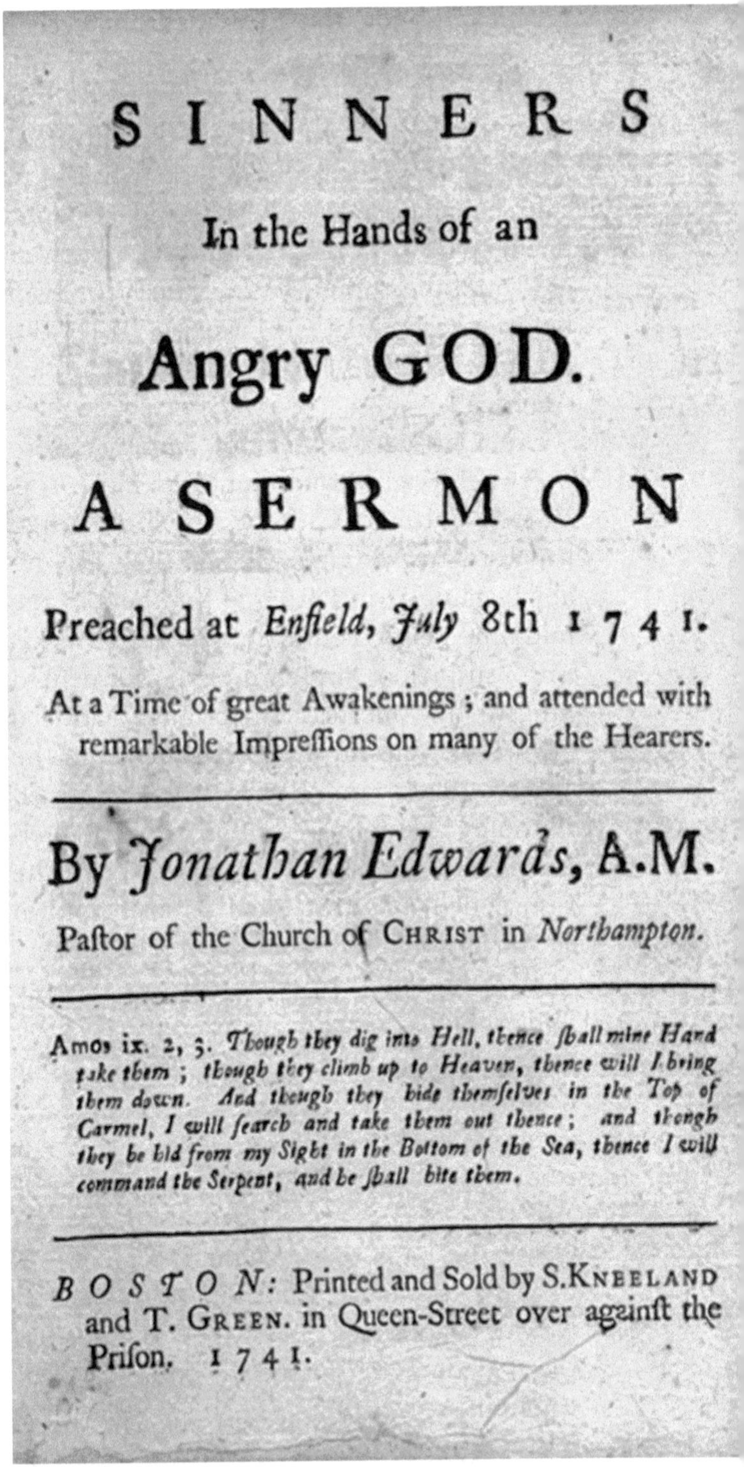
SINNERS

In the Hands of an

Angry GOD.

A SERMON

Preached at *Enfield, July* 8th 1741.

At a Time of great Awakenings; and attended with remarkable Impreſſions on many of the Hearers.

By *Jonathan Edwards*, A.M.

Paſtor of the Church of CHRIST in *Northampton*.

Amos ix. 2, 3. *Though they dig into Hell, thence ſhall mine Hand take them; though they climb up to Heaven, thence will I bring them down. And though they hide themſelves in the Top of Carmel, I will ſearch and take them out thence; and though they be hid from my Sight in the Bottom of the Sea, thence I will command the Serpent, and he ſhall bite them.*

BOSTON: Printed and Sold by S. KNEELAND and T. GREEN. in Queen-Street over againſt the Priſon. 1741.

Figure 36. This sermon was delivered at Enfield, CT, July 8, 1741, by Rev. Jonathan Edwards during the First Great Awakening.

United States

The first wave of Christians to arrive in North America (Jamestown, 1607) were entrepreneurs looking for economic opportunities. The second wave were Puritans, Protestants, fleeing persecution in England. They arrived at Plymouth on the *Mayflower* in 1620. Even before the English Civil War (1642–1651), as many as 10,000 Puritans fled England for America.

The Christian settlers of America were overwhelmingly Protestant, and more specifically Calvinist. Catholics in North America were rare initially. When they eventually began arriving in large numbers in the mid-nineteenth century, they were viewed with suspicion and were a persecuted minority in America. For instance, modern groups like the Ku Klux Klan (active in the 1860s, 1920s, and 1950–1960s) targeted Catholics and Jews as well as African Americans. The eighteenth century also saw the resurgence of Protestant enthusiasm, known as the **First Great Awakening**. The history of the settling of America explains why the United States today is overwhelmingly Protestant (approximately 50%), with a Catholic minority (about 20%).

Canada/Australia/New Zealand

Owing perhaps to their shared Commonwealth experience, Canada, Australia, and New Zealand have much the same story when it comes to Christianity. They are overwhelmingly Christian, in that non-Christian religions amount to a tiny percentage of the population, and yet they are also among the most secular countries, with 24%, 30%, and 42% respectively identifying as non-religious. Thus, they also share the experience of being cultures in which Christianity was once culturally and politically dominant, but has waned steadily over the last century.

These three countries also share a history of regret in their dealings with their indigenous populations. As with the rest of the colonial world, Christians arrived in Canada, Australia, and New Zealand believing they were bringing a superior culture and salvation in addition. They thus largely eradicated indigenous cultures, evidenced most pointedly in the use of residential schools. Several studies, attempts at reconciliation, and in some cases belated apologies for past abuses were undertaken by various governments in Canada, Australia, and New Zealand between 1996 and 2008.

Latin and South America

When the Spanish (in 1492) and the Portuguese (in 1500) arrived in Latin and South America, they brought Catholicism with them. The role of Roman Catholicism in Latin and South America is complex. On the one hand, as with Protestants in North America, Catholics treated the land as theirs for exploitation and the indigenous peoples as the enemy. Christian culture was seen as vastly superior, so there was no reason to preserve indigenous culture. When revolutionary fervor arrived in South America from France and the United States in the nineteenth century, the Catholic Church was in a difficult situation: should it think locally, supporting the people who wanted change, or think globally, supporting Spain and Portugal, very strong allies, who wished to maintain their colonial holdings? Even

Desde ya ofrezco mi sangre
Por la redención y
resurrección de El Salvador...
Que mi sangre sea semilla
de libertad.
(Romero, marzo 1980)

Figure 37. Mural depicting Óscar Romero, the fourth Archbishop of San Salvador, who was murdered on March 24, 1980.

Vatican has had a very tense relationship with Liberation Theologians and Catholic political activism.

The vast majority of South and Latin Americans are Catholic (as many as 80%), although the missionary efforts of Protestants (particularly Baptists, Methodists, and Lutherans) and Mormons have increased the number of non-Catholic Christians there.

Africa

Christianity in Africa is extremely varied, in part because of the size of the continent and in part because of the different colonial histories of its regions. Coptic Christians have existed in Egypt since the second century CE, and are now closely aligned with the Orthodox Church. They were instrumental in the conversion of Ethiopia. Nonetheless, while North Africa was once Christian, Christianity largely disappeared with the conquest of Muslims in the seventh century. The Portuguese brought Catholic Christianity into sub-Saharan Africa in the fifteenth century, and Dutch Protestants brought Christianity into South Africa in the nineteenth century. As a result, Islam dominates in North Africa (from Egypt to Mauritania, including Sudan, Niger, and Mali), while Christianity dominates in the south. Between the south and the north, Christians and Muslims have long competed for control. Thus, many countries in Central Africa contain equal parts Christians and Muslims, which more often than not is the source of tension, not cooperation (e.g., Nigeria).

when the Vatican finally chose to recognize the new states in the mid-nineteenth century, the Catholic elite generally supported the status quo, including when military and totalitarian dictators took over. Their goal, understandably, was to protect the Church and hopefully, from there, Catholics. Many people therefore came to associate Catholicism with the oppression of the dictators.

On the other hand, it was Catholics who created Liberation Theology. These priests and nuns used the image of Jesus found in the gospels to fight political and economic oppression. Liberation Theology championed the poor and the dispossessed, and was openly critical of the dictators' oppression, greed, and extortion. Many Catholic priests were executed for their political activities in the twentieth century, and the

One cannot discuss Christianity in Africa without referring to the creation and export of slaves, the Rwandan genocide, and Apartheid in South Africa. Christians were central in the African slave trade (they were also, it must be pointed out, eventually central in the eradication of slavery and the slave trade), often seeking to convert them before trading them to the United States and Europe. Christians (mostly Catholic since over 60% of Rwandans were Catholic, but also Protestants and Anglicans) were quite involved in supporting the 1994 Hutu slaughter of Tutsis in Rwanda. And the white Dutch Protestant settlers of South Africa, a tiny minority, were behind Apartheid, which took all political freedom away from all non-white South Africans. At the same time, South African Christians were often active in anti-Apartheid activism, and suffered for it.

Christianity in Africa ought not to be reduced to the event of colonialism alone. It can also be characterized by positive contributions. As elsewhere, Christian missions were responsible for contributing to education and literacy, medical and technological change, and supporting the many poor and oppressed in a period when Europe was vastly more advanced and wealthy. The negative side of this can be expressed with the phrase "white man's burden," the assumption that white Europe was superior in all ways to non-European cultures and had an obligation, for that reason, to enlighten the world, even if that meant destroying other cultures and ways of life at the same time. The positive side is that real people often benefited from real medical, technological, and scientific assistance.

Christianity in Africa continues to develop, now with the ever-increasing numbers and influence of Pentecostals (a Protestant denomination known best for speaking in tongues and other forms of spirit possession). In many parts of Africa, Pentecostal churches now compete effectively with once dominant Protestant churches and the Catholic Church. This is particularly evident in South Africa, where the Apostolic Faith Mission rivals the heavily Calvinist Dutch Reformed Church, and in Zimbabwe, where the Assemblies of God has almost as many members as the Catholic Church in that country, but is being replicated in Ghana, Kenya, Zambia, Rwanda, and Nigeria.

South and East Asia

Christians in India maintain a tradition that Christianity was brought to them by Thomas, one of the apostles of Jesus. At the very least, Christianity was fully present there by the sixth century, and Christian colonialism exacted a heavy price on India as it did elsewhere. Today, only 2–3% of Indians are Christian, though the southern tip of India (Kerala) is heavily Christian (90%). India's Christians are very diverse: Catholicism is the largest Christian denomination by far (because of Jesuit missions there), but there are also large populations of Orthodox, Protestant, and Anglican Christians too (the latter because of British colonialism).

Counting Christians in China is notoriously difficult. The Pew Research Center estimates that Christians make up 5% of China, and all studies agree that there are twice as many Protestants as Catholics there. Conversely, the Philippines is over 90% Christian (and heavily Catholic), and South Korea is 30% Christian (18% Protestant and 11% Catholic). While only 1% of Koreans were Christian in 1900, now Seoul is home to the world's largest Pentecostal Church (in 2007, numbered at 830,000 members), and Christianity (especially Catholicism) continues to increase its numbers there. In contrast, Christianity is nearly entirely absent from Japan.

Vatican II

The Catholic Church is a church of councils. Its leaders meet periodically to review its positions, opinions, and doctrines. Sometimes new positions are added, at other times they are altered, more commonly they are upheld. The Catholic Church accounts for this by claiming that God continues to communicate with "His" church. That is, while scriptural revelation is over, other forms of revelation are ongoing. When Catholic bishops meet at councils, they believe that God is guiding the proceedings. The decisions of the council are therefore God's will for the Catholic Church. This is related to the Catholic position called Papal Infallibility: that when a Pope speaks for the Church as Pope, his position is beyond criticism and doubt. The Council of Nicaea was the first such council (in 325 CE), and the most recent one, known as **Vatican II**, happened between 1962 and 1965. Not all councils are equally productive, but these two were especially so. The first one established the doctrine of the Trinity (see Chapter Six), while the most recent one introduced

many changes into the modern Roman Catholic Church.

Vatican II was significant for the concessions it made towards modernization. Latin was replaced by local languages for worship services. People could now understand what was happening at Mass (see Chapter Nine). Music was also allowed to be modernized; it is commonly less choral and organ-based than it used to be. And the Bible was made a stronger focus of Catholic life, moderately more in line with Protestant attitudes. Before Vatican II, Catholics might have had little opportunity to encounter the Bible, but afterwards, more scripture was included in lectionaries, and the study of the Bible was encouraged at the scholarly and popular level (in lay Bible studies). Bibles are more commonly found in Catholic homes than they were before Vatican II, and there are now special Catholic translations and editions.

Vatican II also recognized freedom of religion, and to that end it ceased the practice, common during Easter Masses, of praying for the conversion of the Jews. In fact, anti-Semitism was soundly condemned in all its forms. In addition, Protestant and

Figure 38. Seal of Vatican II.

Orthodox Christians were acknowledged as genuine Christians, and non-Christian religions were recognized as being legitimate and different expressions of devotion to the same God, with Jews, Muslims, Hindus, and Buddhists being named in particular with approval. From this point onwards, Catholics have been involved in interfaith dialogue and have apologized to many groups for a history of violent encounters with non-Catholics.

Other features of Catholicism were upheld at Vatican II: women could not be priests, and therefore neither bishops, cardinals, nor popes; birth control and contraception are wrong; the Pope is infallible. It is unlikely these things will be changed, for Catholicism is growing fastest in the global South, and shrinking in North America and Western Europe. This is significant because the global South is much more conservative religiously than the global North. That is, despite the increasing liberalism of North American and European Catholics, they are not demographically the most powerful. There is a growing tension between liberal and conservative tendencies in the global Catholic Church, and people wonder whether it is time for another Vatican Council.

Christians in a Political World

Two different revolutions – one in the United States and the other in France – determined how and why Christianity functions differently in America and in Europe. When the French revolted against monarchic rule (1789–1799), they were also revolting against the Roman Catholic Church, for the Church was firmly on the side of the monarchy against democracy and social change. As a result, many French people, and by extension Europeans, were left suspicious about religion. They sought a stark separation of church and state, and religious affiliation dropped and has remained low. In France fewer than 5% attend church weekly. The average for religious belief throughout Europe is likewise low: around 50% on average positively affirm belief that there is a god, and 20% are atheists.

In contrast, when Americans revolted against British rule (1765–1783), Protestant churches that had developed in America were very much in support of the revolt. Thus, there was a close relationship between religion and political activism in America because of the revolution. Religion would thus have a central place in the formation of a national identity, unlike in Europe where national identity more or less meant the rejection of religion. A Pew Research Center study revealed that 90% of Americans positively affirm belief that there is a god (this of course includes non-Christians, as Christians comprise approximately 73% of American society), while only 6% identify as atheists.

Religious belief is so high in America that the idea of an atheist becoming President is almost inconceivable. This makes the notion of church–state separation in America a highly contested issue. Governmental bodies in some states frequently debate whether intelligent design should be taught in schools within the science curriculum, which typically assumes Darwin's theory of evolution by natural selection.

The very high rate of religious belief and affiliation in the United States cannot be accounted for solely by the role of Christian churches in its revolution. Another important factor is the response of many American Christians to the global trend towards secularization at the end of the twentieth century. Secularism insists on the strict separation of church and state: government cannot be involved in either the promotion or persecution of any particular religion. All people must be equal before the law, so that one group's religious law cannot be allowed to determine what is legal for other groups. For example, between 1960 and 2005 laws against homosexuality and sodomy were struck down by Supreme Courts and/or democratic legislatures, and prayer was removed from most public schools. In addition, North American and European curricula were becoming increasingly science-oriented, leading many people to read biblical accounts of miracles and creation very much against the grain of Christian tradition.

Some Protestant Christians felt under attack: non-religious people were pushing Christianity out of the public sphere it had once dominated, and science was undermining the authority of the Bible. In response, they established some "fundamentals" of Christian faith, which revolved primarily around the absolute authority and accuracy of the Bible. That position came to be known as inerrancy, and the movement as **Fundamentalism**.

Christian Fundamentalism has spread around the world, but it is most prevalent in the United States, where Fundamentalist Christians have their own bookstores and publishing houses, radio stations and television channels, schools and universities, and networks of businesses. Fundamentalism, and Evangelicalism which is closely related, have spread to Africa (e.g., Uganda, Zimbabwe, Senegal) and South Korea, where they are seeing tremendous growth and are being allowed to influence the public sphere once again.

Chapter Summary

An illegal religion for three hundred years, the fortunes of Christians changed when they found favor with Constantine. After Constantine, Christianity was a religion of empire: European Christians carried Christianity into Russia, Africa, and India, and Christian empires ruled the seas. In those days, a separation of church and state was inconceivable. A couple of hundred years of wars of religion in Europe, however, provided the impetus to imagine just that: freedom of religion, and religion without state sanction or interference. Nonetheless, Christianity's encounter with modernity has been varied and complex, owing to its incredible size and cultural diversity.

Glossary

Byzantine Empire. The name of the Christian empire after the fall of Rome. Its seat of power was in Constantinople, and its territories included what are now Eastern Europe, Turkey, Syria, Lebanon, Jordan, Israel, and North Africa. It diminished in power as the Holy Roman Empire rose in power, and dissolved in the fifteenth century.

Colonialism. The ascendancy of Europe culturally, scientifically, and militarily resulted in its expansion into Africa and Asia. European countries established colonies with interests that were equal parts economic, political, and theological. The negative effects on indigenous populations were permanent.

Council of Trent. Held between 1545 and 1563, this was the Catholic Church's response to the Protestant Reformation. The Council of Trent reconsidered some but not all aspects of Protestant criticism.

Creed. A formal, and usually formulaic statement of religious belief, like an oath. Creeds are instrumental in establishing theological unity and consistency, the obverse of which is the exclusion of difference or diversity.

Fundamentalism. This form of Christianity draws its name from an original attempt to lay out the "fundamentals" of Christian faith and identity, one of which was a commitment to inerrancy: that the Old Testament and New Testament contain no errors and are as a whole completely accurate and literal descriptions of the past, including especially creation as depicted in Genesis.

Great Awakening. A series of Protestant revival movements, mostly in eighteenth–nineteenth century America. They tended to focus on personal morality and inspiration by the Holy Spirit. Extremely influential on the current American Evangelical movement.

Gutenberg Bible. Johannes Gutenberg was a German blacksmith who invented the printing press, and moved quickly to print the Bible, which he completed in 1455. The printing press also allowed political and social ideas and information to spread more quickly, resulting in a more educated populace.

Heresy. Its origins are neutral, in that it derives from a Greek word for "sect." It later became a theological category and derogatory label used by groups claiming to represent correct belief to denigrate their opponents.

Holy Roman Empire. The Christian empire that comprised, at its height, much of Central Europe north of and including Italy (962–1806). Rome was its capital, so it represents the height of papal political power.

Indulgences. Likely the most controversial of medieval Catholic practices, and one of Luther's points of disagreement, the purchase of indulgences promised donors quicker access to heaven; the higher the cost – that is the greater the buyer's generosity – the more effective they supposedly were.

Orthodoxy. Refers to correct (*ortho*) thought or belief (*doxy*). Orthodoxy is a term used readily by religious groups as a way to set themselves apart from competing groups. This term can also be used to describe those parts of religion relating to proper belief, as opposed to proper action.

Patriarch. The highest theological authority in the various Orthodox churches. It is not an equivalent position to Pope, as each Orthodox group (Armenia, Constantinople, Antioch, Russia, etc.) has its own Patriarch.

Vatican II. The most recent of Catholic Councils (1962–1965), Vatican II took major steps towards modernizing the Catholic Church and towards partial recognition of Protestants, Jews, Muslims, and others (called ecumenism).

Other Important Vocabulary

Anabaptists	Constantinople	Eusebius of Caesarea	Mendicant monastics
Anthony of Egypt	Consubstantial	*Filioque* Clause	Papal Infallibility
Arius	Crusades	Franciscans	Prester John
Athanasius	Cyrillic	Great Schism	Secularism
Avignon Papacy	Desert Fathers	*Homoiousion*	*Sola scriptura/ Sola fides/ Sola gratia*
Benedict of Nursia	Dominicans	*Homoousion*	
Calvinism	Edict of Milan	Iconoclasts	Theodosius
Carolingian Empire	Edict of Toleration	Iconodules	Trinity
Cenobitic monastics	Eremitic monastics	Martyrdom	

Discussion Questions

1. Most textbook chapters on Christian history open with a discussion of the life and teachings of Jesus Christ. Compare the benefits and costs of that approach with the benefits and costs of the approach taken here.

2. Modern Western readers are accustomed to thinking about religion as a stand-alone institution, independent of economics and politics. What does the history of Christianity reveal about how embedded religion is in economics and politics?

3. Communities need boundaries, for without boundaries there is no way to distinguish members of the community from non-members, the culture and values of a community from the world around it. Consider examples from this chapter where this is in evidence. How do the Salem Witch Trials, the Great Schism, and the Protestant Reformation all relate to this feature? Can you think of other instances from this chapter.

4. A common assumption would probably be to think of the French and American Revolutions as "political" events, and the Protestant Reformation as a "religious" event. Explain why these categories do not work as well as commonly thought.

Recommended Reading

Adair, James R. 2008. *Introducing Christianity.* London: Routledge.

Bowden, John, ed. 2005. *Encyclopedia of Christianity.* Oxford: Oxford University Press.

Koschorke, Klaus, Frieder Ludwig, and Mariano Delgado, eds. 2007. *History of Christianity in Asia, Africa, and Latin America, 1450–1990: A Documentary Sourcebook.* Grand Rapids, MI: Wm. B. Eerdman's Publishing.

Recommended Websites

http://www.pbs.org/wgbh/pages/frontline/shows/religion

- The American television station PBS did an outstanding survey of scholarship on Christian Origins and the Historical Jesus. The broadcast and other resources can be found at this website.

http://www.virtualmuseum.ca/virtual-exhibits/exhibit/anno-domini-jesus-through-the-centuries

- This website is a virtual art history museum showing the many different ways that Christians have depicted Jesus visually.

http://www.projectwittenberg.org

- Web resources offering primary sources and other resources related to the Protestant Reformation.

—4—

History of Islam

Chapter Overview

Islamic history begins, arguably, in Medina with the establishment of a religio-political charter and a discrete community. From there, we can trace the expansion and spread of the movement to form, eventually, the Islamicate. But establishing an empire and leading an empire are different enterprises, so much of this chapter focuses on the challenges Muslims faced when it came to leadership. The history of the Islamicate reveals little agreement concerning the nature and qualifications for leadership. Although some Arab features will likely always remain in Islam because of its Arab origins, we will see that Islamic history (and, in a later chapter, Islamic culture) has been shaped even more profoundly by Persians, Berbers, and Turks, but also by interactions with Jews, Christians, and Hindus.

Talking about Islamic Origins

In the previous chapter, we saw that Christianity the religion does not start with Jesus. This was the case for two reasons. First, much has to happen for Christianity the religion to take shape: it has to become a religion of empire, and it has to complete its development of Trinitarianism. Second, there is so little that historians can know with certainty about the life of Jesus that starting any historical discussion of Christianity is impossible. Rather, all theological discussions start with Jesus.

The challenges in discussing the history of Islam are not identical, but they are similar. Islam did not begin as a Jewish sect, which means it is almost certain that Muhammad intended to start a new religion, unlike Jesus, and that he did so more or less successfully within his own lifetime. Also, it is quite certain that Muhammad strove to dismantle the tribal political system in Arabia and replace it with something more centralized, with him at its head. That is to say, Islam was a religion of empire almost from the start, while Christianity took several hundred years to arrive there.

Nonetheless, sources that tell about the life of Muhammad were written 140–200 years after his death. Like Christian sources about Jesus, Islamic sources about Muhammad are deeply theologized accounts of his life, which makes distilling historical facts about his life difficult. But these sources have the additional problem of being even more separated from the life of Muhammad than Christian sources were separated from Jesus (which were written 40–70 years after the death of Jesus). In addition, like with Christianity, the figure, person, and mission of Muhammad matters more for pious theological reflection and theological debates than it does for the historical reconstruction of a religion. What matters, for reconstructing history, is not who Muhammad was, or what he was like, or what his followers believed about him, but what he accomplished. And his accomplishments, relative to establishing Islamic religion and the Islamicate, begin with the Constitution of Medina in 622 CE. This is not to say that nothing happened in Mecca. Clearly, something did, and that will be covered, along with a discussion of the prophetic figure of Muhammad, in Chapter Seven.

Starting Islamic history in Medina does not imply that Islam was fully formed this early as the religion we know; a tremendous amount of change was yet to come as an Islamic Arab empire emerged and then expanded culturally and geographically out of Arabia. It is also not the case that our sources about the Medinan period give us un-theologized historical accounts – Islamic stories about the Battle of Badr (624 CE), for instance, describe angels on the battlefield helping Muhammad's fighters! So, while we might have sources for that period, we still need to read them critically.

Medina

Islamic theological tradition maintains that in 622 CE Muhammad was invited to a city named Yathrib to mediate in a long-standing dispute. The event of Muhammad and his followers leaving Mecca to settle in Yathrib came to be known as the **Hijra**. Umar, the second caliph after the death of Muhammad, was the first to use that event to mark the start of Islamic time (e.g., Baghdad was sacked by the Mongols in 655 Anno Hijra, or 1258 CE in the Christian calendar). Because of the role the city played in the foundation of Islam, the name of the city was changed to Madinat Nabi, or the City of the Prophet, eventually shortened to just Medina.

Evidently, one of the first accomplishments of Muhammad in Medina was the formation of a Constitution, or Charter. This document, lost but recorded in numerous early Islamic sources, is a series of amendments governing relations in Medina among the Arab tribes, Jews, and followers of Muhammad who came with him from Mecca. Among other things, it seems to establish a freedom of religion (it claims that "the Jews have their religion and the Muslims have theirs") and also establishes provisions for the peaceful resolution of conflicts between religious groups. Yet it attempts to bring everyone together in the formation of a single unified community: an Ummah. The term Ummah therefore originally included Jews and non-Muslims in Medina, and only later came to refer solely to an Islamic community when this became unmanageable.

It was from Medina that Muhammad gained control of Arabia, primarily by negotiating treaties of peace, protection, and taxation with Arabian tribes. This included conquering and controlling Mecca, several cities in northern Arabia, and even a few Byzantine cities at the south-eastern edge of the Byzantine Empire. Some of these places also accepted Islam, but just as he had done in Medina, Muhammad appears not to have required conversion, only political or military loyalty and a willingness to pay a tribute tax.

The most critical of these early victories and the most difficult to attain was that over Mecca. Muhammad and his men battled Mecca initially by raiding caravans traveling between Mecca and Syria, thereby disrupting Mecca's economic supply lines. This period witnessed three major battles: the Battle of Badr in 624 CE, which the Medinans won, the Battle of Uhud in 625, which the Meccans won, and the Battle of the Trench in 627, which ended in a stalemate. Mecca and Medina agreed to peace at that point, but when that was broken by Mecca, Muhammad arrived with a large army in 630, and Mecca surrendered. Controlling Mecca solidified Muhammad's control over most of Arabia.

Building the Islamicate: from Medina to Arabia, from Spain to the Indus River

Muhammad died in approximately 632 CE without having explicitly appointed a successor. The process of selecting those who would lead the Muslims fractured the community

Islamicate

Within a hundred years of the Constitution of Medina, Muslims had conquered territories from Spain to the Indus River. What should we call this area? There are many options, none of which are perfect. Dar al-Islam, Ummah, Muslim Empire, and the Muslim or Islamic world are the most common options. Dar al-Islam, which means the Abode of Islam – the opposite of which is Dar al-Harb, the Abode of War – reflects an insider theological perspective. Like Christians who referred to non-Christians as Pagans or Heathens, the category Dar al-Islam presupposes the superiority of the in-group. Similarly, Ummah is insider language, as it refers to the community of people united by their recognition of Muhammad as God's messenger. But not only is Ummah insider language, it also imagines a unity that never existed: Muslims were constantly fighting each other for control. "Muslim world" and "Islamic world" are problematic for the same reason: they imply a level of unity that barely existed in a single location let alone across the whole collection of Islamic lands. But more than that, "Muslim world" and "Islamic world" are simply inaccurate: the lands ruled over by Muslims also contained Christians, Jews, Zoroastrians, Buddhists, Shamanists, and Hindus in all their endless varieties, and others in addition. To refer to it as the Muslim or Islamic world implies a homogeneity that never existed; that world was much more than Islamic and more diverse than merely Islamic. Nonetheless, we need to be able to refer to that expanse of lands in which Islamic groups were the dominant shaping force politically and culturally. I have adopted and adapted an adjective first coined in the 1970s, Islamicate, to refer to the collection of places – the boundaries of which were in nearly constant flux – where Islam was politically, culturally, and religiously dominant.

Rightly Guided Caliphs

Sunni Muslims have a theological category for the first four leaders of the Islamic community after the death of Muhammad: the four Rightly Guided Caliphs. That they were "rightly guided" carries with it two connotations: that these four were the correct leaders in the correct order (against the claim that Ali should have followed after Muhammad) and that their divine guidance makes them worthy of great reverence and respect. They were not prophets, so they did not take over from Muhammad in that regard, but they were "rightly guided." They thus hold a level of honor lower than Muhammad, but higher than the many caliphs and leaders who came after.

Abu Bakr (caliph 632–634 CE) was one of the first followers of Muhammad. He was also said to have been present on the Hijra, to have replaced Muhammad as prayer leader when the prophet was dying, and he was the father of Aisha, Muhammad's favorite of his later wives. Abu Bakr is primarily credited with re-establishing the authority of Islam among the Arabian tribes after the death of Muhammad. Umar

(caliph 634–644 CE), appointed by Abu Bakr, was said to have been a fierce opponent of Islam, but after reading verses of the Qur'an he converted and became a fierce defender. He is primarily credited with initiating a soldier-ethic that allowed for the very rapid spread of Islam out of Arabia. He took the title "Commander of the Faithful." Umar was assassinated, but before he died he appointed a committee to select the next caliph. That committee selected Uthman, who reigned for twelve years. On the one hand, Uthman was a poor political leader; he fomented resentment and revolt even among his allies. On the other hand, he also oversaw the collection and creation of the official written Qur'an. Lastly, Ali was the fourth and final Rightly Guided Caliph (656–661 CE). Cousin and son-in-law to Muhammad, he had to handle the civil war that started under Uthman, some of it directed against him personally. He too was assassinated by his own people. Ali, is not only counted among the "Rightly Guided" by Sunni Muslims, but also as the first Imam by Shi'a Muslims.

into two groups: those who believed that Muhammad had appointed Ali, his cousin and son-in-law, to take over after him, and those who did not. The former group came to be known as Shi'a Muslims, the latter group Sunni Muslims. The former group followed a descent from Ali, as the first rightful Imam, through his sons and ending at a twelfth Imam. The latter group began with four "Rightly Guided Caliphs," which included and ended with Ali. After this, Sunni Muslims develop into a very politically and militarily robust caliphate that comes to dominate over Shi'a Muslims through most (but not all) of time since.

If the movement was going to survive the death of their prophet, the primary task was to re-establish the treaties of alliance and taxation that Arabian tribes had made with Muhammad. It was Abu Bakr – the father of one of Muhammad's wives, the young Aisha – who carried out the campaign to renew the Arab treaties. Islamic tradition gave this the highly theological moniker Ridda Wars, or Wars of Apostasy. Before Abu Bakr's term ended in his death in 634, he had shifted his campaign from renewing treaties to establishing total control over the Arabian Peninsula, and beginning forays into Syria. Umar, who led the community

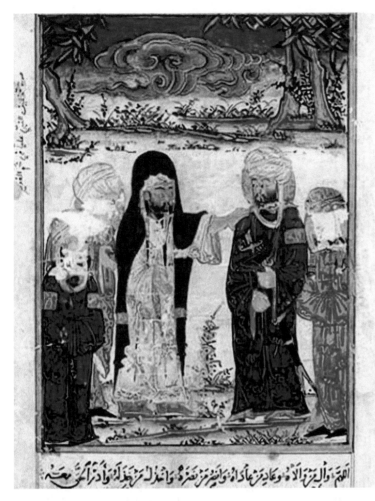

Figure 39. The Investiture of Ali at Ghadir Khumm by Ibn al-Kutbi. Ali is the fourth of the four Rightly Guided Caliphs.

imperial expansion out of Arabia therefore entailed a war with two theaters: westward to wrestle territory from the Christians, and eastward to wrestle territory from the Sasanians. The westward expansion took them as far as Spain while the eastward expansion took them as far as India.

The westward expansion came quickly. Islamic armies under the direction of Umar controlled Damascus by 636 CE, all of Syria and Jerusalem by the following year, the important seaport of Caesarea Maritima by 640, and Alexandria and with it all of Egypt by 641. Happy to leave most of North Africa alone, Muslims did not expand beyond Tripoli until taking Carthage successfully in 698, converting the **Berbers** at the same time, and then crossing Gibraltar into Spain (Iberia at the time) in 711. Berbers eventually controlled most of what is now Spain by 720.

In contrast, the simultaneous eastward expansion into the mountainous Sasanian Empire proved much more difficult. Sasanians were more resistant to conversion and more capable fighters. Muslims won at Nahavand in what is now western Iran in 642 CE, Fars in the south by 650, and Khorasan in the north-east in 654. Because of the Umayyad-Alid civil war that culminated in the Battle of Karbala in 680 (more on that below), movement further east was slowed, though it resumed with vigor afterwards: by 713, Muslims controlled the territory as far east as modern-day Pakistan.

next (634–644 CE), carried on this policy of imperial expansion.

The rapid spread of Islam out of Arabia owed less to the military supremacy of Islamic soldiers and more to geopolitical coincidence. The Christian Byzantine Empire and the Persian Sasanian Empire had been fighting with each other for more than a century, and although the Byzantines had by this time repelled the Sasanians, both sides were exhausted. When Islamic armies arrived, they encountered very little resistance. Islamic

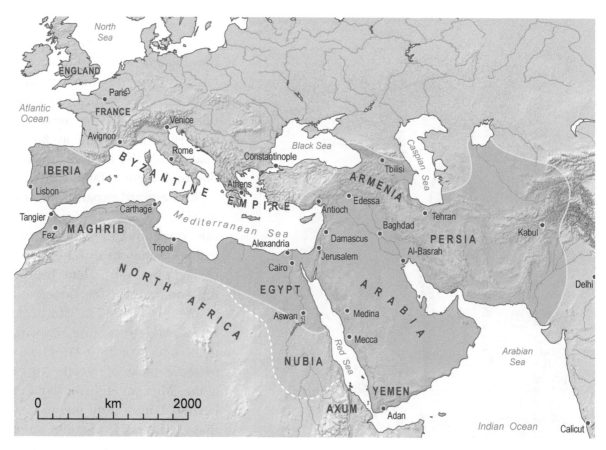

Figure 40. The Islamicate, c. 750 CE.

Muslims had gone from controlling the Arabian Peninsula in 634 CE to controlling and governing everything between Spain and the Indus River by 713, an Islamicate of nearly 5000 miles established in less than a century. It was a process initiated by Umar, carried on by Uthman, who led the Muslims from 644–656, and then completed under the Umayyads (661–750). This metamorphosis increased the complexity and variety of Islamic life and rule exponentially, and brought with it many growing pains.

Governing the Islamicate

Governing the expanse of land won in under a century was far more difficult than winning it in the first place. Arab culture was largely nomadic and heavily tribal, not urban and sedentary, and it had a long history of disliking centralized government, which is what Muhammad initiated and Abu Bakr demanded. Ruling the new empire was made difficult by two features. First, the sheer cultural and historical diversity of the lands and people between Spain and the Indus River made it impossible to follow a single model of rule, let alone the one used by the Arab Umayyads. Second, the speed with which the expansion happened left hardly any time to adapt to and prepare for the complexity of ruling an empire.

While the Islamic movement was spreading both west and east, it was also experiencing

Figure 41. The Arabic inscription carved into this rock crystal seal is an example of Shi'a devotion. It asks God to bless Ali (son-in-law and cousin of Muhammad) and Ali's wife Fatima (Muhammad's daughter) along with Hasan and Husayn (both sons of Ali) and also to bless Jafar (a descendant of Ali) and Moses. (See the discussion on p. 94 of the Alid succession.) The seal was purchased in Afghanistan in the 1830s but is undated.

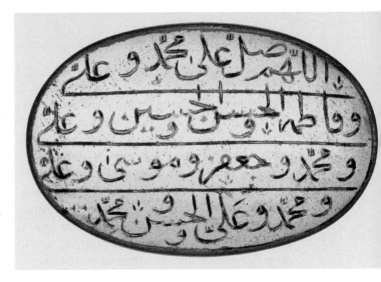

perpetual internal fighting. Thus, while people often tell the story of Islam as if there were two great dynasties – the Umayyads and Abbasids – the reality is that there was never much unity at all. Not only did one violently overthrow the other, as we shall see below, but neither one actually enjoyed uncontested governance. Leadership was constantly contested, a fact that goes back even to the period of the so-called "Rightly Guided Caliphs," only one of whom died of natural causes.

Unlike his predecessors, Ali accomplished almost nothing during his caliphate (656–661 CE). All his energy was directed at defending his rule. When Ali replaced Uthman as caliph, he chose amnesty over revenge for Uthman's killers. This decision appears to have offended two parties. First, it offended Aisha; she led an army against Ali that included others who had been close followers of Muhammad. They met at the Battle of the Camel (656) within months of Ali's assumption of the caliphate, at which Ali prevailed. Second, some of Uthman's relatives, from a clan known as the

Figure 42. "The Mosque of Omar Shewing the Site of the Temple," by David Roberts (1842–1849), who traveled extensively in Egypt and the Levant. Although his images were based on his direct experience, they offer a highly idealized view of the places in question, and have come to epitomize Western artistic views of the Orient (see "Orientalism" text box, p. 94).

Orientalism

Orientalism is a particular way that the "Orient," or the East (which for this topic includes everything from Egypt to Japan) is imagined and represented by the West (for this topic, mainly Christian Europe and America). Western scholars and Christian missionaries in the nineteenth century traveled to the Middle East and "the Orient" and wrote about what they saw. Sometimes they wrote with great admiration and sensitivity, but imagined they had stumbled upon life as it was in the Garden of Eden: original, idyllic, and pure, hearkening back to a time when society was unspoiled by the complexities of modern (especially urban) life. That is to say, the people they found there were "simple" but in the best sense of the word. Sometimes, however, they wrote with hostility, seeing these people as primitive, barbaric, uncultured, and uncivilized. These people were in desperate need of civilization and culture, sometimes expressed as the highly racial and ethnocentric "white man's burden."

Though "unspoiled" sounds more positive than "barbaric," both are in fact ethnocentric perspectives. Orientalism is a specific kind of ethnocentrism. Orientalism can be seen in the very famous collection of short stories called *One Thousand and One Arabian Nights*: magical flying carpets, genies from Aladdin's lamp dispensing wishes, the term "Open Sesame" to unlock a door, Ali Baba's forty thieves, or Sinbad the Sailor. The stories conjured up a magical and superstitious land in the imaginations of the West. It may have been a romantic perspective, but it was also one lacking the intellectual rigor, discipline, or scientific sophistication of the West. For the adult reader, the stories also allude to women of potent but restrained sexuality and unparalleled exotic beauty, though this is epitomized most effectively in Hollywood depictions of the tales. These are the epitome of orientalistic thinking about the Islamicate.

Umayyads, also took offense. Mu'awiya, who was governor of Syria and head of the Umayyads, engaged Ali in battle at Siffin in 657, but conceded defeat during it and asked for arbitration. When Ali agreed to the request, a group of his own supporters defected. They called themselves Kharijites, and four years later in 661, one of them assassinated Ali.

Umayyads, Alids, and Abbasids

Well before Ali was killed, he was powerless. The caliphate was being claimed by Mu'awiya and maintained in Damascus, and he passed it to his son, Yazid. The two sons of Ali, Husan and Husayn, were little match for the power

of the Umayyads. The end of Ali's life for Sunni Muslims marks the end of the period of the four Rightly Guided Caliphs and the start of the Umayyad Dynasty (661–750 CE). As was suggested above, the Umayyad Dynasty was far from uncontested or secure.

Opposition to the Umayyad Dynasty was based on three different objections. The first point of objection was that they had turned the caliphate into a dynasty. A dynasty is rule that passes from one family member to another. Some ancient Islamic witnesses claim that the very reason Ali was not chosen to take over after the death of Muhammad was that the earliest Muslims wanted to avoid dynastic succession. Instead, it is said they wanted succession to be based on

Figure 43. The Umayyad Mosque at Damascus as depicted in the *Book of Wonders*, a late-fourteenth-century Arabic manuscript.

appeared too attractive to let go of once the precedent was established. The Umayyad Dynasty was replaced with another dynasty – that of the Abbasids.

The second objection to the Umayyads concerned their Arab-centrism, which revealed an assumption that Islam was a religion for and from Arabs. Most in the Umayyad leadership were Arabs who felt that Arab culture was superior and Arab identity key to the religion and empire. Though Islam was attracting many converts from other cultures and religions – Iranians, Zoroastrians, Christians, Jews, and polytheists – there was a widespread disdain for them among the older and original Arab Muslims. By the early eighth century, the Arab-centric Umayyad Dynasty could not hold. At the western end of the Islamicate, Berbers had risen up in revolt already in 740. This helped bring about the demise of the Umayyads, but it was at the eastern end that the Umayyad Empire was totally dismantled by a competing clan, the Abbasids.

A third challenge to Umayyad rule was that they did not have a blood relationship to Muhammad (the Umayyads could, on the other hand, claim family bonds: Mu'awiya's grandmother was an aunt of one of Muhammad's wives). Clearly, this did not matter to the Umayyads, but that the Umayyads were defeated can be attributed, at least in part, to the fact that claims of familial relationship to Muhammad resonated deeply with many Muslims in Islam's first century and a half. The first group to make this case was composed of those who felt that Ali should have been the one to lead after Muhammad. Ali was a cousin of Muhammad, so shared his

piety and merit. Perhaps this is why Mu'awiya lost much support and many allies when he appointed his son Yazid to take over after him. Medinan leaders refused to recognize Yazid's caliphate, and both Medina and Mecca had to be brought under control by Yazid's forces. The Kabah (see Chapter Ten) was even destroyed during one of Yazid's sieges of Mecca. Of course, the irony is that though many objected to dynastic rule, it

Martyrdom

By now you know that martyrdom is part of religious discourse for nearly everyone. Jews began using the language of martyrdom under persecution from the Seleucids, which led to the Maccabean Revolt in the second century BCE. Christians used it of their own faithful who died at the hands of Romans. In truth, any group whose members die because of their loyalty to the group tend to be considered a martyr by their group. People in different groups will, of course, have contesting martyrs. One group might consider the death of their enemy to be the death of villains, but to insiders, the death of fellow insiders, of defenders of the group, is the death of heroes, those whose courage is to be emulated.

And therein lies the power of the rhetoric of martyrdom: when death is valorized, martyrdom represents the highest form of devotion to the group, and the highest form of courage in a person. The rhetoric of martyrdom thus functions in the survival and often the identity of a group: a group facing violence – either because it is being persecuted despite its innocence or because it is engaging actively in war – needs its members not to fear death. Heroizing the dead helps to ensure that members will be willing to die in defense of the group. It is very potent stuff.

The 2007 death of former President of Pakistan Benazir Bhutto offers a fascinating example of how the rhetoric of martyrdom is often contested. Her supporters claimed that she was killed by gunshots or an explosion and was therefore a martyr. Her opponents claimed that she hit her head ducking through her sunroof, and therefore was not a martyr because she died accidentally. Her opponents were pleased she was dead, but they did not want to create a martyr.

blood, and in addition had married Fatima, one of Muhammad's daughters. Their sons, Hasan and Husayn, were therefore the only direct descendants of the prophet himself. The community that developed around them took the position that familial descent from Muhammad was the most important feature of Islamic rule.

The second group to claim a blood relationship with Muhammad, and to use that as the basis for their resistance to Umayyad rule, were the Abbasids, so named because of their claim to be descendants of Muhammad's uncle Abbas. It was they who succeeded ultimately in overthrowing the Umayyads. This shift in power is critical in the shaping of Islam because Arab centrism diminished and the influence of Persian culture increased.

After the death of Ali, the Alid community rallied around Husayn to resist Mu'awiya's appointment of his son Yazid to inherit the caliphate. This resistance came to a head at Karbala in 680, which Husayn and his men lost. Husayn's death, considered by his supporters a martyrdom (see "Martyrdom" text box, above), was the trigger that would solidify a new Islamic group, the **Alids** or Shi'a, a name that derives from their original description as the *shi'at 'Ali*, or the faction of Ali. But Alid opposition to the Umayyads did not end with the devastating loss at Karbala. It shifted back to Medina, from where the sons of Husayn revolted unsuccessfully. They were killed too. Each successive death was considered a new martyrdom, and each one strengthened Shi'a resolve and the notion that the deaths were spiritually, almost cosmically, significant.

The Alids and the Origin of Shi'a Islam

The following description of Shi'a origins requires a caveat: much of what we teach about how Shi'a Islam developed, and what they believed and practiced in their early centuries, is very speculative. There is a tremendous amount we do not and cannot know. This is because Shi'a Muslims were so heavily persecuted by majority Islam that much of their life happened in secret. No less, persecution often involved the destruction of sources as well. But it can also be difficult to describe Shi'a identity in certain periods because sometimes no such identity exists. This is because identity requires some consensus, and sometimes there were so many competing Alid groups that it is impossible to find a consensus or majority opinion at all.

By 750 CE, when the Abbasids took over from the Umayyads, Islam was extremely diverse and deeply divided. There were Arabs, Persians, sub-Saharan Africans, Iberians, Berbers, and Turks, nomads and city dwellers. And the division over leadership continued. This is evident within the development of Alid sects, and also evident within the broader Islamic world, which quickly devolved into a number of smaller competing empires and dynasties. The end result is that the Abbasid Dynasty faced constant resistance and was never able to rule the entirety of the territory they took from the Umayyads.

Shi'a Islam does not agree with the legitimacy of the four Rightly Guided Caliphs. In fact, they prefer the office of Imam over caliph, and for them, Ali was the first Imam, followed by his two sons, and then Ali-Zayn, Husayn's son. The deaths of Ali, of Husayn, and of Shi'a rebels under the Abbasids contributed to a highly speculative and innovative theology. Rationalism and pragmatism

---

Language

Islamic culture during the Abbasid period was so advanced, and so attractive, that its influence on the West is easy to see. This is especially the case in Spain, and especially the case with respect to architecture. But it is visible in language as well. The Spanish have a word, *ojalá*. It means "hopefully," as in "Hopefully the picnic won't be ruined by rain." But it comes directly from Arabic, and reflects the presence of Muslims in Spain for so long. *Ojalá* is how *insha'allah* (Arabic for "God willing") came to be pronounced in Spanish. Given that Spain is about 70% Catholic and about 20% atheist, it is very interesting to think of Spaniards using the Arabic word for God without realizing it.

English too has hundreds of words that come from Arabic. In some cases – like camel and giraffe, or the artichoke and the type of cloth called muslin – this is because Europe did not have these things, so English simply adopted the Arabic name for them. These words testify to cultural contact; cultured Christians wanted luxury cloth, so they used the Arabic term "muslin" for it, and they wanted fine gold, so they adopted the Arabic way of assessing its quality: carat. Other examples are more interesting because they testify to the extent to which Christian Europe benefited from Islamic superiority in war and science. Here are a few of those words, and merely the ones beginning with A and Z: admiral, alchemy, alcohol, alcove, algebra, algorithm, alkali, amalgam, almanac, arsenal, atlas, average, azimuth; zenith, zero.

Cultural Competition

Two Islamicate cities exemplify the phenomenon of cultural competition: Baghdad and Cordoba.

Abbasids began building Baghdad in 762 CE where the Tigris and Euphrates rivers come closest. Originally one-and-a-half miles in diameter, the city attracted so many people that within two hundred years it had grown to 24 square miles, several times larger than Constantinople at the time. In part the location of the city articulated the Abbasid interest in moving Islam beyond its Arab-centrism. The Abbasids built, promoted, and supported the House of Wisdom so that it become the leading place of research and learning in the world. Here Muslim, Jewish, and Christian scholars alike excelled in science, mathematics, medicine, astronomy, philosophy, cartography, and geography. Cordoba was the capital of an Umayyad caliphate (756–1031 CE) called Andalus. The Umayyads sought to build a city that would rival Damascus and Baghdad as beacons of Islamic culture and civilization. They built 300 mosques in the city, including the famous Great Mosque of Cordoba, many palaces and public buildings, elaborate bridges, botanical gardens, and monuments. Cordoba, along with all of Islamic Spain, was also an extremely fertile place intellectually: they led the world in the study of medicine and philosophy, mathematics and theology, science and technology, and boasted of one of the largest and richest libraries in the world at the time. Many of the leading intellectuals of Judaism and Islam were produced in Islamic Spain – Maimonides, Ibn Rushd (known as Averroes in the West), and Ibn Arabi, among others.

Figure 44. During the Abbasid period Baghdad was legendary for the beauty and richness of its sequestered pleasure gardens. Here revelers are shown preparing a feast.

gave way to the belief that martyrs and leaders of the groups were imbued with a divine spirit, capable of new prophetic revelations and were uniquely guided by God.

This speculative theology, which we shall look at in more detail in Chapter Seven, was emerging strongly among Shi'a Muslims in the early eighth century when a dispute arose between two half-brothers: Al-Baqir, a learned proponent of this theology, and Zayd, who was more politician and military leader than theologian, and who rejected these recent theological innovations. A group developed around Zayd, proclaiming him the rightful fifth Imam, becoming known as Zaydis (sometimes also as Fivers). Today, they comprise nearly half of Yemeni Muslims, but are found in few other places. The remainder of the Alid community supported al-Baqir.

Al-Baqir carried on, as did his son from him, and both were highly regarded. Yet a dispute arose concerning which of Jafar's sons should be the seventh Imam. Of his two sons, Ismail was the elder, Musa the younger. On the principle of succession known as primogeniture, namely succession by the first-born, it could be assumed that Ismail was the heir-apparent, and indeed his father had said as much. But Ismail died before his father did. Others therefore assumed that succession ought to move to Jafar's other son, Musa, who was still alive. But Ismail's supporters disagreed; they felt that once one was named Imam, this could not be rescinded. Those who continued to support Ismail became known as Ismailis, or Seveners.

Musa was supported by the majority of the Alid community, as were his descendants, until confusion and disarray erupted in 874 CE when the eleventh Imam, al-Askari, died without a successor. The solution was a theological move adopted from competing Shi'a predecessors: the eleventh Imam *did* have a son and heir after all – the twelfth Imam – but in order to protect him, God had hidden him away. We shall return to this idea in Chapter Seven, since the solution and its maintenance are a complex and key feature of Shi'a theological identity. Suffice to say here that the majority of Shi'a Muslims came to accept the solution, and are thus known as Twelvers, or better as **Imami** Muslims.

Multiple Competing Empires

One ought not to assume that because the Abbasid period lasted so long (750–1258 CE) that it comprised a unified empire. Far from it. There may have been Muslims from Spain to India during the Abbasid period, but there was almost no unity within, and the Abbasids, much as they might have wished it was different, lacked supreme political (or military) authority. Between Spain and India at various times there were numerous caliphates who refused to accept Abbasid authority: the Umayyads, whom the Abbasids defeated, resurfaced in **Andalus** (modern Spain and Portugal); Berbers controlled what is now Morocco and Algeria; **Fatimids**, a family of Ismaili Shi'a Muslims, controlled what is now Libya, until they expanded into Egypt by defeating yet another caliphate, the Tulunids; and the Saffarid caliphate operated in Iran (until 1003 CE). In fact, though it is said that the Abbasids governed from Baghdad, even this is not entirely true: in the late tenth century, the Twelver Shi'a group known as the Buyids conquered Baghdad

The Catholic Crusades against Muslims and Orthodox Christians

Starting in 1095 CE, seeking redemption for a 1071 loss to Seljuq forces and capitalizing on schisms between Seljuqs and Fatimids, Christians set out to capture Jerusalem from Muslims hands. By this time, recall, Eastern and Western Christianity had already split after centuries of political tension and developing theological differences. As a result, Catholic Crusaders were as suspicious of Orthodox Christians as they were of Muslims. Conversely, Orthodox Christians had a mutually beneficial detente with the Seljuqs. So, when it was found out that the Orthodox emperor in Constantinople had surreptitiously worked to save the Seljuq royal family from harm, relations with the Crusaders were forever poisoned. Constantinople was first sacked not by Muslims, though it was eventually, but by Christians in 1204, during the Fourth Crusade.

The First Crusade, led largely by Franks (from what is now France), won Jerusalem in 1099, killing people indiscriminately, regardless of their age, sex, or religious affiliation. Though a few Islamic attempts were made to expel the Christians, they all failed. This was not due to Crusader military prowess, but because Islamic divisions ran too deep. Indeed at times, some Muslims cooperated with the Crusaders in order gain a political or military advantage over rival Muslims. In the end, it was Saladin, decorated leader of the **Abbuyids**, who expelled Christians from Jerusalem in 1187, which triggered the Third Crusade in response. In 1192, Richard the Lionheart and Saladin signed a truce, but Christians controlled very little territory in Palestine by then. Nonetheless, they were not fully pushed out of Palestine until 1291. There were additional crusades, as many as nine, but few of them ever made it to Jerusalem.

The Crusades maintain almost mythical status in the modern Islamic world. American and British soldiers in the twenty-first century wars against Iraq and Afghanistan have been called "Crusaders" by Islamic opponents. Regardless of the very different context, the Crusades remain potent in Islamic cultural memory of Christian aggression.

and took control of Iran and Iraq away from the Abbasids, though they left the Sunni Abbasid caliph in place as a figurehead.

This complex political picture becomes even more complex with the arrival of the Seljuqs. The previous groups mentioned were Muslims competing for control of the Islamicate. The Seljuqs were foreign invaders, Turks by culture and language, but like the Mongols in the coming centuries, they quickly converted to Islam. Preferring Sunni Islam, the Seljuqs ended the Shi'a Buyid control over Baghdad by 1060 CE, driving them underground. There was an Abbasid caliph in place in Baghdad under the Seljuqs, but as before he was merely a figurehead. Real power was held by a new figure called the sultan.

Despite this, there are two ways that the Abbasids could be considered an *empire*: economic and cultural. Trade and commerce connected the entire Islamicate. Andalusian merchants traveled to Iran and craftsmen from Baghdad traveled to Andalus. Technological advances increased agricultural as well as material production, which increased goods available for trade, which increased wealth, which increased the demand for quality goods from afar. Fashion trends, personal items, interesting new foods and new tools, building supplies, art, and steel blades were introduced in new locations. Trade caravans and ships were in constant motion, as commerce was happening both at the individual as well as the state level. The competing caliphs were apparently quite willing to set aside their political differences in the interest of economic needs and aspirations.

Trade and commerce not only brought coherence to an Islamicate that utterly lacked it politically, but was also the motivation for expansion. Islamic expansion into West and Saharan Africa was about controlling the gold trade, and the Islamicate during the Abbasid period had an almost unquenchable thirst for gold. In addition,

Islamic merchants were appearing as far away as China for trade eastward as well, travel made easier by the Silk Road.

Christians, Mongols, and the Plague

As we have seen, the Islamicate witnessed nearly constant internal pressures and resistance – the Umayyads of Cordoba, Berbers, Fatimids, Tulunids, Buyids, Saffarids, and finally Seljuqs resisted, cajoled, controlled, and eventually supplanted the Abbasids and each other. Starting in the eleventh century, however, that constant internal pressure

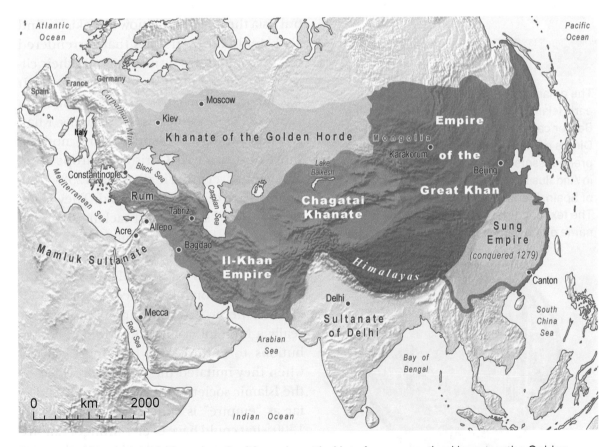

Figure 45. After their initial invasion, the Mongols settled into four competing khanates: the Golden Horde, Il-Khanate, and Chagatai were all subservient to the Great Khanate.

was exacerbated by external pressures at both ends of the Islamicate: Christians at the western end in Andalus and Mongols at the eastern end. The geopolitical world was shifting, and the many of the gains Muslims had made in their expansion would be lost, or as we shall see, transformed.

Christian Europe's discovery of its own military ability to push back at Islamic prowess began at the end of the eleventh century: Christians took Toledo in the Spanish north from Muslims in 1085 CE and Jerusalem in 1099. Nonetheless, taking Andalus in its entirety, an event Christians called the Reconquista, took several centuries. By 1249, Muslims were living under Christian control everywhere in Spain except in the

south, yet it took until 1492 for Ferdinand and Isabella to complete the expulsion of Muslims. Though Spain was the only Islamic land lost entirely to Christians, and though European Christian colonization had negative and lasting effects on the Islamicate, what was happening at the eastern end of the Islamicate – the arrival of Mongols – had an even more profound impact on Muslims. The Islamicate was about to be entirely redesigned.

The Mongols came from the east and the north in relentless waves, wreaking total destruction on land, infrastructure, and populace. From 1219–1222, Genghis Khan led them on a campaign of domination, fresh from victories over China and entering central Asia through what is now Uzbekistan and Turkmenistan. Even cities that surrendered saw their buildings dismantled and their citizens murdered in the tens of thousands. It was far worse for cities that resisted. From 1236–1242, descendants of Genghis Khan reached western Poland, where nothing short of luck saved Christian Europe from also being overrun. Finally, from 1253–1260, a third wave of Mongols arrived. They made short work of sieging and sacking Baghdad in 1258 and by 1260 had arrived at Egypt, where a combination again of luck and the military prowess of the Mamluk soldiers stopped the Mongol advance.

There never was a Mongol Empire, nor really a Mongol civilization. Mongol contributions to culture and learning occurred when they imitated the models provided by the Islamic societies they conquered. And as far as "empire" is concerned, in reality, by 1300 what could have been a Mongol Empire was four mutually hostile Mongol khanates – smaller political entities each ruled over

Dinar

The dinar was the gold unit of currency in early Islam. This example was issued by the Berber caliph Abd al-Mumin (1130–1162 CE). Dinars minted by the Almohads and by their predecessors were a unit of currency not only in Andalus but also in the Christian kingdoms of Spain, France, Germany, Italy and England. The text on the coin does not include the name of the mint or its date.

by a khan. Mongol territory was huge, but would have been much larger were it not for key losses they suffered to Christians in western Poland (1241), to Mamluks in Palestine (1260) and Syria (1281 and again in 1303), and the Sultanate of Delhi (1290–1327).

The devastation of Islamicate culture and society because of and following the Mongol invasion was immense. The Mongols' wanton destruction of people and culture, of libraries, monuments, and entire great cities, had a similar effect on Islam as the Holocaust had on Judaism: many things were lost forever, scholarly and cultural production was set back significantly, and in some places, evidence of Islamic presence was completely erased. But just as persecution in Western Europe forced Jewish people into new lands (e.g., Eastern Europe, America), so too did Mongol violence force Muslims, particularly

intellectuals, artists, merchants, craftspeople, tradespeople, farmers, theologians, and other citizens, into lands free of the threat of Mongol violence. Thus, the Mamluks in Egypt, an emerging Ottoman Empire in Turkey, and the Sultanate of Delhi benefited from an influx of immigrants who brought their culture and learning with them. Thus, it must be recognized that while the suffering of Muslims was great in this period, Islamic advances were nonetheless still happening in other places.

The Mongols were animists, which means they believed that the world (e.g., sky, water, animals, plants) was animated with spirits that could be accessed and needed to be cared for (see Chapter One). When those spirits were neglected, sickness ensued, and a shaman was needed to strike a new balance. The Mongols did not demand that

Mamluks

Among the various groups that influenced Islamic history and culture, few are as fascinating as the Mamluks: a class of soldiers created from captured and enslaved Turks. Two features worked together to ensure the fierce loyalty of the Mamluk soldiers. First, because they had no ties to or familial history in Islamic lands, generals did not have to worry about them following orders that might involve killing their own people. Second, they were granted limited rights after their military service. They were the perfect soldiers in that their only loyalty was solely to their Abbasid caliph.

That loyalty, however, began to evaporate when they realized the power they wielded. In 961, Mamluks took over the city of Ghazna and established their own Ghaznavid Dynasty in what is now Afghanistan, preferring the Sunni over Shi'a version of Islam. Then, although

Seljuqs defeated the Ghaznavids in 1040, Mamluks retained their prestige because Seljuqs and Buyids both relied on them heavily in their armies, as the Abbasids had. Mamluks then arrived in Egypt in the late eleventh century, playing a minor role in establishing the Fatimid Empire. But their presence at the eastern end of the Mediterranean led to even greater prestige in coming centuries. Mamluks formed the core of Ayyubid military power, which reigned in Egypt, Syria, and Yemen until 1250. It was Mamluks then who expelled Crusaders from Jerusalem 1187 and stopped the Mongols from extending into Egypt and North Africa in 1260. In 1260, they again seized control in Egypt, establishing what is called the Mamluk Empire, which lasted until 1517, and included Egypt, Syria, and the western strip of Arabia known as the Hijaz.

Figure 46. The mosque at Bole, situated in the territory of Gonja (northern region of Ghana).

Europe, following the Silk Road.

Even before the arrival of Timur, the Mongol khans were politically unstable, so life under them was unpredictable. Some khans were politically and religiously lenient and interested in culture-building, at which point societies flourished, while other khans were more interested in raiding and looting, and cities and culture would be neglected, or outright harmed: some khans plundered cities in their very own realms.

conquered people take on their animisms, and while Genghis Khan did initially forbid circumcision and the practices of kosher and halal eating, this restriction likely eased as his descendants converted to Islam.

Oddly, the conversion of the Mongols and their descendants to Islam did not mean peace for the conquered Islamicate. Indeed, one of the bloodiest periods of Islamic suffering happened at the hands of a Turkish Mongol convert to Islam named Timur (1336–1405 CE). In the late fourteenth century, he set up the **Timurid Sultanate** over modern Pakistan, Afghanistan, Turkmenistan, Iran, and Iraq. The Timurids crushed Mamluk soldiers in Syria, Ottoman forces in Turkey, and the army of the Sultanate of Delhi in India. And keep in mind that this suffering was only exacerbated by the Plague, which swept from China to Northern

Global Expansion

There have been two periods of pronounced growth of the Islamicate: the first occurred in the Umayyad period, and resulted in a territory that reached from Spain on the Atlantic to the Indus River at the eastern edge, and from the Caspian Sea in the north to the Sahara Desert and the Arabian Peninsula in the south. The Abbasid period saw occasional forays beyond these boundaries, but they never resulted in any long-term gains; for the most part, the shape of the Islamicate was stable in this period.

The second period of expansion happened as a result of the Mongol invasion. At the same time that Muslims lost Spain in the west, the central and eastern parts of the Islamicate experienced unprecedented growth. Islam became fully established in two territories that had long eluded them: Turkey and India. Despite the loss of Spain, the Islamicate doubled in size from 1400–1750. The shape of the Islamicate today – how Muslims came to be in Africa, Eastern Europe, Central Asia, South Asia, and finally, but significantly in South-East Asia – owes everything to this period of expansion, trade, and settlement.

Africa

The loss of Spain to Christians drove Islam back across Gibraltar into North Africa, an area known as the **Maghrib** – which comprised what is today Mauritania, Morocco, Algeria, and Libya. Long-standing Islamic dominance there, under the Berbers, had already facilitated southward expansion into western Africa. Trade in salt, slaves, and gold made crossing the Sahara into West Africa lucrative. After the expulsion from Spain, this region of Africa became increasingly Islamized as Islamic merchants sought out new markets and opportunities. They then spread eastward across sub-Saharan Africa, until by the 1600s, Central Africa from the Atlantic to the Red Sea was brought into the Islamicate. Most of these places remain majority Muslim nations today.

Eastern Europe

The presence of Islam in Eastern Europe occurred because of the Ottoman Empire, the longest-lasting of the post-Mongol Islamic empires. Though the Ottoman Turks had been soundly defeated by Timur in 1402, his death three years later allowed the Ottomans to rebound, and by 1453 they even captured Constantinople. Once again Muslims were on the doorstep of Christian

Europe, who because of this branded the Ottomans the "terrible Turks." Ironically, however, Europeans were also enamored of the cultural prowess of the Ottomans. The epithet of the Ottoman king Suleiman I (ruled 1520–1566), "the Magnificent," was given to him by Europeans. Nonetheless, it was the threat of the Ottomans that perhaps persuaded European kings, princes, and popes to cooperate on technological and military development. Such cooperation helped to defend European cities such as Vienna from Suleiman in 1529, and to repel the Ottomans almost entirely in the late seventeenth century.

In addition, by 1514, the Sunni Ottomans had defeated a new Shi'a state in Iran called the Safavid Empire (not to be confused with the Saffarid Empire). A battle on the border of what is now Turkey and Iran ensured that

Figure 47. The names on this Ottoman ceramic tile are those of God, the Prophet Muhammad, and the Prophet's first four successors, Abu Bakr, Umar, Uthman, and Ali. Sunni Muslims honor all four successors. Shi'a Muslims believe Ali was Muhammad's only rightful successor. This tile therefore marks the Ottoman Dynasty's adherence to Sunni Islam.

Figure 48. Portuguese discoveries and explorations (1415–1543).

the Safavids were kept out of Anatolia, leaving it to the Ottomans. And finally, the defeat of the Mamluks in 1516 transferred control of North Africa, Egypt, and the **Hijaz** (the western coast of Arabia) to the Ottomans as well. These three victories, all coming a little more than a century after the Mongol defeat, established the Ottoman Empire.

The slow collapse of the Ottoman Empire, completed in 1923, left millions of Muslims in Eastern Europe, now part of Christian Europe: Hungary, Bulgaria, and eventually states that were carved out of the former Yugoslavia (Croatia, Bosnia-Herzegovina, and Serbia). As Yugoslavia disintegrated (1992–1995), civil war and a program of ethnic cleansing erupted among its very distinct ethnic groups. Serbs, who were Orthodox Christian, participated in the ethnic cleansing of Bosnians who were Muslim. This was

the worst of negative Islamic experiences in Eastern Europe, which also included periodic expulsions, such as from Bulgaria early in the early 1900s.

Though the Ottoman Empire was a threat to Christian Europe, it was also a threat economically, particularly to Italy and France in the fourteenth and fifteenth centuries. The Ottomans were also political allies of France against what is now Austria. Also, Ottoman culture (particularly architecture, historical writing, and cartography) and science (particularly medicine, mathematics, and astronomy) were the envy of Europeans. For many reasons, some internal and some external, the Ottoman Empire had stagnated by the seventeenth century, and Europeans started to dominate in trade with India, which strangled the Ottoman economy. Europe also made military innovations that the

Ottomans could not match. By its demise in 1923, the Ottoman Empire controlled less territory than modern-day Turkey.

Central Asia

Central Asia encapsulates the lands between the Black Sea and China, particularly Azerbaijan, Turkmenistan, Uzbekistan, Tajikistan, Kyrgyzstan, and Kazakhstan. These territories became heavily populated with the reign of Timur and the conversion of the Mongols. The Islamization of this area was helped by two things: the rise of Russia, pushing Muslims east and south, and the economic trade routes connecting Europe and China – the fabled Silk Road.

In the fifteenth–sixteenth centuries, Russia came into existence, pushing eastward from Moscow and taking over much of what was previously Mongol territory. Moscow capitalized on a relationship with the Orthodox Christian Church to drive out the Islamic Tatars. In the seventeenth century, Russia advanced technologically and militarily, and quickly expanded all the way to the Pacific Ocean through Siberia. Russia pushed as far south as the border of Afghanistan, but eventually pulled back from all of these Central Asian Islamic territories. There continues to be tension between the Russian state and an Islamic territory it still controls in the area of Azerbaijan, namely Chechnya.

Islamic Central Asia became culturally and economically rich under Turkic-Mongol rulers, who nurtured trade with Europe and China. This economic strength withered, however, when the Portuguese discovered an ocean route to China and India (see Figure 48). After that, the Silk Road was replaced by water routes and those places became cut off.

The most significant development of this period, however, occurred in the region of Iran. A collaboration – not always peaceful – between Sufi and Shi'a Muslims resulted in the Safavid Empire, which emerged into power in 1501 when Ismail I took control of Iran and gave himself the title shah. The Safavids, as we saw above, challenged – though never defeated – the Ottomans. A series of teenaged shahs, most of whom claimed both divine status and to be the Hidden Imam (see Chapter Seven), were apparently wise and capable leaders for their age. The Safavid Empire was far enough away from the Ottoman and the Mughal Empires to discourage invasion, but its ability to defend itself ensured peace.

The Safavid Empire declared open war on Sunni Muslims, forcing conversion or expulsion on them, and it eventually turned on Sufis, even if they were Shi'a (see Chapter Seven). When the Safavid Empire lost a large portion of Afghanistan in 1736, it was reduced to the size of modern Iran and stripped of its political autonomy. Because of the exclusive and often violent imposition of Shi'a Islam on the Safavid population, modern Iran remains the largest and most powerful representative of Shi'a Islam in the world.

South Asia

The profound Turkic-Mongol influence over Islam can be seen in the fascinating Mughal Empire. Boasting linear descent from Timur and of being "son-in-laws" of Genghis Khan, the Mughals left the plains of northern India in 1526 and quickly gained control over most of South Asia.

The Mughal Empire differed from other Islamic empires and dynasties in one important manner: the others all ruled over majority Islamic populations. Conversely, the Mughals ruled as minorities over the majority Hindus in India. This, naturally, required either brutal force or creative governance, and both are in evidence in the Mughal Empire. The careers of the first Mughal emperors were spent entirely in military conquest. But the Mughals also proved adept at negotiating among the many ethnic identities present in India, which included Mongols, Turks, Afghans, Iranians, Uzbeks, Hindus, and eventually Sikhs.

Early Mughal governance revolved around rewards for loyalty rather than threats of force, and local elites, regardless of their religion or ethnicity, participated in the Mughal system of governance. Taxation appears rarely to have been extortionate, and early Mughal emperors shared the honor and wealth that came with ruling. Hindus in the first century of the empire received many elite positions in government, and the Mughals never tried to force Islamic religion upon them. In fact, Akbar the Great (1556–1605) was viewed with suspicion by conservative Islamic scholars for his unorthodox Islamic views and practices: he apparently objected to the *jizya*, that is the tax imposed on non-Muslims (*dhimmis*).

Economy was one of the reasons the Mughals ruled as long as they did, for prosperity fosters stability. Mughals negotiated well at first with the Portuguese, who had already set up colonies in India when the Mughals rose in power, and then with the British, French, and Dutch. Trade with Europe and China was immense. Interestingly, economy was also one factor in the demise of the Mughals, as increased wealth

Figure 49. Earthenware plate with Islamic inscription made specifically for sale in countries with a significant Muslim population by William Taylor Copeland, in Stoke-on-Trent, Staffordshire, England, 1853.

brought increased powers and political ambition to their opponents.

Another factor in the demise of the Mughal Empire had to do with religion, however. More conservative rulers reversed Akbar's policies of religious pluralism, including the reinstitution of the *jizya*. Aurangzeb, who was emperor 1658–1707, adhered to Islamic shariah law (see Chapter Ten) more strictly than Akbar but had also discriminated against Hindus, whose temples were destroyed and who had conversion to Islam forced upon them. Rulers who came after attempted to reverse the damage with the Hindu community, but it was too late: Mughals had lost the much-needed power that comes with consensus. Once they lacked the army and the finances to rule, the empire fragmented. Mughals held symbolic power until 1857, though mostly in the north where they had started. The after-effects of Islamic rule over Hindus in India are still evident in the violence and angry political rhetoric in current India. The Islamic population in India comprises the third-largest Islamic population in the world, yet remains a minority population there.

South-East Asia

The Islamic experience in South-East Asia provides a compelling example of the interplay between religion and economics. Portuguese, Spanish, Dutch, and finally British colonialism in the Indian Ocean, starting in the late fifteenth century, was motivated by economics, but they all brought Christianity with them. European colonialists found Muslims in and around India, who had likewise settled there for economic reasons.

The Portuguese wished to control the entirety of the spice trade to Europe. From the African coast to Indonesia, the Portuguese conquered cities – Mombasa in Kenya, Aden in Yemen, Hormuz in Iran, Kozhikode in India, Aceh in Indonesia, and Melaka in Melanesia – in order to monopolize trade. But these cities were Islamic and the Portuguese were Catholic, so religion was part of it too. Muslims were massacred in a number of cities and driven out from many of them, and Catholic missionaries followed.

Portuguese violence and missions against Muslims drove them further east and south, which is how they ended up in such high numbers in Indonesia. Islamic resistance to Portuguese economic and political power attracted non-Muslims, who converted to Islam. This is how Islam came to be the majority religion of Indonesia, eventually also comprising the largest Islamic population of any country in the world.

When the Portuguese and Spanish were replaced by the Dutch and British, nothing changed for Muslims in these areas. Colonialism was a chokehold on the indigenous economies, eventually destroying them and then directing funds towards Europe. Countless cities in India, Iran, and Central Asia, once as populated, as culturally impressive, and as economically wealthy as any European city, became marginalized and economically depressed. If Islamic imperial expansion into Europe, Africa, Central Asia, South Asia, and South-East Asia from the seventh–sixteenth centuries can be said to represent a pendulum swing in their favor, the rise of European and Christian military and cultural power from the sixteenth century onwards represents a pendulum swing against Islam. Christian Europe went from fearing Muslims to ruling them.

Clearly, there was a shift in more than mere global power: colonial Europeans not only controlled trade, but also treated Islamic merchants as second-class citizens. Muslims were not only pushed out of honorable and elite social positions but also denied upward social mobility and lucrative careers as merchants, both of which they had long enjoyed. Poverty and discrimination became the primary experience of many Muslims in this area. Once the rulers of much of the world, they were now the ruled.

Islam after Colonialism

Islam in the modern world is as diverse and fractured as it ever was. The encounter of

Competing Modern Reformers

Two competing approaches to Islamic reform are illustrated in Syed Ahmad Khan (1817–1898) and Jamal al-Din al-Afghani (1838–1897). Khan, a descendant of Mughal nobility, argued openly that India was lagging and that only Western-style education and political reforms could save it. He founded the Aligarh Muslim University in 1875, which he imagined as a "Muslim Cambridge." His approach was to accept the superiority of British culture, even while acknowledging the damage done by failed and unjust British practices in India. The Islamic world would prosper, he argued, by embracing Western culture and leading like, but better than, the British. The solution to troubles in India, then, was to use Islam to improve upon British culture, but not to reject it outright. Khan was even given a knighthood by Britain.

Sir Syed Ahmad Khan

Al-Afghani was a charismatic Iranian who posed as an Afghan (hence his name) in order to be more palatable to the majority Sunni Muslims. He became active in India after the British crushed an Islamic rebellion there in the 1850s.

Sayyid Jamal al-Din al-Afghani

World travel had inspired in al-Afghani an awareness of Islamic unity and superiority, which he shaped into a program called Pan-Islam. Muslims should appropriate Western science and technology, he argued, without in any way accepting Western superiority. In this way, colonial oppressors would be violently evicted and Islam could return to its past glories. After al-Afghani, Pan-Islamic spokesmen emphasized rigorous adherence to shariah and demanded a conservative theological uniformity

individual countries with colonial powers, the varied experiences of liberation, and the assertion for some of an international economic power of their own based in oil has contributed to considerable division among Muslims.

Nearly every corner of the Islamicate experienced colonial rule with the rise of Europe: the British were in India, Nigeria, Egypt and east and south Africa; the French were in Algeria, Morocco, and West Africa; the Dutch displaced the Portuguese in Indonesia, and were displaced by the British in South Africa; Russians were in Central Asia; and the British and Russians eventually divided Iran. Americans were late arrivals, but made their international presence felt everywhere they had an economic or political interest.

As colonial power and wealth rose, political, social, and cultural autonomy for Muslims in colonial territories fell, and with it the promise of prosperity. In addition, because colonial powers wished to maintain control, they ensured that the sorts of things that might empower indigenous populations to improve their condition and exercise autonomy – education, as well as technological, political, and social innovations – were withheld. The result was a vicious cycle in which colonial power exploited land and people, and these lands and people fell increasingly behind European power.

Islamic responses to European rule can be divided broadly into two categories: assimilation and isolation. Some Islamic reformers argued that in order for the Islamicate to compete with the West, it needed to adopt Western culture, particularly education, language, and political formation. Thus, Western-style universities and curricula focusing on mathematics and science were established in Egypt, Lebanon, and India. The logic was that Western-style education could be used to advance Islamic autonomy, and prosperity would follow.

An alternative route to reform was to reject all things associated with the West. On this model, greater attention to tradition, stricter adherence to shariah, and the exclusive promotion of Islamic culture and religion was needed in order for Islamic lands to return to the power they once enjoyed. Here, religion was used as a protective barrier from what these reformers worried were secularizing and Christianizing influences. This approach is evident in the creation and widespread proliferation of the **Deobandi** madrasas, which championed a single theological approach to Islam, and at the same time rejected both alternative theological interpretations and traditional university subjects. In these areas too, then, the Islamicate fell increasingly behind.

There are three locations that serve as examples of the Islamic experience of the post-colonial world: Iran, Bangladesh, and the United States.

Iran

In 1907, Russia and Britain split up Iran. Just over a decade later, the British left, leaving Russia to exercise its imperial aspirations there. In 1920, Reza Khan Pahlavi took control, and took the mantle of shah, or king. He eventually became powerful enough to cease the special treatment of British oil companies in Iran and to assert a national identity. Part of this national identity was as a modern secular state. In the 1950s, the United States facilitated a coup that installed his son, Muhammad Reza Shah, as the sole and undisputed authority in Iran, a position he maintained with American support. His reign as shah was both increasingly secular and increasingly violent against dissenters. He made educational and social reforms in an attempt to modernize Iran, and to create a European culture there, but he did this by marginalizing and demonizing Islam.

One of the most strident critics of the Shah's autocracy, violence, and marginalization of Islam was a jurist and Ayatollah (see Chapter Ten) named Khomeini. Though punished and exiled for his criticisms, he continued to be an effective leader of the opposition. Resistance to the Shah eventually grew in all quarters, secular and Islamic, rich and poor, male and female, and in 1979, a popular revolution ended the Shah's rule, ended American influence in Iran, and ended secularism in Iran. Khomeini returned in victory, and became the first in a long line of Ayatollahs who govern

Figure 50. The 1978 Iranian Revolution: a row of men holding photos of Khomeini.

Iran with the backing and blessing of the Shi'a ulama, or body of religious scholars. Unfortunately, violence did not disappear but merely shifted: under the Shah, Muslims suffered, but under the ulama those who supported the revolution but still wanted a secular state suffered. The Islamic Republic of Iran had been born.

Iran contains the largest number of Imami Shi'a Muslims in the world, though sizeable and significant Shi'a populations are also found in Bahrain, Azerbaijan, Iraq, Yemen, Lebanon, and Syria. In addition, Iran is the only country in the Middle East in which Shi'a Muslims comprise the majority, at over 90%. Close relations among many of the Shi'a communities in the Middle East enables Iran to be a powerful political presence in other locations, such as Syria and Lebanon.

Bangladesh

The tiny region of Bengal, which sits at the north-eastern corner of India was originally Buddhist, rather than Hindu, until Muslims conquered the region in the thirteenth century. The territory of the Bengals, like the territory of what is now Pakistan, was originally part of India. By the twentieth century, a long history of Islamic rule and a new history of Portuguese and then British colonialism had left India politically fractured. Tensions and violence between Muslims and Hindus were frequently high. A two-state solution seemed increasingly unavoidable, but no less messy than any other solution: Muslims were to be found throughout India, not merely in the north, and millions of Hindus lived in what is now Pakistan. The partition plan executed by the British in 1947

Figure 51. September 1947: Muslim refugees clamber aboard an overcrowded train near New Delhi in an attempt to flee India.

the popular rebellion, killing and displacing millions, until the Bengalis called on India for help. Thus, East Pakistan became Bangladesh and West Pakistan became merely Pakistan.

The predominantly Sunni Bangladesh continues to have a very close and peaceful relationship with India; Pakistan continues to have very a tense relationship with India. Bangladesh contains the fourth largest Islamic population in the world. In fact, combined, Bangladesh and Pakistan contain 20% of the global Islamic population.

created Pakistan in two parts, separated by 1000 miles: West Pakistan and East Pakistan, the latter comprising approximately what is now the country of Bangladesh. It also created thousands of Muslim and Hindu refugees and casualties.

That West and East Pakistan were both Islamic was not enough to ensure unity. The Bengal region was different from the northwest part of India culturally, geographically, ethnically, and linguistically. In addition, while West Pakistan appeared to value East Pakistan for its strong economy, it allowed them little opportunity to participate in the governance of Pakistan. Bengalis who agitated for independence were consistently jailed or killed under the authority of West Pakistan, until in 1971 violent rebellion erupted. West Pakistan attempted to crush

United States and Canada

The experience of Muslims in the Islamicate involves the trajectory from supremacy to defeat, from wealth and autonomy to poverty and colonialism. But there are millions of Muslims outside of the Islamicate who arrived as refugees, or who converted to Islam from their original religion, and the experience of these Muslims will be very different. This is seen in the United States and Canada.

Muslims comprise approximately 1% of Americans, and just over 3% of Canadians. In the US, Islam is the fourth largest religion, is currently the fastest growing, and Muslims will soon outnumber Jews there. The number of Muslims in Canada more than tripled from 1991–2011, and they comprise the

Islamism

Islamism is a political ideology that situates itself in the religious claims of Islam. Originally, it implied nothing more than the call for Muslims to be politically active, to work within and against local and global political channels in order to create political change in favor of Islam, and to work towards the creation of societies grounded in the religious principles of Islam. But Islamism no longer refers to politico-religious activism. It now refers to a political ideology that ranges from the Islamic conquest of modern nations to gang-like reveling in violence, chaos, and anarchy.

Jihad (see Chapter Ten) is a term meaning "struggle." Theologically, jihad refers to the personal struggle to set aside one's will for God's will; politically, it refers to the struggle to defend one's community against outside military attack. The political use of the term has positive associations in the minds of many Muslims because it was used to characterize resistance to the abuses of colonialism, and in the Afghan expulsion of Russians, both perfectly legitimate enterprises. However, Islamists have blurred some of the term's traditional meanings: attack is a form of defense, and civilians (because they elect their leaders) are considered soldiers, and are therefore legitimate targets in war. There are many Islamist groups, but none more widely known than Al-Qaeda and Daesh.

second largest religious group there, after Christianity, though obviously Muslims are still very much in the minority. Being such a small minority means sometimes being invisible, which Muslims in the United States and Canada largely were until Islamism arrived in North America on September 11, 2001. After that, North Americans were rather suddenly aware of Muslims, and many viewed Islamic practices with alarm and suspicion.

Table 1. Recent and projected Muslim population. Population estimates are rounded to thousands. Percentages are calculated from unrounded numbers. Figures may not add up exactly due to rounding. Data courtesy of Pew Research.

Muslim population by region	2010		2030	
	Estimated Muslim population	Estimated percentage of global Muslim population	Projected Muslim population	Projected percentage of global Muslim population
World	1,619,314,000	100	2,190,154,000	100
Asia-Pacific	1,005,507,000	62.1	1,296,625,000	59.2
Middle East/North Africa	321,869,000	19.9	439,453,000	20.1
Sub-Saharan Africa	242,544,000	15.0	385,939,000	17.6
Europe	44,138,000	2.7	58,209,000	2.7
Americas	5,256,000	0.3	10,927,000	0.5

Figure 52. Elijah Muhammad addresses followers, including Cassius Clay: the famous boxer joined the Nation of Islam in the early 1960s and eventually changed his name to Muhammad Ali.

it is certain that their Islam was either forcibly replaced by Christianity or was maintained but hidden for generations.

Early in the twentieth century there was a reawakening and reassertion of the Islamic heritage of the descendants of slaves. This movement was led by W. Fard Muhammad, who in 1930 founded the Nation of Islam. Fard was initially represented by his followers as a new Prophet but was soon regarded as God by his apostles. There are even references to a new scripture, though none were ever produced. In this regard the Nation of Islam differs considerably from other groups of Muslims, who believe Muhammad to have been the final Prophet. The Nation of Islam also holds a more exclusive view of race than most Muslims adhere to, in that it believes that black people are superior to whites and that after centuries of racial mistreatment and oppression, God will intervene to end white rule. But in most other respects, the practices of the Nation of Islam resemble the practices of many other Muslims: submission to God, prayer five times a day, avoidance of pork and alcohol, Hajj, and so on. This group is interesting as a religiously creative response to colonialism, slavery, and racism.

About half the Muslims in the US are Sunni, and about 15% are Shi'a. The Nation of Islam, which can now also be found in

In this regard, observance of the hijab by many Islamic women became an issue of contention in a way that would not happen in a majority Islamic country.

The rapid growth in the number of Muslims in Canada and the US is due primarily to immigration of Muslim refugees for humanitarian purposes. But the arrival of Islam into the United States, and the experience of Muslims in Christian America, is also tied inextricably to the American slave trade of the seventeenth–eighteenth centuries, and has had one very interesting effect. It is estimated that 10–15% of the African slaves brought across the Atlantic were Muslims;

Chapter Summary

Canada, is very small but growing, at 50,000 members at most. They are, however, a very visible group, with charismatic figures like Malcolm X (1925–1965) and Louis Farrakhan, who organized the Million Man March. Their rhetoric about military training for their men makes them suspicious in the eyes of some observers.

The history of Islam is the shortest of the three religions discussed in this section, and yet that history is as complex and diverse as any. From the Middle East, to Africa, Central Asia, India, and into Indonesia, Islam has developed into many forms. Though Arab cultural and theological expressions – as we shall see in later chapters – carry considerable influence still, the fact is, Islam has already been profoundly shaped by its encounters with the people it ruled.

Glossary

Abbuyids. A Kurdish-Sunni dynasty that ruled Egypt and most of the Middle East in the twelfth and thirteenth centuries. It was set up by the military victories of Saladin, who successfully won Jerusalem back from Christian Crusader armies.

Alids. The descending families and dynasties of Ali. The name is distinct from Shi'a on a number of levels. Shi'a Islam is theologically complex and takes some time to develop, so Alid can refer to the early forms of that movement. Also, people could convert to Shi'a Islam, so Shi'a refers to more than the descendants of Ali. And finally, not all dynasties that descended from Ali were Shi'a.

Andalus. After the Umayyad Dynasty was toppled by the Abbasid Dynasty, the last surviving Umayyads relocated to Al-Andalus in 756, in what is now Spain, and set up a new dynasty. Umayyads ruled Andalus until the early eleventh century, but were replaced by other Islamic rulers, until Christians took over in 1492.

Berbers. An ethnic group located in North Africa. They were converted to Islam but frequently had tense relationships with Arab Muslims. This was visible not only in Berber–Arab violence in North Africa but also in Andalus, which was first conquered by Berber Muslims in 711 CE, only to have Umayyads take over.

Deobandi. A revivalist Islamic movement dating to the eighteenth century, and developing especially in India, Pakistan, and Bangladesh. Because this movement began in opposition to British colonial rule, and championed a return to Islamic culture, Deobandi groups tend to have an anti-Western perspective.

Dhimmis. Non-Muslim citizens of Islamic states who were protected and who were sometimes allowed to follow their own practices, even when those practices were forbidden to Muslims (e.g., eating pork, drinking alcohol).

Fatimids. A Shi'a caliphate that developed in Egypt, the Maghrib, and the Hijaz, during the tenth–twelfth centuries.

Hijaz. The strip of mountainous land along the west coast of the Arabian Peninsula, from Jordan to Yemen. At the founding of Islam, the

Hijaz contained Christians and Jews. Because Mecca and Medina are in the Hijaz, any dynasty that ruled Egypt also tended to extend its rule to the Hijaz (e.g., Fatimids, Abbuyids, Mamluks, Ottomans, etc.).

Hijra. The flight of Muhammad and his followers from Mecca, which was no longer safe, to Yathrib where they were invited in 622 CE. Because Yathrib (later renamed Medina) was the location of the first Islamic community, or Ummah, the Hijra took on a highly symbolic significance: it came to mark the beginning of the Islamic calendar.

Imami. The formal name for mainstream, or Twelver, Shi'a Islam.

Jizya. A tax levied on *dhimmis,* or non-Muslims living in Islamic states. Complex and controversial, the *jizya* could function differently in different locations: it could be used to generate revenue, punish non-Muslims, encourage conversion to Islam, but it could also be used to mark protected communities.

Maghrib. A cultural, ethnic region of North Africa, generally not including Egypt. Berbers were one group in this region.

Timurid Sultanate. The Timurid Sultanate marked a combination of Persian and Mongol heritage, claiming through the leader Timur to be descended from Genghis Khan. It lasted from 1370–1507, and encompassed what is now Pakistan, Afghanistan, Turkmenistan, Iran, and Iraq.

Other Important Vocabulary

Abbasids	Genghis Khan	Malcolm X	Sasanian Empire
Abu Bakr	Iranian Revolution	Mamluk Empire	Ulama
Battle of Badr	Islamicate	Mughal Empire	Umar
Battle of the Camel	Islamism	Orientalism	Umayyad Dynasty
Battle of Uhud	Ismailis	Ottoman Empire	Ummah
Dar al-Harb	Karbala	Pan-Islam	Yathrib
Dar al-Islam	Kharijites	Safavid Empire	Zaydis

Discussion Questions

1. As Islam first spread out of Arabia, it was assumed that being Muslim meant also being Arab: "Arab" culture was by default superior, and people were expected to adopt it. Describe how it affects the history of Islam that eventually one could become Muslim without ceasing to be Persian, or Turkic, or Mongol, or Bengal, or Malay, and so on.

2. As a feature of life, religion intersects with political, economic, and social realities. Can you think of ways in which the spread of Islam was sometimes helped by and sometimes hurt by economic realities?

3. Scholars of religion once distinguished between Eastern and Western religions, and they designated Islam a "Western religion." After reading this chapter, how would you challenge that designation?

4. A question that can easily be applied to any of the religions covered in this book concerns violence. When someone observes that violent people are not proper representatives of a religion, or are not truly religious people, what assumptions are they making about "religion"?

Recommended Reading

Ernst, Carl W. 2011. *How to Read the Qur'an: A New Guide, with Select Translations.* Durham: North Carolina Press.

Haider, Najam. 2014. *Shi'i Islam: An Introduction.* New York: Cambridge University Press.

Safi, Omid. 2003. *Progressive Muslims: On Justice, Gender, and Pluralism.* London: Oneworld Publications.

Recommended Websites

http://islam.uga.edu

- Alan Godlas, Professor of Islam at the University of Georgia, offers many resources related to the academic study of Islam. Topics covered range from art to history to law.

http://www.islamicity.com

- A wide-ranging website offering media commentary, theological reflection, and prayer time calculators.

—Part Two—
Orthodoxies

Orthodoxy has to do with correct (ortho) thoughts (doxies) or beliefs. The term "orthodoxy" requires options. For instance, "correct" belief implies there are beliefs that are incorrect. According to whom? Here is the first critical aspect of orthodoxy. The claim to be "right-believing" is a rhetorical ploy. It is a claim. Muslims have other terminology for expressing this, but Jews and Christians both use the word "orthodoxy," and the student of religion must learn to see it for what it is: one group's claim of supremacy over competing groups' claims of supremacy. It is a claim of unique legitimacy: "We are right, and the rest of you are wrong."

As orthodoxy has a root meaning of "correct belief," the chapters in Part Two, and the corresponding sections in the final chapter, will focus on the beliefs of Jews, Christians, and Muslims. Some people think of Christianity as a more orthodoxic religion than Judaism or Islam. This is likely because Christians seem to put more energy into delineating correct belief, while Jews and Muslims seem to put more energy into

delineating correct practice or action. This is largely an unhelpful way of distinguishing among Jews, Christians, and Muslims. Some Jews and Muslims care more about belief than action, some Christians care more about action than belief. There is too much variety within each religion to make such generalizations helpful. The bottom line is this: each religion has beliefs its members are supposed to hold. They have therefore put energy into clarifying those beliefs

Figure 53. Shofar, a Jewish ritual horn (made of ram's horn), traditionally blown on Yom Kippur and other occasions to announce the defeat of Satan.

Figure 54. "Helping a Dying Impenitent," a painting by Francisco Goya of 1788 depicting the exorcism of a dying patient.

the orthodoxic position of monotheism. Monotheism is an uncommon notion among almost all the other religions of antiquity, and so it required a tremendous amount of justification, explanation, and defense. But monotheism itself raises so many issues that differences of opinion naturally form, for not all members of a group will find the same explanations satisfactory. Thus, though all three of these religions are monotheistic, they are monotheistic in surprisingly different ways, and there are also surprising ways in which they are not fully monotheistic all the time.

The most obvious way in which the first point is visible concerns the status of Jesus. For most Jews, Jesus is just one of a dozen men who claimed to be the messiah that Jews still await. In other words, most Jews were not persuaded by the messianic claims of the others, and they were not persuaded by Jesus' claims either. They do not even accord him the status of prophet, because for Jews, Malachi was the last of God's prophetic messengers. Islamic texts, on the other hand, reflect the belief that many prophets came between Malachi and Muhammad, and that Jesus was one of them. No less, they hold Jesus in very high regard, first on the grounds that he was a *rasul*, like Muhammad, and second, that God so loved

against members of other religions, and against members of their own religion they think are believing incorrectly. This is what the history of theological and philosophical debate within each religion reveals.

The foundation, or subject matter, of a good deal of that theological debate is

Jesus that he did not let Jesus die. As you will see in Chapter Seven, many Muslims believe that Jesus and not Muhammad will return at the end of time. This is possible for Muslims because Jesus did not die, while Muhammad did.

Figure 55. A representation of a demon in Islamic mythology from the fifteenth century by Mehmed Siyah Kalem.

Christians, not surprisingly, have the highest view of Jesus' status. For most Christians, Jesus was not only the Messiah promised in Israel's texts, and resurrected from the dead. He was also the incarnation of God. According to the Nicene Creed, Jesus and God are the same substance. Jesus was not created, but took on human form in order to save humanity. Jewish and Islamic opponents to Christianity found it very hard to understand how Christians could be monotheistic, in that they talk about Jesus as the son of God, as two different beings, and yet they worship them both as God/gods. This is the heart of the challenge of the Trinity, and Christians have worked very hard over the centuries to make sense of it, to themselves as well as to outsiders. Think of it this way: it is as if Christians have been saddled with a theological conundrum – a monotheistic Trinity – that cannot be explained, but one that they *must* explain. Ineffability is the word most commonly used here: words cannot be used to explain the experience.

The Trinity is not the only way in which the monotheism of the three religions is not total and complete. Yes, there are no other gods acknowledged to exist, so they are monotheistic in that sense. But there are plenty of superhuman beings within these three religions. Some of them are believed to have a positive influence in the world, and can therefore be the object of devotion and prayer (angels, saints). Others are believed to have a negative influence in the world, and are thus the object of fear and loathing.

Satan/Shaytan is that object of fear. But the origin of Satan is a very interesting story in the history of religion. Like all religious ideas, the idea of Satan goes through many transformations, but they all stem from two issues related to monotheism. First, a monotheistic religion that believes in one God who is also all-powerful and all-knowing must be able to explain evil and suffering, especially when they befall seemingly innocent people (e.g., children, people who follow all the rules, or believe all the right things). Satan provides that answer for these three religions. Second, monotheism seems unable to divest itself of its early dualistic roots in Zoroastrianism. From Zoroastrian religion came the dualistic idea of a personified evil, so powerful that the power of good, or God, is constantly threatened, limited, or undermined. Put differently, it would appear that monotheism requires dualism for its survival.

— 5 —

Jewish Theology and Theological Writings

Chapter Overview

Jewish mythological and theological narratives of their origins reveal the view that God was active in the world, creating it, teaching it, punishing it, choosing a people to be uniquely loyal to him and serve as beacons in the world, and promising to stand by them. These foundation narratives tell us about the Jewish view of God. Jewish theology has a long and rich tradition, but this short chapter can offer just a few of the central components of Jewish theology: monotheism, covenant and election, sin and repentance, messiah, Kabbalah, and afterlife. From there we turn to a survey of the writings that are central of the construction of Jewish religious life: Torah and Talmud.

Core Theological Ideas

The core expressions of Jewish theology – the Jewish understanding of God – are found in the narratives about their founders and foundations, in their development of monotheism over henotheism, their belief in covenant and **election**, in how they understand the relationship among law, sin, and repentance, the office of messiah, the development of mysticism in Kabbalah, and finally the changing beliefs of what happens after death.

Founder Narratives

The narratives of any religion's founders and foundations will always be, and can only be, theological, if you recall that a theological narrative is one the primary intention of which is to express something about God. In the case of Judaism, those founding narratives are found in the biblical books between Genesis and 2 Kings, and what is expressed about God is that God was and remains active in the world.

Two caveats must be offered immediately. While some of them are mythological, not all of them, I would argue, are. The books of the Bible slowly transition from mythological (containing stories that are deeply meaningful but have no basis in historical or geological reality) to legendary (containing stories that sound in some respects

Cutting a Covenant

A covenant is a treaty, and the Israelite covenant is closely modeled in language and form on Ancient Near Eastern treaties made between unequal parties: a newly ruling empire and a local defeated king, for instance. In any treaty, two sides agree to terms: they will not attack one another, or they will pay tribute in exchange for not being sacked, or they will trade in peace and good faith. God cuts covenants with Noah, Abraham, Moses, and David, and they all concern basically the same thing: the people promise to be good and God will protect them from harm.

plausible but for which we possess no evidence outside of those stories) and finally to historical (containing stories of events that did likely happen, though perhaps not precisely in the way they are reported). The second caveat is that though there might be historical books in the Bible, they too were written, edited, and shaped with a theological purpose. If a community believes that God is present in their past, their recording of the past will be imbued with that belief, and so it is.

Biblical mythology is limited to the first eleven chapters of the book of Genesis. A loving God creates a good world (Genesis 1–2) and seeks to sustain its goodness. Sometimes this goodness must be sustained with punishment, as when God kicks the people he has created out of the garden he gave to them (Genesis 3), or when he sends a global flood to kill all humans and animals but a select righteous few (Genesis 7–8), or when people are made to speak different languages so that they cannot cooperate again to build a tower to heaven (Genesis 11). These stories also narrate that God sustains the world positively, not merely by creating it, but by "cutting" a covenant with Noah.

Starting at Genesis 12, the narratives switch from mythological to legendary. A man named Abraham takes his family and moves from Ur to Canaan, and he brings his god with him. Migration is common; there is nothing inherently mythological in that. What makes the story legendary (among other things) is that there is no external evidence of this happening. In fact, the archaeological record suggests that the Israelites were not foreign settlers among Canaanites, but rather a break-away group of Canaanites. The story is not meant to relay history as it actually happened, but to tell the story of how God's choice of one man explains the origins of the Jewish people. It also narrates a second covenant: loyalty to God and circumcision are required from the people, and God will reward them.

The biblical narratives that follow, which I will summarize as briefly as I can, are not grounded in the mythological, but they are the legends that comprise the origin narratives of Israel and the Jewish people and are thus thoroughly theological. Theology is the whole point of these origin narratives. God's people move around, and they suffer various calamities, but God never abandons them. And that really is the gist of the stories: one may feel alone in one's suffering, but God is always with you.

Abraham has two sons, one whose mother is Hagar the servant, and the other whose mother is Sarah, Abraham's wife. They

124

are called Ishmael and Isaac. In the Israel-ite narrative, the boys are playing, and for some reason Sarah becomes angry and kicks Hagar and Ishmael out. After God ensures they survive in the desert, by giving them a well, they more or less disappear from the story, but will form the origin narrative for Islam, which claims theological descent from Ishmael.

The biblical story follows Isaac, whose son Jacob has a dream in which he wrestles with an angel, and wins. Because of this, Jacob's name is changed to Israel, meaning "God struggles." Thus, those who descend from Israel come to be called Israelites, and in some periods (see Chapter Two) they will call the land they claim Israel. One can chose to consider these stories historical in the strictest sense of the word, but that would be missing their more important point: to situate God in the founding of their community. Abraham, Isaac, and Jacob are called the Patriarchs of Judaism – the founding fathers – and the God of Abraham, Isaac, and Jacob is active in history.

Figure 56. First record of the precursor of the name YHWH in the list of Shasulands of the temple of Soleb (Sudan).

The Israelites struggle with the Canaanites to live there, and migrate to Egypt because of famine. In Egypt, they flourish, but are eventually enslaved when Egypt comes under new leadership. God guides an infant

Tetragrammaton

Muslims and Christians do not have a special name for God. Greek-speaking Christians called God *theos*, Latin-speaking Christians called him *deus*, and Arabic-speaking Muslims *al-il-lah*, which came to be abbreviated as *Allah*. All these are simply nouns for "God" in different languages, but they are not *names*. While God and Allah might sound like personal names, and might for some function as names, they are in fact merely nouns (like chair, car, and book).

Jews are unique in having a name for God: YHWH. It was probably originally pronounced Yahweh, but it is hard to know for sure. Jews held the name in such reverence that they avoided saying the name out loud. When reading their Bible, Jews came to say *adonai* (meaning "Lord") rather than read out the name when it appears in the text. This explains also the practice in English translations of rendering YHWH as "the LORD." **Tetragrammaton**, mean-ing "the four letters," is another way of referring to the word without saying it. A form of this name for God is reflected in any Jewish name that ends in *yahu*, such as Netanyahu ("Yahweh gives"), Shemaryahu ("Yahweh guards"), and Eli-yahu ("Yahweh is my god").

to be saved by a princess of the Pharaoh, and she raises him in secrecy: Moses. As an adult, Moses must flee Egypt for killing an Egyptian who was beating a Hebrew slave. While on the run in the wilderness, he sees a bush that is on fire but is not being burned away. The same God who called Abraham now calls to Moses from this bush.

This event is significant in the theological narrative of Judaism for two reasons. First, God reveals to Moses his unique name: YHWH (probably pronounced Yahweh). This name will have great theological significance in Judaism, and sends the theological message that the Jews have a unique relationship with God. Second, God persuades an initially reluctant Moses to lead the Hebrews out of Egypt. And so begins the story of the **Exodus**, a story that will be central in the memory and identity of Jews. God defeats Egypt and leads the Hebrews to freedom. Despite his Egyptian name, Moses is the foundation of all Jewish theology that follows.

The Exodus story epitomizes the promises that God keeps to protect and favor his people, and in later periods when Israel is chafing against foreign rule under the Syrians or the Romans, this narrative provides hope that salvation from God might come again. It will also motivate and inspire messianic resistance movements in which an individual tries (always unsuccessfully) to lead the Israelites to freedom from Roman occupation. These messiahs will commonly use Moses as their model.

God is represented in these ancient narratives very much in the role of father: he

The Wisdom of Solomon

King Solomon was remembered for his wisdom as a judge and ruler. This is the most famous story illustrating that wisdom (1 Kings 3:16–28):

Later, two prostitutes came to the king and stood before him. The first woman said, "Please, my lord, this woman and I live in the same house; and I gave birth to a child while she was in the house. On the third day after I was delivered, this woman also gave birth to a child. We were alone; there was no one else with us in the house. During the night this woman's child died, because she lay on it. She arose in the night and took my son from my side while your maidservant was asleep, and laid him in her bosom; and she laid her dead son in my bosom. When I rose in the morning to nurse my son, there he was, dead; but when I looked at him closely in the morning, it was not the son I had borne." The other woman spoke up, "No, the live one is my son, and the dead son is yours!" But the first insisted, "No,

the dead boy is yours; mine is the live one." And they went on arguing before the king. The king said, "One says, 'This is my son, the live one, and the dead one is yours'; and the other says, 'No, the dead boy is yours, mine is the live one.'" So the king gave the order, "Fetch me a sword." A sword was brought before the king, and the king said, "Cut the live child in two, and give half to the one and half to the other." But the woman whose son was the live one pleaded with the king, for she was overcome with compassion for her son. "Please, my lord," she cried, "give her the live child; only don't kill it!" The other insisted, "It shall be neither yours nor mine; cut it in two!" Then the king spoke up: "Give the live child to her," he said, "and do not put it to death; she is its mother." When all Israel heard of the decision that the king had rendered, they stood in awe of the king; for they saw that he possessed divine wisdom to execute justice.

(New Jewish Publication Society Translation, 1999)

is protector and disciplinarian. Immediately after saving the Hebrews, he must punish them when they are found to be disloyal to God. The punishment is twofold: they must wander lost and landless in the deserts of Sinai for forty years, and Moses will die before he can re-enter "the promised land."

The stories of the Hebrews resettling into Canaan are also likely legendary. They tell of dramatic military victories, which cannot be corroborated archaeologically, the transition from a loose amalgamation of twelve tribes, each ruled by a judge, to a united monarchy under Saul, David, and then Solomon. As we saw in Chapter Two, it is likely that Saul, David, and Solomon existed, but the stories we have of their lives and accomplishments are literary, so difficult to corroborate, and therefore theological: thus it is more responsible to discuss them in this chapter. But the fact is: these figures sit right at the cusp between material that is legendary and material that is in all probability historical.

We must remember that every single one of the books of the Hebrew Bible is theological, otherwise it is hard to imagine what it is doing in the Bible. That is, each book says something about the writers' or communities' views of God. And the stories of Israel's beloved kings do this no less than the book of Genesis. Put differently, David's currency as a theological symbol vastly outweighs questions of historical reliability. He provides the model of the "Lord's anointed," or messiah, that will inform every Jewish discussion and controversy related to the Messiah. The same applies to Solomon, legendary for his wisdom and for building the First Temple.

Monotheism

Monotheism is the belief that there exists only one god; anything else that claims to be a god is nothing more than an illusion, a childish superstition, and belief in another god or gods is attributed to pure ignorance. As I said in Chapter 1, the religion of the ancient Israelites was not monotheistic. Neither, of course, was it polytheistic; **polytheism** appears always to have been strictly prohibited by the writings of the ancient Israelites. But there is a position in between monotheism and polytheism, and it is was the first hallmark of Israelite religion: henotheism.

Henotheism is the belief that although many gods exist in the world, one of them is greater than all, and most worthy of loyalty. In much of the Tanakh, Israelites are henotheistic. Consider the following examples:

- Exodus 20:3 – "Let there be among you no other gods beyond me."

- Psalm 86:8 – "There are none like you among the gods."

- 1 Kings 18 narrates a contest between the Israelite prophet Elijah and 450 prophets of the Canaanite god Ba'al to see whose god is more powerful. The God of Israel wins.

These clearly indicate an exclusive loyalty to the God of Israel alone, but they also clearly assume that other, lesser gods exist (see also Exodus 15:11).

At some point, it appears during and because of the Babylonian exile, the shift was made from henotheism to monotheism. Yahweh becomes not only the god of Israel, but God of the universe, and from there, the only God.

Competing Monotheisms

Jewish monotheism comes to be expressed in the Shema, which can be translated in a number of different ways, owing to the ambiguous Hebrew original:

Listen Israel! The LORD our God, the LORD is one.

Listen Israel! The LORD is our God, the LORD alone.

Listen Israel! The LORD is our God, the LORD is alone.

In a henotheistic context, one might understand this sentence to say that Yahweh (the Hebrew behind LORD) "is our god alone" from among others (the second option), while in a monotheistic setting, "Yahweh our God is one/alone" (the first and third options). Imagine how this passage takes on greater significance after the first century CE when Jews are arguing about God with Christians, who believe in a three-part God (made up of Father, Son, and Holy Spirit). God is a god alone for Christians, but God is not one.

Christians and Muslims found their monotheism in Judaism, but Judaism retains one interesting feature not found in either of the other two: a personal name for God. According to the theological history of Judaism, the god that Abraham and his descendants, eventually the Israelites, had been following for nearly seven hundred years finally revealed his name to Moses from the midst of the burning bush just prior to the Exodus (Exodus 3:14). Here we find the origin of Judaism's named God.

Moses asks who is speaking to him from the bush. One way (out of several) of translating what the voice says is "I am who I am." The next sentence has the voice tell Moses, "Tell them that 'I am sent me to you.'" "I am" in Hebrew is spelled *ehyeh*, wherein the *h-y-h* is the root of the verb "to be." Yet, in the very next verse, God is not called *ehyeh*, but *yhwh*. The two words seem to be related in some way, but they are clearly different. From this narrative, Jews derive a name for God, Yahweh (see Figure 56 and "Tetragrammaton" text box, p. 125).

Covenant and Election

The Israelite covenant relationship with God is complex. On the one hand, the relationship is voluntary: neither side is forced to agree to terms. On the other hand, Israelites in the past and many Jews in the present understand God to be loving and fierce in equal parts, showing that disloyalty to God has serious implications. Adding to the complexity, how is the covenant to be enforced when one of the treaty partners is God? To whom can you appeal if you feel wronged by God?

This question takes up a good deal of Jewish thought because the fact is, though the Israelites and the Jews were promised protection in return for their loyalty, they have been conquered and ruled over by other nations for more years than they have been free: Egyptians, Assyrians, Babylonians, Greeks, Romans, Syrians, Christians, and Muslims (in rough chronological order). And then there are the expulsions from England (1290) and Spain (1492) and the Holocaust. Each bout of suffering raises the question anew: is God still protecting Israel, and if so, where is the evidence of it? In the wake of the Babylonian exile, prophets such as Isaiah, Jeremiah, and Ezekiel solved this problem by proclaiming that God had not broken his agreement. Rather, he was punishing the Israelites for having sinned against him, and used the Babylonians to deliver that punishment. Above all, their point was that despite appearances to the contrary, God is never disloyal nor unreliable. In the wake of the Holocaust, there have been no shortage of ways in which Jewish theologians have struggled with the notion of a caring God.

This is the classical solution to a theological problem called theodicy. Theodicy refers to the problem of why bad things happen to good and righteous people, and it is a problem for any monotheistic (or henotheistic) religion that believes in a good and just god. It is premised on the assumption (or hope) that a loving and powerful god would be able to and would choose to protect a righteous and loyal people. Isaiah claimed that Israel as a whole paid for the sins of its fathers, and of a few leaders. The book of Job offers a different solution: righteous people suffer because God (with the help of Satan) is testing their faith to see whether they are faithful only because their life is good and comfortable.

These explanations for theodicy prevailed for much of Jewish time, but the Holocaust challenged this notion considerably. It was not uncommon to feel that an event made so monstrous by its sheer enormity, in which Jewish men, women, and children were either worked to death while being starved or executed en masse for nothing more than their religion, cannot have been part of any loving god's plan for a people. The Holocaust forced many Jews to re-evaluate their relationship with God, and God's engagement with this world. Some abandoned their religion and God altogether. Others felt that to do so would give the Nazis what they wanted all along: to destroy Judaism. Yet others remained in Judaism, but not under any illusion that God protects the Jews. For them, such a thought is incomprehensible after the Holocaust. It is no understatement to say that modern Jewish theology has been consumed with how to comprehend, how to digest, and how to exist after, the Holocaust.

Related to covenant, and similar in its complexity and tension, is the idea of election. From the call of Abraham and the promise to establish a nation, to the protection Israel

Putting God on Trial

Elie Wiesel, a Holocaust survivor, scholar, and novelist, relates an event he witnessed at Auschwitz and later fictionalized in a play called *The Trial of God*: a few Rabbis gathered one night to put God on trial. At stake was whether God had abandoned the Jewish people, and thus whether God was guilty of breaking the covenant. In the midst of a concentration camp, arguments were made in God's defense, and also against God. They argued and debated through the night, going back and forth. As night was drawing to an end, the men came to the decision that God was indeed guilty. Yet, as daylight began to appear, the men immediately set about to their morning prayers, as if the guilty verdict changed nothing. God might be dead, but Judaism goes on.

Moses Maimonides

Moses Maimonides (c. 1135–1204 CE), as he is known by his Latinized name, remains one of the most widely admired Jewish theologians. In his own lifetime, he was admired too, but even more so by Muslims than by Jews. Moshe ben Maimon, as he was known among Jews, was also known as Musa ibn Maymun among Muslims, who read his works in Arabic before Jews read them in Hebrew. This was a period of fruitful interaction on theological matters between Jews and Muslims. Scholars debate whether and to what extent Maimonides read the works of his Islamic predecessors (Al-Ashari, al-Farabi, Ibn Sina, Ibn Rushd, and al-Ghazali), but there is no doubt that he was fully immersed in the culture of Islamic philosophy and theology.

In about 1160 CE, Maimonides did something quite novel for Judaism: he created a list of thirteen articles of faith, consisting of those things he felt every Jew must believe in order to claim to be a Jew. What is most interesting about this list is that it represents a moment in Jewish history when they dabbled in orthodoxy, that is in the attempt to prescribe correct belief. Despite Maimonides' deep impact on current Jewish theological identity, it is noteworthy that this attempt at orthodoxy never did displace Judaism's tendency towards **orthopraxy**.

1. God is the sole creator of all things
2. God is the essence of oneness
3. God has no body
4. God is the first and the last
5. It is right to pray to God, never to anything else
6. All the words of the prophets are true
7. Moses is the greatest of all prophets, and his words are true
8. The Torah as it stands was given to Moses
9. The Torah will not be added to and there will not be another
10. God is all-knowing
11. God rewards the righteous and punishes the disobedient
12. The messiah will come eventually
13. The dead will be resurrected

has felt it has received from God (e.g., in the Exodus), it has been part of Israel's self-understanding that it was chosen by God. Rarely has this been presented with a sense of superiority, except perhaps in the moral sphere. Of course, every group believes its ways are morally superior, that other people are sinners, barbaric, and immoral, and the ancient Israelites did too! They felt that their God-given law made them uniquely moral; it made them a light in a world of darkness and immorality, from polytheism to sexual licentiousness. The idea of "election" in Judaism most commonly means that God chose the Jews to carry this burden of offering an example of what right living before God looks like.

Torah, Sin, and Repentance

The medieval theologian **Moses Maimonides** counted 613 *mitzvot* (or commandments) in the **Torah**, and there are yet other laws in the **Talmud**. These are the laws by which Jews were traditionally expected to live. Because they were given by God, and because they represented the practices that set this community apart from others, adherence to them was considered extremely important. Israelite prophets blamed the loss of the First Temple on the failure to keep God's law, and medieval theologians praised those who could keep them. Rabbinic Judaism developed an approach that recognized the sanctity of each law, namely to "build a fence around the Torah" (see Chapter Eight). Christians caricatured Jewish observance to the law, erroneously claiming that if one broke even one of the smallest commandments, a person was lost from God forever.

In Judaism, God forgives sin, just as in Christianity and Islam. Many Jewish theologians have taught that forgiveness is granted when individuals sincerely repent, when they seek to make recompense with those wronged, and when they participate in the annual holy day that pleads to God for the atonement of the sin of all God's people (see Yom Kippur in Chapter Eight). The Jewish perspective on sin, then, is that it entails a transgression of God's commandments, stepping over a boundary that separates righteous and unrighteous conduct. Sin is not inherent to humanity for Jews; it is simply (though seriously) something they do when they become forgetful, self-centered, or led astray. Adherence to God's law requires concentration, faithful devotion,

and the occasional reminder. It is possible in Judaism, theoretically, for a human being to be wholly sinless. Yet, as we will see in Chapter Eight, there is great variety in Judaism about how best to follow God's law.

Messiah

The ideas of the messiah and resurrection run like a thread through the theology of Jewish religion, waxing and waning in importance, and shifting and developing as time passes and historical settings change. The Hebrew verb *mashach* means "to anoint," an action that involves rubbing oil on someone's head as a way of installing them into an important role (not unlike a coronation ceremony, during which someone becomes king or queen). The noun that derives from the verb is *mashiach*, that is "one who has been anointed." Greek-speaking Diaspora Jews kept the Hebrew word, but rendered it with Greek letters, producing the word *messia*, which English adopts as "messiah." Greek had its own verb for the act of rubbing oil on one's head, and that is *chriō*, from which the noun *christos* derives, with the same meaning as *mashiach*, namely "anointed one." *Christos* becomes the central title Christians apply to Jesus.

Jewish Influence

The notion of messiah developed over many centuries within Judaism, and this development was extended considerably in Christianity and Islam (and, as we shall see in Chapter Eleven, Mormonism and Baha'i as well). The title *Christos*, the root of the name for the religion of Christians, is the Greek word for "anointed one." This figure in Christianity is very closely related to the Jewish figure of messiah, so much so that Christians always believed that Jesus the Messiah was the messiah Israel had always been expecting. Islam is indebted to but independent of this stream. Islam's term *mahdi* has nothing to do with anointing, but with the figure who ushers in the final judgment day.

When Israelite Jews first used the terms related to messiah, they were always applied to living people: David, Solomon, the High Priest, and so on. Being a messiah was somewhat like being a king: one can only be king while alive. Once one dies, the office of messiah, like that of kingship, passes on to someone else. Unlike the office of king, however, there can be more than one messiah at a time: the king and the High Priest were often messiahs at the same time. The term was even used of some utensils at the temple, and once of a non-Israelite. Because the Persian king Cyrus was so helpful in returning exiled Jews to Judah after the Babylonian conquest, and in rebuilding the temple, he is called "the LORD's messiah" (Ezra 1:2). It is interesting to note there that this whole period ends up being one in which God uses foreign nations to deal with Israel, either negatively (Babylonia) or positively (Persia).

The Babylonian conquest had another effect on messianic thinking. In the aftermath of the conquest, which involved ending the line of Davidic kings, Jews remembered 2 Samuel 7:13 ("He shall build a house for my name, and I will establish the throne of his kingdom forever"), which they came to interpret as a prophecy that the line of Davidic kings would in fact never end. Taking this as a divine promise, they began to hope for the restoration of the Davidic monarchy, which would be enacted by a future figure: the messiah, a king like David. Thus, the office of messiah was transferred from a present office, always currently filled, to a future office, waiting to be filled by some future figure.

Kabbalah

Though known as the Jewish form of mysticism, Kabbalah is not in fact like other forms of religious mysticism, which we will see are concerned with achieving unity with the divine, an experience that seeks to dissolve the boundaries between the self and the deity. Few Kabbalists are interested in mystical unification. Rather, Kabbalah is an expansive system of creative thought that invented new ways of imagining how God created and actively sustains the universe, and of relating that to the interpretation of scripture. Jewish mystics claimed to have a

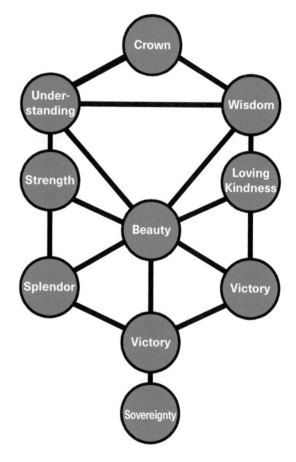

Figure 57. The Tree of Life, on which can be found the ten Sephirot, or emanations, of God.

higher ideal than merely reading and obeying the Torah, and they sometimes also claimed to have the only proper way of doing so.

The core of Kabbalistic thinking about God is that God has an essence that is wholly hidden and unknown. They call this divine essence *Ein-Sof*, or that which is infinite. While it is common for Jews, Christians, and Muslims alike to think of God as transcendent – that is, existing above and apart from the created world – Kabbalistic theology places God even beyond this. For them God is so transcendent that he cannot interact directly with the created world at all. God and world can only interact indirectly through ten emanations that come from God, called Sephirot. These Sephirot are aspects of God, characteristics drawn from passages in the Tanakh and Talmud. Access to them reveals new, deeper meanings in creation, in the Torah, and in understanding the nature of God.

Kabbalah developed among Jewish communities in France and Spain in the twelfth and thirteenth centuries CE, though many early texts from and supporters of Kabbalah claim explicitly that they invented nothing, but merely transmitted ancient wisdom. For instance, the Zohar, one of the key texts of Kabbalistic theology, claims itself to have been written by Simon bar Yochai in the second century CE. The work is even written in Aramaic, the language of second-century Jews, but uncommon in the Middle Ages. It is quite clear, however, that the work is a thirteenth-century product of the creative

Figure 58. Hasidic Jews in Stamford Hill, London.

genius of Moses de Leon of Guadalajara, Spain. The ascribing of texts and sayings to an earlier period or past authoritative person is a common practice in religions.

Though in many respects an elite, idiosyncratic, and extreme approach to religion and scripture, Kabbalah has had a discernible influence on Judaism. In the sixteenth century, Isaac Luria influenced modern Kabbalah, despite writing very little. His perspective influenced many aspects of Jewish theology, including his ideas about the Messiah, God, and creation. For instance, writing after a number of catastrophes had hit the Jewish people, including expulsions from Western Europe and the Inquisition, Kabbalists were certain that the arrival of God's Messiah must be imminent. Inspired by this, Shabbatai Zvi, from Turkey, claimed to be the long-awaited Messiah, gaining the support of several prominent Rabbis. In 1666, Zvi was forced to choose between conversion to Islam or death. He converted.

Eastern Europe was the site of a new development in Kabbalah, known as Hasidism. Allegedly founded by a mysterious miracle worker from the Ukraine known as the Baal Shem Tov (1700–1760), Hasidism sought to inject joy into Jewish suffering, especially as that suffering grew more extreme in the context of seventeenth- and eighteenth-century massacres in Poland and Ukraine. This group of Jews rejected the learning-centered approach of the powerful but also rich and comfortable Rabbis, an approach that brought little consolation to suffering communities. Hasidism championed emotion over learning, by singing, dancing, and telling stories in the midst of their suffering. We see in this summary also an explanation for how this originally Sephardic (Spanish and Mediterranean) movement came to be almost exclusively associated with Ashkenazi (Eastern European) culture: because of the expulsions of Jewish communities into Eastern Europe, and because of the additional catastrophic suffering they encountered once there.

Kabbalah's interest in emotion over learning, and in spiritual over legal reasoning, has made it attractive to people outside Judaism. This is most apparent in the trend involving Hollywood celebrities wearing a red thread as a bracelet and calling themselves devotees of Kabbalah. These include the singer Madonna, actors Gwyneth Paltrow and Ashton Kutcher, and sport star David Beckham. This popularity in the West makes red threads easy to purchase in all the tourist areas of Jerusalem. The origins of wearing a red thread are unclear, though they are certainly neither biblical nor Talmudic. The practice probably derives from "folk" religious practices related to protection from evil spirits.

There are currently a dozen Hasidic groups in the world, accounting for as many as one million adherents. The largest and most visible Hasidic communities are found in New York City, Montreal, and Israel. Lubavitch (or Chabad) and Ger share a distinctive style of dress, which most people associate with them.

Afterlife

What happens after death was another set of ideas in Judaism that took many centuries to develop. Originally, Israelites believed that God rewarded the righteous and punished the evil in this life. To have many cattle, many sons, and health and wealth was a sign that God was pleased. To be poor, sick, childless, or to die an early death was a sign of God's displeasure. In this system, called Deuteronomistic, the dead all went to the same place: Sheol. Sheol was neutral; it was neither paradise nor hell.

The greatest blow to this way of thinking came during a time of persecution. If a good life is the reward for righteousness, then torture and death at the hands of a godless enemy is clearly a problem. The second-century BCE persecutions under the Seleucid king Antiochus IV Epiphanes (see Chapter Two) were possibly the first experience of martyrdom in Judaism. Jews were killed for doing the things required by their religion, such as reading Torah, sacrificing, and praying. If people were dying precisely when God should protect them most – when they are being loyal – then where was the reward for righteousness? Clearly, a new system was required.

This new system was resurrection, and it replaced the idea of Sheol. This life is random – sometimes the good suffer and the evil gain – but justice is delayed until after death. The righteous will be resurrected, and the evil will not. In the earliest form of development, resurrection first applied to Israel as a people. We call this corporate resurrection. This eventually turned into individual resurrection, a system built much more upon individual piety and culpability.

By the time the book of Daniel was written (c. second century BCE), resurrection belief was growing, but was still not widespread. In the first century CE, Pharisees were known for accepting the idea, whereas Sadducees did not, possibly on the grounds that the idea cannot be found in the Torah. Christians did the most with the idea, claiming not only that Jesus himself was resurrected, but that while he was alive, he resurrected others.

Jewish Theological Writings

Judaism holds a fairly expansive view of the term "scripture." In some respects, it refers to writings revealed directly from God, in other instances to a collection of humanly created though authoritative texts.

Tanakh/Midrash

Jewish collective memory maintains that when Ezra the Scribe returned from the Babylonian exile, either in 458 BCE or 398 BCE, he collected and standardized a canon of scripture: the Torah. While it is possible that the process of thinking canonically – that is, ascribing some works greater authority than others – had been happening for some time before Ezra, it is certain that most of the work in this direction was done after, and probably because of, the exile. This canonization was, of course, limited to the "five books of Moses," since the rest of the works that make up the Tanakh had not yet been written. Clearly, the creation of a Jewish canon was a very lengthy process involving many stages, not least because the process of authorization generally takes some time, but because the individual writings that came be to canonized represent different types of

---

The Books of the Tanakh

The Jewish Tanakh and the Christian Old Testament contain the very same writings, though sometimes they are differently arranged. In addition, sometimes the Hebrew names and English names for the books are the same (e.g., usually when it is a personal name), sometimes the names are different but obviously related (e.g., with the translation of the Hebrew title, such as Judges or Kings), and sometimes they are completely different (e.g., Deuteronomy is a Latin word referring to a "second" [deutero] collection of "law" [nomos]; the Hebrew name is Devarim [meaning "words"]).

Torah:
Genesis, Exodus, Leviticus, Numbers, Deuteronomy

Nevi'im:
Joshua, Judges, Samuel A, Samuel B, Kings A, Kings B, Isaiah, Jeremiah, Ezekiel, Hosea, Joel, Amos, Obadiah, Jonah, Micah, Nahum, Habakkuk, Zephaniah, Haggai, Zechariah, Malachi

Ketuvim:
Psalms, Proverbs, Job, Song of Songs, Ruth, Lamentations, Ecclesiastes, Esther, Daniel, Ezra, Nehemiah, Chronicles A, Chronicles B

Figure 59. Torah scroll inside the former Glockengasse Synagogue in Cologne.

Narratively, the Torah ends with the Israelites about to re-enter Canaan, and it is the books that follow that continue the story: the transition from twelve tribes to a united monarchy, the dissolution of the kingdom and the conquest and dispersal of its parts, and so on.

But in addition to mythological and possibly historical narratives, the Torah also provides Judaism with its laws. For Israelites at the time, and for many Jews today, these are divine laws, in that they come directly from God. They prescribe the behavior God expects of the community, in gratitude for their election and as a sign of their loyalty. By the Common Era, Jews enumerated these laws (*mitzvot*) at 613. They cover such things as diet and dress, domestic life and neighborly relations, sex, temple purity and administration, and proper engagement with God. These laws include requirements (what members of the community must do) and prohibitions (what they must avoid doing). As we shall see in Chapter Eight, modern Jews do not agree on how best to keep these laws, but they agree universally that one's relationship to them is an important element in defining communal and individual Jewish identity.

writing produced in a wide array of settings, periods, and geographical locations.

Torah

The five books that Jewish tradition credited to Moses came to be known as **Torah**, meaning "teaching" or "instruction." These books provide Judaism with its myths of origins (e.g., the creation of the universe and of humanity, the call of Abraham and the creation of a nation descending from him and his descendants) and its legendary history (e.g., the time spent in and the exodus from Egypt, the revelation of the Torah).

Prophets

The Torah makes up the first section of the Jewish Bible. It comes first because in the process of Jewish canonization these books were understood as God's direct revelation. The next two sections were also often considered "divine," but in a less direct manner. The word *Nevi'im* means "prophets," and they claimed to speak on behalf of God. Isaiah, for instance, condemned his own and preceding generations for acts displeasing to God as a way of explaining the tragedy of the Babylonian conquest and the destruction of the temple and establishing hope for Judah's restoration. The Former Prophets (Joshua, Judges, Samuel, and Kings) narrate the period from the conquest of Canaan after the Exodus to the monarchy of David and his united kingdom. The rest are known as the Latter Prophets, and are divided up into Major (Isaiah, Jeremiah, and Ezekiel) and Minor because they are so short (the remaining twelve). What unites the "prophetic" writings is that their writers claim to speak for God in condemnation of some aspect of contemporary Israelite society – such as treatment of widows, relapsing away from monotheism, or general iniquity, and so on. Prophets condemn on God's behalf,

What is in the Talmud?

Each page of the **Talmud** contains one or two short passages from the Mishnah, with its corresponding Gemara below. These sit in the center of the page. Surrounding them in rings leading to the outside edge of each page are commentaries by esteemed Rabbinic interpreters (such as Rashi), as well as cross-references and later commentaries. Since the center, and heart, of each page is the passage of Mishnah, the Talmud as a whole follows the structure of the Mishnah, which revolves around six topical headings: Seeds (material related to agriculture and tithes); Times (material related to Shabbat and the holy days); Women (material related to purity, marriage, and divorce); Damages (material related to civil and financial law); Holies (material related to the temple, priesthood, and sacrifice); and Purities (material related to the laws of impurity and practices leading to purity). Similar to the spirit of Midrash, the traditions of Talmudic interpretation retain conflicting opinions among the Rabbis, rather than imposing uniformity, and there is even some blank space on every page, symbolizing the potential to add to the diversity of voices. In addition, each heading is further divided up into ten individual sub-topical elaborations, called tractates.

A page of the Talmud illustrating its complex layout.

but they also reveal God's love, that he would seek to rectify actions that offend him among his people.

Writings

The final section of the Tanakh is a collection of miscellaneous Ketuvim, or "writings." In this section we find poetry (Psalms), riddles and anecdotes (Proverbs), stories that sound historical (Ruth), and some that are clearly mythological (Job). These writings could be considered divine in some ways, though not in the same way as writings in the preceding sections, either because they come from revered figures who enjoyed divine approval (David, Solomon) or because they depict proper human responses to the divine (Ruth, Job).

The word "Tanakh" is an acronym deriving from these three sections: the T from Torah, the N from Nevi'im, and the K from Ketuvim.

Midrash

When the Rabbis interpreted the Tanakh, they wrote down and collected those interpretations, and called it Midrash (referring to the activity of "seeking" or "investigating"). One limitation of this is that it authorizes certain interpreting voices over others (e.g., those not included), but Midrash is interesting because the collectors enshrined a diversity of opinion: little attempt appears to have been made to impose a uniformity of opinion on Jewish interpretation of the Tanakh.

Midrash is often quite creative. For instance, there are *midrashim* (the plural of midrash) on Exodus 4:10. This passage claims that Moses complained to God that he would be unable to lead his people. In the narrative, he claims, "O my Lord, I have never been eloquent, neither in the past nor even now that you have spoken to your servant; but I am slow of speech and slow of tongue." Nothing more is said, here or elsewhere, about Moses' speech

---

Rabbinic Innovation in the Mishnah

The Oral Torah, and the Mishnah that was an extension of it, is not merely the Torah in an oral form. Often it involves innovative ways of thinking that are only distantly based on the Torah itself. Here is an example. The Torah forbids work on the Sabbath (Exodus 31:13), but it is rarely very specific about itemizing the kinds of work prohibited, or of defining work. The Rabbis took it upon themselves to create a list of prototypes of work prohibited on the Sabbath, which is found in the Mishnah text on Festivals (*Mishnah Shabbat* 7.2). This list of 39 prototypes is interesting because within each treatment there is a discussion of how to define each type, and how much of each type one could do before being guilty of transgressing Shabbat. These 39 prototypes are: Carrying, Burning, Extinguishing, Finishing, Writing, Erasing, Cooking, Washing, Sewing, Tearing, Knotting, Untying, Shaping, Plowing, Planting, Reaping, Harvesting, Threshing, Winnowing, Selecting, Sifting, Grinding, Kneading, Combing, Spinning, Dyeing, Chain-stitching, Warping, Weaving, Unraveling, Building, Demolishing, Trapping, Shearing, Slaughtering, Skinning, Tanning, Smoothing, Marking. Rabbinic interpretation prohibits these kinds of work, anything related to these, and anything analogous (see Chapter Eight).

The Oven of Aknai

Here is an interesting portion of the Talmud (from Baba Metzia 59b). In it, the Rabbis are having a debate over a question of Law: is a certain type of oven susceptible to impurity or not? In the debate, the esteemed and widely adored Rabbi Eliezer not only believes he is right (the oven cannot become impure), and not only can he perform miracles in support of it, but even God speaks from heaven in support of him. Watch how the debate unfolds.

Why [the oven of] Aknai? – Said Rabbi Judah in Samuel's name: [It means] that they . . . proved it unclean. It has been taught: On that day Rabbi Eliezer brought forward every imaginable argument, but they did not accept them.

Rabbi Eliezer said to them: "If the *halakhah* agrees with me, let this carob-tree prove it!" Thereupon the carob-tree moved a hundred cubits to another place – though others claim it was four hundred cubits.

"No proof can be brought from a carob-tree," the other Rabbis retorted.

Again Rabbi Eliezer said to them: "If the *halakhah* agrees with me, let this stream of water prove it!" whereupon the stream of water flowed backwards.

"No proof can be brought from a stream of water," they rejoined.

Again Rabbi Eliezer urged: "If the *halakhah* agrees with me, let the walls of the schoolhouse prove it," whereupon the walls inclined to fall. But Rabbi Joshua rebuked them, saying:

"When scholars are engaged in a *halakhic* dispute, why do you interfere?" Hence they did not fall, in honor of Rabbi Joshua, nor did they resume the upright, in honor of Rabbi Eliezer; and they are still to this day inclined.

Again Rabbi Eliezer said to them: "If the *halakhah* agrees with me, let it be proved from Heaven!" whereupon a heavenly voice cried out: "Why do you dispute with Rabbi Eliezer, seeing that in all matters the *halakhah* agrees with him!"

But Rabbi Joshua arose and exclaimed: "It is not in heaven." What did he mean by this? – Said Rabbi Jeremiah: That the Torah had already been given at Mount Sinai; we pay no attention to a Heavenly Voice, because Thou hast long since written in the Torah at Mount Sinai, After the majority must one incline.

Rabbi Nathan met Elijah and asked him: What did the holy one, blessed be he, do in that hour? – He laughed [with joy], he replied, saying, "My sons have defeated me, my sons have defeated me."

This story reveals a central characteristic of Rabbinic Judaism: that consensus is more important than charisma. Eliezer has power over nature, and even has the support of God, but no other Rabbis agreed with him. Rabbinic Judaism decided that the days of revelation – God speaking to his people – were long past, and thus all that was left for the community was reasoned argument and persuasion leading to consensus.

impediment. Later Jewish traditions created *midrashim* in order to resolve this lack of explanation.

One of them claims that when Moses was a child, the Pharaoh suspected that he was Jewish, so to test him, he placed two pots before him: one filled with gold pieces and the other with hot coals. Pharaoh felt that if the boy reached for gold, this would prove his Jewishness, but he also knew that any child would avoid reaching for the coals. As the boy Moses was reaching for the shiny coins, as any child would, God intervened. Moses touched the coals, and putting his burnt fingers into his mouth burned his tongue. According to this midrash, this was how Moses' tongue was injured, making him slow of speech. This story, one of several on this particular passage, shows how creative and free the Rabbis could be in interpreting their scripture.

Talmud/Gemara

Recall that the Pharisees, whom we met in Chapter Two, were a Judean sect of the Second Temple period. One of the features that set them apart from other sects around them (e.g., Sadducees, Essenes, etc.) was their belief that they were in possession of a body of laws told to Moses on Mt. Sinai, but not included in the Torah. Because it was claimed that these laws were transmitted in oral form only, they became known as the Oral Torah. This was not, it must be emphasized, the Torah in oral form; they were an entirely different set of laws, and the Pharisees alone had access to them. Needless to say, Sadducees sharply contested this claim.

After the destruction of the Second Temple, however, only the Pharisees remained of these sects, and thus it was their form of Judaism that survived, and, of course, their unique text. Jewish tradition maintains that around the start of the third century CE, one leading Rabbi in particular, Judah ha-Nasi, oversaw the move to commit the Oral Torah to writing and editing, producing what is called the **Mishnah**.

Mishnah

The Mishnah is not to be confused with Midrash. It is not an interpretation of the Tanakh. It also not a collection of laws and legal opinions exclusively pertaining to post-Temple Judaism. It is, in some ways, all of those at once. Sometimes the Mishnah comments on Torah. Sometimes it comments on legislation pertaining to the Temple, which no longer exists. Sometimes it deals with laws unique to the fourth century. The text is sometimes thought to be a compendium of material helping Jews live in the real world, and in some ways it is, but it is also more expansive than that.

Just as the Tanakh came to be interpreted, so too did the Mishnah. And since there were two distinct Rabbinic communities in the early period of post-Temple Judaism, there are as a result two different interpretations. These are called Gemara, and there is a Gemara that comes from the Babylonian Jewish community, and a Gemara that comes from the Jewish community in Palestine. The Mishnah along with each Gemara forms a Talmud, and since there are two Gemarot (plural of Gemara) there are two Talmuds: the Palestinian Talmud (completed around the fifth century CE, but fragmentary in places), and the longer, more revered Babylonian Talmud (completed in the seventh century CE). When Jews refer to "the Talmud" today, they invariably mean the Babylonian Talmud, and even have a nick-name for it: the Bavli.

Chapter Summary

The sacred writings of the Jews, the Hebrew Bible, containing Torah, Prophets, and Writings, and the Talmud, sit at the foundation of Jewish theology. These writings also give Jewish people their sense of origins in a cosmos created by God as essentially good, and over which God watches. These writings not only inform a community's sense of its origins and its place in the universe; they also inform the components of belief. Yet no writing can accomplish any of these purposes without being interpreted, and we looked at the interpretive tradition in Judaism. Jewish tradition often retains the voices of opposing theological opinions, not only as they pertain to core theological components but also the interpretation of sacred writings.

Glossary

Ein-Sof. In Kabbalah, it is said that before God gave shape or form to anything in creation, God was formless, merely a divine essence. They call this *Ein-Sof*, meaning "without end." The ten Sephirot are the emanations of energy from the *Ein-Sof*.

Election. A core Jewish theological idea articulating the belief that God chose the Israelites (hence: the chosen people) to establish a covenant with. Having been chosen by God is sometimes understood as an honor, but more often the burden of it is stressed, in that God placed on the Jews a heavier burden (613 *mitzvot*) than he did the rest of the world (seven laws of Noah).

Exodus. Refers to the legends of the flight of the Israelites from slavery and oppression in Egypt in the second millennium BCE, narrated in the book of Exodus. This narrative forms the foundation of the Pesach celebration, and articulates the profound Jewish conviction that God watches over and protects the Jews.

Moses Maimonides. The paramount Jewish philosopher and theologian (c. 1135–1204 CE). Born Musa ibn Maymun, fluent in Arabic and comfortable in Islamic society, Maimonides benefited immensely from his interactions with Islamic philosophy and theology. His career is emblematic of the close relationship between Judaism and Islam in the medieval period, and his most influential writings were originally in Arabic.

Mishnah. When the Rabbis put into writing the oral legal traditions of the Pharisees, they called it Mishnah, which means "secondary," marking its place as second only to the Torah.

Orthopraxy. Refers to correct (*ortho*) practice or actions (*praxy*). Orthopraxic debates are those debates that seek to establish or challenge correct practice.

Polytheism. Especially prominent in antiquity, polytheism stems from the twofold conviction that different groups have their own gods, and that different gods govern different aspects of life: travel, fertility, love, weather, agriculture, and so on. Thus, one goes to particular gods depending on need.

Talmud. A product of Pharisee tradition, the Mishnah is the written form of Oral Torah. The first Rabbinic interpretation of and commentary on the Mishnah came to be called Gemara. Together, Mishnah and Gemara are the subject of several interpretive traditions. All of these are contained in the pages of the Talmuds, one from Palestine and one from Babylonia.

Tetragrammaton. Means "four letters," and it refers to the four Hebrew letters that comprise the name of God. This term exists because of a common Jewish hesitation to say the name of God, either in prayer or in reading the Tanakh.

Torah. A Hebrew term meaning "instruction," Torah most technically refers to the first five books of the Bible, which establish the legal foundation of Judaism. More loosely, the term is also used to refer to the entirety of Jewish teaching.

Other Important Vocabulary

Ba'al	Kabbalah	Nevi'im	Sephirot
Baal Shem Tov	Ketuvim	Shabbatai Zvi	Theodicy
Gemara	Midrash	Shema	Yahweh
Hasidism	*Mitzvot*	Sheol	

Discussion Questions

1. Using the origins narratives of Judaism, how might you articulate the relationship and difference between history and mythology?

2. What might explain the fact that theological concepts like monotheism, messiah, and resurrection took so long to develop? Can we be certain that these developments are now complete?

3. Notice how developments in Jewish theological positions (e.g., prophecy, Kabbalah) often occur in response to historical events, such as suffering and the loss of autonomy. What lessons do we learn about "religion" from this?

4. There is a common, and not very funny, joke: where there are three Jews collected you will find five opinions. Consider how our discussion of Midrash, Gemara, and the Talmudic page might lead to this perception of Judaism.

Recommended Reading

Dorff, Elliot N., and Louis E. Newman, eds. 1999. *Contemporary Jewish Theology: A Reader.* Oxford: Oxford University Press.

Halbertal, Moshe. 2013. *Maimonides: Life and Thought.* Princeton, NJ: Princeton University Press.

Morgan, Michael L. 2001. *Beyond Auschwitz: Post-Holocaust Jewish Thought in America.* Oxford: Oxford University Press.

Recommended Websites

http://www.jtslibrarytreasures.org

- The Jewish Theological Seminary has a digital collection of Jewish sources and rare books numbering in the hundreds of thousands.

http://www.jewfaq.org

- An excellent resource for Orthodox explanations of Jewish theological concepts and practices.

http://www.jewishencyclopedia.com

- An old resource now part of the public domain, this site offers countless thoroughly written entries on all sorts of topics relating to Judaism. Especially useful for its entries on historical figures and texts.

—6—

Christian Theology and Theological Writings

Chapter Overview

In this chapter you will learn the theological narrative of the origins of Christianity, which can be found in the New Testament stories of Jesus Christ and Paul of Tarsus. These narratives are a central element of Christian theology, along with other key elements, such as the Trinity, justification, resurrection, salvation (life after death), mysticism, and eschatology. We shall also explain the content of the New Testament.

Core Theological Ideas

Founders and Foundations

To place a discussion of Jesus' life here in a theology chapter does not deny the historicity of Jesus. Rather, it recognizes the profound theological importance of the model of Jesus to Christians. Put differently, it is not an academic lecture on first-century Judea under Roman occupation that Christians seek when they turn to the gospels, but rather a deeper understanding of God's role in and rule over the world. Christians turn to the gospels to reflect on what God intended by sending Jesus, to understand how they might come closer to God by imitating Jesus, and to understand how to relate to the world around them. In other words, by understanding and embracing the evidence of how God was present with a community in the past, Christians can find confidence in how God will be present with the community in the present and in the future, and that is a fundamentally theological process. Thus, most Christians turn to the stories of Jesus for theology and not history.

The stories of Jesus in the gospels are, like many of the stories found in the Tanakh in the previous chapter, possibly historical events that have been deeply theologized in their retelling. Jesus of Nazareth was, for his followers (as too for Christians today), Israel's long-promised Messiah, or Anointed One (see Chapter Five): *Mashiach* in Hebrew and *Christos* in Greek. He is therefore known

Figure 60. A page from the eighth-century Lindisfarne Gospels, the most spectacular manuscript to survive from Anglo-Saxon England.

in the Hebrew Bible pointed towards Jesus Christ. Since Jesus could be found anticipated and even predicted in each of these roles throughout the Hebrew Bible, his followers thought of him as the culmination and fulfillment of Judaism. This is an attitude that would eventually result in anger against Jews: many Christians until the twentieth century felt that because Christianity was the rightful inheritor of Judaism, it was stubborn and hateful for Jews to persist in their own religion.

Stories of Jesus found in the gospels can be divided into two categories: those that look backward, establishing Jesus as the fulfillment of Jewish prophecy, and those that look forward, articulating a new message and promising a new world order. The Jesus of the gospels calls this new world order the "Kingdom of God/Heaven." The **Kingdom of God** appears to have privileged the poor and the downtrodden, condemning and mocking the rich and powerful. In the Kingdom of God, the first would be last and the last would be first (Matthew 20:16; Mark 10:31; Luke 13:30), truly a new world order.

In the gospels, the Kingdom of God is discussed in two ways: in stories of Jesus' healing/miracle mission, and in stories about his teaching mission. The gospels depict Jesus healing many people: frequently the blind, those who cannot walk or use their hands, and people with skin diseases. He can even raise the dead. None of these events is depicted as the result of his own innate abilities, but are presented as evidence that God was working through Jesus in a unique way. All of Jesus' acts, therefore, are miracles, including many that have nothing to do with healing – such as walking on water and calming a storm.

to Christians as Jesus Christ, short for Jesus the Christ. The process of defending Jesus' identity as the Messiah was one of theological contestation: Jews who followed Jesus and Jews who did not argued, sometimes with great anger, over the correct interpretation of the Torah and the Prophets.

The followers of Jesus found proof through their interpretations of the Torah and the Prophets that Jesus was the Son of God, the Messiah, the Suffering Servant, the Lord, and the Son of Man. For them, everything

Mary and Virginity

Part of the theological narrative for some Christians is that Jesus was *really* (not merely metaphorically) the Son of God. All of our biblical texts agree on calling Jesus the Son of God, and many passages have Jesus calling God *Abba* (the Aramaic word for "father," not as sometimes claimed, "Daddy"), but two of the gospels narrate how this came about. Mary was made pregnant by the Holy Spirit, from God. Mary was a virgin when she became pregnant, and therefore Jesus had no human father. On this theological point Protestant, Catholic, and Orthodox Christians agree.

But they disagree in an interesting way on a related topic: did Jesus have brothers and sisters? Protestants have tended to argue that when ancient writings (which include biblical texts, non-biblical Christian texts, and non-Christian historical texts) refer to brothers or sisters of Jesus, they really were his brothers and sisters. That is, after the virgin Mary bore Jesus, she went on to have other children with Joseph. So, Jesus had brothers and sisters through his mother.

Most Catholic and Eastern Orthodox Christians (and a few Protestants) on the other hand argue that references to brothers and sisters of Jesus in ancient writings are not literal. For example, "brother" could be a term used of a fellow follower of Jesus, because Jesus created a new "family" around him, so naturally they called each other brother and sister. Catholics also speculated about more complex kinship arrangements, such that Joseph was an elderly man with children from a previous marriage. Thus, his relationship with Mary was never sexual (because he was too old) and Jesus' "brothers and sisters" were children of Joseph but not Mary. For these Christians, which include Orthodox Christians, Mary remained "ever virgin." These differences exist because different Christians have different ways of interpreting the same texts.

The final key events in the theological story of Jesus are his trial, death, and resurrection. The gospels tell a story of Rome prosecuting Jesus, but finding him innocent, and the Jewish mobs threatening to riot and calling for his execution. Afraid, the Romans acquiesce. This is one of many instances in which historians doubt the accuracy of the gospel stories: it is unlikely that the great and unflinching Roman empire would worry about a small riot in Jerusalem, and Rome did not like to be threatened by its subjects. More likely, such a story derives from a later period during which followers of Jesus were breaking away from Judaism, their parent religion, and seeking approval in Roman society. Nonetheless, the gospel stories are agreed: Rome killed Jesus at the behest of the Jews, and three days later, God raised his son from the dead. The resurrection is the key theological event in Christianity.

The gospels, and other early Christian sources as well, relate encounters with the resurrected Jesus – or to use the language of Easter (see Chapter Nine), the "risen Christ." In the estimation of one gospel writer, "God so loved the world that he gave his only son" (John 3:16), and he so loved his son that he raised him from the dead (Acts 2:24).

Trinity

The Christian understanding of God is extremely complex. God is imagined as equal parts merciful and punishing, personal and transcendent, loving and yet allowing suffering. God can be described as a friend (James 2:23), father (John 14:1), mother (Deuteronomy 32:18), judge (2 Timothy 4:1), midwife (Isaiah 66:9), and king (Jeremiah 10:10). As you can see, some of these characteristics are consistent with the Jewish sense of God, as they come from Jewish sources. The Islamic sense of God is not dissimilar either. But far more complex, and in sharp contrast to Jewish and Islamic understandings of God, is that for some Christians the God who is one is also three at the same time.

Centuries of theological writing, from the New Testament (50–120) to the Church Fathers (100–400) and on through the medieval (500–1500), Reformation (1500–1700) and modern (1900–present) periods, reveal that the Christian understanding of God is born in experience. It was the experience of Jesus Christ among his followers that must have forced a re-evaluation of their conception of God, namely as triune God. It is this belief that is expressed in the doctrine of the Trinity.

The task before Christian theologians was monumental: to explain how the one God was to be experienced as a Trinity. They were, after all, unequivocally monotheists, and felt themselves called by the one true God of Israel. Could one worship both Jesus and God and be considered a monotheist? The answer developed by Christians was yes, but not without tremendous effort being

Figure 61. A medieval woodblock depicting scenes from the Old and New Testaments.

Allegory

For many Christians the text of the Old Testament was taken as coded allusions, an allegory, rather than literally. This kind of exegesis was popular in the classical world and remained so in the Middle Ages. Abraham's near-sacrifice of his son Isaac in Genesis 22, for example, was understood to prefigure Jesus' own sacrifice. The medieval woodblock (Figure 61) shows Abraham raising his sword above Isaac (on the right) and Jesus bearing the cross (on the left) with special attention drawn to the wood that each of the victims carried.

spent on explaining, defining, and developing the idea of the Trinity. It has been the source of much controversy. Indeed, this element of Christianity is so complex that many Christians cannot explain it and do not understand it.

Developing Theology

Theological ideas never appear out of thin air. They develop, change, and adapt by interacting with historical events. For instance, starting in the first century, followers of Jesus believed that Mary the mother of Jesus was a virgin when she bore Jesus. This developed into the doctrine of the Virgin Birth. The decision at Nicaea that Jesus and God were *homoousion*, the same substance, required a re-evaluation of the identity of Mary. Some Christians claimed that the elevation of Jesus to godhead required an elevation of Mary: if Jesus is God, then Mary must be the mother of God. They used the term *theotokos* to describe Mary, literally "the bearer of God." For other Christians, placing Mary above God was intolerably illogical. For them, Mary was the mother of the Messiah, or *christotokos*. The first position, *theotokos*, was the winning position at the Council of Ephesus in 431.

But this position led to a new theological problem. The doctrine of Original Sin claims that humans are born innately sinful. Given this, how can a sinful human be the mother of God? This is what leads to the doctrine of the Immaculate Conception: the position that Mary the mother of Jesus was born without sin. Theologians had been speculating on this doctrine starting in the fourth century, and the idea became commonplace by the eighth century, but it was not until 1854 that it received official dogmatic articulation.

It is interesting to see how one theological solution opens up another problem: the problem of monotheism leads to the development of the doctrine of the Trinity (325), which leads to the development of *theotokos* (431), which leads to the doctrine of the Immaculate Conception (1854). What theological developments await?

Recall that at Nicaea in 325 Athanasius's opinion was preferred over Arius's, and so the Trinity was set out in the Nicene Creed: Jesus and God were **homoousion**, of the same substance, and therefore co-eternal (see Chapter Three). The mystery of the Trinity is that to worship Jesus is to worship God, not a second or additional god, and yet Jesus and God are still distinguishable from one another. Likewise, the Holy Spirit. How are they one and yet distinguishable?

Christianity in its first centuries emerged in two locations: the Greek eastern part of the Mediterranean, and the Latin western part. As a result, they each used and developed different terms when trying to work out the idea of the Trinity, and eventually these terms came together in a relatively universal Christian expression of the Trinity. *Homoousion* and *homoiousion* were Greek terms, referring to the relationship between Jesus and God. They also used the term *hypostasis*, referring to the essence or substance of God as an individual. Though Greek, these terms were extremely influential on later Latin-speaking theologians, who used the interesting and puzzling term *persona* to translate the Greek word *hypostasis*.

The Latin term *persona* sounds like it should mean "person" as it does today, and eventually it does come to carry some of the same connotations, but originally *persona* meant "mask." It was a term borrowed from Roman drama: rather than have many actors each playing a different role, in Roman drama a few actors would play many roles and wear different masks to indicate the different roles. Used theologically, the term was apparently intended to refer to the different

Figure 62. Stained-glass window depicting the doctrine of the Holy Trinity in Latin with symbols of circle and triangle.

roles that God plays, that is how God interacts with others: as Father, as Son, and as Spirit. Substance was also a term contributed by Latin-speaking theologians as a way of thinking about how God is constituted.

Shield of the Trinity

In the thirteenth century, Peter of Poitiers depicted the relationships within the Trinity in a way that remains popular (Figure 62). It attempts to show how Jesus and God can be one and yet distinguishable, how they can be distinct without amounting to different gods (e.g., Jesus/Son is God, but he is not the Father).

Thus, Greek-speaking Christians expressed the Trinity as "three individuals (*hypostaseis*)

Trinitarian and Non-Trinitarian Christians

Tertullian (c. 160–c. 225 CE) was a North African theologian who was among the earliest and most influential champions of Trinitarianism. Evidence of his influence, but also evidence of how novel his position was, can be found in the fact that he needed to invent words in order to express his beliefs. For example, Tertullian had to coin the words *trinitas* (Trinity), *persona* (mask), and *substantia* (substance) in order to arrive at the analogy of God as a single actor with three roles.

Trinitarianism has been controversial from its very beginnings. Tertullian himself acknowledged that many of the things Christians claimed to believe were absurd, and he would surely have included the emerging Trinitarian thought in this. But other Christians could not go so far into the absurd. Though the vast majority of Christians affirm the Trinity, not all do. Arius opposed it in the fourth century, claiming that Jesus was similar in substance to God,

but not consubstantial, and although he lost the debate that happened at Nicaea in 325 CE, his ideas continued to enjoy significant support among Christians for the remainder of the fourth century. The rising power of Protestantism and Anglicanism in the sixteenth through eighteenth centuries led to a decreased confidence in the doctrine of the Trinity in some locations, since it is difficult to see the presence of the Trinity in the New Testament. And finally, there are modern Christians who reject the Trinity, typically on the grounds that it cannot be found in the New Testament. Modern non-Trinitarian Christians include (but are not limited to): Jehovah's Witnesses, Doukhabours, Unitarians, some Pentecostals and Quakers, Christian Scientists, and some mainline liberal Protestants, as well as Mormons, to be discussed in greater detail in the last chapter. Together, non-Trinitarian Christians comprise a not-insignificant number: 41 million, or 1.6% of Christians.

in one being (*ousia*)" while Latin-speaking Christians expressed it as "three persons in one substance." Not surprisingly, the Greek version of this is still dominant among Orthodox Christians and the Latin version among Protestants and Catholics. All of these groups are Trinitarian, but not, as you can see, in precisely the same way. This is evidenced most forcefully in the controversy generated by the Catholic addition of *filioque* to the Nicene Creed, which Orthodox Christians rejected, contributing to the split between Eastern and Western Christianity. As was suggested above (see "*Filioque* Clause" text box, p. 67), Eastern Greek-speaking Christians objected to the addition of *filioque* to the Nicene Creed because it jeopardized the important conviction that divinity emanates from God alone. Divinity deriving from God "and the Son" simultaneously presented too great a logical challenge for Eastern Christians, for it implies two sources of divinity. While those who objected to

the *Filioque* Clause were trying to protect the identity and unique position of God, those who supported it were trying to explore the relationship of Jesus and spirit as "persons." One can see here how profoundly complex the notion of the Trinity was and why it took Christians so much energy to work it all out.

Jesus

One of the core theological convictions of Christianity is that the entire religion goes back to the *man* Jesus Christ: he is the foundation and the fount of Christianity, the route to a wholly new way of engaging with God. Many Christians speak of having a personal relationship with Jesus Christ, speak of Jesus with deep emotion, as if he is their closest friend and confidant. For other Christians, Jesus is not an intimate and personal friend, but a dignified king and judge. Yet others see in Jesus a fierce liberator

---

Orthodoxy vs. Heresy

A common theological enterprise that groups pursue is to represent the past in such a way that supports their view of things and denigrates competing views. The official Christian view of history is that Jesus of Nazareth established a religion that was expanded and defended by **Paul of Tarsus**, the Apostle to the Gentiles. This "right-thinking" – or *orthodox* – form of Christianity soon found itself under attack from "heretics," that is Christians who had perverted the true message of Jesus.

The most well-known of the "heresies" was a movement that began taking form in the second century: Gnostics. These were Christians who felt that faith in Jesus was not what led to salvation but rather a specific "knowledge" about

Jesus. These Christians also felt that they alone were in possession of that saving knowledge, namely that Jesus was not truly human, but only appeared in human form. Jesus was pure spirit with no actual body. It goes without saying that Gnostics also had a version of the past that showed them to be "right-thinking" and their opponents to be in error. There was, in other words, from the very beginning many different ways of being Christian, not just one proper (orthodox) way. Categories like "orthodox" and "heretic" are always rooted in power struggles and politics: the winner is declared orthodox, and then declares the losers heretics. Which one of them was the correct way is *not* for scholars of religious studies to decide.

Islamic Criticisms of Christianity

A passage in the Qur'an leads many Muslims to misunderstand Christianity. Consider how different the Qur'anic depiction of the Trinity is from the Christian depiction of it. Sura 5.116 reads:

> (Remember) when God said, "Jesus, son of Mary! Did you say to the people, 'Take me and my mother as two gods instead of God alone'?" He said, "Glory to You! It is not for me to say what I have no right (to say). If I had said it, You would have known it. You know what is within me, but I do not know what is within You. Surely You, You are the Knower of the unseen."

(Translation from A.J. Droge, *The Qur'an*. Sheffield: Equinox Publishing, 2012)

The passage accuses Christians not only of being polytheistic, but of straying from the original monotheism that Jesus himself naturally taught: according to the Qur'an, Christians worship Jesus, his mother Mary, *and* God all as separate deities. The passage also depicts Jesus himself denying teaching his followers to do this.

It is unclear where Muslims acquired this understanding of Christianity. One option is that it is simple polemics: rivals knowingly twisting facts in order to make their enemies look ignorant or ridiculous. But it is possible that Muslims got this idea from actual Christians. While we know early Muslims were in contact with Christians in the Arabian Peninsula, it is not always clear which ones and what their beliefs were. But since these groups had beliefs about Jesus that were different from the orthodoxy of Imperial Christianity, it is possible that this description describes some Christians. On the other hand, the common Christian veneration of Mary (known as Marianism) might easily have been misunderstood by Muslims as worship of Mary. At any rate, it does seem likely that the Qur'anic misunderstanding (or misrepresentation) of Christian monotheism derives to some extent from religious rivalry.

from oppression and tyranny, a friend and defender of the downtrodden. It is remarkable that so many mutually exclusive images can adhere to a single character.

Jesus not only plays many roles for Christians; he also has many titles. And though there are periods when Jesus' Jewishness was denied or downplayed by Christians, the names and titles that the earliest Christians used of Jesus were all drawn from Jewish tradition. In his famous oratorio, "Messiah" (1741), Handel referred to Jesus with the following names: "Wonderful, Counsellor, the mighty God, the everlasting Father, the Prince of Peace." Handel was quoting Isaiah 9:6, and in so doing reflected a common Christian practice of interpreting passages from the Old Testament that they felt referred to Jesus (see "Allegory" text box, p. 146). This is because, for Christians, Jesus fulfilled the prophecies, hopes, and expectations of Israelite tradition. Therefore, it was only natural that they would see Jesus referred to, alluded to, echoed, and anticipated everywhere in their Old Testament.

Christians believe in Jesus in a way that Jews do not "believe in" Moses and Muslims do not "believe in" Muhammad (though Jews and Muslims may believe many things about Moses and Muhammad respectively). But what is it that various Christians have believed about Jesus? That he is God, Son of God, Messiah, Lord, and Savior.

God

At the heart of the doctrine of the Trinity sits another related doctrine: the **Incarnation**. The Incarnation is the belief that God took human (fleshly) form in Jesus Christ. In other words, to say that Jesus is God means also that God became flesh. In the first few centuries of Christianity, there were some Christians who felt that Jesus only appeared to be human but was not really human (**Gnostics**). For them, Jesus was spirit and only seemed human, but this view was rejected in favor of an alternative: that Jesus was truly human, capable of love, sorrow, pain, death, and the full range of human emotion and experience. Christians are Christian because they feel that Jesus Christ revealed something new about God, and this was possible because Jesus was God in human form. So, for Christians the Incarnation is not some curiosity of God; rather, it reveals something important and unique about God's special interest in humans, expressed through the person of Jesus Christ.

Religion and Gender

Christianity, like Judaism and Islam, is commonly said to be a patriarchal religion, meaning that power and influence tend to rest with males – popes, bishops, theologians, Church Fathers, Desert Fathers. Were there any Desert *Mothers*? As a matter of fact, yes there were, and many of them! Like the Desert Fathers, they left often wealthy families and lives of comfort to seek God in the desert. But, unlike the Desert Fathers, their sayings and reflections were not collected, published, and read widely in male monastic settings, so those collections are less well known and less influential on later Christianity as a whole. That we refer to this group of ascetics and mystics as Desert Fathers instead of, say, Desert *Saints*, says something about the male orientation of Christianity.

In addition, in the Middle Ages, women established monasteries, and at times Catholic orders of nuns have clashed with the Vatican, which attests to their power and voice. And women mystics are among the most well known of Christian mystics: Teresa of Avila, Joan of Arc, Mary of Egypt, Catherine of Sienna, and Hildegard von Bingen. Joan of Arc and Catherine of Sienna even exercised considerable political influence. Recall that Catherine of Sienna moved from mysticism to political activism, campaigning for peace among popes and kings, and pressing for the return of the papacy to Rome (see Chapter Three, pp. 66–67). Joan of Arc led and inspired French military forces in several of the battlefields of the Hundred Years' War against the English.

What do we make of the fact that women are quite present in the history of Christianity, yet quite often overlooked? That historical perspective is dependent on who is doing the observing. Male church historians conducting historical surveys for male church leaders, assuming elite male influence will naturally focus on the male past. This could be described as the "Great Man" approach to doing history. Consider my own chapter on history in this volume: such an approach is also in evidence here. No less, I have placed this discussion of gender in a text box, perhaps signifying that it is a specialty topic, not deserving to be in the main body of the chapter. To what extent have I, as a male author, replicated that male-oriented framework that I am critiquing here? Conversely, to what extent am I constrained by the genre in which I am writing (e.g., introductory survey to a patriarchal religion)?

Son of God

The earliest followers of Jesus called him the Son of God. This is a term with a variety of meanings in the ancient Mediterranean. In Jewish circles it was commonly used to refer to the nation of Israel, and so Israelites could be called "children" of God if they were righteous. Particularly effective teachers, healers, and miracle workers were also given the honorific "Son of God." In a Roman context, however, "Son of God" was understood quite literally: when the deified emperor had a son, that son was obviously the "son of God." Early Christian use of this title encompasses all of these aspects: Jesus was the extraordinary healer and miracle worker, he was perfectly righteous, and he was literally the *son* of God. Jesus' own use the Aramaic term *Abba* (father) is also interesting here. But would he have meant it in the Jewish sense, or the Roman sense when he used it?

Messiah

Christians also believe that Jesus was Israel's long-promised Messiah. This belief connects and intertwines the histories of Judaism and Christianity, past and present. For Christians, the God of Israel followed through on a promise to send a messiah, but it was not the type of messiah that most Israelites hoped was coming. Thus, a new religion grew out of an old religion, and the two religions would continue to contest the interpretation of that title. But for Christians, Jesus' messianic status situates him indelibly in Jewish salvation history.

Lord

One of the most common Christian proclamations is that "Jesus is Lord." The primary connotation of the term "Lord" concerns authority and power (akin to master). But this term also carries connotations of divinity. In a Jewish environment, while "lord" was a common enough term for an authoritative man, it was also the word Jews used of God rather than speaking the name (the tetragrammaton; see Chapter Five). *Adonai* (Hebrew) was read out instead of Yahweh by Jews, and *kurios* (Greek) was used both as the translation of *adonai* (in the Septuagint) and as a title for Jesus in the Greek texts of the New Testament. It is not entirely clear whether the earliest Christians meant to say that Jesus is God when they called him Lord, but there should be no question that when they called him Lord, they understood Jesus to have an authority perhaps tantamount to that of God.

Savior

Interestingly, although Jesus is directly addressed as "Savior" only once (John 4:42), and associated with the idea of salvation only a few other times in the New Testament, Christian tradition comes to see this as one of Jesus' primary identities and functions: "Jesus saves," and "Jesus is Lord and Savior" are far more popular expressions of Christian identity than Trinitarian statements (e.g., "Jesus is God"). Salvation has much to do with the forgiveness of sins, which in turn relates to the attainment of everlasting life and resurrection at the end of time.

Justification, Atonement, and Salvation

The role, the place, and the understanding of **justification** has been bitterly contested throughout Christian history. It divided followers of Jesus from other Jews in the first century, and supporters of Luther from other Catholics in the sixteenth century and beyond. These divisions, though real and deep, have rarely been arrived at from positions of mutual understanding and respect. For example, when Paul the Apostle to the Gentiles championed "justification by faith" he did so by contrasting it with "justification by works," by which he implied that Judaism was a religion of works-righteousness, not of faith in God. But Paul's position is more caricature and parody than reasoned critique, perhaps because Paul was trying to establish a distinct identity for his community over against other forms of Judaism.

Luther likewise claimed that Catholicism taught that justification by God had to be earned through actions. In the other direction, Catholics could cite biblical passages supporting the importance of actions and conduct in the proper response to God. For them, the Protestant idea of justification by faith alone could result in the position that one could act anyway one pleases (no matter how sinful) since one is justified by faith only.

Needless to say, neither Catholics nor Protestants were working very hard to understand each other. Today Catholics and Protestants agree on a great deal when it comes to the Doctrine of Justification. In 1999, the Catholic Church and the Lutheran World Federation agreed on the following definition of justification:

> In faith we together hold the conviction that justification is the work of the triune God . . . Together we confess: By grace alone, in faith in Christ's saving work and not because of any merit on our part, we are accepted by God and receive the Holy Spirit, who renews our hearts while equipping and calling us to good works (Joint Declaration on the Doctrine of Justification 3.15).

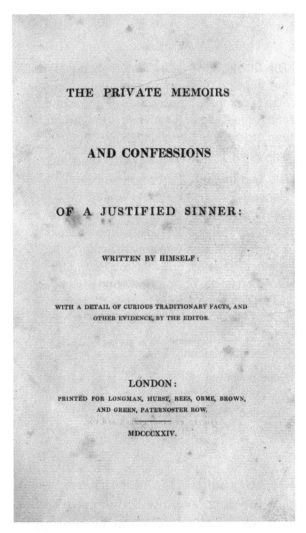

Figure 63. *The Private Memoirs and Confessions of a Justified Sinner* by James Hogg (published anonymously in 1824) is a fictional memoir set in war-torn eighteenth-century Scotland. Hogg's sinner, justified by his Calvinist conviction that his own salvation is preordained, is suspected of involvement in a series of bizarre and hideous crimes. The book explores religious bigotry and the duality of good and evil, and has been cited as the inspiration for Robert Louis Stevenson's *The Strange Case of Dr. Jekyll and Mr. Hyde.*

The Books of the Christian Bible

The Tanakh and the Old Testament contain all the same books. It can be an interesting exercise to compare how they are arranged differently (see Chapter Five). Here is the structure and order of the Christian Bible, commonly called The Bible, or the Holy Bible.

Old Testament:
Genesis, Exodus, Leviticus, Numbers, Deuteronomy, Joshua, Judges, Ruth, 1 Samuel, 2 Samuel, 1 Kings, 2 Kings, 1 Chronicles, 2 Chronicles, Ezra, Nehemiah, Esther, Job, Psalms, Proverbs, Ecclesiastes, Song of Solomon (same book as the Song of Songs), Isaiah, Jeremiah, Lamentations, Ezekiel, Daniel, Hosea, Joel, Amos, Obadiah, Jonah, Micah, Nahum, Habakkuk, Zephaniah, Haggai, Zechariah, Malachi

New Testament:
Matthew, Mark, Luke, John, Acts of the Apostles, Romans, 1 Corinthians, 2 Corinthians, Galatians, Ephesians, Philippians, Colossians, 1 Thessalonians, 2 Thessalonians, 1 Timothy, 2 Timothy, Titus, Philemon, Hebrews, James, 1 Peter, 2 Peter, 1 John, 2 John, 3 John, Jude, Revelation

Catholic bibles often have additional books, which are placed between the Old and New Testaments. They consider these to have some value, but not quite the same value as the canonical books. Protestants place no theological value in these books, and thus often are unaware of their existence. These writings are known as the Apocrypha, or Deuterocanonical writings. Orthodox Christians, like Catholics, also have additional canonical books, though they place even more theological value in them than Catholics. The New Testament of the Ethiopian Orthodox Church, for instance, contains thirty-five books rather than the twenty-seven New Testament books of Catholics and Protestants (see also "Canon" text box, p. 160).

To be "justified" is a judicial term, analogous to being "acquitted" in a court of law. It means that all charges have been dropped by the mercy and grace of the court. In the Christian theological estimation, humans have sinned against God by virtue of being human and they can do nothing of their own accord to make that relationship right again. Justification is God's free, unearned gift given to humans to right that relationship. All people are sinners equally, and all are in equal need of God's forgiveness. On this, Catholics, Protestants, and Orthodox Christians tend to agree.

Even faith is not an "activity" by which Christians are justified. Rather, the most common expression of this is that faith is the only proper response to the fact of having been justified by God. Nonetheless, Protestants and Catholics also agree that pious or righteous actions, while not earning justification, are the fruits of justification. Thus, there is in most forms of Christianity an intrinsic and causal relationship between actions and justification, but it is that justification results in appropriate behavior, not that appropriate behavior leads to justification by God.

Atonement is another key feature of this theological system. Here, that Jesus the Son of God lived a human life (Incarnation), died and was resurrected is thought to have some relationship with justification. But there are different ways of explaining this across Christianity. From some perspectives, atonement involves a cosmic battle between God and the forces of evil. The good news is that this is a battle that Jesus Christ won when he conquered death (by being raised from the dead). If one believes in Jesus, then one can, like him, conquer death.

This first model dominated in Christianity for most of the first millennium, and was replaced in the eleventh century by a model that focused less on Christ as victor and more on Christ as vicarious sufferer. In this model, when humans do wrong against God, they dishonor God and God requires "satisfaction," a term that combines the meanings of "restitution" and "justice." So here, Jesus took on the sins of humanity so that God would not have to punish all humans. This model is found in Catholic and Protestant theology for much of the second millennium.

Eastern Orthodox Christians, on the other hand, tend to view this model as too legalistic, preferring a model that stresses the transforming power of faith. In this model, Christians are invited to become like Christ and united with God – a process and goal they call *theosis*. This experiential and mystical approach to atonement stands in stark contrast to the intellectual scholastic approach of most Catholic and Protestant theologians.

Jesus is considered "savior" by most Christians, with salvation as the primary promise of Christianity. What is the Christian saved *from*? Most commonly: sin and death. Sometimes sin and death are two distinct problems, and sometimes they are construed causally: the wages of sin is death (Romans 6:3). This promise of salvation revolves around the incarnation and the death of Jesus. That God became human in Jesus and

Figure 64. Detail of the right-hand panel from "The Last Judgment" triptych, 1504–1508, by Hieronymus Bosch. Satan receives the damned souls within a dark landscape dominated by flames and devilish figures.

Figure 65. "The Rapture: One at the Mill," by Jan Luyken, an etching of 1795 depicting Matthew 24:41.

died is key here: when Christians believe in Jesus, worship God, and live faithful lives, they are said to be saved, and, wanting to avoid appearing over-confident, hoping they *will be* saved. Salvation happens at judgment day.

Eschatology

Christian time, like Jewish and Islamic time, is linear: it had a beginning (creation) and it moves towards an inevitable end. Thinking about that end time – what will happen to the world, what will happen to righteous and evil people, what will the role of God be, what happens next, and so on – is a form of theological study called eschatology. Christian eschatology commonly associates

The Rapture

The doctrine of time ending with Judgment Day is nearly universal in Christianity. Some Protestant denominations (usually referred to as Evangelical or Fundamentalist, both imperfectly named categories) have additional beliefs about this end-time event. They believe that rather than face judgment before God with the rest of creation, some Christians will be selected to bypass judgment altogether. This event, which they call the Rapture, is not described in the New Testament; the idea developed from interpretations of certain New Testament passages in the nineteenth century, but entered Christian theology most forcefully under the influence of a number of creative works of fiction, especially and most recently a best-selling thirteen-part series entitled *Left Behind* (published 1995–2007).

Belief in the Rapture also inspires some people to calculate when it will occur, and to prepare for it accordingly. Believing there will be signs that appear first (thus one can know when it is coming), and that some New Testament passages need decoding, these Christians settle on a date and then wait. Most recently, a Christian radio broadcaster named Harold Camping proclaimed May 21, 2011 as the day of Rapture, and through his radio shows encouraged listeners to prepare. Many sold their belongings and spent their savings in order to spread the news and attract new members. Others simply invested themselves emotionally, full of hope, conviction, and confidence in Camping's prediction. When this prediction proved to be inaccurate – it was his third incorrect calculation – he promised to stop making such predictions, and died in 2013.

four events with the end times: the return of Jesus Christ, divine judgment, resurrection of the dead, and the commencement of everlasting life.

The return of Jesus, called the **Parousia**, the Second Advent, or the Second Coming, ushers in the end of time. Christians disagree on whether Jesus Christ will reign on earth for a thousand years at this point, or whether he will establish the Kingdom of Heaven after the judgment of creation. They also disagree on whether certain signs will indicate that the end is near, including a mass conversion away from Christianity (called apostasy), the conversion of the Jews to Christianity, the appearance of the Antichrist, earthquakes and/or famines, and trumpets. Christian art, literature, and theology reflects a nearly unquenchable thirst for creative speculation of this sort.

The primary purpose of Christ's return is, in the words of the Nicene Creed, "to judge both the living and the dead." Here, too, Christian imaginations differ: for some, Judgment Day is a terrifying day of torment, wailing, and anguish for the damned, and a day of joy for the righteous and vindication for those who suffered to be faithful; other Christians have objected to the image of Jesus/God as vengeful and angry, and hope for more of God's love, forgiveness, and redemption, and less judgment at the end time.

The two final features of Christian eschatology are resurrection and eternal life. Some schools of thought on resurrection are that all people will be resurrected, into the bodies they originally lived in, in order to be judged. The good will go on to eternal life, lived in the presence and glory of God, and the evil will go from there to hell. For much of Christian history, heaven and hell were imagined as locations, places one went to. Most modern Christian theologians now speak of heaven and hell as relative proximities to God: heaven is closeness to God while hell is separation or distance from God. Some Christian theologies imagine that eternal life and communion will entail a complete knowledge and experience of God, which is merely fragmentary until then, while others imagine that eternal life means becoming one with God. A different understanding of hell can be found in Orthodox Christianity: God will reveal himself, his love, and his glory to all at the end of time, believer or not. This revelation will be wonderful for the believer, and punishment for the non-believer. That is what hell is: having to face God's love and rejecting it.

Mysticism

As seen above, much of Christian theological identity presupposes a personal, and somewhat intimate, relationship with Jesus Christ. Yet, for a religion to survive, and to function as an empire, it must have rules, order, hierarchy, and it must exercise power. In Christianity, as in Islam (see Chapter Seven), mystics are often those who feel the rules and a concern with power have taken precedence over the raw experience of the divine.

At its most basic, mysticism is a religious movement that champions the experience of God over lawful obedience and religious ritual or sacrament. That experience most commonly involves various kinds of unification with God: either the mystic claims to have left the body behind (called ecstatic experiences) to become one with God,

Figure 66. A sixteenth-century painting of the mystic Teresa of Avila by Peter Paul Rubens. Mysticism tends to allow for a greater role for women than other forms of patriarchal religion.

very slowly) from oneself, or by the use of music (chanting, drumming).

Mysticism has had a different history in the various parts of Christianity, but ultimately can be found throughout it. In Orthodox circles, monastic and ascetic tendencies have had a more broad-based influence. As we saw above, the term *theosis* describes the goal of Orthodox Christians: to become united with God, and by virtue of that unification deified. Interestingly, while in Catholic Christianity participation in mystical pursuits has long been considered to be naturally limited to those select few capable of such discipline, in Orthodoxy it is the goal of each Christian to achieve this mystical state of *theosis*.

The difference between Orthodox and Catholic mysticism is perhaps due to the fact that in Orthodox Christianity, mystics were not officially co-opted into the church to the same extent as they were in Western areas. Mystics were thus able to have a stronger influence on the formation of Christian practice and identity in the East. In the West, mystics were brought into the church, in the form of "orders," such as Dominicans and Franciscans. This had the simultaneous effect of marginalizing them, since admission into the orders was special and ascent through the ranks even more so, and controlling them, encouraging a greater focus on ritual and sacrament than was normally the case among mystics. In short, it made Christian mystics in the West less radical, and also gave them less influence on Christian laity.

After the Reformation, Protestant Christians tended to see in Catholic monastic discipline too much work. From a Protestant perspective, it looked like Catholic

returning later when finished, or the experience brings God or some aspect of God down into the mystic. Thus, what makes an experience mystical is generally that it is described as profound, personal, and intimate. Sometimes these experiences are said to involve visions and auditory experiences, and sometimes merely profound spiritual clarity. It seems that one can be an accidental mystic, but generally mystical experiences are achieved with deliberation and discipline, either through prolonged periods of intense prayer, and by withholding food, water, sleep, or oxygen (by breathing

Thomas Aquinas

The shape of Christian theology in the West owes a great deal to a particular trend in Christian history known as Scholasticism. Scholasts were theologians who attempted to solve major theological puzzles using logic and critical intellectual thought. This was a development made possible by earlier movements in this direction that occurred in Judaism and Islam, with Maimonides and Ibn Rushd (see text box, p. 130). Thomas Aquinas (1225–1274) represents the pinnacle of Scholastic thought in Christianity, and his debt to Maimonides is explicit in his work. Aquinas is well known for his attempt to prove the existence of God using only logic. This he did with his Five Proofs for the Existence of God.

These five proofs still echo in current Christian theology and in university campus debates about the existence of God. Aquinas's proofs also heavily influenced C.S. Lewis, a modern theologian popular among many Christians.

First Proof: From Motion
Anything in motion had to be set in motion by something else. Since an infinite chain of moved movers is impossible, there must be an unmoved source of all motion, which Aquinas calls God.

Second Proof: From Causation of Existence
Anything created exists because something caused it to exist. But an infinite chain of created causes is impossible. Hence, there must be a first source of all things that is itself uncreated. Aquinas calls it God.

Third Proof: From Contingency and Necessity
Nearly all things are contingent, meaning that it is possible for them not to exist. But if all things were contingent, there would have been a time when nothing existed, which is impossible. Therefore, if contingent things exist, there must be something that exists in virtue of its very nature. Aquinas calls this necessary being God.

Fourth Proof: From Degrees of Perfection
Many things display relative degrees of perfection like goodness, justice, and beauty. But this is possible only if an absolute form of such perfections exists. For Aquinas, God is that absolute form.

Fifth Proof: From the Order of Nature
All natural bodies, including those lacking intelligence, aim for something – their best state – and almost always achieve it. This cannot be due to chance. Rather, an intelligent designer – whom Aquinas calls God – must direct all natural bodies to their best states.

monastics thought their salvation was being earned by this work, so this was another of the many Catholic practices that Protestantism rejected. As a result, mysticism in Protestant Christianity is not found in organized and official orders with systematic structures, but it can be found as tendencies within individual groups. For instance, Pentecostals tend to stress unmediated experience of God through engagement with the Holy Spirit, clearly a form of mysticism. The difference is that Pentecostal mysticism is individualistic and spontaneous, observed most commonly in sporadic and inspired outbursts of glossolalia (speaking in tongues), prophecy, and healing.

Lived Theology

Much of the preceding discussion about Christian theology will strike many Christians as foreign. They might have difficulty seeing their own beliefs represented, despite my attempts to represent Protestant, Catholic,

Canon

Canon in a religious context is a thoroughly theological concept. To create a canon is to champion certain works and reject others. In the process, one creates a dichotomy between legitimate and illegitimate works. Sometimes this process is completed and permanent, as with Protestants and Catholics who hold the position that the Bible cannot be changed in any way. In contrast, canonization can be an on-going process, as it is in the Orthodox churches. Nonetheless, for all considered, canonization is still a process whereby approved works are imagined to be holy or divinely inspired, and rejected works theologically dangerous and heretical. Behind these categories there can very often be a context of religious rivalry: canons might tell us which works a religious community valued, and which works their opponents valued. Clearly, these are exclusively theological categories, and by no means perfectly demarcated ones. Despite the attempts of canonizers to proscribe certain works, we do see those works sometimes being used and valued by Christians who were not supposed to be using them! So canonization is not only a theological exercise but also a contested one.

Non-canonical writings can be extremely useful for the historian. The *Gospel of Thomas*, which claims to have been written by the twin brother of Jesus, shows us something about the diversity of Christian belief in the second century. The *Infancy Gospel of Thomas* shows us what some Christians were imagining Jesus Christ might have been like as a very young boy. In other words, canon is not a category that speaks of historical value, but only of theological value for a particular community.

and Eastern Orthodox theological positions. This is because in addition to these sectarian divisions, there are also differences between the theological developments and doctrinal debates of elite theologians, official representatives of Christianity, and the beliefs of common Christians on the ground. There can also be a vast difference between theologically conservative and liberal ways of being Christian, which influence not only how one interprets scripture, but also one's knowledge of and even acceptance of doctrinal debates. So, for some Christians, their identity as Christians has nothing to do with the Incarnation, **theotokos**, sin, judgment at the end of time, or with defending the inerrancy of the Bible, all of which have to do with correct belief. These Christians might frame their Christian identity around social-justice concerns, care for the world's poor and dispossessed, resistance to political and economic injustice, protection of the environment, and education. Some might associate these activities with Liberation Theology (see Chapter Three). That is to say, some Christians place more emphasis on world-affirming and assisting practices than on the intellectual debates and philosophical speculation that this chapter has emphasized.

Christian Theological Writings

The Holy Bible, as it is most commonly called among Christians, comes in two parts: the Old Testament and the New Testament. The Old Testament comes first, and is what the Jewish people call the Tanakh. The content of each is identical, but the books are arranged differently. Christians value the Old Testament because of the belief that its writings predict and anticipate Jesus as Israel's Messiah. Also, although there was no Jewish canon in the time of Jesus, it is likely accurate to say that many books of what is now the Tanakh were scripture to Jesus and scripture to his Jewish followers. Therefore, these writings were included as part of the Christian Bible.

The second part is the New Testament, and it contains writings created by followers of Jesus within a century of his death. Put differently, all the Old Testament comprises writings from before the life of Jesus, and all the New Testament comprises writings from after the life of Jesus. None of the writings came about when Jesus was alive, and most scholars do not think any of them were created by anyone who knew Jesus personally. The twenty-seven books of the New Testament are arranged in four genre sections:

Parables

The primary method that Jesus used to speak about the Kingdom of God was the parable. **Parables** are narrative stories with two levels of meaning: a surface meaning (one is a story about how seed grows best in good soil, another is about a woman who puts yeast into bread so that it rises) and a deeper, hidden, *real* meaning. Because the "true" meaning of the story resides beneath the surface, there is a long history of Christians disagreeing about what that "true" meaning is and how to get at it. Some preferred a metaphorical approach, while others read parables as allegories, but these each spawn a nearly endless range of possible interpretations. Consider this parable, commonly called "The Parable of the Wedding Banquet," found only in Matthew 22:1-14:

1 Jesus spoke to them again in parables, saying:
2 "The kingdom of heaven is like a king who prepared a wedding banquet for his son. 3 He sent his servants to those who had been invited to the banquet to tell them to come, but they refused to come.

4 "Then he sent some more servants and said, 'Tell those who have been invited that I have prepared my dinner: My oxen and fattened cattle have been butchered, and everything is ready. Come to the wedding banquet.' 5

"But they paid no attention and went off – one to his field, another to his business. 6 The rest seized his servants, mistreated them and killed them. 7 The king was enraged. He sent his army and destroyed those murderers and burned their city. 8

"Then he said to his servants, 'The wedding banquet is ready, but those I invited did not deserve to come. 9 So go to the street corners and invite to the banquet anyone you find.' 10 So the servants went out into the streets and gathered all the people they could find, the bad as well as the good, and the wedding hall was filled with guests.

11 "But when the king came in to see the guests, he noticed a man there who was not wearing wedding clothes. 12 He asked, 'How did you get in here without wedding clothes, friend?' The man was speechless.

13 "Then the king told the attendants, 'Tie him hand and foot, and throw him outside, into the darkness, where there will be weeping and gnashing of teeth.'

14 "For many are invited, but few are chosen."

This parable is typically puzzling and challenging. For instance, what does it say about the Kingdom of Heaven that it can be compared to a person (a king)? What does it mean about the Kingdom of Heaven that an unsuspecting man can be pulled off the street into a wedding and then punished for not being appropriately dressed?

Gospels, Acts, Letters, and Apocalypse.

The gospels are narrative works focusing on the life of Jesus, offering stories and many sayings of Jesus. Taken together, they cover the life of Jesus from birth to death, and some of them from there to resurrection. These works, traditionally ascribed to figures named Matthew, Mark, Luke, and John, are the works that form the foundation of the theological narrative of Jesus outlined at the start of the chapter. They show Jesus healing, teaching, casting out demons, disputing the Torah with Pharisees and Sadducees, and performing many miracles. And importantly for many Christians, Jesus' life is bookended by the miraculous, from virgin birth to resurrection.

One challenge for many Christians is how to come to terms with the miraculous. For Christians in the ancient Mediterranean, where miracles and miracle workers were common, the miracles associated with Jesus illustrated his divine approval: that God's power was at work through him, that Jesus had the legitimacy and authority that Christians ascribed to him. Many Christians in the modern day continue to read these stories this way, but struggle with the miraculous aspect. Are these stories meant to be read literally? Did Jesus really did raise Lazarus from the dead (John 11:1–44)? Or are they meant to be read as stories that give honor to Jesus, show him to be worth following? Was Jesus really conceived without a human father (Matthew 1:18–20 and Luke 1:26–31), or is that story an attempt to depict Jesus as having a truly significant (but not biological) relationship with God? On these difficult questions, modern Christians disagree. Interestingly, though miracle traditions also exist in Judaism and Islam, they play a far

more significant role in Christianity, and so not surprisingly, the debate about miracles among Christians can be very intense.

The book known as the Acts of the Apostles offers, in a way, the first history of the Church, and presents itself as a continuation of the Gospel of Luke. The book credits two apostles (hence the title) with the survival of the group: Peter the chief disciple of Jesus (who is the main subject in the first third of the book) and Paul the Apostle to the Gentiles (the sole subject of the remainder of the book). The book of Acts, therefore, is a popular theological source for the life of Paul, who wrote many letters contained in the next section of the New Testament.

Twenty-one letters comprise the third section of the New Testament. Of these letters, thirteen claim Paul the Apostle to the Gentiles as their author. They are letters written to churches and a few individuals around the Mediterranean to address crises that arose in their communities. These letters address practical matters (e.g., how worship services should be ordered, whether it is proper to marry, how to choose leaders of their communities) as well as theological matters (e.g., the importance of believing in the resurrection, how sin is to be conquered), but above all, they are about establishing Paul's authority over these churches. The remaining letters claim to be written by important Christian figures: two of Jesus' brothers, James and Jude, and two of his disciples, Peter and John (the only other letter, Hebrews, does not in fact name an author, so no one knows who wrote it).

The final book of the New Testament, and therefore of the entire Bible for Christians, is the book of Revelation, which is an apocalypse. "Apocalypse" is the Greek word for revelation, because it claims to have been revealed to a seer from the divine. Ancient Jewish apocalypses contained tours of heaven or visions of the cataclysmic end of the world, and the Christian book of Revelation contains both. In it, judgments in the form of plagues and calamities fall upon the world, destroying it many times over, and the armies of Jesus and the armies of Satan meet for the final victory of God over evil, and the dawning of a New Jerusalem.

Chapter Summary

Like all theology, Christian theology is complex and vast. It is also diverse, an unavoidable outcome of imperial expansion leading to interaction with others and internecine rivalries. Theological developments are always grounded in the real world, even when they are attempting to contemplate a reality beyond this world. The foundation of Christian theology is the conviction that God took human form, Incarnation, in Jesus Christ, a radical and world-transforming event. Christian theological writings about Jesus and the formation of Christianity all represent attempts to articulate and comprehend this experience.

Glossary

Atonement. Christianity focuses on the intro-duction of sin into human existence by Adam and Eve, which separated humans and God. Just as, in ancient Israelite religion, temple sac-rifice aided in the forgiveness of sins, which is what atonement refers to, so too the sacrifice (suffering and death) of Jesus results in the for-giveness of sin, and hence the reconciliation of God and humanity.

Gnostics. A group of Christians in the second through fourth centuries who believed that it was knowledge of Jesus' true nature that led to salvation and not, as other Christians believed, faith in the resurrection. That saving knowledge consisted in the fact that Jesus was pure spirit, and no part human.

Homoousion. Meaning "same substance," this term expresses the belief that Jesus is the same substance, and therefore co-eternal with God. This position was advocated by Athanasius and was put into creedal form at Nicaea in 325.

Incarnation. The Christian doctrine that God took human form in Jesus Christ. The position contrasts with the Gnostic position that Jesus was pure spirit. For Incarnation Christians, Jesus' actual humanity is important because it gives meaning to the resurrection.

Justification. To be justified is to be forgiven for wrongdoings, to be acquitted of all sins. In Christianity, justification is said to rely equally on the faith of the contrite sinner and on the willingness and generosity (or grace) of God.

Kingdom of God/Heaven. Jesus' message appears to have centered on the Kingdom of God, a radical reorientation of worldly values in which the downtrodden, powerless, poor, and dispossessed would win glory over the wealthy, powerful, and elite. Jesus preached this king-dom mostly in the form of parables.

Parables. Short narratives, and sometimes rid-dles, that carry multiple levels of meaning: a surface-level meaning (e.g., a story about a mus-tard seed that grows into a plant), and symbolic, metaphorical, and sometimes allegorical levels of meaning.

Parousia. The second coming of Jesus, also known as the Day of Judgment and the Second Coming. Some Protestants have developed notions of the "Rapture" with this event, and millenarianism (belief that the event will hap-pen at a 1000-year mark), but these are absent in Catholicism.

Paul of Tarsus. A first-century Pharisee who was an opponent of Christians in the years after the death of Jesus. He converted and became the Apostle to the Gentiles, responsible for estab-lishing Christian groups in several Mediterra-nean cities. Over half of the New Testament is either by Paul or about him.

Theosis. In Orthodox theology, *theosis* refers to the mystical goal of Christian life, which is to become a perfect reflection of God, not gods *per se* but a being very much in the image of God.

Theotokos. A Greek word meaning bearer of God. The term came to express the belief that as the mother of Jesus, Mary must also there-fore be the Mother of God, since at Nicaea Christians proclaimed Jesus as *homoousion* with God.

Thomas Aquinas. Lived 1225–1274, and was the foremost theologian of the Catholic Church. He was sainted, and there are many Catholic churches and schools in his name. His pro-found contributions were made possible by Christianity's encounter with Ancient Greek and Roman philosophy, inherited through Jew-ish and Islamic interlocutors.

Other Important Vocabulary

Abba	Christ	Heresy	Rapture
Acts of the Apostles	*Christotokos*	*Homoiousion*	Reformation
Apocalypse	Dominicans	*Hypostasis*	Resurrection
Apostasy	Eschatology	Liberation Theology	Satan
Arius	*Filioque*	Messiah	Savior
Athanasius	Franciscans	Nicene Creed	Scholasticism
Canon	Glossolalia	Order	Tertullian
Catherine of Sienna	Gospels	Orthodox	Trinity

Discussion Questions

1. With the narratives of Jesus in mind, how might you articulate the relationship and difference between history and mythology?

2. Think about the theologized stories of Jesus in the New Testament, and the use of the Hebrew scriptures that are reinterpreted to describe Jesus. What do you think those stories, and attempts at their reinterpretation, were intended to communicate to Christians?

3. Think of some ways in which Christian theological debates, ideas, or developments are directly related to historical experience. Can you relate this at all to the incredible diversity of Christian ideas and positions over time?

4. The New Testament is a collection of different genres of writing, with different authors and written at different times. In what way can it be considered a single book?

Recommended Reading

Ehrman, Bart D. 2015. *The New Testament: A Historical Introduction to the Early Christian Writings.* Sixth Edition. Oxford: Oxford University Press.

Keller, Rosemary Skinner, and Rosemary Radford Ruether, eds. 2006. *The Encyclopedia of Women and Religion in North America.* Bloomington, IN: Indiana University Press.

Leinsle, Ulrich Gottfried. 2010. *Introduction to Scholastic Theology.* Washington, DC: Catholic University of America Press.

Recommended Websites

http://www.newadvent.org
- Hundreds of articles on topics of traditional and modern Catholic theology.

https://www.biblegateway.com
- Offers excellent access to the New Testament in hundreds of translations, as well as in the Greek. Makes it easy to compare translations.

http://www.goarch.org/ourfaith/ourfaith7063
- A rich collection of articles on topics of Orthodox theology.

http://www.ntgateway.com
- Introductory resources for biblical studies.

http://geezmagazine.org
- A modern, liberal community that contemplates Christian identity in a complex world.

—7—

Islamic Theology and Theological Writings

Chapter Overview

This chapter introduces the theological narrative of the origins of Islam and Islamic beliefs about the life and figure of Muhammad, as well as the core positions that inform much of Islamic theology, the six pillars of faith. Next, we learn about Islamic mysticism, called Sufism, and the productive, though controversial, encounter between Greek philosophy and Islam. In the second part of the chapter, we shall look at the foundational texts that provide the basis of almost all of Islamic theology: the Qur'an, the incarnate word of God for Muslims; the hadiths, the sayings, stories, and example of a prophet believed to be incapable of error in his knowledge of God's will; and tafsir, or commentaries on the Qur'an. Muslims rarely agree on how to interpret these various texts, but they all agree that these are the key sources for their competing theologies.

Core Theological Ideas

Founders and Foundations

When Christians in the medieval period referred to Muslims as Mahometans or Muhammadans, they did so not out of disrespect, but by analogy: they themselves were called Christians because they worshipped Christ, so they assumed that Muslims worshipped Muhammad similarly, and thus were best called Muhammadans. They were wrong, of course, but they can be forgiven for making this mistake: Muslims may believe that Muhammad was merely a man, born and deceased like any other, but the theological treatment and telling of Muhammad's life casts him as a man unlike any other.

Details about the life of Muhammad are gathered from three types of sources: the *siras* or biographies, written 100–200 years after his death; the sayings or actions of Muhammad, or *hadiths* collected by those around him; and finally the Qur'an (which gives some but not a lot of biographical information on Muhammad). These sources all reflect a similar pattern, much like what

The Image of the Prophet

A 2005 controversy involving a Danish newspaper made many non-Muslims aware for the first time of the question of depicting the face of Muhammad. They solicited twelve artistic images of the Prophet Muhammad. Those images, some attractive and respectful, others disturbing and critical, set off a global outrage. Violence and damage to property ensued, and most mainstream media outlets refused to reproduce the images to allow people to see what had set off such controversy. Repeatedly, Muslims explained in the media that it is forbidden to depict the face of the Prophet. In fact, there is no explicit Qur'anic or Hadith passage making this prohibition.

Muslims who hold this position relate the concern to idolatry. Some Islamic jurists have felt that depicting the face of Muhammad, being the most beautiful and perfect of men, could lead people into worshipping the image, which is idolatry, a most serious sin in Islam. Notice, for instance, that mosques around the world can be beautifully and elaborately decorated, yet none of them contain images of humans, let alone of Muhammad. So much Islamic art follows the same trajectory, creating elaborate art based on calligraphy, sometimes even in the form of animals, but usually avoiding the depictions of people one commonly sees in Christian and Jewish art (see Chapter Ten). A glimpse at the history of Islamic art, however, reveals a much more complicated state of affairs. In thirteenth–fourteenth-century Persian art, the face of Muhammad is frequently depicted. So the fact is, as with all issues relating to religion, one can find a variety of positions on this topic over the history of Islam.

The other issue raised by the Danish cartoon controversy, and another controversy relating to the satirical French magazine *Charlie Hebdo* ten years later, is the extreme sensitivity some Muslims feel over satirical or outright disrespectful depictions of or comments about Muhammad. The violence raises a number of difficult issues: does constitutionally enshrined freedom of speech allow for religious figures to be lampooned? Or should mocking religious figures be understood as a form of hate-speech, and therefore be illegal? The answers to these questions are not obvious, but the Islamic response to these depictions, even when entirely non-violent, is rooted in their reverence for Muhammad as the perfect and faultless prophet of God (see also "Figurative Art" text box, p. 259).

we see in the narrative biographies of Jesus found in the Christian gospels: a narrative that in places sounds reasonable but throughout has been shaped and colored by a profoundly theological agenda. Many of the stories and sources agree, in broad outline, on the mundane life of Muhammad: he was born in Mecca in approximately 570 CE into the dominant Quraysh tribe, was orphaned at five years old, became a merchant in adult life, married an older wealthy widow named Khadijah, his first wife, and made spiritual retreats into the mountains around Mecca.

But the stories of Muhammad's life were not written merely in order to deliver accurate biographical information; they were written to make two key theological points.

The first theological point of these narratives is to provide a framework for the divine revelation of the Qur'an. In the Islamic narrative, God chose Muhammad to receive a revelation that was meant to remind humans – primarily Arab polytheists, and Arab Jews and Christians as well – what they once knew but had forgotten or altered: how to conceive of and worship God properly. Many of the stories about Muhammad relate to the act of God's revelation: how it happened, and how to know it was an authoritative event. For example, stories are told in which Muhammad's heart is removed from his chest and cleaned by an angel (see Figure 6, p. 25); the intent of such a story is to claim that Muhammad had no evil in him. Stories are told of a "night journey and ascension" in which Muhammad travels on a winged horse from Mecca to Jerusalem and then from Jerusalem through several levels of heaven where his mission and identity are authorized by figures like Abraham, Moses, Enoch, Jacob, Jesus, and John the Baptist. There are also stories about how a Christian monk acknowledged the prophetic status of Muhammad when he was only nine years old, based on the presence of the "seal of prophecy," a small mark on his back between his shoulder blades. Even the detail of Muhammad being illiterate carries theological currency related to the revelation and authority of the Qur'an: if Muhammad was illiterate, he cannot be the author of the Qur'an, as opponents might commonly charge. Only God can be its author. It is clear that most of these stories were created in order to show the divine legitimacy of a new prophet. From a history of religions perspective, these narratives function no differently from stories of Jesus in the New Testament, because Christians had to defend and explain the legitimacy of Jesus.

The second theological point of the narratives of Muhammad is to provide Muslims with the quintessential model of the perfect and perfectly faithful man. He is the perfect Muslim in every way. Even his physical appearance is claimed to be perfect: neither too tall nor too short, neither too large nor too thin, hair both curly and flowing, and with the finest chest and most eloquent speech of any man. He spoke without error and without malice or evil (evidenced in part by the cleaning of his heart by angels). No man was greater, for he is the perfect example of honesty, compassion, justice, courage, mercy, and truth. Many Muslims, when they refer to the Prophet in any manner in writing or speech, add a number of epithets, such as "peace be upon him." All this reveals the degree of reverence many Muslims have for Muhammad: he was just a man, but he was a man like no other and is to be emulated in every manner. This, in part, can explain the violent response of some Muslims to any slight, real or perceived, against the character or nature of Muhammad.

The theologization of Islamic origins is also applied to the period prior to the rise of Islam in Arabia. The time before Islam in Arabia is characterized as one of ignorance and darkness; the term used to describe this

Imitation

When the renowned Sunni and Sufi theologian al-Ghazali wrote in the late eleventh century, there was already a long tradition of imitating the Prophet. Nonetheless, al-Ghazali articulated it thoroughly and eloquently. His instructions reflect the position that Muhammad was the perfect man.

Know that the key to happiness is to follow the example of the Prophet's speech and actions and to imitate the Messenger of God in all his coming and going, his movements and rest, in his way of eating, his attitude, his sleep, and his talk . . . That means you have to sit while putting on trousers, and to stand when winding a turban, and to begin with the right foot when putting on shoes.

period is *jahiliyya*. Yet early Muslims have a complicated relationship with this past. Sometimes Arab practices were rejected as immoral or backward, and were used as evidence of the necessity of God's new revelation to Muhammad. At other times, however, Muslims took over Arab practices almost unchanged. For example, pre-Islamic Arabs circumambulated the Kabah in Mecca (see Hajj, in Chapter Ten). In this case, elaborate theologies were generated, in which it was claimed that these Arab practices in fact derived from Abraham and Ishmael doing them long before Arab polytheists took them over and, from an Islamic perspective, corrupted them. The view that Islam was a light in a world of darkness influenced Islamic understandings of pre-Islamic Arabia, as well as descriptions of Muhammad.

The biographical narratives of Muhammad contained in the siras and hadiths also commonly depict his time in Mecca as one of strife. It is said that the Meccan elite, his own Quraysh tribe, were offended by his prophetic messages, which included social and theological criticisms and challenges to their political authority. They were also threatened, as his theological message undermined their ability to profit economically from polytheistic worship. They attempted to silence him, but as long as Muhammad enjoyed the protection of an uncle, Abu Talib, he was safe. The death of Abu Talib in 619 CE, however, apparently made things difficult for Muhammad, a situation that would have been exacerbated further by the death of Khadijah in the same year. It is the call to a city named Yathrib, whose name was soon changed to Medina, that gave the group a new direction and new protection. Their success in Medina resulted

in a political-religious **Ummah**, or community. For this reason, the Hijra came to be considered the start of the Islamic calendar.

I close this brief discussion of the theological origins of Islam by clarifying, as I did for Judaism and Christianity, that there is certainly some history buried or embedded in these theological sources. However, the stories of Islam's founding, particularly those stories focused on Muhammad, had as their first purpose a theological message. Islamic scholars have long acknowledged the fanciful nature of many stories in the biographies, or siras, of Muhammad; this is why they are not relied on for shariah rulings (see Chapter Ten). But even some hadith stories have been transmitted and shaped by their theological purpose, just as for Jewish and Christian stories too. It is simply the way religious narrative and memory works. From a scholarly perspective, it is interesting to note the long-standing and rich history of debate among Islamic scholars concerning the historical reliability and the chains of transmission of many hadiths and sira stories of Muhammad.

Six Pillars of Faith

The well-known Hadith of Gabriel prescribes for many Muslims a threefold structure for Islam: *Iman, Islam,* and *Ihsan. Ihsan,* which refers to perfection or beauty, is commonly associated with mysticism and esoteric thought, and is the domain of Sufis, though it is certainly not theirs alone. *Islam,* which refers to action or submission, is commonly associated with establishing lawful (and unlawful) action, and might be said to be the domain of jurists (see Arkan in Chapter Ten). *Iman,* which refers to faith, is

The Muslim God?

It is and should be uncontroversial to claim that Muslims believe in, worship, and submit to Allah. One sees the use of the word "Allah" everywhere in the media, and Muslims do it as often as non-Muslims. It is rare, conversely, to hear about Muslims believing *in God*. The effect of this, whether intentional or not, is that Muslims are set apart from Jews and Christians. It is thought that Jews and Christians worship God, while Muslims worship Allah. People often talk about "the God of Islam," which makes it sound as if it is a different god. In fact, a controversy erupted at an American Christian university in 2015 when a political science professor claimed that Muslims and Christians both worship the same god. She was forced to resign.

As we saw in Chapter Five, the Arabic word Allah is more like the Greek *theos*, Latin *deus*, than the Hebrew name Yahweh. Allah is a contraction of two Arabic words, *al ilah*, meaning "the god" (like Greek). While in Islamic culture and piety, Allah has *become* a personal name for God, technically it is not the Muslim name for God, nor is Allah "the Muslim God."

"Allah" is the word used by Arabic speakers of any religion to refer to or address God, rather than indicating that the speaker is Muslim. To illustrate, Arab Christians who pray in Arabic also pray to Allah, yet they are not Muslim! Using the word "Allah" rather than "God" when speaking in English, perpetuates the notion that Muslims worship a different god.

commonly associated with establishing correct (and incorrect) ways of believing, and might be said to be the domain of theologians. There are different versions of the Hadith of Gabriel, and one of them presents six items of belief that are required of Muslims: belief in God, angels, revelation, prophets, afterlife, and predestination.

The first pillar of Islamic faith is belief in God. Here, Muslims share much more in common with Jews than with Trinitarian (which is to say most) Christians: Jews and Muslims share a sense of God's oneness that makes the Christian tripartite division of God incomprehensible. God for Muslims is indivisible. God is not just one, but the essence of oneness. In Islamic theology, this principle is called **tawhid**. If the acceptance of *tawhid* is a virtue, that is accepting God's oneness totally and worshipping God only and unconditionally, its opposing vice is said to be **shirk**. Many things qualify as *shirk* to

different Muslims: the refusal to worship God; the act of worshipping something in addition to God, such as another god, an idol, mountains, or the stars; worshipping God in the wrong way (which many Muslims claim of Christianity); claiming that someone else has greater power or wisdom than God; and praying to anything lower than God (e.g., angels, saints, spirits, etc.). Some Islamic theologians have even claimed that racism, elitism, materialism, and ambition can be understood as sub-categories of *shirk*. Modern radical Islamists (such as Daesh, al-Qaeda) consider democracy as *shirk*, because it takes authority away from God to govern society and gives it to humans.

The second pillar of faith concerns angels. In Islamic theology, angels are heavenly beings, made of light. They have no free will, in that they can do only what God commands of them, and they serve most commonly as messengers from God. Some angels play key roles in the mythic narratives of Islam. For example, the angel Gabriel – Jibril to Muslims of practically any Islamicate language – was the intermediary between God and all of the prophets, and was the one who revealed the Qur'an to Muhammad. Gabriel is one of the few angels mentioned by name in the Qur'an. The angel Uriel – Israfil to Arabic-speaking Muslims – is tasked with announcing the arrival of Judgment Day, which he will do by blowing a trumpet. There is an angel of death too, whose role it is to watch over the dying and to carry the extracted souls of the dead to God. Some Islamic traditions have given this angel the name Azrael, borrowed from Jewish tradition.

There is in addition another kind of non-human entity in Islamic cosmology, the jinn. Jinns are made of smokeless fire, and unlike angels, they have free will. There is debate in Islam about whether Satan was an angel or a jinn. Muslims who argue Satan was a jinn do so on the grounds that he defied God's command that all the heavenly beings should bow down before humans. An angel, they claim, cannot defy God. Satan on the other hand objected to the command, on the grounds that humans were beneath him – being created from mud, rather than fire – and so was cast from heaven. That would suggest he was an angel.

The third pillar of faith concerns the existence of revealed books. The tradition of Islamic theology expands on this to refer to the belief that God communicates with people in stages through revealed scriptures or books. God's revelation for Muslims culminates with the Qur'an, but it includes earlier revelations, such as the Torah, which was revealed to Moses, and the gospels, said to have been revealed to Jesus. In both cases, Islamic theology maintains that the original revelations to Moses and Jesus survive only in fragmentary form in the Torah and New Testament gospels, because that revelation was changed by Jews and Christians. This is in part what – in the Islamic way of thinking – necessitated the Qur'an, the final, perfect revelation of God to Muhammad.

The fourth pillar of faith is related to the third: the role of prophets. Islam, however, has two figures in this role where Judaism and Christianity have only one: *nabi* and *rasul*. Though confusing, it is best to translate

Revering the Prophet

Earlier in the chapter we encountered some evidence of Islamic reverence for Muhammad, in the form of theological narratives about him and the modeling of behavior based on his example. Another form of reverence can be seen in the epithets many Muslims say or write every time they refer to Muhammad. In speech, it is common to hear *salla llāhu 'alayhi wa-alehe wa-sallam* (prayer of God be upon him and his family and peace) or the shorter *alayhi as-salām* (peace be upon him).

There is a strong tendency in Islam to think of Arabic as the superior language, so some Muslims will speak the Arabic blessing even when they are English speakers. In writing, one commonly sees these blessings, Arabic and English alike, abbreviated: SWT, SAWS, PBUH. It can become a contest in piety to see if one can do this every time one refers to him by name, by title, or even pronoun, and to claim that abbreviations are lazy and not reverential enough.

nabi as prophet. This is the figure that brings a message to humanity from God. Generally, the "message" of a prophet claims that God is displeased in some way with the generation receiving the message. Prophets rarely deliver praise.

There are twenty-five prophets mentioned by name in the Qur'an, many of them shared with Jewish and Christian tradition, such as Adam, Abraham, Moses, David, Jesus, and John the Baptist. But some Islamic traditions claim that there have been 124,000, and in some circles over 200,000, prophets sent. In fact, the Qur'an (16.36) claims that a prophet has been sent to every community and group in the history of the world.

But there is a higher office than prophet, and that is occupied by the **rasul**. As a type of prophet, the *rasul* brings not only a message from God, but also something innovative, such as a new law or a new book, though it is not always known what the innovation was. So, for instance, Abraham, Moses, David, and Jesus were *rusul* (plural of *rasul*) for they brought forth books. It is important to remember that while all *rusul* are also *anbiya* (plural of *nabi*), not all *anbiya* are *rusul*; that is, *rasul* is the role with the greater honor.

The fifth pillar of faith concerns the Day of Judgment, also known as the Day of Resurrection and the Day of Reckoning. Judaism, Christianity, and Islam have very closely related understandings of eschatology, a term that refers to the study of the "last things" or the end time. So, much of what follows can be found in all three religions. Judgment Day brings time to a close, and brings all souls together to be judged by God. At the trumpet blast, all people will die in order to be brought before God for judgment according to their deeds. It is

said that good deeds and bad deeds are balanced by a merciful, just, and loving God, and those with a favorable balance will enter paradise, an everlasting life of bliss free of toil and death. God, however, is not only merciful and loving, but also demanding, so that those with an unfavorable balance on the Day of Judgment will be sent into hell, a place of torment and suffering. This last group, it is claimed, failed to heed the many warnings God sent through prophets and scripture to worship God and act justly.

Another way in which Christian and Islamic eschatology intersect revolves around signs and the return of Jesus, as well as the role of an Antichrist, or *Dajjal.* Theological speculation among Muslims and Christians concerning the nearing of the end imagines a surge in widespread violence, injustice, and sin. There is agreement among Muslims on the arrival of two figures in the final days: the **Mahdi** and Jesus. The *Mahdi* is the "guided one," who with God's assistance prepares the world and Islam for the end. Both Shi'a and Sunni Muslims expect the *Mahdi* to inaugurate the end time, but have one important difference: Sunni theologians do not think the identity of the *Mahdi* is yet known, whereas Shi'a theologians believe that the twelfth Imam is the *Mahdi.* The return of Jesus in Islamic eschatology, along with the *Mahdi,* is possible because of the Islamic belief that Jesus was taken up into heaven before he died on the cross.

The sixth and final pillar of faith is predestination, namely that all things are known to God. Next to *tawhid,* this is the most complex of the pillars, and as we shall see below, one of the more controversial. It comes down to the question of God's omniscience: do humans act freely, that is, can a person ever surprise God, or does God know what each human will do in advance of it happening? Most classical Islamic theologians came to the conclusion that if humans have true free will, such that even God does not know what they will do before they do it, then God is not omniscient, or all-knowing. This position seems to have been intolerable, so they tended to go further than their Jewish and Christian counterparts in the direction of **predestination**: God knows every event and decision in a person's life before she or he is even born. Whereas Jews leave the question in the form of a paradox, an unsolvable riddle, and Christians come to a myriad of different conclusions, Islam has gone the furthest in trying to produce a systematic theology to resolve the tension between free will and divine determination. This is the suggestion that God exists outside of time, without future or past. Thus, God simply knows. God does not know the future because there is no future for God, there is just knowledge. The relationship, therefore, between free will and divine determination is only difficult for humans, who live with a sense of present and future. It is this belief that informs the common Islamic practice of intoning *insha'allah*, meaning "If God wills it," before driving a car, starting a journey, or making future plans or promises. It articulates the notion that people do not know what lies in their future, but they believe that God does.

It is important to note that these six pillars of faith pertain to Sunni Muslims. Twelver Shi'a Muslims have what they call five foundations of the faith. Three of them closely resemble the Sunni pillars: *tawhid*, prophethood, and Judgment Day. The remaining two belong to them alone: justice (that

God is always fair and just) and leadership (that God approves of the line of twelve Imams, who were infallible). Shi'a Muslims reject outright the Sunni principle of predestination.

Sufism

Mysticism can be found in many religions. As a way of being religious, mysticism tends to privilege unification with the deity, ecstatic or out-of-body experiences, and trance states. These states and experiences tend to be achieved through the body: by self-denial of food by fasting or oxygen by breathing very slowly, by ingesting drugs, through meditation, or by becoming immersed in repetitive drumbeats, music, dance, or spoken words. As we saw above, Jewish mysticism is called Kabbalah and Christian mysticism does not have a special name.

Mysticism in Islam goes by the name Sufism. It is important to note that the term Sufi is not precisely equivalent to the terms Sunni and Shi'a. Sufism does not comprise a sect within Islam, but to a way of worshipping God. Thus, while it is inconceivable to imagine someone claiming to be both Sunni and Shi'a, Sufism can be found among Sunni and Shi'a Muslims alike. Needless to say, the sectarian animosity that usually exists between Shi'a and Sunni extends also into the ways each practices its Sufism.

The primary characteristic of Sufism is that the mystic seeks to love God unconditionally and to be united with God. Love of God might be said to start out with remembrance of God, or **dhikr**. To remember God is nearly to think of nothing else, to have every breath, thought, and action strive to be a remembrance of God. *Dhikr* also commonly involves the repetition of the ninety-nine names of God. In addition, Sufi writings lay out a process through which the love of God leads to nearness to God, which leads to bliss, which leads ultimately, for the saint, to *fana*. In *fana*, the self is annihilated because the mystic has been completely swallowed up by God. Once one has achieved this state, one can teach others how to achieve it. Indeed, Sufis reject the idea that these things can be learned in books, and instead insist that they can only be learned from teachers and with practice. Today, nearly a dozen Sufi orders claim to trace their origins back to one or another charismatic teacher or saint in the thirteenth or fourteenth century (and there are several other orders that developed more recently).

Sufis believe that the Qur'an is filled with mystical experiences and references, and that Muhammad himself is their model. For example, they see in the Night Journey (Sura 17 and 53), in which Muhammad travels to the heavens on his horse and encounters God and all the former prophets, as a model of the ultimate mystical experience to which they aspire.

Two features of ninth-century Islam seem to have stimulated the development of Sufism. First, while Islam was developing

Rumi

Rumi, whose full name was Jalal al-Din Muhammad Rumi, was a thirteenth-century poet, jurist, theologian, and Sufi mystic. He spent his adult years, and did all of his writing, in what is now Turkey, though he was born and raised in what is now north-east Afghanistan. He wrote mostly in the Persian language, but his works have been translated into many other languages. His greatest work, *Mathnawi* (sometimes also spelled as *Masnavi*) is widely considered one of the literary masterpieces of Persian culture. In fact, in 2014, Rumi was the best-selling poet in the United States. Examples of his poetry are as follows:

Wealth has no permanence:
it comes in the morning, and
at night it is scattered to the
winds.

Physical beauty too has no importance,
for a rosy face is made pale by a single
thorn-scratch.

Noble birth also is of small account, for such a one is befooled by money and horses.

There is many a nobleman's son who in riot and mischief has disgraced his father by his wicked deeds.

Do not court a man full of talent either, even if he be exquisite in that respect, and take warning from the example of Iblis.

Iblis had knowledge, but since he had not religious love, he beheld in Adam nothing but a figure of clay.

(*Mathnawi* VI: 255–260; From Reynold A. Nicholson, ed. London: Gibb Memorial Trust, 1925–1940, pp. 171–172)

Figure 67. The Whirling Dervishes are Sufis who are so called because they "whirl" as an expression of their remembrance (*dhikr*) of God.

a robust legal tradition and deep respect for the divine law, some felt that too much effort was being put there and not enough into a pure and simple love of God, regardless of law. Second, these people appear to have objected to the wealth, opulence, worldliness, and corruption that came with imperial expansion under the Abbasids. Sufism then originally involved the rejection of wealth and power, the self-denial of comfort, the love of God without fear, reward, or self-interest, and the minimization of Islamic law. The name Sufi possibly derives from the fact that the earliest Islamic mystics wore rough and uncomfortable wool clothing (*suf*), a form of self-denial that was surely influenced by the Islamic encounter with Christian ascetics.

The Sufi privileging of love over legal observance sometimes took on the rejection of legal observance altogether. This tendency can be called antinomian, and it was a source of great distrust from other Muslims.

So, for instance, a tenth-century Sufi mystic named Al-Hallaj is famous for coming out of an ecstatic trance in which he had been unified with God, and proclaiming "I am the Truth." It was a claim that sounded, to the non-Sufi ear, like a claim to be God. He was promptly executed. Al-Ghazali, in the eleventh century, gave up a promising career as a Sunni jurist to follow the Sufi path, and he eventually succeeded in legitimating Sufism in the eyes of most Sunni Muslims. If the early instantiations of Sufism can be called "intoxicated" mysticism, al-Ghazali's was definitely a "sober" mysticism. But even though it could be claimed after al-Ghazali that Sufis upheld every aspect of shariah (or Islamic religious law), there remained an antinomian strain, which can be seen in the ruminations of a fourteenth-century Persian poet named Hafez concerning the spilling of wine on a prayer rug. In addition, despite the generally widespread appreciation of Sufism among most Muslims, strains of violent rejection of Sufism can be found in many modern Islamist groups, because they see their beliefs and practices as religious innovation and *shirk*.

Sufism was not merely a set of ascetic and mystical practices. It also came to have profound political implications, for Sufism had a critical role in the spread of Islam. Sufis spread from Baghdad eastward into Persia, South Asia, and India, as well as into Africa with missionary zeal. Often, along with merchants, Sufis were the first Muslims to arrive in new lands. They would settle and interact with local populations, and their teachings of universal love and harmony among people was very attractive. Conversions naturally followed. Thus, Sufism continues to have a significant influence on the Islam one finds from Bangladesh to Indonesia. Not surprisingly, this influence continues to be met with suspicion and hostility in some Islamic circles.

There have been many well-known, widely admired, and influential Sufis over the course of Islamic history. For instance, **Rabia Basri** was an extremely poor woman in eighth-century Iraq. She became one of the most influential Sufi mystics, which illustrates how women can hold positions of prominence in mystical circles that are normally unavailable to them in more orthodox circles. But by far the most well known of Sufis is the poet and storyteller Rumi (see text box, p. 175). Rumi's writings are widely appreciated among Muslims and by non-Muslims also, especially in North America. Likewise, Western non-Muslims have been especially fascinated by the Whirling Dervishes, the most recognizable Sufi order to non-Muslims. Interestingly, the Whirling Dervishes belong to the Sufi order founded by followers of Rumi, known as the Mevlevi Order.

Islamic Philosophy and Speculative Theology

Islam, no less than Judaism and Christianity, has struggled with the inherent tension between revelation and reason. The question comes down to this: how are those who worship God to know about the world around them? By what has been revealed in scripture or by what they observe in the natural world? And by extension, how much room is there for creative or innovative theological speculation? Among Sunni Muslims, Al-Kindi (d. 870 CE) was an early supporter of the movement to translate classical Greek authors (e.g., Plato and Aristotle) into Arabic. He himself wrote treatises on Aristotelian philosophy. He was convinced that classical philosophy could be used to address Islamic questions, and also to enrich one's understanding of God's creation.

The most famous of Islamic philosophers in the Sunni tradition is the Persian Ibn Sina (d. 1037). Ibn Sina was the first to posit an argument for the existence of God later used by the Christian theologian Thomas Aquinas (see Chapter Six). Developing and advancing ideas found also in Aristotle, Ibn Sina deduced the existence of God by distinguishing between necessity and contingency. Simplified, the logical argument claims that many things in the world come and go; their existence is contingent on something necessarily creating and sustaining them. This produces a chain of necessary beings and the contingent things they cause. This chain must logically start somewhere, namely with God, the original necessary and uncontingent cause.

The work of these philosophers was and continues to be controversial for three reasons. First, it suggests that the Qur'an is not sufficient as the sole source of one's knowledge of the world. Second, many Muslims consider it problematic to import something "foreign" (that is, non-Islamic philosophy) to understand any feature of Islam. This might have been made worse by the final source of controversy: Islamic philosophers often arrived at conclusions that contradicted the Qur'an. Thus, philosophy has faced much criticism throughout the history of Islam. The battle against philosophy, and Ibn Sina in particular, was led by al-Ghazali's eleventh-century work, *Incoherence of the Philosophers*. He did not have the last word, however: a generation later, Ibn Rushd retaliated with a work entitled *The Incoherence of the Incoherence*, and Ibn Sina's philosophy continued to exert profound influence on Islam.

If philosophy was controversial in Sunni circles, **kalam** was even more controversial. *Kalam* was an approach to Islamic theology that considered itself rational. *Kalam* was adopted and honed by the Mutazilites, who emerged in eighth-century Basra. Total commitment to the principle of divine unity (that God is one and indivisible) and to divine justice (that God is just and fair) drove Mutazilites to adopt some highly controversial theological conclusions. For instance, they outright rejected one of the pillars of faith,

predestination, because they could not reconcile that principle with divine justice. Predestination claims that God programs the future and humans act out their parts, good and bad. Put differently, humans are not actually in control of their actions, for even before their birth, their actions have been preordained by an all-powerful and all-knowing God. Yet Mutazilites asked, how is it just for God to punish humans for actions they were unable to avoid doing because God created them predisposed to those actions? For them, a just God would require people to be freely righteous and to submit, and then punish them for choosing unrighteous conduct.

Shi'a theology has not tended to be as troubled by innovative and speculative theology as has Sunni theology, and indeed Shi'a Muslims embraced a good deal of the Mutazilite thinking that Sunni Muslims rejected. Though such openness to innovation was sometimes resisted by concerned Shi'a theologians, it did despite that become a key component of Shi'a identity. To this end, Shi'a Muslims developed highly innovative theologies concerning the divine knowledge to which their Imams had unique access, the idea of occultation to explain how their twelfth Imam had not died but been taken by God into hiding, and the role of Bab, who served as agent between the Hidden Imam and the Shi'a community. Much of this innovative thought can be traced to the oral traditions of the teaching of the sixth Imam, Jafar.

Figure 68. The 20 Somoni banknote from Tajikistan carries the image of Ibn Sina, though he was born in what is now Uzbekistan. Renowned for his work in philosophy, medicine, and mathematics, Ibn Sina is also memorialized throughout Iran, in the names of universities, medical research institutes, and schools.

Islamic Theological Writings

Islamic theology largely rests on three collections of writing: the Qur'an, the Hadith, and the Tafsir.

Figure 69. Tree of life mosaic in the reception hall of the bath complex at Khirbat al-Mafjar, an Umayyad palace complex of the Early Islamic Period, 724–743 CE or 743–746 CE. West Bank, Palestine.

Qur'an

According to Islamic tradition, when Muhammad was about forty years old, he began to receive revelations from God delivered by the angel Gabriel. These revelations continued to come over the next twenty-two years, until Muhammad died. Further, Islamic tradition maintains that the material of the Qur'an was memorized perfectly as it was recited by Muhammad after each revelation, and that the creation of the written text under the command of Uthman, who was caliph 644–656 CE, was nothing more than a device to stabilize that memory.

There are a few interrelated beliefs embedded in this set of narratives. First, the Qur'an was not a performance or a composition, but a recitation, which is the meaning of the word Qur'an. Second, Muhammad had no creative role at all in the creation or composition of the Qur'an, nor in its recording and collection; he merely recited to those around him perfectly and dutifully what was recited to him. And finally, Muhammad was illiterate and uneducated. This last point is key, for on it hinges the key miracle of Islamic tradition, a religion with few foundational miracle claims. Because Muhammad was illiterate and uneducated, the beauty and power that many Muslims see in the Qur'an cannot derive from his own creativity or genius. It derives, therefore, exclusively from God. And because Muhammad was undefiled – according to a common Islamic way of putting it – by worldly knowledge, he represents the perfectly pure conduit for the message of God. There is then a highly complex and developed Islamic theology about the Qur'an and the role of Muhammad in its revelation to humans.

Another key theological belief about the Qur'an is that the arrangement of suras (chapters or sections) was chosen by Muhammad and sanctioned by God, though

The Mutazilites

The Mutazilites were a ninth–tenth-century Islamic movement renowned – and controversial – for their reliance on rational as opposed to dogmatic argumentation. So, for instance, while most Muslims believed that humans lacked free will and that God knows all things in advance – a doctrine called predestination – the Mutazilites were of the opinion that this made God unjust. That is, commitment to the belief that God is just requires, they argued, human freedom to act faithfully or badly, and to be rewarded or punished accordingly on account of their decisions. For Sunni opponents of Mutazilites, predestination was a position that derived from God's omnipotence and omniscience. Opponents argued that the Mutazilite position of human free will directly undermined God's power.

Another famous debate concerned the nature of the Qur'an. Mutazilites argued that though the Qur'an was the word of God, it was so by virtue of having been revealed by God to Muhammad in real time. That is to say, the Qur'an did not exist until it was created by the act of God's "speech" and revelation to Muhammad. Against this, Sunni opponents of the Mutazilites maintained that the Qur'an was eternal, there with God as a "heavenly tablet" since creation.

The Mutazilites were defeated, and their positions branded heretical. This happened in part because the positions of their Sunni opponents were more popular, and because Mutazilites were influential with the Shi'a in the eleventh century – something that naturally made them suspect to Sunni Muslims. In the end, the Sunni position of the eternal and uncreated Qur'an sounds surprisingly like the language most Christians use of Jesus – *homoousion*, one being and co-eternal with God.

the version of the Qur'an that came to be most widely used by Muslims was the one Uthman produced and distributed.

Many people find the Qur'an difficult to read. The arrangement of the suras appears generally (though far from consistently) to have been governed by order of length, longest to shortest, rather than by chronology, by theme, or by genre. The effect is that the material jumps from prophetic indictments of unrighteous behavior to reinterpretations of Israelite prophets to legal material and from location to location and one time to another. Theologians have devised ways to justify this arrangement. For example, some observe that the suras each sit independently in their order and are not reliant for meaning on the suras around them. Alternatively, some Islamic commentators claim that the Qur'an's coherence is found in a ring structure, rather than in sequential structure.

It is also the case that while the shorter suras have a certain topical coherence, the long suras frequently shift abruptly from one topic to another. In addition, there are many narrative gaps in the text, which the reader must fill in. This characteristic of the text was the source of one of the first polemical attacks against the legitimacy of Islam from Christians in the ninth century: how can a text that, from the Christian perspective, is so chaotic and shows so little concern for clarity and pleasing arrangement reasonably claim divine origin? By the end of the tenth century, Islamic apologists settled on two defenses of the Qur'an, and therefore of Islam: inimitability and miracle. The first, drawn from certain verses within the Qur'an, argued that God had created a text the qualities of which no human could ever hope to imitate, so sacred and beautiful was it. The gaps in the text that Christians complained about, Muslims claimed were virtues, an economy of language that is God's own prerogative and ability. Their secondary defense against Christian criticisms entailed the claim that, since Muhammad was wholly illiterate, the Qur'an itself is a miracle. This was useful particularly against Christian critics who felt that miracles were the mark of true religion. And, needless

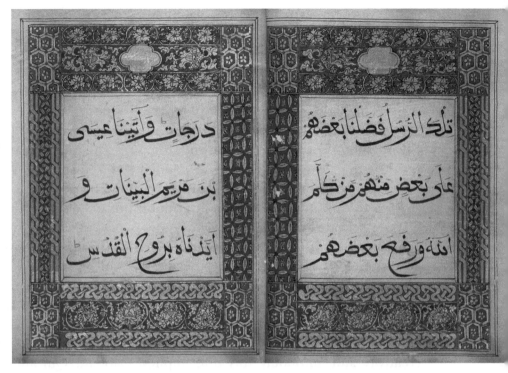

Figure 70. Illustration on a page of an illuminated Qur'an from the seventeenth-century Ottoman Empire. The passage shown here is the Fatiha, the opening sura of the Qur'an.

The Fatiha

The Fatiha is the opening sura of the Qur'an, and as such holds pride of place. This short sura is the most recited segment of the Qur'an, being said seventeen times a day (the total number of rakas in Islamic prayer; see Chapter Ten), at births, weddings, and at funerals, official events, or the start of a journey.

As a summary of the Qur'an, note the following themes from the Fatiha. First, there is only one God, master of all. Second, people can be separated into two groups: those who are blessed by God and those who go astray and thus incur God's anger. Third, there is one straight path to God, thus anyone not on that path has gone astray. Fourth, taking the straight path requires guidance, which God grants. And finally, while God is loving, merciful, and compassionate, he is also prone to anger, and people need to worry about Judgment Day. Of course, the Qur'an says much more than this, but these five themes are repeated countless times throughout it.

In the Name of God, the Merciful, the Compassionate. Praise (be) to God, Lord of the worlds, the Merciful, the Compassionate, Master of the Day of Judgment. You we serve and You we seek for help. Guide us to the straight path: the path of those whom You have blessed, not (the path) of those on whom (Your) anger falls, nor of those who go astray.

(Translation from A.J. Droge, *The Qur'an*. Sheffield: Equinox Publishing, 2012)

to say, Muslim polemicists were able to level many of their own attacks against the divine legitimacy of the New Testament. One ought not to think that medieval Christians had the last or definitive word in the rivalry between these two religions!

One key difference between Judaism and Christianity, on the one hand, and Islam on the other concerns the origins of their scriptures. Jews and Christians argue for and assume the divine authority or inspiration of their scriptures, but ultimately acknowledge that their scriptures had *several authors*. The common view of the Qur'an among Muslims is different: it is not a collection of writings by different people, and the sole person involved in it – Muhammad – is not conceived of as an author, with the authorial creativity and autonomy this title implies. Because the Qur'an is thought of as the unchanged and unchangeable word of God, many Muslims consider both the content and the object itself to be deeply sacred. This is reflected in a variety of practices and beliefs that different Muslims around the world have developed concerning the treatment of the Qur'an: a translated Qur'an is not really a Qur'an, in part because too much of the power and beauty of the Arabic original cannot be replicated in any other language, and by extension, God is no longer present in a text that has been translated; only someone who has recently done ablutions, that is, purification rituals, should be allowed to touch a Qur'an, which naturally eliminates all non-Muslims; a Qur'an should not be carried below the waist, should never have other books stacked upon it, and should never be carried into impure places, such as a bathroom; the Qur'an is commonly adored and kissed, and is sometimes worn in

miniature form around the neck as an amulet; one might pass under a Qur'an when beginning a long journey, and passages from it carried on the body are believed to have protective and also healing qualities; the Qur'an is made exquisitely beautiful by illumination, by calligraphy, and with the voice.

The Arabic of the Qur'an is best described as a rhymed prose: not quite poetry but not always merely prose because of the frequency of rhyme and rhythm. There are a number of different kinds of material one finds within the Qur'an. Much of it is concerned with eschatology, or the end of time. Central here are the topics of the Day of Judgment (also called the Last Day) and the afterlife, and in several places in the Qur'an, the end of time is imagined to be close at hand and violent. Qur'anic statements on the afterlife imagine a bodily resurrection for those who gain eternal life. One also encounters a good deal of prophetic material, that is strict instructions on ethical, moral, and legal conduct: the just treatment of widows and the poor, attacks on polytheism and illustrations of proper belief in the one God, prohibition of usury and the consumption of alcohol and other laws, and treatment of key practices like prayer and fasting. It also has much to say about many previous prophets, like Moses, David, Isaac, and Jesus, though naturally it offers a unique perspective that sometimes differs quite markedly from Jewish and Christian perspectives on these figures. And finally, one finds in the Qur'an narratives on and allusions to the early history of the Islamic movement (e.g., battles, persecution in Mecca). As a whole, the Qur'an provides the foundation of Islamic thinking about God, monotheism, creation, the nature of human experience and the plight of the human soul, in other words the place of humans in an unfolding cosmic history in which good and evil are in constant battle.

Hadith

A hadith is a report concerning a saying or an action of Muhammad when he was not reciting the Qur'an, but also includes reports not of things he said but of things he allowed to happen in his presence. These sayings and reports relate to his role as religious and political leader of the community, and it is almost universally assumed by later Muslims that if something happened in Muhammad's presence and he did not comment negatively on it, then that thing must be permitted. Because Muhammad came to be considered the very best example of what it meant to be faithful and pious to God, and because future decisions about correct practice and directions for Islamic communities were based on the example, or **Sunnah**, provided by the actions and sayings of Muhammad, the motivation was very high for traditions of Muhammad to be fabricated. Islamic scholarly tradition clearly acknowledges this fact in two ways: the first was the need to develop criteria intended to distinguish reliable from unreliable sayings; the second is the claim that hadith collectors encountered several hundred thousand sayings of Muhammad, yet accepted as authentic only a small percentage of them.

In attempting to filter the authentic hadiths from fabricated ones, collectors focused on the support, or *isnad*, for that saying or example of conduct. The *isnad* is always a chain of transmission, from the most recent moving backwards to reach someone in Muhammad's inner circle. Each hadith has two parts: the chain of transmission followed by the saying or act of Muhammad. The following comes from the hadith collection of Muslim ibn al-Hajjaj. It does not report a saying of Muhammad, but an action. This hadith would have been used to establish that it was permissible to drink milk fresh from an animal.

> Abd Allah ibn Muadh al-Anbari told us that he was told by Shuba on the authority of Abu Ishaq on the authority of al-Bara who said that Abu Bakr the Truthful said, "When we went from Mecca to Medina with the Prophet, we passed by a shepherd. God's Messenger had become thirsty, so I milked [an animal] and brought some milk to him. He drank it until his thirst was quenched."
>
> (From Juan E. Campo, ed. *Encyclopedia of Islam*, New York: Facts on File, 2009, p. 278)

Sometimes investigative work was used by the early compilers to assess the legitimacy of the *isnad* claims. For example, an investigator might ask whether there is evidence that Shuba ever encountered Abu Ishaq, or that they passed though the same city at the same time, such that one might be able to hear a saying of Muhammad from the other. Or one might search for missing or invented links elsewhere. Problems like these would undermine the reliability of a hadith. In addition, the investigators claim to have been interested in the reputations of the transmitters – if they were deemed to be good and pious Muslims, their credibility was assumed. Given that the hadith collectors were working 200–300 years after the death of Muhammad, the historicity of these encounters and the reputations and piety of the transmitters cannot have been easy to assess. Two contradictory positions

Figure 71. The Mausoleum of Imam al-Bukhari near Samarkand, Uzbekistan, is a common site of Islamic pilgrimage.

arrive at different conclusions than the early compilers.

Nonetheless, the most common position among religious Muslims is that the hadiths as found in the current collections were thoroughly investigated by the compilers and found to be reliable (they call them "sound"). Eventually ten different collections of hadiths were produced, six that are revered by Sunni and Zaidi Muslims, and four that are revered by Imami Shi'a Muslims. As a rule, Imamis reject the criteria used in the collection of the Sunni hadiths, so they use those collections sparingly. Of the six Sunni hadith collections, two stand out as the most respected: one by Muhammad al-Bukhari (d. 870 CE) and the other by Muslim ibn al-Hajjaj (d. 874 CE), who lived in ninth-century Uzbekistan and north-east Iran respectively. Shi'a Muslims turned to hadith collection a little later than Sunni Muslims did. Shi'a hadiths are found in what are called the Four Books, each of which they revere equally. The earliest of them was written by al-Kulayni (d. 941 CE).

The hadith collection of al-Bukhari has ninety-three chapters and a total of 7563 individual hadiths. The topics covered range widely, from the theological (revelation, belief, monotheism, creation, prophecy, and so on) to the practical (prayer, pilgrimage, charity, fasting, business, justice, conflict resolution, marriage, diet, apostasy, and many more). They offer an interesting glimpse into what concerned Muslims most in the third century of the development of Islamic religion and community.

on the reliability of the hadith collections can be seen in Islamic tradition: one is the belief that men speaking about sacred matters would not lie, and the second is that the collectors were surely susceptible to human limitations. Not surprisingly, increased historical scrutiny is being paid to the *isnad* claims and the text of the sayings today by scholars of Islam, and sometimes they

If the Qur'an represents the word of God, the hadiths represent the word of

Muhammad. Because of the deeply held belief that Muhammad was incapable of error, however, those sayings are considered as good as the word of God for many Muslims. In fact, as we shall see in the discussion of shariah (see Chapter Ten), the hadith are second in authority only to the Qur'an in establishing lawful and unlawful behavior. Thus, al-Bukhari, the compiler of the most revered Sunni hadith collection, is himself adored in Islam (see Figure 71).

Tafsir

As the authority of the Qur'an developed, and as it came to serve as the primary source for determining proper and ideal Islamic conduct and setting legal precedent, it also became apparent that serious scholarly attention had to be devoted to the text, its structure, its meaning, and its qualities. The Qur'anic commentary tradition was the result, and that tradition is vast, diverse, and extremely influential in Islamic theology. The author of a *tafsir*, or commentary, tended to comment on each chapter and verse, explain the origin, meaning, and significance of words and phrases, always following the order of the Qur'an, and commenting upon the entirety of the text.

While early Islamic scholars focused on the difficulties of the Qur'anic text – creating lists of passages the meaning of which was made ambiguous by gaps, by subject–verb disagreement, by nouns with shifting gender, and by variant readings – Christian polemic forced Muslims to rally around the text, and as a result concern for these issues fell away. Instead, interpreters began to focus exclusively on meaning. Sometimes the commentators were most interested in the language, literary qualities, and grammar of the Qur'anic Arabic, sometimes in reconstructing the earliest history of Islamic origins, sometimes in the juridical or legal aspects of the text, sometimes in explaining the surface meaning of the passages, and sometimes in discovering the mystical or esoteric meaning of the passages. Those most commonly involved in this last type of commentary were usually either Sufis or Shi'a; both traditions were motivated to explore esoteric readings: that is, readings that sometimes depart quite creatively from the surface meaning of the texts. Arguably the most respected Sunni commentary is that by al-Tabari (who died in 923 CE). The teachings of Jafar, the sixth in the line of Shi'a Imams, were compiled into a highly respected Shi'a commentary. And when the Sufi poet Rumi titled his work *Mathnawi* he implied that it was a mystical commentary on the whole of the Qur'an.

All commentaries focus on the Arabic text, and most of the classical commentaries were written in Arabic, but there are also a number of highly influential Persian commentaries. The writing of commentaries continues into the present day, where now they might address themes like the challenges of modernity. Here, the tafsir can be separated into two categories: those that seek to modernize the meaning and interpretation of passages that might strike the modern ear as problematic (e.g., passages pertaining to the control and discipline of women), and those that argue that God's timeless word cannot be made to fit into passing fads and mores. Thus, Qur'anic commentaries are commonly a reflection of the theological needs and interests of the community.

Chapter Summary

Islamic texts represent Muhammad as the final and perfect messenger in a long line of messengers and prophets, including Moses, Isaiah, John the Baptist, Jesus, and some non-biblical figures as well. Islamic theological sources all revolve around Muhammad: they are biographical (siras and hadiths) and revelatory (Qur'an), or they are interpretations of these (tafsir). Throughout these theological sources, Muhammad is pure, without error, a perfect model of faithfulness and submission to God. This can be seen as well in the pillars of faith, of which in the Sunni tradition there are six: belief in God's oneness, angels, revelation, prophets, afterlife, and predestination. Islamic eschatology is quite like Jewish and Christian eschatology, in that it involves the coming of a messianic figure to inaugurate the end of linear time. This chapter also considered Sufism, its early radical history and its later, subdued history in which it comes to infuse many parts of Islamic religion.

Glossary

Dhikr. Can apply to any instance of silent repetition of phrases, often Qur'anic, but most commonly it refers to the Sufi goal of constant remembrance of God, as the best strategy against forgetfulness of God.

Fana: a Sufi term meaning annihilation, it refers to the annihilation of the boundary or distinction between God and self, and it is a state achieved when the self has been completely swallowed up by the divine. The result is said to be an awareness of the total unity of God and creation. This is the highest state of mystical experience.

Isnad. The chain of transmission that informs the claims of authenticity concerning the sound hadiths. Thus they are commonly constructed in this way: "so-and-so heard from so-and-so who heard from so-and-so who was a companion of the Prophet that . . ."

Kalam. A form of rationalist theology, most evident among the Mutazilites. It was called rationalist because proponents of the approach were willing to accept logical conclusions even when they contradicted divine revelation. For instance, their position that God is just led them to conclude that God cannot know and determine what humans will do before they do it. Yet this was understood to contradict Qur'an and Hadith, which claim that God is all-knowing.

Mahdi. Meaning "guided one," the *Mahdi* will appear and rule for a period just preceding the Day of Judgment, and this will happen at the same time as the Second Coming of Jesus. Sunni tradition claims that the identity of the *Mahdi* is not yet known, while Shi'a tradition claims that the *Mahdi* will be the twelfth Imam having come out of hiding.

Predestination. The sixth, and most theologically complex and divisive of the pillars of faith. At its simplest, predestination rests on the conviction that God's knowledge is not limited in any way. Therefore, if God is all-knowing (omniscient), then God must know what each individual will do before she or he has done it, even before that person is born.

Rabia Basri. Born in Basra (in what is now Iraq), and therefore Persian culturally, Rabia

Basri was a Sufi mystic and poet. Her poetry, like much Sufi poetry, expresses a wholesale rejection of fear (of judgment) as the motivation for worshipping God, and in its place puts only love.

Rasul. A type of prophet, but more than a prophet (*nabi*). A *rasul* brings something new, something innovative, most commonly a "book." Thus, Moses, David, and Jesus are designated as *rasul* in Islam, because of the "books" associated with each of them (Torah, Psalms, and New Testament respectively), as is of course Muhammad.

Shirk. The sin of associating anything with, or placing anything above, God. The charge of committing the error of *shirk* has been applied to polytheists or idolaters (because they place other gods alongside God), atheists (for placing nothingness alongside God), as well as to Muslims who follow a law or teaching other than God's law. Christianity, because of the Trinity, can also be considered *shirk*.

Sunnah. Refers to custom, as in the custom of Muhammad. The hadiths record sayings by and stories about Muhammad, which together provide a collection of examples of how Muhammad lived and taught others to live in submission to God. This word is the origin of the term Sunni. It articulates the belief that unlike the Shi'a who rallied around Ali, they (the Sunni) followed the customs of Muhammad.

Tawhid. The Islamic principle of monotheism. God is not only one, but is wholly, completely, and thoroughly one. God cannot be partitioned, divided or split off in any manner.

Ummah. The community of Muslims, it carries political and religious overtones equally, since an Ummah imagines people living in unity, which requires governance and a legal structure, in submission to God.

Other Important Vocabulary

Antinomian	al-Ghazali	*Jahiliyya*	*Nabi*
Bab	Hadith	Jinn	Omniscience
al-Bukhari	Ibn Sina	Al-Kindi	Rumi
Dajjal	*Ihsan*	Mevlevi Order	Sira
Eschatology	*Iman*	Mutazilites	Tafsir

Discussion Questions

1. Using the narratives of Muhammad, how might you articulate the relationship and difference between history and mythology?

2. One feature of Islam is that it is the last of these religions to develop. It thus inherits all that came before it, but of course it also reshapes it. Consider the history, historical context, and the rhetorical claims that direct the Islamic reshaping of the past.

3. Some might observe that there are many fewer miracles (e.g., events that defy the limitations of nature, or supernatural experiences) in Islam than in Christianity. Setting aside the question of quantity, how might you assess the function of the miracle claims themselves (the cleaning of Muhammad's heart, the Night Journey, the claim that Muhammad was illiterate)? Do Christian and Islamic miracle stories do the same work?

4. The Qur'an is to Islam as Jesus is to Christianity. Can you think of ways the Qur'an–Jesus analogy works, and ways in which it breaks down?

Recommended Reading

Ali, Kecia. 2014. *The Lives of Muhammad*. Cambridge, MA: Harvard University Press.

Nasr, Seyyed Hossein, ed. 2015. *The Study Quran*. New York: HarperCollins.

Schimmel, Annemarie. 1975. *Mystical Dimensions of Islam*. Chapel Hill, NC: University of North Carolina Press.

Watt, Montgomery. 1962. *Islamic Philosophy and Theology*. Edinburgh: Edinburgh University Press.

Recommended Websites

http://www.sandowbirk.com/paintings/recent-works

- American Qur'an is an artistic enterprise which depicts American political and cultural scenes in traditional Qur'anic calligraphy.

http://quran.com

- An easy-to-use and accessible source for the text of the Qur'an.

http://www.sahih-bukhari.com

- Contains images of mosques from around the world, as well as abbreviated *isnads*.

http://www.muslimphilosophy.com/index.html

- Introduction to Islamic philosophy and philosophers.

—Part Three—
Orthopraxies

Orthopraxy means correct action, and as such pertains both to the concern that some actions be done correctly, but also to a concern with delineating which actions are allowed and which are not. Orthopraxic is a term commonly used to describe religions with *laws*, such as Judaism and Islam. Jews and Muslims over the centuries have put considerable effort into matters of law. At its most basic, the question becomes: how does one live according to the law of God? This debate is complex enough when it occurs among people from different parts of the world with different cultural traditions and practices. It becomes exponentially more complex when we add *change* to the equation. What I mean is this: when coffee, cell phones, in vitro fertilization, artificial contraception, and high-rise apartment towers are all developed, those who strive to live by God's law must revisit the question anew every time: namely, is this new thing, activity, or practice lawful in the eyes of God? Since change is constant, so then is the religious debate about what is lawful or unlawful.

Jewish tradition maintains that there are 613 *mitzvot* (or commandments) in the Torah, and the interpretation, defense, and execution of these laws has required the constant presence, preparation, and attention of High Priests, Rabbis, and theologians. The Talmud is almost entirely concerned with religious law as it relates to daily living, and the interpretive and apologetic tradition relating to the Talmud is every bit as rich as for the Torah. Jewish legal debates have sought to establish proper dress and diet, proper handling of animals and money, marriage and purity, proper actions of prayer, and so on. And although the resolutions to these various religious debates – or halakhah – differ from one Jewish community to the next, the debates themselves are very common.

Like Judaism, Islam has a religious law – shariah. And, like Jews, Muslims characteristically wonder how to live by God's law, not only in fifteenth-century Persia but in twenty-first-century Canada, United States, and Great Britain. Muslims face many of the same challenges today that Jews faced in Europe and North America in the nineteenth century: namely, how to live by God's law as minorities. Of course, every Muslim

Figure 72. "Talmud Readers," an early-twentieth-century painting by Adolf Behrman.

But what is religious *practice*? What makes a practice *religious*? When someone is *being* religious, that is, when she is practicing her religion, what does that look like? How would an observer *see* that person being religious?

The answer to these questions is surprisingly straightforward: any action or activity that is grounded in a person's religious convictions is a religious practice, no matter what that action is, and no matter whether anyone else likes it. It might well be that fellow members of a religion disagree on what constitutes proper "religious" practice. Some, for instance, might argue that lighting a candle and praying to a saint are not appropriate actions. But for the scholar, this disagreement itself is something worth studying, and we do not determine who is right. For us, if a person claims some action is religious, it is religious. If there is debate, it is there to be analyzed.

When thinking about religious practice, it is also important to consider more than the obvious: holy days and law. The decision to be vegetarian could be a religious one, though your religion makes no such demand. So too with the decision to get a tattoo, or *not*, the decision not to shave your beard or the decision to shave your head, your choice of career, how to vote in elections, whether to drive a car, what movies you watch or music you listen to. If religious motivation shapes a person's actions, those actions are religious. It is as simple as that.

The term orthopraxy might not, therefore, apply in precisely the same way in Judaism, Christianity, and Islam, but the difference is one of degree, not of kind. One does not need religious law in order to *practice* religion. Just because Christians do not observe kosher or halal eating restrictions does not

answers this question differently, but the concern is paramount for many.

It can seem intuitive to claim that Christianity is different in this regard from Judaism and Islam. After all, Christianity does not have an equivalent term for shariah or halakhah. What is more, the energy that Jews and Muslims have directed towards legal thinking and debate Christians appear to have directed towards creedal thinking and debate. It would be a mistake to conclude from this that Christians are not concerned with practice. They are, every day. What is more, Catholic Christians do have a very rich history of legal development, in Canon Law. So it really cannot be claimed that Christianity lacks a law. It is merely the case that law and practice function differently for Christians than for Jews and Muslims.

mean that practice matters less in Christianity than it does in Judaism and Islam. In the chapters that follow, we shall look at how religion is practiced by Jews, Christians, and Muslims alike.

Another feature of practice relates to time, and to mark time one needs a calendar. But calendars do not merely mark time; they also mark a community. Should we be surprised that Jews, Christians, and Muslims all have different calendars? Even Western and Eastern Christians have different calendars. Some Eastern Orthodox Christians are considering adopting the calendar used by Catholics and Protestants, and predictably, the discussion is causing tension among the Eastern churches.

It makes sense to start with the Islamic calendar, for it is the simplest. The Islamic calendar contains twelve months of 29–30 days each, and follows an exclusively lunar cycle. The sole Islamic holy day that adheres to the solar calendar is the Persian New Year called Nowruz. The lunar calendar is eleven days shorter than the solar calendar. Thus, to those who follow a solar calendar, Islamic holy days appear to cycle backwards through the year, for each one happens eleven days earlier than in the previous year. This works because most Muslim holy days are not tied to the agricultural or season cycle. That is, there is no Islamic holy day connected to the harvest.

But this is not the case with Jewish holy days. Though Judaism prefers the lunar calendar, many of its holy days do have seasonal significance as well as theological significance. This requires the Jewish calendar to

Figure 73. The Christian liturgical calendar marks important events, such as the feast of Epiphany (the visit of the Magi), as portrayed in this tapestry, "The Adoration of the Magi," by Edward Burne-Jones (1904).

be a hybrid of lunar and solar cycles, which is accomplished with the introduction of an extra month added every two to three years. That additional month is called an intercalary month. Thus, following the lunar calendar, a Jewish holy day will be eleven days earlier each year, until an additional month bumps the holy day back up a month. This allows a holy day with connections to the fall harvest to stay in the general season of autumn, while still following a lunar cycle.

In contrast to Islam and Judaism, the Christian calendar is solar, but not exclusively. The exception is Easter. Because Easter celebrates the resurrection of Jesus, who was in Jerusalem for Pesach when he died, it came to be important to Christians for Easter to occur near Passover. Thus, the timing of Easter has to be calculated, unlike the other Christian holy days.

Figure 74. Nowruz in the Kurdish-Iranian village Toop Aghaj.
(See also a more contemporary celebration of Nowruz in Figure 95.)

—8—

Jewish Practice and Holy Days

Chapter Overview	
Discussing thousands of years of Jewish practices would be impossible in so short a survey, so this chapter focuses on modern Jewish practices, though some of the practices do go back, in some form, thousands of years. Understanding religious practice is important because much can be expressed in practice, such as one's understanding of God and one's relationship with competing	groups, whether inside or outside of the religion, whether majority or minority. In addition, practice is one of the key ways that communal identity is expressed. This chapter summarizes some common Jewish practices and the widely observed holy days. Finally, to speak of practice is also to speak of Jewish culture, Jewish homes, and Jewish life.

Jewish Practices

Modern Jewish Practice

Europe in the eighteenth and nineteenth centuries was changing. The power of the Catholic Church in France was reduced, and Protestants and Jews were given equal political rights. So started the **Jewish Emancipation**: the gradual removal of state-sanctioned discrimination against Jews in many Christian European countries. Many Jews eagerly embraced the opportunity to participate in society, in culture, and in politics fully, freely, and legally. Some of them eventually came to the position that Jewish traditions and laws relating to dress, diet, and liturgy could be,

and indeed needed to be, modernized. Taking their cue from Protestants around them, they took the position that religion was an internal state, a mind-set, not an external set of requirements relating to dress, diet, ritual practices, and language.

Some Jews, however, while doubtlessly pleased at the prospect of being free from discrimination and persecution, perhaps worried that these new freedoms and the attractiveness of modern secularism would erode and eventually destroy Jewish identity and religion. It is almost as if for these Jews

Figure 75. An 1806 French print depicting Napoleon Bonaparte emancipating the Jews.

be more open to modernization than Orthodox Jews, but reject the radical changes of some groups of Reform Judaism.

These labels, however, are far from perfect. First of all, they invite people to imagine a uniformity within each group that simply does not exist. Not all Reform Jews feel the same way about traditional practices, and nor do all Orthodox Jews. In fact, some Reform Jews follow the very same traditions as Orthodox Jews, but they might do so because they choose to, or because doing so is part of their cultural heritage, not because the divine voice of God revealed in scripture commands them to, as might be the case for an Orthodox Jew. In other words, sometimes the difference between a Reform Jew and an Orthodox Jew resides only in what motivates their practices.

One must avoid the mistake of seeing Orthodox Judaism as the more authentic expression or form of Judaism, and Reform Judaism as less authentically Jewish. It is true that Orthodox is generally seen as more strict, and Reform more relaxed concerning the observance of **halakhah**. But "strict" religion is not in itself more authentic than "relaxed" religion. Orthodox and Reform Jews agree on their reverence and respect for the Torah. They disagree on how to embody that reverence, and how to interpret what both groups consider to be the word of God, the Torah. This naturally leads to differences in how that interpretation is expressed in practice. As with all religion, the rhetoric of authenticity is always an insider argument, and its resolution is best left to them.

there was a silver lining to being confined to the Jewish ghettos: the walls that kept the community in also kept the forces of change and the draw of **assimilation** to Christian culture (and sometimes Christian religion) out. So some members of the Jewish community in Europe strenuously resisted even the slightest changes to Jewish cultural traditions, liturgical practices (e.g., prayers), and Torah interpretation.

The first group, those who were eager to modernize and assimilate and who were willing to depart significantly from tradition, can be included within a movement referred to as Reform Judaism, and are commonly characterized as liberal. At the other end of the spectrum, those who resisted all form of change are commonly referred to as Orthodox Judaism, and tend to be characterized as very conservative. Between these two sits Conservative Judaism. They tend to

Torah, Mitzvah, and Halakhah

To say that Judaism is an orthopraxic religion is to say that typically Jews are deeply

194

concerned with action and practice. For some, this is a matter of cultural tradition and for others it is about choosing actions that are acceptable to God. But on what is this pleasing action and practice to be based? First and foremost, correct practice is based on the law that God gave to the Israelites and commanded them to guard and to follow. These laws are found throughout the **Torah** (see Chapter Five). The word "torah" does not mean "law," though it is often thought to because one finds so much law in the Torah. "Torah" means "instruction" or "teaching." The Torah is believed to contain the laws of God, given to Moses in order to instruct the Israelites in every aspect of life: worship, sex, marriage, diet, dress, social justice and interpersonal relationships, business, judiciary, war, and many other topics.

Maimonides famously counted 613 *mitzvot*, or commandments, in the Torah, though many of them can no longer be practiced, since they relate to Temple practices. Taken together, the rules that govern practice in any Jewish community is called halakhah. Halakhah is legal reasoning and tradition relative both to Torah and Talmud, and contains much that is grounded in the contemporary culture of the interpreter.

There is no authoritative body in Judaism that sets laws and punishments for transgression. But communal and peer pressure can be very strong. Thus, different Jewish groups have different practices, or different ways of undertaking common practices, and membership in that community might be jeopardized by failure. In other words, establishing rules about practice is part of the process

Building a Fence around the Torah

Rabbinic legal reasoning appears to have revolved around two principles: to transgress God's commandments is a serious thing, and an inadvertent or small transgression is still a transgression. This might explain a strategy the Rabbis developed, called "Building a fence around the Torah." It works by taking a commandment, and expanding upon it. For example, Exodus 23:19 commands: "Do not cook a young goat in its mother's milk." Rabbinic kashrut dictates that dairy and meat cannot be consumed together, or even separately during the same meal, which as you can see goes much further than the original commandment. The reasoning is simple: one never mixes any form of dairy with any kind of meat, one will never, even inadvertently, transgress God's commandment found at Exodus 23:19.

Yet note how intellectual these decisions and discussions are: a goat comes from a mother that makes milk, as does a cow. The biblical prohibition can therefore be applied to cheeseburgers by analogy, if not by the letter of the law. Yet Rabbinic debate and Jewish practice also came to apply the prohibition to chicken, but chickens do not produce milk. On the other hand, fish was not included in the prohibition, so mixing fish and dairy is acceptable. The fact that dairy together with fish is acceptable yet dairy with chicken is not nicely illustrates the creative and somewhat unpredictable human intellectual effort that characterizes this religious process. The same process is repeated many times over in Orthodox circles, such as concerning definitions of work and the Sabbath. These rules are unrelated to biblical law or divine commandment, but they are developed in order to protect that law.

of establishing boundaries between communities (whether among groups of Jews, or between Jews and Christians, Jews and Muslims, and so on). Clearly, whether one follows Jewish legal traditions and how one does so is integrally related to establishing a group's identity.

Circumcision

In the legendary narratives of Israelite religion, God's call of Abraham and the establishment of that first covenant required a reminder: Abraham, all the males of his household, and from there on all of his descendants, were to cut the flesh of their foreskins, an act that would mark God's covenant with Abraham and his descendants into male flesh. This ritual came to be performed on the eighth day of a boy's life, and also on all adult males who wished to convert (proselytes). Circumcision was practiced occasionally by other groups in the ancient world, but it came to be most commonly associated with Israelites because of its widespread practice among them.

Though the longest-standing and most universal indicator of male Jewish identity, circumcision has been an occasional source of controversy since antiquity. Ancient Greeks and Romans strongly objected to circumcision, and since significant portions of Greek and Roman culture happened in the nude (e.g., public baths, Olympics), Jews tended to be ostracized. In the Hellenistic period, the practice of epispasm – creating a new foreskin for oneself – happened often enough to raise the theological and cultural concern of more conservative Jews in ancient Israel. The earliest Christians abandoned circumcision as a requirement of conversion, though the practice was never wholly forbidden, and has been practiced and endorsed in Christian society intermittently since. In the nineteenth century, more radical Reform Jews included circumcision among those archaic rituals that needed to be set aside. Most recently, Jews can even be found among the growing numbers in Western societies who object to circumcision as an affront to the human rights of children, though it is still widely practiced and fiercely defended by the majority of Jewish communities. Attempts from some modern Jews to find a comparable rite to mark female inclusion in the Jewish community have failed to find any thing resembling a consensus.

Kashrut

Certain dietary restrictions relating to meat appear to go back to the earliest forms of Israelite religion. The Torah indicates which animals can and cannot be eaten, as well as how they are to be killed, handled after death, and prepared for eating. Food that adheres to these laws is called **kosher** (all fruits and vegetables are kosher), and the body of laws and traditions (halakhah) surrounding kosher eating is called kashrut.

The Torah specifies that certain animals are unfit for human consumption: pigs and camels are forbidden; cows, sheep, and goats may be eaten. If a fish has scales, it may be eaten, which eliminates not only shellfish (lobsters, oysters, shrimp, clams and crab) but also marlin, eel, shark, and swordfish. The Torah is less clear concerning birds: chicken, duck, goose, and turkey are permitted, but birds that kill or that eat dead things (e.g., eagles, vultures) are not to be eaten. Reptiles, rodents, amphibians, and most, but not all, insects are also forbidden. In all cases, it is not solely the forbidden animal that cannot be eaten, but anything the animal produces, such as dairy, eggs, and fat is also forbidden.

Kashrut also includes rules about killing animals: first and foremost, an animal for eating must be killed for the purpose of eating (in other words, they cannot have died of natural causes nor have been killed by another animal); second, the killing of the animal must involve a quick, deep cut across the throat with a sharp clean blade (obviously this only applies to birds and mammals). Also, since the Torah forbids the consumption of blood, birds and mammals must be hung upside-down after being killed, so as to drain the blood from them. Any blood left in the meat is removed by other means (e.g., with salt).

In some circles, for meat to be considered kosher, a Rabbi must be on hand at the slaughtering in order to certify that proper Rabbinic procedures were followed. As a result, a kosher slaughterhouse would have a Rabbi on staff for this purpose, as would many factories producing kosher food (e.g., chocolate, cereal, crackers, etc.). Any factory lacking a Rabbi but wanting to be certified as producing kosher food would need to pay a local Rabbi to provide that certification. The certification, resulting in a symbol placed on the grocery item, is what tells a concerned Jewish shopper that the food item meets Orthodox standards of kashrut.

It is possible for kosher foods to be prepared in non-kosher ways, so there are also laws and traditions relating to how food is cooked and served. The most well-known law here pertains to the mixing of dairy products and meat, and for that reason can relate not only to how meat is cooked (e.g., whether the meat is cooked in a sauce with dairy in it), but also how it is served. Here again we encounter the sheer variety of Jewish practice. For some, not mixing dairy and meat means not eating a cheeseburger; for others it means having separate pots, pans, dishes, utensils, and kitchen sinks: one for meat preparation and consumption and the other for dairy. Dairy products and meat are not even mixed at the molecular level in the latter household.

In less orthodox kitchens, on the other hand, a family might keep kosher, but use the same set of dishes and utensils, believing that washing them between dairy and meat meals or courses is sufficient (while taking care to leave a proper amount of time between dairy and meat consumption). In still less orthodox settings, a Jewish family might make an entirely different set of decisions: some will not follow the laws of kashrut at all. Others might apply those laws to the consumption of pork, shellfish, and the mixing of dairy and meat, but not to ensuring that their crackers, cereal, and cookies, for instance, are certified kosher. Still others might keep kosher at home, but make no attempt to be kosher when they eat at restaurants or friends' homes. For some Jews, the point of biblical kosher law has to do with ethics, not diet, and in today's world, they consider it unethical to eat meat, or to eat at certain fast-food chains that treat the environment with contempt. For those Jews, a vegetarian (and even more so, a vegan) diet might be a way of creatively and spiritually redefining the laws of kashrut, while also eating in a kosher manner. By some estimates, fewer than 20% of North American Jews self-identify as keeping fully kosher. The challenge might not be solely cultural, either, but could well be socio-economic as well. The expense of having two fully functional sides of a kitchen (one for dairy, and the other for meat) would be considerable.

Purity

The laws of kashrut are part of the system of Jewish ritual purity. Ritual purity includes not only avoiding foods that make one impure but also objects and actions that have the same effect. For instance, many Jews believe that coming into contact with semen, menstrual blood, a dead body, or skin lesions (on oneself or on someone else) makes one ritually impure. In terms of actions, some Jews believe that menstruation and childbirth make women ritually impure. It is also a common belief among Jews that a variety of forms of sexual contact forbidden in the Torah make one ritually impure: adultery, pre-marital sex, homosexuality, masturbation (for men), and incest.

Impurity is thought to be contagious. If a Jewish person believes that a woman becomes impure during menstruation, then it follows that anyone who touches her while she is menstruating will also become impure. Thus, most Jewish men at the conservative end of the spectrum avoid touching their wives in any manner while they are menstruating. Laws of purity specifically related to menstruation are called **niddah**, so called because Jewish practice came to call for the separation of women in a state of impurity.

When Judaism was a temple religion, purity was a ritual state one must have in

Figure 76. Mikveh inside a house in Boskovice, Czech Republic.

order to approach the altar. Ritual purity presupposes ritual impurity, of course, which in turn requires a process to become ritually pure when one has come into contact with impurity. When the Temple stood, certain sacrifices such as an offering to heaven and ceremonies such as **tithe** offerings were believed to return one to a state of ritual purity. Today, the only option available to Jews concerned with purity and impurity (by no means all) is the mikveh, a ritual bath. The use of the mikveh varies across Judaism. In some instances, a woman must wait for five days after the last sign of blood in order to qualify for purification; in other instances, she may visit the mikveh immediately after the cessation of bleeding.

Today, the laws of niddah are contentious in Judaism. Orthodox forms of Judaism tend to seek the wholesale maintenance of traditional biblical purity, and "build a fence around it" (see text box, p. 195). So close inspection for blood, and waiting additional days to ensure menstruation is complete, are common expectations of Orthodox women. Reform Jews tend to reject the laws of niddah altogether as archaic and patriarchal, and as a sign of old-fashioned male mistrust of – and interest in controlling – women's bodies. Orthodox Jews might counter that the laws of niddah are not about a woman's inherently inferior status (as liberal opponents claim), but about upholding the sanctity of marriage (e.g., when a married couple spends one week of every month apart, they will reunite with increased ardor). Conservative Judaism generally takes a middle position, perhaps opting to avoid sexual contact during menstruation, but not prohibiting all forms of contact (e.g., holding hands).

Shabbat Practice

One of the Ten Commandments is that every seventh day is to be a day of rest, a day without work. But because defining terms like "rest" and "work" is so difficult, many additional expectations about what can and cannot happen on the Sabbath have developed over the centuries.

The Talmud expands considerably on what is prohibited on the Sabbath, listing thirty-nine types of activity. These are commonly identified in English as "work," but might more accurately be described as "chores." These are activities relating to and extending beyond: a) the field (e.g., from sowing seed to harvesting and grinding grain for baking); b) creation of clothing (e.g., from shearing wool to dyeing, weaving, sewing, and also tearing apart); c) killing animals (e.g., from slaughtering to salting meat to dealing with the hide). In addition, writing and erasing, building and tearing down, lighting and putting out a fire, hitting with a hammer, and finally, carrying something outside of one's home are also Talmudic categories of work (see text box, p. 138).

This complicated and expansive list was made more so by the practice of building a fence around the Torah. One way of doing this was to prohibit not only those things listed above, but also anything that can be likened to them. For example, it was decided that

---

Kiddush

The traditional way of opening the Sabbath is with a set of prayers: welcoming the Sabbath, remembering why it is observed, praying over the bread, the dinner; and before everything else, candles (typically at least two) are lit. These candles are not to be blown out, but must be allowed to burn out. They are therefore not very large (larger than a birthday candle, much smaller than a common dinner candle). This is the traditional ritual prayer spoken over the lighting of the candles:

Barukh atah Adonai Eloheinu melekh ha'olam, asher kidishanu b'mitzvotav v'tzivanu l'hadlik neir shel Shabbat

Blessed are you Lord our God, king of the universe who sanctified us with his commandments and commanded us to light the lights of Shabbat

electricity is "like" fire, and so Orthodox Jews avoid the use of anything that requires electricity on the Sabbath – lights, computers, microwaves, cell phones. Starting a car requires fire (in the form of a spark), so driving is prohibited too. Handling money is prohibited, so an Orthodox Jew cannot ride the bus on the Sabbath. Hospitals in major cities often have "Sabbath elevators." They stop at every floor without buttons needing to be pressed, since pressing the button is like turning on a light switch. As you can see, Orthodox observance of the Sabbath requires thoughtfulness and creativity for communal living.

But Sabbath observance is, for religious Jews of any denomination, much more than a long list of actions one must avoid. Sabbath is a time to be free: free from the worries and activities that take up the rest of the week, free to rest, free to spend quality time with family, and free to spend time in prayerful reflection. How this is accomplished will differ among different Jewish communities.

An Orthodox Sabbath might look like this: prayers and the lighting of candles some minutes after sundown on Friday, a short service (less than an hour) at the synagogue, a meal with family and friends, home Torah study before bed, Saturday-morning synagogue worship (sometimes three hours), afternoon meal, then leisurely family time together.

A less orthodox Sabbath might start with prayers, candles, and dinner, some synagogue time on Saturday, leisure sports like tennis or golf, riding a bike, or seeing a movie. In this instance, a Reform Jew might interpret the avoidance of work as relating to their jobs, and thus all forms of leisure are acceptable, no matter how strenuous or reliant on electricity.

Synagogue Practice

The transition from Temple to Synagogue was simultaneously a gradual one and a traumatic one. While the Temple stood, it was the central location for the execution of Judean religion. Reimagining Jewish practice after the Second Temple was destroyed took ingenuity. The Rabbis replaced the priesthood, sacrifice, and the altar with a decentralized network of Rabbis, the wholesale absence of

Rabbis

Jewish worship is most commonly led by a Rabbi, an ancient Hebrew word originally meaning "my teacher." Consistent with this, Jewish people commonly understand teaching and interpretation of halakhah, or law, to be the primary role of the Rabbi. But it is not necessary to have a Rabbi for a religious service: though trained in the language and in the reading and interpretation of religious texts, a Rabbi has no special power or authority beyond what any member of the congregation has. That is to say, a member of a congregation can, and often does, lead services. Rabbis are trained in a specific tradition, coinciding with the various sectarian categories of Judaism: Reform, Conservative, and Orthodox, but also Ultra-orthodox, Haredi, Hasidic, Reconstructionist, and so on. Congregations towards the orthodox end of the liberal–orthodox spectrum are less likely to allow women to be Rabbis, those at the liberal end more likely. Larger synagogues that can afford it also often have an additional leader: the cantor, or chazzan. This person leads the prayers, which often have a musical aspect. Sometimes this person is a paid professional, and sometimes members of the community take turns in the role.

sacrifice and all the practices and traditions that revolved around it with the home and synagogue. Purity was no longer the domain of the Temple, but could be guarded in the home, through the application of kashrut, with the dining-room table replacing the altar as a location of Jewish devotion. Sacrifice was imagined as metaphorical. It is important to note that the synagogue took on new functions: it did not take over any of the Temple's functions.

Synagogues are primarily now places of prayer, but they are also places of community socializing, education, and social welfare. The different names Jews use for these places tells us something interesting about the groups in question. Jewish communities at the Orthodox end of the spectrum commonly refer to their synagogues with the Yiddish word *shul*, meaning "school," a term that construes the synagogue as a place of study and learning. Conservative communities tend to use the word "synagogue," because the synagogue is a place for the community to assemble as a community. These tendencies apply most commonly to informal speech, which can be hard to assess. The terms "synagogue" and "congregation" are the most common words that appear in the names of both Orthodox and Conservative synagogues themselves. What is certain, however, is that Orthodox and Conservative synagogues never use the word "Temple" in their titles; Reform synagogues on the other hand commonly do use Temple (though, of course, not always).

This reflects different ways of responding to the destruction of the Second Temple: Reform Jews often hold the opinion that the synagogue replaced the Temple, perhaps even that the synagogue is the new Temple; Orthodox and Conservative avoidance of the

term suggests a different way of seeing the relationship between Temple and synagogue.

There is no evidence that women were separated from men in any form of synagogue worship until the medieval period. Before then it appears that women were present and active in it. In the medieval period, segregation by sex was happening in mosques, so it is possible that synagogues emulated them for reasons of cultural assimilation. In Christian lands, Jewish segregation of men and women in the synagogue likely owes more to the general segregation of men and women socially, since in churches sexual segregation does not occur. Jewish segregation took the form of galleries, from which Jewish women could hear but not see the service, and separate rooms with female prayer-leaders, but not female Rabbis. In modern synagogues where men and women are separate, the common practice is to divide the space down the center, putting men and women on each side, rather than giving women the rear 20% of the space, as was done in the past.

Reform Judaism began ordaining women as Rabbis in the 1970s. In Conservative circles, there was intense debate and resistance to female ordination, but eventually the majority came to accept the ordination of women too. Some who did not approve broke away from the mainstream Conservative movement. Ordination of women does not happen in Orthodox communities.

Synagogue services happen seven days a week, but the central services happen on the Sabbath: Friday after sundown, Saturday morning, and Saturday afternoon. Which of these three is the focus is for each community or individual to decide. Services are usually an hour, but special services can be

The Tools of Prayer

Many Jews use certain devices that are meant to enhance focus during prayer. The first of these is called **tefillin**. These are two small black boxes, each with a scroll of Torah within it, that are placed on the body: one on the left bicep (close to the heart), and the other at the top of the forehead (close to the mind). The scrolls in the tefillin boxes must be written in Hebrew in a special style of writing, and the boxes are wrapped in leather, and fastened to the body with straps of leather that comes from a kosher animal. The placement of the boxes and the straps is not haphazard: generally ritual movements and activities are not haphazard, but undertaken with great precision and thought.

The second tool for focusing one's prayer is the **tallit**, a prayer shawl that is placed over one's head in order to block out sound and motion in one's peripheral vision. Some Jews, wishing to express and illustrate a deep devotion to God, choose to wear the tallit at all times, as a way of showing that in their daily routine they are in a constant state of prayer. Commonly, a few tassels (*tzitzit*) of the tallit are left visible as an external indicator of their piety. In this regard, the tallit and the kippah (a skull-cap, also called a yarmulke) are related. What began as a practice of covering one's head in the presence of God (e.g., during prayer or sacrifice) became a common practice outside of worship settings as well. Today, the Orthodox tend to wear a kippah whenever in public, Conservative Jews sometimes when in public and almost always when in worship, and Reform Jews at their discretion. It is a common feature of religion for clothing to function as a marker of identity.

as long as four hours. They are a mixture of reading/hearing the Bible, singing and music, standing, bowing and sitting, and formulaic prayers. If a Torah scroll appears, it is sometimes paraded around the room, and congregants might attempt to get near enough to kiss it.

Prayer

Prayer at a synagogue requires a minimum number of people to be present, called a **minyan**. The idea of a minyan derives from the belief that worship of God, prayer, and the reading of scripture is more effective when done as a congregation than when done individually (though, of course, individual worship and prayer can happen in Judaism). The theological goal is to be a "holy congregation" that invites the divine presence. The question then becomes: how many people are needed to constitute a holy congregation? The Orthodox Jewish answer to the question has been ten adult males. In Conservative synagogues, whether women can count in the minyan depends on the individual Rabbi and congregation. In Reform synagogues, women are almost always part of the minyan.

This threefold division applies as well to the Bat Mitzvah, the female counterpart to the Bar Mitzvah in which a Jewish boy becomes a Jewish man in order to count as one in a minyan. Orthodox communities have no need for a Bat Mitzvah (except as a modern novelty item), while Conservative and especially Reform congregations would have Bat Mitzvah opportunities for girls, since the latter can count in the minyan.

Holy Days

Recall (see p. 191) the Jewish calendar is an adapted lunar calendar, in that it follows the lunar cycles but has an intercalary month added every two to three years so that the holy days can remain anchored to the solar agricultural seasons. This is what explains why Jewish holy days have specific dates in Hebrew months and month ranges (e.g., November–December) in solar months.

Rosh Hashanah

Many who read this book know already that there are different ways of marking "a year." There is the academic year (which commonly starts in September, but sometimes starts in August or October, depending on location), the secular calendar year (which starts in January), and the fiscal year (which varies from location to location, but often starts in May).

Similarly, Judaism has two calendars. The Jewish calendar begins with the month of Nissan, yet the New Year is celebrated on the first day of the seventh month (called Tishri), a ritual known as Rosh Hashanah (lit: the top of the year). One commonly hears wishes of *shanah tovah* (meaning "[have a] good year!") exchanged between religious and non-religious Jews for the two days on which Rosh Hashanah is observed. On the solar calendar, Rosh Hashanah falls in September–October.

Commonly, for a period including the month of Elul (preceding Rosh Hashanah), Jews take on a mind-set of contemplation and penitence, known as the Days of Awe. The ten days between Rosh Hashanah and Yom Kippur mark the final, and most intense, days of this period, and are known as the Days of Repentance. Here Jews reflect on the failings of the past year and promise to strive to do better in the coming year. Together, the thirty days of Elul, plus the ten days from Rosh Hashanah to Yom Kippur total forty, the same number of days that Moses is said to have pleaded to God to forgive the Israelites. One sees in this the creative theological thinking of religious tradition.

Rosh Hashanah is a day of rest, and most of it would be spent in a synagogue, with a longer service than a typical Sabbath, and with much prayer. Prayers on Rosh Hashanah recall a God who is judge and protector, king and creator. In this regard, one key

Jewish Time	
Jewish holy days are marked on a lunar calendar that has been adapted through the use of an intercalary month so that each holy day "floats" within a range of months in the solar year. Adar is the sixth Hebrew month, and every two to three years one finds an Adar I plus an Adar II, the intercalary month. This is what it looks like for Rosh Hashanah, which is observed in September–October:	1st of Tishri 5780 starts on Sept 29, 2019 1st of Tishri 5781 starts on Sept 18, 2020 1st of Tishri 5782 starts on Sept 6, 2021 1st of Tishri 5783 starts on Sept 25, 2022 1st of Tishri 5784 starts on Sept 15, 2023 1st of Tishri 5785 starts on Oct 2, 2024

practice in the synagogue on this day is the blowing the shofar, which happens at various times (and in various styles) during the long service. The shofar is a horn made from a ram's horn and is blown, with difficulty, like a trumpet (see Figure 53). Originally part of the coronation of ancient Israelite kings, the ritual now signifies the sovereignty of God.

Rosh Hashanah is a solemn day; one might say it is "observed" more than it is "celebrated" (so too of Yom Kippur). But it is not an unhappy day either. Both Rosh Hashanah and Yom Kippur are characterized by hope and confidence: hope for a sweet coming year and confidence that God will forgive. At dinner in the home on Rosh Hashanah, Jews typically eat (among other things) bread and apples dipped in honey, in order to symbolize the hope for an extra "sweet" coming year. In liturgy, three stages are the focus: recognizing God's kingship over the world, acknowledging that God remembers every human action, and the blowing of the shofar. One therefore maintains a serious, somber, and reflective mind-set.

Yom Kippur

When Judaism was a temple religion, Jews regularly sought God's forgiveness by sacrifice. Ten days after Rosh Hashanah (10th of Tishri), on Yom Kippur (lit. Day of Atonement), they did so collectively under the guidance of the High Priest. In those days, two symbolic rituals were central to atoning for the sins of Israel before God. First, the High Priest would heap the sins of the people onto a goat, and then drive the goat into the wilderness where it would die (taking the sins of the people away with it). Second, the High Priest would enter the Holy of Holies,

located at the very heart of the temple, to utter the otherwise unspeakable name of God, Yahweh. Only this figure was allowed to say the name of God, and only on this day. It was believed that doing so would bring God's forgiveness over the whole nation.

The destruction of the Temple completely changed how Yom Kippur is observed. Now, it is no longer orchestrated by a High Priest, but is in the domain of every individual to seek atonement from God. Now, sacrifice is understood metaphorically, in the form self-discipline. This is expressed in five ways: a fast that starts half an hour before the sunset that begins the Day of Atonement and ends half an hour after the next sunset; anointing with oil; sexual abstinence; avoidance of bathing; and the avoidance of leather shoes. The day is also spent in deep prayer by religious Jews.

God is seen in Judaism as judge, and though it is believed that God's justice is fair, it is also acknowledged to be severe. But God is also seen as merciful and forgiving. Nonetheless, this mercy and forgiveness are not to be taken for granted. Therefore, serious and introspective contemplation on how one has sinned against God and against other people, and the sincere prayer sent up to God for forgiveness, typically fill the day of Yom Kippur. Confident that God has forgiven the sins of the people, a feast breaks the fast, and after forty days of the solemn Days of Awe, this feast is meant to be truly festive.

The language of sin in Judaism is couched in terms of paths and whether one is walking in the correct direction: toward God rather than away. Halakhah, the law that guides correct living, derives from the Hebrew word for walking. *Shuv* is part of the language of conversion, that is "turning" to God. The Jew who has sinned transgresses God's law

– another image involving the feet. When one is repentant and seeks to do better in the eyes of God, this is called *teshuva*, or "re-turning" to the straight path that God has laid out. The Day of Atonement is about standing before God expressing deep and sincere repentance, and praying for God's loving kindness to be shown in the act of forgiveness.

Sukkot

Sukkot begins on the 15th of Tishri (September–October), and lasts for a week. It marks a sharp change in the mindset of the observer. Whereas Rosh Hashanah and Yom Kippur and the period between them are characterized by somber repentance and self-reflection, Sukkot is intended to be joyous. Historically, Sukkot recalls when the Israelites wandered in the desert living in tents (or booths) for forty years; agriculturally, it recalls a time when Israelites brought in their final harvest of the year, such as grapes, figs, pomegranates, and olives. Israelites would guard their crops by sleeping out with them in temporary huts, called booths. Hence, Sukkot is sometimes called the Feast of Booths, and also as the Festival of Ingathering. Today, one might build a *sukkah*, and the children of the family might sleep in it. Of course, not all Jews have backyards, and some Jews in live in climates that make sleeping outside in late October challenging, so one can find creative solutions: building a sukkah in the living room, garage, or community center. As is so common in religion lived in the real world, tradition and even legal requirement sometimes have to be creatively interpreted and relaxed.

Figure 77. "The Feast of the Rejoicing of the Law at the Synagogue in Leghorn [Livorno], Italy," by Solomon Alexander Hart (1850).

Sukkot is festive, since it involves the bounty of fruitful crops being successfully harvested. But it is of course also serious. Since God is creator and sustainer of the earth, celebration of Sukkot involves thanking God for the bounty and also acknowledging that God is the protector of the Israelites – allowing them to live in temporary dwellings and yet not perish, as would also apply to their memorialization of the period of wandering in the Sinai desert.

Simhat Torah

The month of Tishri is certainly a busy one on the Jewish calendar. Rosh Hashanah on the 1st, Yom Kippur on the 10th, Sukkot on the 15th, lasting for a week, and then, the day after Sukkot ends, Simhat Torah. Literally, the "Joy of the Torah," Simhat Torah celebrates the gift of the Torah that God gave to Moses on Mt. Sinai. By the medieval

Adaptation

The only thing that never changes is that everything always changes. Sometimes change is incremental, which suggests some stability, but sometimes things are more fluid and adaptable, and change is therefore more significant. The meaning of one particular Jewish holy day is an example of fluidity: Tu B'shevat, also known as the 15th of Shebat or New Year for Trees (which occurs in January–February).

In the Talmud, this date was set for assessing the age of fruit-bearing trees, considered important because of a belief that the Torah dictates that no one may eat the fruit of a tree for its first three years, that the fruit from its fourth year must be given to God as a tithe, and that humans may eat its fruit from the fifth year

onward. Thus, this would be a good day to plant those trees. Focus shifted in the sixteenth century from trees to eating fruit when a mystical symbolism was sought in the festival: eating the various fruits of Israel helps correct the sin of eating the forbidden fruit from the Tree of Knowledge (Genesis 2–3). A seder (see p. 208) much like Passover was even developed for this day, and it was enshrined as a joyful day. In the twentieth century, focus for many has shifted from fruit to soil, as the day became a way for people to articulate a deep spiritual connection to the land of Israel. In yet other iterations, this day is celebrated as Arbor Day, with many taking the opportunity to relate environmental concerns with their religion.

period, it was common for Jewish people to read the whole Torah over a yearly cycle. Simhat Torah came to be designated as the day on which that yearly reading cycle would be completed. In modern synagogues, one might observe Torah scrolls being carried around the room as many as seven times, with people dancing, singing, and rejoicing in their presence.

Hanukkah

Hanukkah is the only holy day not referred to in the Bible. For this reason, it was not observed widely for most of Jewish history. It has become more broadly observed most likely because of recent political and cultural pressures.

From the September–October range that marks the time frame from Rosh Hashanah to Simhat Torah, we move to November–December, or on the Jewish calendar, the

25th of Kislev. Historically and theologically, Hanukkah remembers the war the Judeans won against the Seleucids (who ruled what is now Syria) in 167–164 BCE. According to the narrative, which is found only in books known as 1 and 2 Maccabees, after the Israelites regained the Temple that had been desecrated by Antiochus IV Epiphanes (an event remembered as "the Abomination of Desolation"; see Chapter Two), the Temple had to be rededicated to the God of Israel. This required the lamps to be lit, and to remain lit. However, there was only enough oil for a single day, and new supplies were, according to the theological narrative, eight days away. At the heart of Hanukkah therefore lies a miracle: a single day's worth of oil lasted for eight days. It is important to note, other than recently in the state of Israel, Hanukkah has been celebrated not as a military victory, but as a miracle of light.

The central ritual of Hanukkah today is the lighting of the Hanukkiah candles on each of the eight nights of the festival. A Hanukkiah is a menorah with nine arms instead of the standard seven. The lighting of the candles invokes the memory of the miracle of light, as well as the rededication of the Temple to the God of Israel. This happens in homes, in synagogues, and frequently in public squares in North American cities in the spirit of cultural inclusiveness.

This latter point also explains the similarity between Hanukkah and Christmas. Many non-Jews (and even many assimilated Jews) think of this holiday as the "Jewish Christmas," adopting many Christmas customs, such as elaborate gift-giving, and instead of a Christmas tree in the home sometimes a "Hanukkah Bush." When one religion borrows features from another, we call it syncretism. The irony, of course, is that the putative historical setting of Hanukkah involves a war of resistance against allowing Jewish practice to be shaped by pressure from a non-Jewish culture. A particularly Jewish cultural practice associated with Hanukkah is the eating of oily foods (related to the oil of the lamps): Ashkenazic Jews commonly eat potato pancakes called *latkes*, while Sephardic Jews commonly eat donuts (often jelly-filled or fritters).

Purim

Purim, also known as the Feast of Esther or the Feast of Lots, is celebrated on the 14th of Adar (February–March). It is one of the most joyous and fun holidays on the Jewish calendar, and commemorates a narrative in which the Jewish people living in Persia in the fifth century BCE were saved from extermination.

The background narrative for this day is found in the biblical book called Esther. A character named Haman, an advisor to the Persian king, comes to hate the Jews. He persuades his king to allow him to proceed with a plan to exterminate them from the land, under the pretense that it is objectionable that they follow a different law than the king's. The king agrees, and to choose the date on which the extermination will begin, Haman draws lots (like drawing a lottery ticket from a barrel), which in Hebrew is *purim*.

The plan is foiled when a Jew named Mordecai learns of it. He persuades his young cousin, Esther, whom he had raised as a daughter, to intervene with the king. She is in fact Queen Esther, married to the king. Esther persuades the king to revoke Haman's plan, and Haman himself is hanged on the gallows he had built.

The Talmud instructs that on Purim, one should drink in such a celebratory fashion that one can no longer distinguish between the statements "cursed is Haman" and "blessed is Mordecai." Some theologians over Judaism's long history have been uncomfortable with the endorsement of such intoxication, and so have suggested that perhaps drinking until sleepy is sufficient. Despite this, there is a common tradition in many Jewish circles to become extremely drunk, noisy, and rowdy on Purim. Under the influence (no pun intended) of Christian culture, Purim has come to share some of the same features as Mardi Gras (see Chapter Nine).

Pesach

Like Yom Kippur, Pesach is the one of the most commonly observed holy days, even by otherwise non-observant Jews. This holy day falls on the 15th of Nissan (March–April). Agriculturally, this day is about spring, the re-emergence of new life and fertility after the dead of winter. Theologically, Pesach recalls the narrative of Moses leading the Hebrews out of Egypt after generations of enslavement. In the story, God sends plagues against the Egyptians as punishment for their treatment of God's people. The final plague is the killing of all Egyptian first-borns. In order for the Hebrews to be spared from this, God instructs them to sacrifice a lamb and to wipe some of its blood on their doorways. Doing this would ensure that the angel of death would "pass over" the Jewish households, sparing their first-borns. The sacrifice of a lamb was, for this reason, the central ritual of ancient celebrations of Pesach.

In modern days, Pesach revolves around a meal rich in symbolism. A child in the house starts off with a question: "Why is this night different from all other nights?" This and three other prescribed questions move the narrative along. The story of the Exodus is told, and, four times, a celebratory glass of wine is taken. The wine represents joy, and small items of food are eaten at the appropriate places in the story in order to represent various parts of the narrative: unleavened bread called matzah (to recall the haste with which the Hebrews fled Egypt), a herb like parsley or lettuce (to recall their humble origins) dipped in salty water (to recall their tears under bondage), horseradish (to recall the bitterness of slavery), and a relish called

Figure 78. Samaritan Passover sacrifice on Mt. Gerizim. The butchered sheep are skewered on long poles ready to be lowered into the roasting pit.

charoset, the thickness of which recalls the mortar used to make bricks while slaves of the Egyptians. The taking of the symbolic foods and the wine in their proper order is called a seder, and the story told is often read from a book called a Pesach Haggadah.

The importance of the absence of leaven in bread, inspired by the Exodus narrative, is taken much further in many Jewish homes. Many Jews avoid foods labeled as *chametz*, but they might disagree on what constitutes such prohibited foods. Most Jewish people likely agree that yeast is certainly to be avoided (which is what explains eating unleavened bread), but in many Jewish homes people assiduously seek out and remove all forms and evidence of leaven (or yeast) for the duration of Pesach. This is commonly extended to wheat, oats, and barley. In addition, Ashkenazic Jews also avoid eating rice, corn, and legumes (e.g., lentils, chick peas, and peanuts) during Pesach, while Sephardic Jews do not. Thus, Sephardic Jews would eat hummus during Pesach, while Ashkenazic Jews would not. Ashkenazic halakhah also requires a greater degree of food purity than Sephardic halakhah before something is declared kosher.

Shavuot

Seven weeks plus a day after Pesach is Shavuot, which is why this holy day is called the Feast of Weeks and also Pentecost. Falling on the 6th of Sivan (May–June), this holy day is an early harvest festival, and hence is also known as the Festival of First Fruits, referring namely to barley and wheat. Barley was harvested starting at Pesach and by Shavuot wheat was harvested. When the Temple stood, Jewish males were expected to offer a sample of their harvest to God as thanksgiving.

Shavuot came to be associated in Rabbinic Kabbalah circles with the day God gave the Israelites the Torah at Mt. Sinai, and this remains the focus of the day. For some, then, the primary activity associated with this day is studying the law all through the first night, though some communities counsel putting your books away at midnight. Shavuot is celebrated for different lengths of time by different Jews. In Israel, it is a one-day celebration; for Jews living outside of Israel, it is usually a two-day celebration. However, Reform Jews outside of Israel usually observe the one-day timeline, and non-religious Jews are commonly unaware of the significance of the day altogether.

In addition to studying the law late into (and sometimes through) the night, other practices associated with this day include the eating of dairy-based foods, such as cheesecake or cheese-filled pancakes. Moroccan Jews traditionally eat a seven-layer cake, while Jews in Yemen do not eat dairy on this day at all. The addition of dairy to bread for this day (e.g., cheese bagels) is interesting, as normally Jewish bread is dairy-free (kosher bagels and challah lack milk and butter) so that it can be had at any meal (e.g., without worrying about the dairy–meat prohibition). There is no consensus among Jewish sources on the reasoning behind dairy consumption on this day. Also, homes and synagogues are commonly decorated with flowers and green plants on Shavuot, because of a midrash that Mt. Sinai blossomed greatly in anticipation of the delivery of God's law, or Torah.

Tisha B'Av

The 9th of Av (both the name and the date of this holy day, which falls in July–August) is a fast of mourning. Mourning is a central practice of Tisha B'Av because Jewish tradition maintains that on this day, various calamities befell the Jews: the destruction of the First (586 BCE) and Second (70 CE) Temples, and the expulsion of the Jews from England (1290) and from Spain (1492).

The fast is, like Yom Kippur, a full fast for twenty-five hours. Since one is meant to be in mourning on this day, mourning rituals are in effect: in addition to not eating or drinking, one does not work, bathe or shave, wear make-up, cut hair, or have sex, all things one would naturally not attend to if in deep mourning. In addition, one ought not wear leather shoes or study the Torah, and weddings are not scheduled for this day (or, for some Jews, at any point in the three weeks preceding Tisha B'Av either). Why is Torah not to be studied on this day? Because studying the Torah is meant to be an act of joy. Only sad biblical texts may be studied on this day. Hence, the biblical book Lamentations is commonly read in synagogues, since it was written in the wake of the destruction of the First Temple.

With its focus on the destructions of the two Temples, interest in this holy day differs among modern Jews. Reform Judaism tends not to lament the destruction of the Temples. These are long-past events with little or no significance to the modern Jewish experience. More conservative or orthodox forms of Judaism, which tend to look forward to the re-establishment of God's Temple in Jerusalem, feel differently about the day. Some spend the day reflecting more abstractly on suffering and loss, and non-religious Jews tend not to be aware of the day (unlike Yom Kippur).

Jewish Culture

Visual and Literary Arts

Jewish visual art has been influenced by the avoidance of aniconism. Aniconic art must above all avoid giving any form to God, whether in sculpture or painting. Jews in the ancient Mediterranean rioted at the sight of Roman religious images in Jerusalem. Jewish art tended to avoid the sculptural medium altogether, which is condemned in biblical language as "graven images," though Jewish communities have tended to accept the depiction of humans in realistic settings in two-dimensional form (e.g., paintings).

In the Middle Ages, Jewish art seems to have been influenced by dominant Islamic approaches, which were even more wary of figurative images. At that point, it was common for Jews to avoid reproducing human faces in their art. Medieval Jewish art is found very commonly in Torah scrolls, prayer books, and gravestones. After the sixteenth century, one would find the same art in Jewish homes as in other homes: painted portraits and biblical scenes. By the eighteenth century, there were Jewish painters making a living from their art. Some of the most famous modern European painters were Jewish, such as the Impressionist Camille Pissarro, though their Jewishness was not always a feature of their art. Today, only the Orthodox and some Conservatives Jews consider human facial depictions in art to be problematic, but this is not universal even among these groups.

Art and the Holocaust

The effect of the Holocaust on Jewish theology and art is difficult to imagine, and artists and theologians alike have grappled with that part of their history. Not every theologian is an artist, but every artist is, arguably, a theologian. Every piece of art, whether visual, dramatic, or literary questions the role of God. Visual Holocaust art can be deeply haunting and troubling, as it forces the viewer to witness the inhumanity. But literary art can also be deeply troubling, and all of it participates in the theological project of understanding theodicy (see Chapter Five). The novels of Elie Wiesel, such as *Night* (1960), offer other powerful examples (see "Putting God on Trial" text box, p. 129). Another is a poem by Dan Pagis, also a Holocaust survivor. Motivated by his Holocaust experience, Pagis, originally Romanian, wrote his poetry only in Hebrew. His most well-known poem is called, "Written in Pencil in the Sealed Railway Car."

Figure 79. Zodiac mosaic floor of the Bet Alpha synagogue (sixth century CE) located in Israel.

Hasidic communities have long produced, and revered, portraits of their Rebbes, the Yiddish version of Rabbi.

Music

Jewish religious music has expanded over its long history. Originally limited to the singing of psalms, instrumental music, and liturgical music lead by a highly trained cantor, synagogue music followed early-modern European trends in hymnal composition. Most Orthodox synagogues avoid using instruments for Sabbath services, Conservative synagogues accept some instrumental music, and Reform synagogues are very musical.

As broad appreciation for music expanded beyond Christian church music in Europe in the Middle Ages and the Renaissance, Jewish culture followed suit. This would be called folk music, that is, the music of the people: bards, troubadours, and so on. The most widely known form of Jewish folk music is called *klezmer*, and it is a product of **Yiddish** Ashkenazi culture. It is a joyous music to which people dance at weddings and celebrations, and quite resembles Eastern European polkas and waltzes.

There have also been some very famous and influential Jewish composers of classical music, such as Gustav Mahler (1860–1911). Hints of Yiddish music can be found in some of Mahler's symphonies. But there have also been many Jewish people in popular music, such as the late Leonard Cohen from Canada, who explores Jewish themes in some of his music, or the American Matisyahu, who blends clearly Jewish themes with hip-hop beats and reggae rhythms, and, for most of his career, upheld Orthodox practices in his life and with his performing schedule.

Architecture

The crowning achievement of Jewish architecture was arguably the Second Temple in Jerusalem. Construction on it began in

515 BCE, with a massive expansion under the reign of Herod the Great that lasted from approximately 19 BCE to 63 CE. The completed temple stood for a mere seven years, destroyed by the Romans in the Jewish War in 70 CE. The remaining western-most wall, now called the **Wailing Wall**, gives one a sense of the grandeur of the original temple. Beyond this, however, there is no parallel in Jewish architecture to the architectural achievements of the Vatican or Mecca's Great Mosque. Nonetheless, Jews built synagogues wherever they lived, when they were allowed to, and many of them are beautiful.

Many breathtaking synagogues in the world today are to be found in Eastern Europe, testifying to the vibrant presence of Jews there before World War II. These are found in Hungary, Czechoslovakia, Russia, Bulgaria, Georgia, and Serbia, though noteworthy synagogues can also be found in Florence, Glasgow, Jerusalem, and New York City.

Judaism in the World

The job of this chapter, to describe Jewish practice, is complicated by yet one more feature of global Judaism: it can be divided, most broadly, into two cultural groups: Ashkenazic and Sephardic. Ashkenazic and Sephardic Jews eat and dress differently, they pray differently, and their music and literature is different. Yet these features are not merely "cultural," as if religion and culture can be distinguished. In all streams of Judaism, liberal and orthodox, Ashkenazic and Sephardic, culture and halakhah are intertwined.

Ashkenazic Judaism developed in Eastern Europe, Germany, and France, while Sephardic Judaism developed in Spain, Portugal, North Africa, and the Middle East.

Jewish life in these two regions was vastly different. Not only are diet and dress obviously very different between, for example, Spain and Poland, but the experiences of the Holocaust were also very different. Many Sephardic Jews did not experience the trauma of the Holocaust as directly as did Ashkenazic Jews. Most Jewish people in Canada and the United States are culturally Ashkenazic. In Israel, Ashkenazic and Sephardic Jews appear in equal numbers, but there are can be sharp tensions between them there because of cultural differences, and because of their different experiences of the Holocaust.

It will take until approximately 2050 for the global population of Jews to reach its pre-World War II number of approximately 17 million. But the Holocaust not only lowered the total number of Jewish people in the world; it also dramatically altered their global distribution. Prior to World War II, the vast majority of Jews lived in Europe; today only approximately 8.3% of Jews live there. Approximately 43% live in Israel, and 40% live in the United States; this latter number rises to just over 45% when North and South America are counted together. The more surprising number, however, is this: though 40% of the world's Jews live in the United States, they make up only 1.8% of the American population.

Keeping in mind that accurate numbers are difficult to get and census data often out of date, one can propose the following: in North America, there appears to be more Reform than Orthodox synagogues, with Conservative synagogues between them in number. In Israel, those statistics point in the opposite direction: Reform Jews comprise the smaller group, Conservative Jews

Figure 80. Polish synagogues between the seventeenth and twentieth centuries were distinctive in Europe. Probably inspired by the Zohar, their lavish interiors often included painted imagery of familiar and exotic animals and landscapes intended to evoke feelings of awe and wonder in imitation of God's creation. Today, there are many abandoned synagogues throughout the country serving as melancholy reminders of the near total destruction of Jewish culture in Poland during the Nazi occupation. Pictured here is the ruined Dukla Synagogue.

number more (perhaps 40% more), and Orthodox Jews dominate among religious Jews. This is in part because the Rabbinate of Israel, which is exclusively Orthodox, does not accord Reform and Conservative Jews full recognition as Jews. Reform and Conservative marriages, for instance, are not legally recognized, Reform and Conservative Jews have difficulty accessing the Western Wall, and their Rabbis are not eligible for government salaries. Interestingly, however, religious Orthodox Jews comprise less than one-third of Israeli Jews. And approximately two-thirds of Israel's Jews self-identify as not religiously observant.

Jews can, of course, be found in all countries around the world. Two features of modern geopolitics push Jews toward Israel: the fact that the government of Israel makes it very easy for Jews to emigrate there, and the fact that worldwide tensions between Judaism and Islam often force Jewish communities out of Muslim-majority countries, where Jews have sometimes lived in peace for several thousand years until recently.

Chapter Summary

A common question asked in any religion is this: how much diversity can a group sustain, or tolerate, before that difference comes to be seen as a threat to unity? In other words, there is always a certain amount of diversity within unity for any group, but at which point is it too much? In Judaism, that question has tended to revolve around practice: how to *be* properly Jewish. While it must be stressed that it would be irresponsible of this book to claim that one set of those practices is best, or most authentically Jewish, one characteristic that Jewish groups around the world and across millennia share is a concern about practice. Much effort has been put into defining proper Jewish practice.

Glossary

Assimilation. Jews in many periods have struggled with a pressure, sometimes external (e.g., political oppression) and sometimes internal (e.g., personal attraction), to abandon or alter their own religio-cultural practices in order to conform to majority religio-cultural practices: Caananite, Egyptian, Babylonian, Persian, Greek, Byzantine, Islamic, German/Christian, secular. Muslims in non-Islamic countries face the same pressure today.

Halakhah. The body of laws pertain to Orthodox Jewish practice. Derives from the Hebrew word for walking or path, reflecting the belief that halakhah involves walking on the path to God. Halakhah derives mostly from the Torah, but also from Talmud and Rabbinic custom. Because these laws represent Orthodox standards, Reform and Conservative Jews have different ways of regarding halakhah.

Jewish Emancipation. After the various national expulsions and ghettoization of the Middle Ages, the nineteenth-century abolition of discriminatory laws in several European countries led to the belief and hope that Jews would be allowed to live freely in Christian lands. Emancipation led many Jews to reject Zionism, believing they were safe in Europe now. The Holocaust changed that perception.

Kosher. Food is kosher when it meets the requirements of Torah and Rabbinic custom. Certain animals are not kosher, meat must be drained of blood, and meat cannot be consumed with dairy. Halal and kosher share similar requirements with respect to blood and pork, but Jews can consume alcohol and Muslims can consume shellfish.

Minyan. The minimum number of people thirteen years and older required in order for certain Jewish prayers to be said and rituals (e.g., Torah readings, funerals, benedictions) to be held. In Orthodox circles, those people must be male, while in Conservative and Reform settings those people can be male or female. The Bar or Bat Mitzvah ritual marks the transition from childhood to adulthood, after which one becomes eligible to count in the minyan.

Niddah. Niddah refers both to a woman who is menstruating and is therefore to be separated from the men around her and to the laws regulating that separation. Sexual intercourse is the most common thing to be avoided while a woman is niddah, but with some couples it can also extend to any form of contact at all. Orthodox couples are more likely to follow laws of separation and be fastidious concerning trace amounts of blood than Reform Jews.

Tallit: A large piece of cloth covering the head and shoulders, used in prayer to aid in concentration by blocking out the sights and sounds of other people praying. The Tallit can also be worn under clothing as an Orthodox expression of piety, commonly with the tzitzit (or tassels) revealed.

Tefillin. Leather-covered small boxes containing small scrolls with Hebrew Bible passages and placed on the head and left arm during Jewish prayer. The technical term for these items is phylacteries, illustrating their relationship to amulets and other items traditionally conceived as "magical."

Tithe. A common form of sacrifice, in which a portion of one's profit, normally monetary or agricultural, is returned to God in gratitude. A form of tithing is found in Judaism, Christianity (e.g., collection), Islam and Baha'i religion (e.g., *zakat*), and the LDS Church.

Wailing Wall. Also called the Western Wall, this is the only part of the Second Temple that remained after the Roman destruction in 70 CE. It thus holds deep symbolic significance for many Jews, and is a common site of pilgrimage and prayer.

Yiddish. An Ashkenazi Jewish language deriving from a combination of Germanic and Hebrew elements. Thus, its letters are Hebrew, but its sounds are quite like German. Yiddish also, however, refers to cultural features of Ashkenazic Jews, such as music (klezmer), food, and civic life.

Other Important Vocabulary

Aniconism	Kashrut	Purim	Sukkot
Ashkenazic	Kippah	Rebbes	Syncretism
Bar/Bat Mitzvah	Klezmer	Reform Judaism	*Teshuva*
Chametz	Matzah	Rosh Hashanah	Tisha B'Av
Conservative Judaism	Menorah	Seder	Torah
Days of Awe	Mikveh	Sephardic	Tzitzit
Epispasm	Orthodox Judaism	Shabbat	Yarmulke
Hanukkah	Pesach	Shavuot	Yom Kippur
Hanukkiah	Pesach Haggadah	Shofar	
Intercalary	Proselytes	Simhat Torah	

Discussion Questions

1. The historian of religion can be struck by the fact that Christians, Jews, and Romans all have a festival of light around the same time: December for Jews (although every three to four years it falls in November), December 25 for Christians, and December 22 for Romans (in the festival of Saturnalia). How might the historian of religion explain this fact?

2. What do you think the relationship is between ritual and religious identity? How might ritual function as a way for a member to claim membership in a community? How might it function to deny membership to someone? How might it function to remember the past and establish group identity?

3. Reflect on the tension caused within religious communities because of different ways of interpreting religious writings (e.g., literal vs. metaphorical) and applying religious tradition (e.g., liberally or conservatively). Drawing on Chapter One's discussion of religion and religions, what might this tension be evidence of?

4. What are the strengths and weaknesses of categorizing religions according to whether they are orthodoxic or orthopraxic?

5. The discussion above about practices and rituals reveals a good deal of variation within Jewish practice. Clearly, variation is natural and unavoidable, owing to cultural and historical variation. Is it possible for there to be too much variation? How much variation do you think a religion can sustain before it starts to disintegrate? Who would decide such a question?

Recommended Reading

Hartman, Tova. 2007. *Feminism Encounters Traditional Judaism: Resistance and Accommodation.* Lebanon: Brandeis University Press.

Hoffman, Lawrence A. 1979. *The Canonization of the Synagogue Service.* Notre Dame, IN: University of Notre Dame Press.

Kraemer, David C. 2007. *Jewish Eating and Identity Throughout the Ages.* London: Routledge.

Segal, Eliezer. 2000. *Holidays, History and Halakhah.* Northvale, NJ: Jason Aronson.

Recommended Websites

http://jwa.org

- The Jewish Women's Archive offers articles on women Rabbis and Jewish feminist thought.

http://www.tikkun.org

- A website representing a progressive Jewish perspective on politics and living in the world.

http://www.myjewishlearning.com

- Offers thousands of articles on a variety of features of Judaism.

http://www.jewfaq.org

- Many articles on Jewish practice, including comments on historical development and future dates, normally representing an Orthodox perspective.

—9—

Christian Practice and Holy Days

Chapter Overview

This chapter describes a variety of Christian practices, particularly liturgical practices involved with church worship. It also examines the key Christian holy days and periods, and considers Christian culture displayed in art, music, and architecture. The chapter closes with brief glance at the numbers and denominations of Christians around the world.

Christian Practices

As we saw in Chapter Eight, and as we shall see in Chapter Ten, Judaism and Islam are legal religions: that is, they each have a law that they claim comes from God, a law that needs to be taken seriously, and a law that needs to be renewed with every generation. It is certainly the case that different Jews and Muslims adhere to these laws to different degrees and in different ways, but nonetheless law functions in Jewish and Islamic life and self-understanding differently than it does for Christians. As a matter of fact, the self-understanding of many Christians, the narrative most familiar to them, is that in the first century followers of Jesus agreed (though with considerable debate) on the rejection of the two key practices of Jewish law: circumcision and kosher eating. This developed quickly into a Christian theology in which it was claimed that practice had little or no effect on salvation. In their own words, they stressed that one could not earn salvation by proper action, but only through faith in Jesus.

To this extent, then, practice features differently in Christianity. But it would be a mistake to conclude that Christians do not also practice their religion. Every day, Christians, like Jews and Muslims, seek to behave or act in ways that they think are determined by, or consistent with, the values of their religion.

It is easy to see that practice forms a significant part of a Jewish and Islamic person's identity, but this is no less the case for Christians, despite the differences just described. For instance, a considerable element of Catholic identity revolves around the practice of not eating meat on Fridays, but fish instead. This was a practice that originally carried the force of law, but since the 1960s no longer does. Yet, despite this, many Catholic families and institutions (e.g., hospitals, schools) still consider "fish Fridays" an element of their Catholic identity. There are many other unique Catholic practices too, and these function in the formation of their identity. Likewise, a major feature of Evangelical identity in the 1990s was bound up in a grassroots movement called "What Would Jesus Do?" Some of them still wear bracelets that were intended to remind them, before *doing* anything, to pause and reflect on the question, and thus choose an action consistent with their loyalty to Jesus. In other words, differences exist between Jewish and Islamic practice on the one hand and Christian practice on the other, but it would be unwise to exaggerate those differences, and

to conclude that Jewish and Islamic practice is about religious identity while Christian practice is not.

While it is important to remember that anything religious people do in the name of their religion is data for a scholar interested in religious practice, a chapter as introductory as this one must keep things simpler. Here I shall focus on the traditional and communal practices most widely seen among Christians. These might be called liturgical practices: that is, the practices associated with Christian church settings.

Liturgy

When Christians speak of ritual and practice, it is generally in the context of **liturgy**: that is, worship. When the very first Christians gathered to worship, they did so in people's

What is Ritual?

There are many different ways that ritual can be understood. On the one hand, a ritual involves a ceremony with a prescribed set of actions, which can involve body positioning, language, or gestures. Put differently, rituals tend to involve actions that are planned and clearly defined rather than spontaneous and creative. Rituals can be simultaneously about social control (e.g., ritual is generally created, performed, and protected by those with power and divine authority, such as a priest or minister), social inversion (e.g., Carnival, which for a day rejects and subverts Catholic morality), the articulation and illustration of social norms, conventions, and expectations. Rituals tend to be practices so deeply entrenched and invested with so much authority that it is nearly impossible to challenge or question them, but they can also be the means by which creative change is introduced into a society.

Perhaps the most fruitful way of looking at ritual is not as a kind of event, but as a *way of acting*. Modern theorists describe ritual as a way of acting that is designed or intended to distinguish itself from other, normal or daily ways of acting. This is because rituals are meant to express power and authority. From this perspective, it may be more fruitful to speak of ritualization rather than ritual. Ritualization is the process by which mundane activities are transformed into significant (e.g., holy, authoritative) activities. This coheres with the approach to the study of religion presented in Chapter One: that there is no thing (artefact or action) that is inherently religious; rather, absolutely anything can be made religious. Similarly, ritualization transforms mundane actions into actions made significant by the fact that *someone* has categorized them as religious.

Figure 81. A Russian Orthodox church in Düsseldorf: the Gifts (bread and wine) prepared during the Liturgy of Preparation before the beginning of the Divine Liturgy.

reading the Old and New Testaments, Eucharist, singing or listening to a choir, hearing a sermon, and communing with fellow worshippers (greeting each other explicitly as Christians, or merely coming together as a community). In fact, it is this last feature that is key: any of those other practices (e.g., praying, singing, reading the Bible) can be and frequently are done alone, but coming together as a community cannot be done alone. Christians in the first few centuries gathered together at great risk because of Roman persecution, suggesting that the act of gathering was as important as any other act. This risk still exists in some places in the world, mostly in the Middle East, but Christians now mostly meet in peace and with government and social acceptance.

Some Christian worship services have a consistent order and structure from week to week and location to location, whereas some do not. For instance, a Catholic mass will have the same structure in almost every location around the world (e.g., entrance hymn, greeting, song, scripture, **sermon** or homily, Eucharist, etc.), which will include reading the same passages from the Bible. When a worship service is this structured, consistent, and predictable, we call it "highly liturgical." But some Christians worship without any structure at all. Such a service is led by people who speak when inspired to do so. One example is a Quaker service, and we would call it non-liturgical. The worship services of other denominations fall in between these extremes: for instance, in the United Church of Canada, which makes up Canada's largest group of Protestants, services are consistent and predictable in individual locations, but might differ from location to location.

homes. While some still do so, most Christian worship happens in churches, even though Quakers (a denomination of Protestants) call their churches "meeting houses." Worship, it could be said, is the primary practice of Christians. It happens most commonly on Sunday mornings, but sometimes frequency is related to one's level of devotion: when a person considers her- or himself truly devoted, he or she might attend a church service every day of the week. Whether individual churches conduct formal worship services more frequently than once a week depends on tradition and demand.

Worship Activities

Worship activities are generally drawn from the following kinds of practices: prayer,

Churches, Cathedrals, and Basilicas

The buildings that Christians worship in have many names: meeting house, church, parish, chapel, basilica, and cathedral. Some of these belong to certain denominations: parish churches tend to be Anglican, meeting house is Quaker, and they tend to be small. Others, such as cathedrals and basilicas, tend to be much larger, and are sometimes positively gigantic (more on that on p. 236). But these churches are not called cathedrals and basilicas because they are large. They are large because of what the buildings signify.

A cathedral belongs not to a local priest but to a higher-ranking bishop. A cathedral is generally so large both in order to provide the bishop with a grand setting fitting to his office and because it is assumed many people will come to worship in his or her presence. When the term "cathedral" is used for Catholic, Orthodox, and Anglican churches, it means there really is a bishop's "seat" (*kathedra*) there. When Protestant churches use the term "cathedral" (e.g., the Lutheran Magdeburg Cathedral in Germany), it is almost always because they took over a cathedral from the Catholic Church after the Reformation, retaining the grand name but not the hierarchical office of bishop.

"Basilica" refers primarily to the architectural form, referring to a long hall with high ceilings and three long aisles. In Catholic tradition, however, the term has come to refer to churches with a special historical significance for Catholics, or churches that contain relics. Hence, they too are large because people will travel to see and worship at such holy sites. A church can be both a cathedral and a basilica (e.g., St. John Lateran in Rome, Notre Dame in Ottawa, Canada) if it houses a bishop and has historical significance or a relic (see "Architecture," p. 236).

Eucharist

The rough outline of the story of Jesus' last night depicts Jesus dining with his disciples for one last time, which happened to be the evening of Passover. The whole meal is not described, only the opening thanksgiving, which in Greek is *eucharistos*. Jesus takes a piece of bread, gives thanks to God for it, and refers to it as his body. He then gives bits of the bread to his gathered disciples to eat. Next, he takes some wine, thanks God for it, refers to it as his blood, and gives it to his disciples to drink. Jesus' final instruction concerning this ritual, found in the Gospel of Luke, is that this is to be done in memory of him.

This is the narrative that sits at the foundation of one of the central rituals of Christian practice: the Eucharist, or the consumption of bread and wine during the worship service. This ritual is evidenced in the earliest Christian records (in Paul's letter, 1 Corinthians 8), and continues. Around the world, Christians eat something bread-like and drink something wine-like when participating in this narrative. The precise details of this practice differ from place to place and from one group to another.

In some churches, members tear a piece from a whole loaf of bread; in others a pressed wafer is placed on the tongue by a priest. The ritual has many names, most of them used interchangeably by Christians, regardless of denomination: in addition to Eucharist, it is also called Communion, Holy Communion, Lord's Supper, and Agape Feast.

There are many differences in the experience of Communion among Christian denominations. Catholic and Anglican churches offer Communion every week, many Protestant churches offer it once a month, and some even less frequently, as low as once a year. Each group has a rationale for their preference. Catholics and Lutherans would claim that the Eucharist is the central ritual of Christian community, and therefore ought to happen whenever Christians gather; Protestants who celebrate the Eucharist once a year might argue that doing it more frequently removes its mystique, lessening the significance.

Another difference relates to the wine. Some Catholic and Anglican churches offer wine every time bread is offered, while other Catholic and Anglican churches offer wine less frequently than they offer bread. Orthodox churches offer wine whenever the bread is offered; they believe the two must always be offered together. Many Protestant churches serve grape juice instead of wine when the Eucharist is celebrated, generally in these cases quarterly not weekly. Catholic and Orthodox Churches insist that only members of their own denominations are allowed to take Communion (and both denominations place further limits on which of their members can, namely those who have been to Confession recently). Protestant churches are more likely to let all comers partake in Communion.

And, finally, there is a difference in the theological understanding of the Eucharist as well. Catholic and Orthodox churches teach that during the Mass (as Catholics call their service) or Divine Liturgy (as Orthodox churches call theirs), the bread and wine become the body and blood of Christ in a way that is both mystical and actual. The term that refers to this is **transubstantiation**, which means that the bread and wine might retain the appearance and taste of bread and wine, but in actuality their substance changes (*trans*) to the body and blood of Christ. The entire process and experience are referred to as a mystery by Orthodox and Catholic churches.

Protestant churches conversely maintain that during Communion, the body and blood of Christ are present with or alongside the bread and wine, but that the bread and wine remain in appearance and substance. Protestants also sometimes stress that Communion represents a memorializing of the last supper of Jesus with his disciples. The term they use to describe the ritual is **consubstantiation** (*con* = with).

Orthodox churches teach that during the Divine Liturgy (as Orthodox churches call their services), the bread and wine simply *are* the actual body and blood of Christ, but they have not developed a doctrine (i.e., transubstantiation) to explain it as Catholics have. They leave it unexplained, preferring to think of it as a mystery.

All these positions, interestingly, can be supported by authoritative texts, an important practice in most religions. The Catholic and Orthodox positions are supported by a saying of Jesus in the gospels: "This is my body" and "This is my blood" (e.g., Matthew 26:26–28), while the Protestant position is supported by Jesus saying, "Do this in remembrance of me" (Luke 22:19). A situation like this provides a good illustration of the role of scriptural interpretation in religion: without it, there can be no religion, which is to say, no religious belief and no religious practice. Everyone has to interpret, every group believes that its own interpretation is correct and reasonable, and no one can do without it.

Baptism

The use of water in a ritual not of daily hygiene but of symbolic cleansing of sin or impurity is common to Jews, Christians, and Muslims. Christians inherited their practice from Judaism, of course, since John the Baptist and Paul were both Jewish. Christians call their practice **Baptism**, a Greek word that refers literally to dunking someone in water. Some forms of Christianity still Baptize by fully immersing the person outside in a body of water (a river or lake usually); other Christians practice Baptism indoors, using water set aside for this ritual and pouring a small amount of it on the forehead.

Baptism is the most common ritual marking Christianity identity, both for those born into Christian families and for those converting. Any convert, regardless of age, would likely be baptized by and into the church they are joining. Baptism has different symbolic meanings for different Christians: for some it represents the washing-away of sin – sometimes the actual sin of a previous life without Jesus, and sometimes the sin of simply being born human, called **Original Sin**. Catholics, Lutherans, Anglicans, and Orthodox Christians – more than half of Christianity – favor infant Baptism. Here, a baby of any age is baptized by the parents in order to have its Original Sin removed or detached, as in the Catholic case, or be protected from the spirit of evil, as in Orthodox theology. Other Christians, all Protestant, favor adult Baptism, arguing that conscious and conscientious dedication to Christ defines

Figure 82. Fresco on the catacomb of Saints Marcellinius and Peter, Via Labicana, Rome, depicting a Baptism.

Christian faith and identity, and infants are incapable of that. Baptism thus is best left, according to these Christians, until a person is old enough to decide for her- or himself.

Interestingly, the single practice of Baptism does the same work as two different practices in Judaism, and the two positions of Christians on Baptism can be aligned with the two Jewish practices. Christians who favor infant Baptism see it as replacing circumcision (also done to infants in Judaism), while those who prefer adult Baptism tend

Gender: Women in Positions of Leadership

One of the most pressing issues today for many Christians (and one that relates to the predictability of liturgy) is whether women can be ordained for positions of ministry, and, from there, whether they can hold higher offices such as bishop, cardinal, pope, primate, or patriarch. Christianity's long history and its present diversity reveals many different practices when it comes to granting women religious authority. In the first century, although technically there was no Christianity at that point, it does appear that there were women leaders of Paul's house-churches (Phoebe, Chloe, Prisca). Yet Jesus appears to have chosen twelve men and no women to be his disciples. 1 Timothy 2:11–15 is commonly read as prohibiting women to be priests or ministers. The cases for and against women's ordination thus rely equally on scripture, and yet arrive at opposing positions.

Those who argue against women's ordination tend to stress the authority of tradition and the male godhead: that God, Jesus, his disciples, Paul, and the Church Fathers were all male illustrates the primary role of men in the establishment of the church. At the same time they might embrace a theology in which women are fundamentally incapable (intellectually or spiritually) of holding such an office.

Those who argue in defense of women's ordination tend to stress the importance of cultural location: the Bible holds archaic views on slavery, but few Christians think slavery should still exist. They argue that those were the views of a different time, and are therefore to be overridden. For these Christians, the Bible's patriarchal tendencies also need to be left in the distant past, replaced by modern positions of gender equality.

Catholic and Orthodox Churches forbid women to be priests, and since one must be an ordained priest in order to be a bishop, cardinal, or pope in the Catholic and Orthodox Churches, those positions cannot be filled by women either. Anglican (or for Americans, Episcopalian) Churches are allowed to decide individually, and there are women bishops in the Anglican Church, but there has not yet been a woman as the Archbishop of Canterbury, the Primate of the Anglican Communion. Since there is no hierarchical structure of any kind over Protestant churches, they too decide individually whether to have a female minister. Baptist churches in the United States, for example, ordain women, while many Evangelical or Fundamentalist churches hold more traditional or conservative views.

to treat it as analogous to the Bar Mitzvah, that is a ritual marking religious adulthood. This is what made Anabaptists controversial: when they broke from Catholic and Lutheran practice, claiming that all people baptized as infants had to be baptized again as adults (hence: Ana-baptists), they were fiercely opposed (see "Luther, Calvin, and Grebel" text box, p. 74).

Baptism also relates to membership in a Christian community. An adult who converts to Christianity will be baptized and thus becomes a full member of the church, with access to all its rites and rituals (where they exist). There is diversity of opinion, of course, on when children are to have access to these rituals. Catholics baptize infants, but the child must wait some years, which includes some preparation and instruction, before being allowed to participate in the Eucharist. First Communion happens for Catholics and Lutherans most commonly at around seven years old. In Orthodox churches, on the other hand, baptized children are allowed to eat the Eucharist as soon as they are old enough to eat, and sometimes it is said that First Communion happens in fact at Baptism.

Other Sacraments

The Eucharist and Baptism, just described, are examples of a sacrament: a ritual during which, it is believed, God becomes uniquely present. Sacraments are, therefore, regarded as extremely holy rituals, and they are intended to be carried out with great attention to detail by priests, bishops, and participants alike. Not every ritual is a sacrament; sacraments are especially significant rituals. So what rituals in Christian religious life are

Figure 83. Mpho, an Anglican deacon and daughter of Desmond Tutu, serves Holy Communion to her mother Leah in Soweto, South Africa, in 2003.

considered sacraments? As with all things religious, it depends on whom you ask.

The Christian Fish

Second only to the cross, the "Christian fish" is one of the most widely recognized symbols of Christianity. Placing this on a tombstone in the third century had the same effect as placing it on a car bumper in the twenty-first century: it identifies a person or family inside as Christian. Jesus is called a "fisher of men" in the gospels, and the fish comes, for a reason no one really knows, to be associated with Jesus. By the fourth century, Christians had made an acrostic from the word itself: the Greek word for fish has five letters: I-CH-TH-U-S, which is said to stand for: I**ē**sous **Ch**ristos **Th**eou **U**ios (pronounced hui-os) S**ō**t**ē**r, or "Jesus Christ, Son of God, Savior."

Early-third-century-CE funerary stele of Licinia Amias, one of the earliest Christian inscriptions from the area of the Vatican Necropolis, Rome.

Almost all Christians agree that the Eucharist and Baptism are sacraments, though, as we shall see in Chapter Eleven, Mormons reserve the term "sacrament" for the Eucharist alone. Most Protestants reserve the designation "sacrament" for just the Eucharist and Baptism.

In contrast, Catholic and Orthodox Christians consider an additional five rituals also to be sacraments, though Orthodox Christians call them Sacred Mysteries. These are Confession, Confirmation, Last Rites, Ordination, and Marriage. Protestants practice some of these (though not all), but they consider these to be rituals, not sacraments. That is to say, Protestants practice marriage as a holy ritual in the church, and they ordain their ministers for a life in church leadership, but they do not consider marriage and ordination to be sacraments.

Let us next consider these five additional Catholic sacraments. **Confession** is the act of confessing one's sins to a priest. Admitting that one has sinned is considered the first step in making things right, both before God and before one's community, family, or friends. The next steps are prescribed by the priest, who might recommend additional prayers, and might also offer advice on how to forgive oneself or seek the forgiveness of those one has wronged. Confession is meant to happen regularly, on the assumption that incidental sins are a regular part of human living. Therefore, the failure to

Theology on the Ground

When religious people suffer, it is very common for them to wonder about, doubt, and even question, the power of God. If God is loving and just, they wonder, why do bad things happen to righteous people? If God is all-powerful, why do the communities that worship God suffer in war and plague? This is the topic of **theodicy**, which refers to beliefs about God's justice. Wondering about God's justice, whether God is just, and what God requires of people often leads to creative theological innovations, such as we saw in the wake of the two destructions of the Jerusalem Temple in 586 BCE and 70 CE (see Chapter Two).

This happened in Christianity too in the fourteenth century, when a plague called the Black Death arrived from China. During the Avignon Papacy, the city was hit with three catastrophic waves of the plague, in which as much as 75% of the population died. People naturally wondered whether it was God's punishment for removing the papacy from Rome. But of course,

all of Europe (and the Middle East – see Chapter Four) had their populations reduced by half. Worried that God had failed them, or ceased entirely to take notice of them, people devised ways to regain God's attention, such as self-flagellation, in which people whipped themselves mercilessly in order to atone for their sins and persuade God to relent in his punishment. Because priests were attending to the sick, so many of them died that there was no one left to administer the sacrament known as Last Rites. The Catholic Church allowed any Christian to hear Confession and perform funerals. But the lack of priests caused such despair among the dying that people were even known to bury themselves alive in holy ground rather than face death without the properly administered rites. The Plague had far-reaching social, political, and theological effects, and may even have laid the foundation of the Protestant Reformation. Theology often develops in direct response to historical events.

attend Confession regularly is considered a problem in the Catholic Church, and can influence one's participation in other sacraments.

First Confession, that is the first time a child participates in Confession before a priest, is often a significant rite of passage in Catholic families. It tends to happen when a child (boy or girl) is seven or eight years old, considered the age at which a child can be expected to take moral responsibility for his or her actions. Catholics are not supposed to participate in the Eucharist if they have not been to Confession recently, so the ability to take Communion (and participate in Confession) implies something about the child's ability to know the difference between right and wrong, and to choose right. When Confession is practiced as a sacrament, it is individual: a sinner with a priest (in Catholicism), with an respected elder (in Orthodoxy), or with a pastor (in Lutheranism).

Confession is an important part of worship for other Christians, however, even if it is not considered a sacrament. Anglicans and non-Lutheran Protestants stress inward Confession, that is the Confession of sins directly to God, not through a human intermediary. During sacramental Confession, a Christian enumerates his or her sins to a priest, elder, or pastor, expresses heart-felt remorse for offending God, is assured forgiveness, and is perhaps instructed on how to be a better Christian.

Confirmation is the sacrament in which a Catholic child becomes a young adult Catholic, confirming membership in and loyalty to Catholic teaching and tradition. Typically this happens around twelve to thirteen years of age, but it can happen as early as seven years old. Preparation for Confirmation

Figure 84. A Venetian doctor during the time of the plague.

involves instruction in Catholic theology, as well as in basic Christian identity.

Confirmation is sometimes thought to be the Western equivalent of the Eastern rite called **Chrismation**. Chrismation involves anointing with an ointment called chrism, a mixture of oil and balsam. Orthodox Christians also consider this ritual a sacrament. Chrismation does not wait until the age of reason (as with Confirmation), but happens as part of Baptism, both of adult converts and of infants brought by their parents to be Baptized into the church. Chrismation alone completes the initiation of someone into the Eastern churches.

Taken together, Baptism, Confession, First Communion, and Confirmation complete a process of initiation into the Catholic Church. It is a long process that recognizes that at different ages, an initiate is capable of different things, but at the end of it, one is considered a full member of the Catholic Church. If one of these stages were missing, one might have difficulty being married in a Catholic Church, as the priest might not consider the person wholly Catholic. In contrast, as you have seen, Baptism, Confirmation, and Communion all happen at the same time for Orthodox Christians, when they are infants. Therefore, they are considered fully initiated into the church much earlier in life than Catholics.

Last Rites refers to the sacrament one undergoes just before death, and involves a series of steps to prepare a person's soul for death. First, the dying or extremely sick person is asked for a Confession of sins. Second, the sick person is anointed with olive oil. This part of Last Rites is reserved for those who are sick or injured; it would not be given to one who is about to be executed (though they too can receive Last Rites). Finally, the Eucharist is administered one last time. The sacrament would end with the priest recommending the person to God, in the hope that God will receive that person (despite being a sinner, as all humans are considered to be) with grace and mercy, granting eternal life to the person. It is important in Catholicism that a person not approach God unprepared, so people who are sick and near death for a long time might undergo Last Rites many times. Orthodox Christians also participate in Last Rites, though for them it does not include anointing, only Confession and the Eucharist. The rationale for the practice is the same as for Catholics, to prepare a person to stand before God.

Ordination, also called the "taking of holy orders" or "the laying on of hands," occurs when a man enters the Catholic or Orthodox priesthood. There are a variety of holy orders for both Catholic and Orthodox Christians: minor orders (a designation that is mostly no longer used among Catholics), deacon, priest, and finally, bishop. A Catholic deacon might perform many functions of a priest (such as preaching and teaching) but he lacks the full authority of a priest. A bishop presides over multiple congregations, while a priest presides over only one. While a priest can perform any of the other sacraments, only a bishop can perform ordination. And when one rises in rank from priest to bishop, several bishops must be present to administer the sacrament. Ordination is another of those rituals that Protestant Christians practice, as entering ministry represents a significant commitment, but they do not consider it a sacrament. It warrants pointing out that initiation into holy orders is different from ordination. It is a sacrament for men who become deacon, priest, or bishop, but it is not a sacrament for either monks or nuns.

Finally, marriage, also practiced before God by all Christians, is a sacrament only for Catholic and Orthodox Christians, though it was not regarded as a sacrament for Catholics until the sixteenth century. For a marriage to occur in Catholicism, the couple must be free to marry (e.g., not be married to someone else) and must be marrying of their own free will. Catholic priests have had

Competing and Imperfect Calendars

Christians inherited from the Romans many things. One was the challenge of trying to create a calendar that accurately measured the solar year. Christians took over the Roman calendar named after Julius Caesar that was adopted in 46 BCE – the Julian calendar. The trouble with the Julian calendar, however, is that it calculates time incorrectly: it was eleven minutes shorter than the calculated astronomical year (or the solar year). In 1582, Pope Gregory XII became troubled by the realization that in the centuries of Christian time, Easter was getting further and further away from the March equinox because of a calendar that was too short. By 1582, the date of Easter was already ten days different than the date Christians had agreed to in 325 CE. So the Gregorian calendar was created. It was significantly more accurate, but still not perfect: it is eleven seconds shorter than the solar year. In the year 4909, the Gregorian calendar will be off calculated astronomical time by a day.

If history repeats itself, it is quite likely that Christians will disagree how to best address that problem. Protestant and Orthodox Christians originally rejected the papal endorsement of a new calendar because it was Catholic. It took until 1700 for Protestant Germany to adopt the new calendar, which was being used in Spain, Portugal, and Italy (Catholic countries at the time), and until 1782 for Britain to adopt it. In 1923, Eastern Orthodox Christians revised the Julian calendar, but not all Orthodox churches accepted the revision. So, in fact, there are three different solar calendars currently in use by Christians, all of them imperfect, but all of them dearly embraced by different groups.

various responses to the question of inter-marriage: sometimes they allow Catholics to marry non-Catholics, and sometimes not. The couple to be married must also consent to the permanence of the marriage, and promise to bring children into the world and into the Church. Before marrying a couple, it is common for the Catholic Church to insist on a lengthy period of time to prepare for married life. This time might involve meetings and conversations with a priest, as well as a marriage preparation course in which the couple learn both of the challenges of living together and building a home and family, and the Catholic laws and traditions that ought to govern certain family and household decisions (such as those relating to birth control). The course is intended, in addition, to ensure a couple are not entering into marriage hastily.

In contrast to Protestant and Orthodox Christians, divorce is not permitted for Catholics. The only option for getting out of a Catholic marriage is annulment. Annulment, however, is not an equivalent to divorce. Divorce cancels a marriage contract, and is a legal decision of the state; annulment is a decision of the Church, and in effect declares that a marriage never actually happened. There are specific conditions that are required in order for an annulment to be granted (e.g., if the marriage was never consummated), and it is an expensive process. If a Catholic's husband or wife has died, however, one is then free to remarry.

Orthodox Christians are permitted to divorce, but this does not necessarily mean a divorced Orthodox Christian is free to remarry. The right to remarry is granted only by special appeal. It does so happen that this special right to remarry may be granted as many as three times in a person's life, but the Orthodox Church tends to declare that no person may marry four times. Nothing, and no one, governs Protestant marriage and divorce.

Holy Days

There are two ways of structuring the Christian liturgical year, Western and Eastern. The Western way is shared by Catholic and Protestant Christians; the Eastern way is represented by Orthodox Christians. It is of course more nuanced than this: because the Western liturgical year originates in the Catholic Church, Protestants have diverse ways of responding to it. Since the Reformation, sometimes Protestants have rejected this calendar outright, but in recent times, Protestant churches have come increasingly to embrace it too. And the Orthodox liturgical year is separate, but is more similar to the Western year than it is different. The Western liturgical year begins with Advent in late-November or early December, depending on the date of Christmas. The start of the Orthodox liturgical year is fixed to November 15. Otherwise, both calendars are structured primarily around Christmas and Easter, and the time outside of the Christmas and Easter seasons is called Ordinary Time.

Rituals and Rivalry I

It is common every December in the West for some Christians to issue a plea: "keep the Christ in Christmas." What they want is for Christmas to be about the Incarnation of God, and not about consumerism and extravagance. Historically, such a statement is perhaps more complicated than they realize. First of all, when Western Christians wanted to choose a day on which to celebrate the birth of the Son of God, one day was as good as any other, since no one knew when Jesus was born. However, there was already in place a popular Roman holy day called Saturnalia. Focused on the winter solstice (December 25 on the Julian Calendar), Saturnalia celebrated the victory of the unconquerable sun. For these people, winter solstice was evidence that the sun brought light and life into the world, and that the sun's cosmic battle against darkness was won again. The language and imagery echoed things Christians believed about Jesus (e.g., they called Jesus Christ "the light of the world"), so they repurposed Saturnalia. Today, some Protestant Christians object to the non-Christian (they use the pejorative term "pagan") origins of this day, and as a result, they do not celebrate Christmas at all. Here, then, are Christians who refuse altogether to put Christ in Christmas because it was not there in the first place.

This objection to the pagan origins of Christmas happened for the first time in England in 1647. The Puritans were strict Protestants, and when they gained political power, they outlawed the celebration of Christmas. Puritan influence in the United States was strong enough that Christmas was illegal in Boston between 1659 and 1681. Though the ban was overturned, it took two hundred years before celebration of Christmas was widespread in America. Behind the seventeenth century Puritan ban and contemporary Protestant rejection there lies a strong anti-Catholicism. Thus, this controversy becomes one not only of theology, but also of identity. A significant part of Protestant identity for some has been the rejection of ritual, which the Catholic Church embraces.

Rituals and Rivalry II

Just as there is rivalry between Catholics and Protestants over the legitimacy of Christmas, so too some Protestant Christians (particularly Puritans, Quakers, and Jehovah's Witnesses) do not celebrate Easter. Their rationale for this is first and foremost that the term "Easter" cannot be found in the New Testament, and only entered Christian usage from Anglo-Saxon in the eighth-century CE. Additionally, it appears that the word "Easter" was borrowed from a non-Christian goddess of fertility called Eostre, and the proliferation of bunnies and eggs are certainly fertility symbols that have greater affinity to non-Christian fertility cults than the New Testament story of Jesus' resurrection. Therefore, these Christians would celebrate Resurrection Sunday rather than Easter, and would participate in none of the egg–bunny traditions so common in other Christian Easter practices.

It is also worth noting that both Christmas and Easter in the West particularly are now also fully secular holiday and rituals, with no religious significance for many. That is, people who were (or whose families were) once but are no longer Christian commonly celebrate Christmas and Easter regardless. Christmas and Easter for these people is no longer about Jesus' birth or his death and resurrection; they are about family, generosity, and celebration, and ideally feasting. Big family dinners are part of this tradition, gift exchanges and Easter egg hunts. There can be something of a rivalry, then, between these people and Christians who feel their holy days have been taken over by secular non-Christian and non-religious culture. Losing the religious meaning of these holy days is not an easy process for many Christian communities.

Advent and Christmas

The Christian liturgical year begins with Christmas and its preparatory period. In Western churches, this preparatory period is called Advent; in Eastern churches it is called the Fast of the Nativity. Advent starts on the fourth Sunday before Christmas Day. The Fast of the Nativity runs the forty days between November 15 and December 24; it also involves abstaining from red meat and other meat products, poultry, dairy products, and oil. Other than these differences, Christians in the East and West alike see this period as a time to prepare for the birth of the Son of God and to celebrate the incarnation.

Advent preparation means not only fasting (though fasting is not part of Advent for Catholics and Protestants), but reading passages from the Old Testament that Christians believe predict the birth and anticipate the mission of Jesus Christ. So, for example, usually late in Advent, Christians will read Isaiah 7:14:

> "Therefore the Lord himself will give you a sign. Look, the young woman is with child and shall bear a son, and shall name him Immanuel."
>
> (New Revised Standard Version)

Christians have long believed that this passage was a prediction of Jesus' birth. For them, that Jesus was born in fulfillment of a Jewish prophecy is part of what proves his status.

For Western Christians, Christmas Day falls annually on December 25. Many Orthodox Christians also have chosen to celebrate Christmas on December 25, in order to share the more common Christian date. Other Orthodox groups have refused to accommodate and so continue to celebrate Christmas only on January 7.

Regardless of whether one celebrates Christmas on December 25 or January 7, it is important to stress that neither date is Jesus Christ's birthday, nor does disagreement over the date arise because of different ways of calculating the date of the birth. On this all Christians agree: the precise date of Jesus' birth is unknown. Christmas is the day on which Christians celebrate the birth of Jesus; it is not his birthday. In point of fact, it is much more than a birthday. This day marks, for Christians, the Incarnation, the day that God chose to make himself human for their sake.

Easter Season

Easter is the next major holy day on the Christian calendar. Like Christmas, it too is preceded by a period of preparation and also followed by a period of time leading to Pentecost. The preparatory period for Easter is called Lent. Almost all Christians observe Lent in some way and of some duration, though there are many variations in that duration, between five and seven weeks. Lent is a period of serious and somber reflection on the coming death of the Son of God. It begins, for most Christians in the West, with Ash Wednesday. Ash was an ancient symbol of grief at tragedy, but also remorse for one's failings or sins.

Before setting the date of Ash Wednesday, Christians must first set the date of Easter. Unlike the other Christian holy days, Easter is not set on the solar schedule. Because Jesus died in Jerusalem during Passover, it

was always important to Christians that Easter fall close to Passover, and since Jews use an intercalary lunar calendar, so too (with adaptations) must Christians. But Christians came to object to being reliant on Rabbinic calculations of Pesach in order to set the date of Easter, so they devised a formula: Easter was to occur on the first Sunday after the first full moon after (never on) the vernal equinox. So, for example, in the year 2015, the vernal equinox was March 20, the first full moon after that was April 4, so Easter was April 5. This means that for Western

Figure 85. Painted in 1632, Diego Velázquez's "Christ Crucified" forces the viewer to see the nearly nude and inert body of Jesus Christ, and the painting itself has inspired religious poetry.

Christians, Easter Sunday will always fall between March 22 and April 25.

During Lent, many Christians around the world – Orthodox, Protestant, and Catholic – practice austerity and self-discipline in order to raise their spiritual awareness and practice community solidarity. Traditionally, Christians, especially Catholics and Orthodox, avoided eating meat and dairy, but in modernity a Christian might also choose to avoid comfort foods like chocolate, soft drinks, or fast food. Others might try to quit smoking or avoid alcohol, cursing, gossiping, or speaking ill of others. Often these avoidances are framed in the language of avoiding vice, or avoiding something one really enjoys. Ultimately, there are very few rules about what to avoid during Lent; Christians can be quite creative in freely electing to avoid something they enjoy. For others, however, Lent is not only about avoiding practices, but also embracing practices: some might pray or attend church more often during Lent, or try to be more calm, generous, kind, humble, or patient with others.

Because of the austerity and discipline associated with Lent, a practice developed of allowing for excess on the day before Lent began. It may have started out as a practical issue – since it was common to avoid meat during Lent, it made sense to use up the meat so that it did not go to waste – but it came to represent a day of excess in more ways than that. In Catholic South

Religion and Popular Culture

Above we saw that Christmas in most Western countries has become a popular holiday with little relationship to its Christian meaning. The same has happened with a number of Catholic saints' feast-days. Many non-Christians celebrate St. Valentine's Day, St. Patrick's Day, and Hallowe'en. St. Valentine, who lived in the third century CE, was martyred for performing marriages among soldiers and for refusing to renounce his Christian religion. By the fourteenth century, he was associated with romantic and youthful love. The legend of St. Patrick is that in the fifth century he converted Ireland to Christianity. In popular culture, people celebrate Irish culture on March 17 by wearing green. Hallowe'en is a contraction of All Hallows' Eve, which occurs the night before All Saints' Day on November 1. Originally the evening was set aside for a vigil in which people would pray for the souls of the recently deceased and all those who attained sainthood. In popular culture, Hallowe'en is a night on which children dress in costumes and go door to door collecting treats.

Popular culture also sometimes inherits features of Catholic culture. For instance, Catholicism has patron saints of every imaginable thing, from things like abdominal pain and Alaska to zoos and Zaire. Madonna del Ghisallo became the patron saint of travelers in Italy in the medieval period, and in the 1950s was made the patron saint of cyclists by the Pope at the time. Today, cyclists with no connection to Catholicism might place the Madonna del Ghisallo medallion on their bicycle frames in order to keep them safe, since the role of the saints is to intercede on one's behalf. Similar, St. Christopher is a patron saint of travelers yet can be found on the necklaces of non-Catholic travelers. And children play at crossing their fingers when they are saying something that is untrue. Most of them do not realize that the origin of this comes from the conviction that making a "cross" (related to Jesus' cross) while telling a lie cancels out the ill effects of lying.

Figure 86. The Sydney Mardi Gras Parade maintains a political flavor, with many marching groups and floats promoting LGBTQI rights, issues, or themes. The historical evidence tells us nothing at all about Jesus' sexuality, and within Christian traditions there are a variety of views on sexual orientation.

America, this day became known as Mardi Gras (French for "fat Tuesday") and Carnival (meaning "the removal of meat"). These festivals carry connotations now of social chaos, promiscuity, and drunkenness more than a meat feast. In a world where austerity and discipline were a standard expectation, Latin American society spent the day before Lent partying.

An alternative but related practice developed in Northern Christian countries. Shrove Tuesday (and in Germany, Denmark, and Austria Shrove Monday), were celebrated in the day or two before Ash Wednesday. Here Christian households would use up all the rich foods in the house (e.g., milk, eggs, butter, sugar, syrup), typically making a feast of pancakes. Hence, in Canada, the United Kingdom, and Australia, this day is known also as Pancake Tuesday.

Orthodox Christians did not develop an analogous practice to Mardi Gras or Shrove Tuesday. Great Lent, as it is called by Orthodox Christians, begins forty-eight days before their Easter date, and it begins with Clean Monday (the equivalent of Ash Wednesday), a public holiday in some European countries.

The last week of Lent is always the busiest for Eastern and Western Christians alike. Protestant, Catholic, and Orthodox Christians refer to it as **Holy Week**. Orthodox Christians stop fasting in this last week, claiming to shift the focus from sorrow and austerity to joyful worship. In the West, the last week before Easter starts with Palm Sunday, commemorating Jesus' final entry into Jerusalem. On this day, Christians come out of their churches carrying a palm leaf. Four days later, on Maundy Thursday, Christians remember Jesus' last supper with his disciples, then the next day is Good Friday, the day on which he died, and then Easter Sunday, the day on which they celebrate his resurrection from the dead.

In the week immediately following Easter, Orthodox Christians feast and celebrate, a period they call Bright Week. The more extended post-Easter season revolves around two days, which many Christians observe: Ascension Day and Pentecost. Ascension is celebrated forty days after Easter, and marks the Christian belief that after Jesus' resurrection, he spent forty days on earth building the Christian community so that it would survive. They believe he then ascended into heaven. Ten days later, Christian tradition maintains that the Holy Spirit descended to take Jesus' place here, which is celebrated on Pentecost. Christians live in the world with the Holy Spirit, which guides them as a place-holder until the Second Coming, the time at which Jesus is to return to earth and inaugurate the judgment.

In addition to the central holy days and periods of Christmas and Easter, Catholics have an elaborate tradition of Saints' Days. Every single day of the year except December 25 has a saint, sometimes more than one, associated with it. These nearly four hundred saints with feast days comprise a mere fraction of the ten thousand or more saints of the Catholic Church. A saint is someone who is believed to have had a unique relationship with, or gift from, God. Orthodox Christians share some saints with the Catholic Church, and also has some saints of its own. Like Catholics, they also commonly pray to these figures, believing that they can work with God on someone's behalf. But Protestants, while they might refer to certain people with the title "saint" (e.g., St. Paul, St. Peter), do not create saints of their own as Catholics and the Orthodox do.

Christian Culture

Visual Arts

Though very often controversial, Christians seem to have used art in religious practice nearly from the beginning. Where controversy arose, it was generally motivated by two concerns. The first had to do with Christianity's historical relationship with Judaism. Judaism is aniconic – that is, it avoids the use of images in its worship of God – and so some aspects of Christianity have shared that perspective. Second, some Christians have worried that the use of images in worship would resemble idolatry, a sin in Judaism, Christianity, and Islam. Worse, it was sometimes supposed that the use of images in worship could lead people into polytheism, that is, worshipping something other than God. So, some in the Orthodox churches objected to their paintings (Iconoclasts), many Protestants objected to Catholic art, and in Hollywood, movies of the life of Jesus originally were forbidden from showing Jesus' face. In fact, the unique look of Orthodox paintings likely derives from their closer interaction with Islam. The stylized (which is to say, non-realistic) paintings of Orthodox Christians were possibly a compromise between Islam's discomfort with iconic art and the contemporary movement toward figurative art emerging in Christianity. Remember that Orthodox Christians were much closer geographically to the Islamicate than were most Western Christians.

But Christians have otherwise embraced art in religion. According to one seventh-century pope, the images in a church are what allow poor and illiterate Christians to know their Bible though they cannot read it. Thus, Catholic churches developed the Stations of the Cross, small engraved images spread throughout a church depicting in twelve scenes Jesus' final walk to his death. Christians produced paintings of theological concepts – such as the Trinity – as well as of individuals, such as Jesus, Mary his mother, or the saints of the Catholic and Orthodox

Figure 87. U2 performing on the Joshua Tree Tour 2017 in Brussels, Belgium, on August 1, 2017. U2 is a politically engaged band that manifests a particular brand of Christianity, through the band's mediation in a global context and for a global audience.

Churches. Whereas Orthodox Christianity, unlike other forms, does not endorse three-dimensional art, other Christians moved into wholly realistic art forms, such as statues and realist paintings. Art could be used to inspire piety, deepen theological reflection, or challenge people's beliefs.

Music

Christians were writing hymns as early as the first century, and Christian music has continued to develop unabated. Christian music was originally done without instrumentation, but secular technological advances that made instruments like violin and piano accessible changed Christian music too. Christians now sing in worship, and also listen to singing (choirs) or music (organ) that is meant to inspire and uplift. Here, less

separates Protestants and Catholics: two of the greatest composers of Christian music were Protestant – Handel and Bach – while Vivaldi was Catholic.

Music too, though originally part of pious expression, could be used to challenge and question the power of Christian religion. Christian themes can be explored in popular music (such as the music of U2), and sometimes religion itself can be expressed and explored. Canadian folk singer Bruce Cockburn and American folk singer Sufjan Stevens are both openly Christian, and explore in subtle ways how their religion can influence social or political change (Cockburn) or be woven into the beauty of art (Stevens). Other musicians take it upon themselves to evangelize through their music: their music is only and always about Jesus, about hope, about God's love, and they hand out bibles

Figure 88. Interior of Chester Cathedral, England.

be grand and awe-inspiring. Church buildings were full of symbolism. The most basic form of symbolism, in terms of design, was the cross-shape of the basilica. More elaborate symbolism came in the technological advances of the Gothic architecture of the twelfth to fifteenth centuries. Vaulted ceilings appeared to float hundreds of feet above the ground in tall towers. Inside walls were gone because of the flying buttresses and ribbed vaults, and the effect was to draw the viewer's eye upward towards heaven. These buildings invoked the wonder of the divine and the power, wealth, and prestige of the Catholic Church. Renaissance architecture brought great domes, seen most vividly in St. Peter's Basilica in Vatican City, the heart of the Catholic world. When the Pope presides over a mass at St. Peter's, as many as eighty thousand people can be hosted using the adjoining square.

After the Reformation, many Catholic churches were taken over by Protestants. Therefore, some Protestant churches, particularly Lutheran and Anglican ones, can be every bit as grand and ancient as the great Catholic cathedrals – because that is precisely what they once were! Most Protestant churches, however, were built after the Reformation, and were governed by a strong desire to forge an architectural identity of their own, independent of Catholic architecture. Many Protestant churches deliberately rejected the grandeur and art, and embraced the simple and austere.

at their stadium-filling concerts. Today, individual churches debate about what type of music is best for worship – traditional hymns, choirs and organs, bands and modern music – but few Christians reject outright the legitimacy of music to augment religious experience.

Architecture

Architecture is an art form that can also create in people an *experience* of religion. The numerical growth of Christianity after Constantine required the construction of many churches, some of them very large, and the power and wealth of the Church (Catholic in the West, Orthodox in the East) allowed, even demanded, that many of these churches

Christianity in the World

Counting the world's Christians is hardly a straightforward enterprise. The estimate offered here is that the total population of global Christianity in 2015 was approximately 2.3 billion, comprising almost one-third of the global population, by far the largest religion in the world. Christians are spread throughout the world: 37% of the world's Christians can be found in North and South America, 26% in Europe, 23% in sub-Saharan Africa, 13% in Asia, and less than 1% in the Middle East and North Africa. Europe, and North and South America are, however, *less* Christian than they were a century ago: Europe used to be 94% Christian, and in 2010 was at 76%; the Americas used to be 96% Christian and in 2010 were at 86%. Conversely, in the same century, the percentage of Christians in sub-Saharan Africa rose by over 50%, and it doubled in Asia. It is interesting to note that Christianity's global numbers reflect its colonial past: there are more than twice as many Catholics in Brazil as there are in Italy, the home of the Vatican. Mexico, Brazil, the Democratic Republic of Congo, and the Philippines are all over 90% Christian, and the United States holds a nearly 80% Christian majority. The United States and Brazil are the two countries in the world with the highest Christian population.

Of the world's 2.3 billion Christians, approximately 1.2 billion of them are Catholic, approximately 800 million are Protestant, and approximately 385 million are Orthodox. Breaking these numbers down more specifically is where one discovers the rich variety and complexity of Christianity. In Catholicism it is relatively simple: 98% of the Catholic Church belongs to the traditional Latin Church. Although there are Catholic denominations from Eastern Europe to Egypt, these comprise a very small percentage of global Catholicism. Orthodox Christianity is dominated by what is commonly known as Eastern Orthodoxy, comprising about 300 million Christians found in fairly independent versions in Russia, Ukraine, Romania, Serbia, Bulgaria, Greece, and Poland. There are about 85 million Oriental Orthodox Christians found in India, Egypt, Ethiopia, and Syria.

Describing the division of Protestants is much more complicated. First of all, Anglicans comprise 85 million, found around the world, chiefly either in England (one-third) or in countries with colonial ties to England: Nigeria, Uganda, Kenya, Sudan, and several other African countries, as well as Australia, the United States, and Canada primarily. Protestant denominations proliferated after the reformation, and are known by some of the following designations: Baptist, Lutheran, Evangelical, Presbyterian, Methodist, Mennonite, and Pentecostal.

Chapter Summary

Though Christian debates about practice have sometimes resembled Jewish and Islamic debates – such as whether beards should be mandatory on clergy – by and large, Christian interest in practice is seen in worship, or liturgical settings. With the exception of debates concerning divorce, abortion, and homosexuality, Christians do not often argue about Christian practice. Nonetheless, Christians *practice* Christianity in a variety of ways, and this chapter looked at some of those practices.

Glossary

Baptism. A ritualized practice related to conversion, Baptism uses water to symbolize the washing-away of sin and failing.

Chrismation. The ritual that brings someone (an adult converting, or an infant) into an Eastern Church by rubbing ointment made from oil and balsam on the forehead.

Confession: all Christians practice Confession in some form, but the most formal of these is Catholic Confession, which is closely tied to Communion. Catholic Confession is formal in that it is a ritual stage of maturity.

Consubstantiation. The Protestant understanding of the Eucharist is that during the sacrament of the Eucharist, the body and blood of Christ are present spiritually *with* (the implication of *con*substantiation) the bread and wine, but the bread and the wine (or juice) truly remain.

Holy Week. In Protestantism and Catholicism, Holy Week starts with Palm Sunday (remembering the entry of Jesus into Jerusalem), includes various observances on Monday, Tuesday, and Wednesday, then Maundy Thursday (remembering the last supper), Good Friday (remembering the trial and execution), and ends on Easter Sunday (celebrating the resurrection). Orthodox Christians also observe Holy Week but commemorate different events of Jesus' last week, and refer to each day as Great Holy Monday, Great Holy Tuesday, and so on.

Liturgy. Refers to the specific structure of a service – readings from the Bible, Eucharist – but also whether there is a structure and whether it is consistent and predictable. Thus, Catholic worship is highly liturgical because it has a structure and it is the same everywhere. Some forms of Protestant worship have less predictable and consistent services, and thus might be called non-liturgical.

Original Sin. A Christian doctrine concerning the fallen nature of humanity. The disobedience of Adam and Eve brought about the fall of humanity, meaning that all people, by virtue of being human, have inherited the sin of Adam and Eve.

Sermon. Many Christian worship services include a sermon (sometimes also called a homily). This is a lesson, or lecture, delivered by a priest, minister, or person so designated, in which a feature of Christian life, faith, scripture, or devotion is made relevant in the present.

Theodicy. A Greek term meaning "justice of God," there are many questions bound up in this term: How is God just? Is God just? How does God punish injustice and reward righteousness? At root, it revolves around the question "Why do bad things happen to good people?" Suffering presents a theological problem for monotheistic people who believe in a good and omnipotent God.

Transubstantiation. In Catholic doctrine concerning the Eucharist, the bread and wine might appear, but their substance has been altered to the body and blood of Christ.

Other Important Vocabulary

Advent

Anabaptists

Anglican

Aniconic

Ascension Day

Ash Wednesday

Basilica

Bishop

Bright Week

Carnival

Cathedral

Catholic

Clean Monday

Confirmation

Communion

Divine Liturgy

Eastern Orthodox

Episcopalian

Eucharist

Fast of the Nativity

Good Friday

Great Lent

Gregorian calendar

Homily

Hymns

Last Rites

Lent

Lutherans

Mass

Maundy Thursday

Oriental Orthodox

Palm Sunday

Pentecost

Primate

Protestant

Puritans

Reformation

Sacrament

Sacred Mysteries

Saturnalia

Shrove Tuesday

Discussion Questions

1. Above, I observed that religious practice is whatever it is that religious people do when they are being religious. Take a moment to consider and list the vast number of practices undertaken by Christians. What does this tell us about religion?

2. Different Christians have different practices, sometimes entirely different practices and sometimes just different versions of the same practice. Either way, each group has a way of defending its own practices as superior. However, which do you think comes first: historical tension and rivalry among groups, or the theological commitment to one's own practices?

3. You might be accustomed to hearing people distinguish religion from culture by saying things like, "Oh, that's not religion; that's just cultural." After reading this chapter, do you think religion and culture can be separated from one another?

4. Some people characterize Christianity as orthodoxic and Judaism as orthopraxic, meaning that Christians care more about correct belief than correct practice, and Judaism cares more about correct practice than correct belief. Having read this chapter, how would you contribute to that discussion?

Recommended Reading

Beavis, Mary Ann, and Michael J. Gilmour, eds. 2012. *Dictionary of the Bible and Western Culture.* Sheffield: Sheffield Phoenix Press.

Foley, Michael P. 2005. *Why Do Catholics Eat Fish on Friday? The Catholic Origin to Just About Everything.* New York: Macmillan.

Maffly-Kipp, Laurie F., Leigh E. Schmidt, and Mark Valeri, eds. 2006. *Practicing Protestants: Histories of Christian Life in America, 1630–1965.* Baltimore, MD: Johns Hopkins University Press.

McDannell, Colleen. 1995. *Material Christianity: Religion and Popular Culture in America.* New Haven, CT: Yale University Press.

Recommended Websites

http://w2.vatican.va

- The official website of the Vatican, in nine languages and offering many original documents and some history.

http://www.archbishopofcanterbury.org

- Official website of the Anglican Church's Archbishop of Canterbury.

http://www.goarch.org

- Official website of the Greek Orthodox Archdiocese of America. Contains many articles explaining practice.

—10—

Islamic Practice and Holy Days

Chapter Overview

Islam is a religion with legal codes the interpretation of which govern the shape of daily life, from religious services to dress and diet. This chapter will illustrate just some of the vast diversity of Islamic legal interpretation. We shall look at the development and characteristics of shariah as it pertains to daily life, the legal schools, and Arkan (or the five pillars of action). We will also look at topics such as diet, modesty, and the pressures of assimilation. This chapter also describes the main Islamic holy days and religious practices associated with them. It closes by looking at various features of art and culture in the Islamicate, and the global demographics of Muslims.

Islamic Practices

As with Judaism and Christianity, the number of Islamic practices is limitless. While there are some that are common among millions of Muslims, there are also local practices that some Muslims fiercely defend and others strongly disapprove of. That is to say, there is not one universal way of *being* Muslim. Because Muslims seek to submit to the will of God, it is common for great effort to be put into establishing laws and codes to guide and govern conduct. The intent is twofold: to offer guidance to people who sincerely wish to submit to God and want to know what to do and what not to do, and to create a society in which people behave in certain, approved ways. Thus, it is imperative that we start by looking closely at how Islamic law is established.

Shariah

One of the most common articulations of Islamic religion is that people are to submit to the will of God, that is do as God commands and avoid what God prohibits. If it is so important to submit to the will of God, then two things must happen to facilitate that: God's will must be ascertained, and that will must be codified in law. Muslims devoted concerted effort and reason, which they call *fiqh*, to express God's will in terms of legal precedent and then codify it into a set of laws, which they call shariah. Shariah, then, refers to the body of laws, rules, and regulations governing Islamic life; abiding by them is how one demonstrates by one's actions that one is submitting to the will of God. Shariah and halakhah (see Chapter Eight) are more or less equivalent terms.

In ascertaining the will of God, two written sources are given priority: the Qur'an and the body of Hadiths. The Qur'an is considered the word of God and thus the interpretation of Qur'anic material has the highest authority in establishing shariah. Next in authority comes the interpretation of Hadiths, which offer sayings of Muhammad, from those around him, as well as reports of his habits and events that he witnessed. Early reliance on the Hadiths in establishing shariah explains the great push discussed in Chapter Seven to establish authoritative collections of "sound" hadiths. Of course, people argued with one another about what the Qur'an or Hadiths *meant*, but the principle that these sources were absolutely authoritative in establishing law was always assumed in those debates. And of course, those debates continue today.

The problem with the Qur'an and the Hadiths is that they are ancient Arab writings: they cannot anticipate life among Byzantines and Persians, nor life in twenty-first-century America. More was needed if one hoped to devise new Islamic laws in the face of constant change. With this as the goal, there are two additional sources of Islamic law: analogical reasoning, or *qiyas* and consensus, or *ijma.*

If a particular practice or issue is not addressed in the Qur'an and Hadiths, but is *like* something that is addressed there, then by analogy, one can draw the same conclusion.

For example, because the Qur'an prohibits wine, one might conclude by analogy that modern drugs such as marijuana, ecstasy, or cocaine are also prohibited, though drugs are not explicitly prohibited in the Qur'an or Hadiths.

Ijma refers to consensus, and it is rooted in a common Islamic belief that God would not allow a majority to agree on an error. Generally, this is thought to be the majority of scholars, though of course this designation will always be contested. For example, the Qur'an and Hadiths do not specify whether one is permitted to play the role of Muhammad in a movie or play, and there is nothing that can provide an analogy either. So, the prohibition against portraying Muhammad in film has been arrived at by consensus alone. It is interesting that Christians felt the same way about Jesus being portrayed in film when movies were first being made.

Shariah covers all aspects of Islamic life, drawing no distinction between secular and religious spheres. Shariah refers to Islamic law, which includes what is allowed or prohibited, and often the prescribed punishments for transgressions. The laws and concerns of shariah can be separated into four groups: those that govern human interaction with God (e.g., when and how to pray, sacrifice, alms, fasting, pilgrimage, proper worship, and festivals); those that govern human interaction with other humans (e.g., lending, theft, slander, land tenancy, assault, murder, war and making peace, marriage and divorce, inheritance, and property law); those that concern individual morality (drinking, gambling, adultery, homosexuality, modesty, and diet); and finally, those laws that govern the shariah penal system itself (what constitutes evidence and testimony, as well as the prescribed punishments for transgressions).

Sunni and Shi'a Muslims have slightly different ways of arriving at shariah. They all agree that the Qur'an and Hadiths are foundational, and they all agree on what the Qur'an says. But they do not always agree on which hadiths are sound, or authentic, and they rarely agree on what the Qur'an means, so there will naturally be differences between Sunni and Shi'a shariah. Also, *ijma* does not carry the same certainty for Shi'a jurists as it does for Sunni jurists. For the first few Shi'a centuries, while there was an Imam, consensus was unnecessary, since the Imam had complete and divinely ordained authority. Yet despite the disappearance of the twelfth Imam, *ijma* still has not attained the same status for Shi'a Muslims. In addition, Shi'a jurists reject analogical or deductive reasoning that is part of *qiyas*. Shi'a jurists have a longer history of privileging the creative intellectual effort, or **ijtihad**, of the individual scholar in the process of *fiqh*. Shi'a scholars then continue to develop followings. Scholars who rise to the top, in modern Iran at least, are given the title "sign of God," or **Ayatollah**.

Legal Schools

Over the first two centuries of Islam, there was a competitive or entrepreneurial spirit among Sunni scholars participating in the establishment of shariah. These scholars would form schools, with generations of students devoted to their particular approaches to *fiqh*. Some of these schools did not survive, and others were absorbed into competing schools. In the end, four Sunni schools, or Madhhabs, emerged as authoritative: Hanafi, Shafi'i, Hanbali, and Maliki. These schools rose to prominence in different regions of the Islamicate, and have come mostly to be associated with those areas.

The Hanafi school is very popular, and dominates in the Balkans, Turkey, Syria, Jordan, Lebanon, Palestine, Egypt, central Asia, Pakistan, and India, as well as a portion of Iraq and most of Afghanistan. The Shafi'i school is strongest in Eritrea, parts of Ethiopia and along the west African coast, Yemen, in Kurdish areas of Turkey, Iraq, Jordan, Malaysia, Singapore, and Indonesia, and can be found in parts of Egypt, Palestine, Lebanon, and Syria. The Maliki school covers the rest of Islamic Africa, particularly Morocco, Algeria,

Halal

Halal refers to food that Muslims are permitted to eat, while **haram** refers to those things (including but not limited to foods) prohibited by shariah. Halal is the equivalent of kosher, but less complex, as there are fewer prohibitions. Kosher and halal meat both exclude pork, blood in meat, any animal sacrificed to another god, and meat not slaughtered specifically for human consumption. Also common to both is that meat that is in principle halal, such as beef, can be rendered haram if it was not slaughtered in the appropriate manner.

In addition, carnivorous animals, such as wolves and lions, are haram, while shellfish is sometimes forbidden, sometimes not, depending on the school of legal interpretation. Beyond this, there are no other foods that are haram, unless they are made with haram ingredients, such as pork fat, wine, or vanilla extract. Even though cosmetics are not ingested, they too can be considered haram if they contain ingredients that are haram (such as pork fat).

Libya, Mauritania to Sudan, and Nigeria. It can also be found in parts of Kuwait, eastern Saudi Arabia, and the United Arab Emirates. Finally, the Hanbali school is limited to Saudi Arabia and Qatar.

In the eighteenth century in what is now Saudi Arabia, a Hanbali jurist named Muhammad ibn 'Abd al-Wahhab, took a particularly puritan approach to *fiqh* and theology. The teachings of al-Wahhab came to be closely associated, and nearly merged later, with the Salafist school that developed in Egypt. Hard-line Salafist thinking can be found around the Islamicate, but has its strongest presence in the radical Islamist movement called **Wahhabism**, in Saudi Arabia.

These four classical schools still exist, but if there was a time when all Sunni Muslims in the Islamicate adhered to one of these four schools, that is no longer the case. Political instability in the post-colonial world and the rise of the political ideology known as Islamism has allowed new teachers and new schools to develop. In Shi'a Islam, Zaidis (but not Ismailis) have their own school of *fiqh*, and Twelver Shi'a ascribe to the school named after Jafar, the renowned sixth Imam. It is found mostly in Iran, but also in Shi'a parts of Iraq, Lebanon, and Syria.

By and large, the four Sunni schools agree on major matters of shariah and differ on how to define and govern exceptions. For example, one is allowed to shorten prayer when traveling, but how does one define "travel"? There are also differences in the finer details of some rituals, such as when certain daily prayers start, or how to calculate *zakat* (see pp. 246–247). But there are also differences with implications on lived experience, especially in North America.

For example, there is a widespread dislike of dogs among Muslims, and this is because they are not spoken well of in the Hadiths. Three of the four Sunni schools of *fiqh* consider dogs to be impure, so that if a dog's saliva or its wet nose touches a person, that person cannot pray in the garments they are wearing. The Maliki school on the other hand has no such position on dogs, and thus have no qualms about praying in a garment that has come into contact with a dog. This perhaps explains why many North American converts to Islam choose the Maliki school, because dogs are such a part of North American cultures, and the Maliki school makes it easier to convert and keep one's dog.

Arkan

Arkan is the formal way of referring to the five pillars of Islamic practice (also known as the five pillars of action). These five pillars of action represent bodily submission, emphasizing that in this formulation, devotion to God is not solely a mental activity, but a corporeal one as well.

Shahada

The **Shahada** requires one to witness or testify. The content of that testimony concerns God and Muhammad: there is no god but God, and Muhammad is the messenger of God. This is the Shahada as it exists in Sunni Islam; Shi'a Muslims add a third clause about Ali being the vice-regent of God. The key here is that this is not solely a creed, stipulating what one is to believe. Its significance resides additionally in the fact that it is something people are to testify to.

Like Christianity, Islam is a missionary religion, seeking actively to convert others. In

Figure 89. Muslim men doing ablution (*wudu*).

and with the intention – *niyya* – of converting.

Salat

While Muslims can pray any time they want, *salat* refers not to spontaneous prayer but to ritual prayer, and it can be either communal or individual. As ritualistic prayer, salat is required, structured, and scheduled. Several times a day many Muslims stop their activities to pray. In Islamic cities, the call to prayer, or *adhan*, rings out, sometimes cacophonously as the calls are issued not in perfect unison but seconds apart. The person who calls others to prayer is referred to as the muezzin. Sunni prayers happen five times a day, breaking up the pattern of the day: sunrise, midday, mid-afternoon, sunset, and evening. While some Shi'a follow this same prayer schedule, most

addition to that, the Shahada is whispered into the ear of a newborn and the dying. It is the object of Sufi meditation and repetition as well as depiction in art, and is heard multiple times a day in the calls to prayer. Conversion to Islam requires only that one say the Shahada three times before witnesses

---

The Formulas of Prayer

There is room during salat for a few moments of personal reflection and prayer, but the prayers of salat are mostly prescribed. The call to prayer consists of an expansion of the Shahada; note how the Shi'a *adhan* is longer than the Sunni one. For both groups, each line is said at least twice before moving to the next line.

In addition, the Fatiha (see text box, p. 173) is said during every raka of salat by Sunni Muslims, and in some but not in every raka by Shi'a Muslims.

God is Great

I bear witness that there is no god but God

I bear witnesses that Muhammad is the messenger of God

    [Here the Shi'a *adhan* adds: I bear witness that Ali is the vice-regent of God]

Hurry to the prayer

Hurry to success

    [Here the Shi'a *adhan* adds: Hurry to the best action]

God is great

There is no god but God

Figure 90. Mosque interior showing *mihrab* and *minbar*.

pray three times a day: sunrise, afternoon, and evening.

There are two types of impurity that Muslims encounter, mostly by living. Minor impurities are encountered in going the bathroom, flatulence, and bleeding from a cut, while major impurities come with ejaculation, menstruation, and childbirth. Even deep sleep renders one impure. The major and minor impurities can both be lifted with a bath, called *ghusl*, while minor impurities can only be lifted by performing *wudu* at the mosque. *Wudu* entails washing the face, hands, forearms, head, neck, and feet in water, commonly uttering prayers with each part cleansed.

In salat, the one praying goes through a number of cycles, each called a *raka*, of standing, bowing, kneeling, and prostration. The precise number of rakas, usually from two to four, depends on the time of day,

but the total for the day is meant to be seventeen.

According to Islamic tradition, salat is best performed with others, though if necessary one performs it alone. As such, the best place to commune for prayer would be a *masjid*, or mosque, though again, one is not obligated to perform every salat in a mosque. There is one weekly salat for which Muslims are expected to gather, and that is the Friday midday prayer, called *jumah*. Most commonly, women pray separately from the men in mosques, either in a separate room, or on the same floor but behind the men. Any time one is praying in a mosque, one faces the *qibla,* usually marked by a *mihrab* or niche in the wall; facing the *qibla* means that one is facing in the direction of Mecca. There are many monumental mosques across the Islamicate, and this is because the ideal was for there to be one mosque for congregational prayers. Therefore, they had to be large.

Before the prayers, the **Imam** delivers the *khutba*. In this part of the ritual, an Imam (or guest designated by the Imam) offers a prayer and a lecture from the *minbar*, expounding on a Qur'anic verse or hadith and relating it to any feature of life as a Muslim.

Zakat

The third pillar of action is an obligatory tax that is used to help those in financial need. And since the poor are the intended

Imams

Shi'a and Sunni Muslims share the term "Imam," and in some tasks they are the same. An Imam is formally appointed and salaried by the community to lead prayer and deliver sermons at a mosque, as well as to represent the Islamic community and serve as a spiritual advisor. Imams are fluent in Arabic, must be familiar with the Qur'an and Hadiths as well as their interpretation, and be knowledgeable in *fiqh*, or legal reasoning. Naturally, Sunni and Shi'a Imams learn the interpretive and legal traditions specific to each group. The training to become an Imam is now roughly equivalent to that involved in earning an undergraduate degree. In smaller or more remote communities, where it is not possible to find someone with formal training, the person who is considered the most knowledgeable in the group would be selected as the Imam. The position of Imam as religious leader is much like the positions of Rabbi in Judaism and Minister in Protestant Christianity.

But Shi'a Muslims (with the exception of Zaidis) also have an understanding of the term "Imam" that is wholly unique to them. In this usage, Imam refers to the highly exalted station of being a blood descendant of Muhammad, and of being declared infallible by the preceding Imam. They have access to divine knowledge, and the unquestioned authority that extends from that. People in this category include Ali, Husan, Husayn, the remainder of the twelve Imams, and Fatima. In the more regular use of "Imam," as religious leader, there is no expectation of descent from Muhammad.

recipients of *zakat*, most legal schools have provisions for exempting the poor from paying it, though Muslims disagree on what one's minimum wealth must be. In addition, there is a small, mandatory *zakat* to be paid at the end of Ramadan, associated with the celebration of Eid al-Fitr. The *zakat* on one's wealth is paid annually, on a date of one's own choosing.

The amount of what is to be paid varies by location, tradition, and the kind of wealth one has (e.g., money, livestock, property). The simplest and most common number given is that one should pay 2.5% tax on the wealth one has beyond what it is needed for sustenance and beyond one's debts. Increasingly, the amount paid is left up to individual conscience.

The traditional role of the state as arbiter, enforcer, and collector of the *zakat* raises the topic of the *jizya*. Because *zakat* is an Islamic obligation, it was never required or collected from non-Muslims. As the Islamicate expanded to include large numbers of Christians, Jews, Zoroastrians, and Hindus, it became common to apply a comparable tax on them. This is the *jizya*, payable by any healthy, sane, and wealthy non-Muslim male, unless he was a soldier in the army. The topic is controversial. In some locations, it appears that the *jizya* was merely a way for non-Muslims to contribute to local social welfare. In other locations, however, it was a way of humiliating and pressuring non-Muslims to convert or join the army. That is, if the *zakat* was considerably less than the *jizya*, there would be a strong incentive to convert to Islam or to serve in the state's military. The *jizya* is rarely seen in Islamic countries any more, but it is part of the rhetoric of modern Islamist movements, who seek its return.

Is Jihad a Pillar of Practice?

Where does jihad fit into Islam? A minority of Sunni Muslims argue that jihad constitutes a *sixth* pillar of practice, but the majority of scholars argue that to add a sixth pillar would change the religion that Muhammad established, which no person has the authority to do. Conversely, Shi'a Muslims do consider jihad a pillar of practice: for Ismailis it is the seventh pillar, and for Imamis it is the sixth pillar. This can be alarming for non-Muslims to hear, especially given the prevalence of Islamist groups claiming that jihad is not merely a pillar but the heart of Islam. What exactly is jihad?

When Islamists use the term *jihad*, they are privileging its secondary meaning: military defense of the religion and resistance to oppression, both of which justify violence. The primary meaning of jihad, however, for Sunni Muslims and for those Shi'a who consider it one of their pillars, resides in the struggle not against opponents and oppressors, but against oneself. Human selfishness and desire make submission to God extremely difficult; the fight to suppress one's own will and to submit to the will of God is called the "Greater Jihad." The "Lesser Jihad" is the one that involves violence.

Sawm

It is said that Muhammad's first revelation came to him during the month of Ramadan, and thus a purifying fast came to be instituted during this month. Muslims may practice *sawm* at any time, and for any number of personal and religious reasons, including other minor festivals and observances, but the main period of fasting, and the one considered the fourth arkan is the month-long fast that occurs during Ramadan.

The fast prohibits the consumption of all forms of food (even things you do not swallow, such as chewing gum and hard candies) and drink (including water, coffee, and tea) while the sun is up. Some even feel that brushing one's teeth once the sun has risen is forbidden, because it would be impossible not to swallow some toothpaste residue, or water from rinsing out the mouth.

Because Ramadan can be extremely arduous, much flexibility exists in Islamic law to ensure that the fast is not dangerous to one's health. If one is sick and needs medication, or is pregnant or breastfeeding and thus needing nourishment, or if one is traveling, fasting is not required. In these cases, one might pick another month when one can observe the fast. Those who are permanently on medication and can never fast can contribute money for the feeding of the poor. Daily during Ramadan, one declares one's intention, or *niyya*, to fast, for it does not count as fasting if it is accidental.

But fasting during Ramadan applies to more than the stomach. Fasting also applies to other behaviors, such as sexual activity, sarcasm, gossip, violence, anger, and lust. In other words, this is a fast in which much of human nature is controlled, not only the need to eat and the pleasure one gets from it. It is a period of self-control and self-denial, the goal of which is, for many Muslims, to mimic the purity Muhammad must have had to be worthy of a revelation from God.

Hajj

The fifth and final pillar of practice, or arkan, is the pilgrimage to the Great Mosque in Mecca, known as the **Hajj**. Every Muslim

Figure 91. Holy Mecca: pilgrims circling the Kabah during Hajj.

on Mecca; they are hosted, guided, protected, and watched by the government of Saudi Arabia, tasked with everyone's safety and security. Part of this entails controlling who is allowed to attend. Pilgrims (Hajji) do not simply show up for the Hajj; they must apply for a permit through travel agents approved by the Saudi government. Part of the process of acquiring a permit is to prove one is Muslim, for only Muslims are allowed into Mecca. Once in Saudi Arabia, pilgrims pass through controlled checkpoints with their permits, otherwise known as "Hajj passports."

who is capable of making the journey is to do so once in his or her lifetime. One cannot incur debt to make the trip and must settle any debts first. This expectation derives from a time when travel to Mecca was long, arduous, treacherous, and sometimes dangerous. When there were reasonable odds that one might not return from Hajj, it was not right to borrow money to make the journey. While modern travel is less dangerous, there are still casualties during almost every Hajj, sometimes numbering into the hundreds and thousands.

Hajj occurs 8–12 Dhul Hijja, the twelfth and final month of the year. Annually, 2–3 million foreign and local pilgrims converge

Preparation for Hajj, taking up the seventh day of the month, involves three rituals. The first is called *ihram*, involving entry into a state of purity and nothingness expressed by donning two white, seamless pieces of cloth. This ritual also expresses the equality of all pilgrims: the simple cloth hides individual markers of status and wealth. The second ritual is called *tawaf*: it is the circumambulation of the Kabah, seven times counterclockwise. The third ritual is called *sa'y*, reliving Hagar's panic – according to Islamic tradition – as she ran between two hills, Marwa and Safa searching for water for Ishmael (see pp. 124–125).

On the eighth day, Hajj begins with a long walk from Mecca to the Plains of Arafat, which may be broken up by a stay in Mina. By noon on the ninth day, pilgrims must be at Arafat, for the ritual of *wuquf*. For at least an hour between noon and sunset, everyone stands still before God, contemplating and repenting their past sins, praying to God for forgiveness, and seeking mercy, symbolizing Adam and Eve begging God for mercy. It is, like Yom Kippur for Jews, a ritual of atonement. At sunset, the ritual ends and the pilgrims move to Muzdalifa, where they pray and gather pebbles for the next day's ritual.

On the tenth day of the month, two rituals happen. In the first, pilgrims arrive in Mina for the stoning of the Jamarat pillars. The pillars represent Satan, and by throwing stones at them, pilgrims remember how Abraham rebuked Satan for trying to discourage him and his son from submitting to the will of God. The second ritual, called Eid al-Adha, involves the sacrifice of an animal, and more will be said on it below. At the end of this third day, some pilgrims will have their heads shaved. The shaved head is meant to resemble an infant's head, for the Hajji, like an infant, is said to be without sin. The stoning of the Jamarat pillars in Mina continues until the twelfth day of the month, at which point pilgrims return to Mecca for one more *tawaf*. From Eid al-Adha onwards, Hajj winds down, and slowly takes on a more festive and social atmosphere for many. Then once pilgrims leave Mecca, the trip often transitions into tourism, as some travel to Medina and others to various shrines and holy sites in the Islamicate, all of which can also happen before Hajj begins.

These five arkan are practiced by all Muslims, regardless of sect, but Shi'a Muslims do have additional practices that are strongly encouraged, such as an additional taxation, expressions of love for God and hatred of evil.

Holy Days

Three caveats are in order before discussing Islamic holy days. First, each Islamic day, including holy days, begins with the setting sun, like in Judaism. Second, most of the holy days discussed below are known by different names to different Muslims around the world. The names below reflect Arab culture, but they often have different names in Turkish, Persian, South Asian, and East Asian cultures. Finally, there are many additional Shi'a holy days not listed below. These tend to be days commemorating the births and deaths of each of the first eleven Imams and the birth of the twelfth Imam, some of which are public holidays in Iran.

Muharram/Ashura

Muslims recognize the start of a new lunar year – the first of Muharram – but do not tend to celebrate it, beyond perhaps attending morning prayer at a mosque. Consciously

Islamic Time	
The Islamic calendar is lunar, and Islamic time begins with the Hijra from Mecca to Medina (see Chapter Four). Here is a list of Islamic New Years.	1st of Muharram 1441 starts on August 31, 2019 1st of Muharram 1442 starts on August 20, 2020 1st of Muharram 1443 starts on August 9, 2021 1st of Muharram 1444 starts on July 30, 2022 1st of Muharram 1445 starts on July 19, 2023

Figure 92. Shi'a Muslims commemorate the martyrdom of Husayn on the Day of Ashura. Shi'a march in the streets, self-flagellating, flailing, and beating themselves. The injury and blood during this festival of mourning serves as a reminder to Shi'a of the sacrifice and pain of Ali.

The meaning of Ashura for Shi'a Muslims is different, and the observance of it is much more elaborate. Nine somber days prior to Ashura reach a peak on the tenth day, on which Shi'a Muslims remember the martyrdom of Husayn at the Battle of Karbala in 680 CE. It is a day of collective mourning and self-recrimination for the fact that the military support promised to Husayn prior to the battle never arrived, and thus his forces were decimated and he was killed and decapitated.

resembling the first Jewish month (Tishri), the first ten days of Muharram are a period of sombre reflection in Islam, a time of increased fasting and prayer. The tenth of Muharram, called Ashura, is significant for Shi'a and Sunni alike, but for wholly different reasons.

Sunni Muslims fast on Ashura (and sometimes also on the ninth) because of a tradition that Muhammad chose this day as a fast day when he observed Jews fasting (Yom Kippur) on it. Like Yom Kippur, Muslims make a connection between fasting on this day and atonement for the sins of the previous year. It is worth noting, however, that fasting on this day is not obligatory.

The rituals of Ashura revolve around the memory of this event: in the days preceding, the narrative of the battle is recited in dramatic fashion and mournful poems are delivered. On the day itself, sermons focus on the character of Husayn and his suffering, passion plays are observed, along with somber parades with floats that contain a coffin, barrels of weapons, and Husayn's horse. The sorrow can reach levels as if the sadness is fresh; some people weep and deliver emotional laments. Typically, over two million people come to Karbala, in Iraq, to observe Ashura, and it is a national holiday in Lebanon, Iraq, Iran, Afghanistan, Pakistan, and India. Shi'a Ashura gatherings are commonly occasions of violence from Sunni opponents.

Mawlid

Mawlid is the abbreviated name that refers to the birthday of Muhammad. Though several

Devotional Mawlid Poetry

Suleyman Chelebi (d. 1411) was a prince in the Ottoman Empire. In his life of political intrigue over the Ottoman throne, he still managed time for poetry. This is a single stanza from his Mawlid poem. Typical of the genre, the poem regards Muhammad as the manifestation of God's mercy and love, and illumination in a dark world.

This night is the night that he, so pure
Will suffuse the worlds with radiant light!
This night, earth becomes a Paradise,
This night God shows mercy to the world.
This night those with heart are filled with joy,
This night gives the lovers a new life.

(Translation from: A. Schimmel, *And Muhammad is His Messenger.* Chapel Hill, NC: University of North Carolina Press, 1985, p. 154)

dates are listed in early Islamic sources, the twelfth of Rabi al-Awwal, the third month of the calendar, is the date designated for this commemoration. Mawlid is festive in spirit, so mosques and sometimes whole cities can be found decorated with candles, lights, banners, flags, and streamers, with sweets distributed to everyone. It is common for gifts to be given to children, and for grand feasts to be held. One might also hear devotional songs that extol Muhammad as the bringer of mercy into the world and praise him for his role as intercessor between humans and God.

There has always been rigorous debate among Islamic scholars concerning whether one is allowed to celebrate Muhammad's birthday, though recently it has come to be observed by many Muslims. Though there is evidence of Mawlid being celebrated for at least

the last eight hundred years, some Sunni groups, particularly but not limited to Wahhabis, object to it on multiple grounds: it is an innovation, and therefore wholly improper; it was invented by Shi'a Muslims; it was not celebrated by Muhammad; and it is nothing but an imitation of the Christian celebration of Jesus' birth. One sees here parallels with Christians who reject the celebration of Easter and Christmas, and Jews

Figure 93. The al-Aqsa Mosque, and the Dome of the Rock, Jerusalem.

Mysticism and Ecstasy

Islamic theologians have long debated whether the *Isra* and *Miraj* of Muhammad were physical or spiritual experiences. Was his body transported, or was this an out-of-body experience? In defense of the physicality of the experience, Sura 17 suggests that the *Isra* involved Muhammad being physically transported. Conversely, there is a Hadith of Aish'a that claims that Muhammad never left the bed on this night, suggesting that the trip was spiritual or visionary, but not physical.

These types of experiences are common in many religions, and often form the foundation of religious experience in general, and of mystical experience in particular. For example, for Sufis, these two episodes inspire the hope that divine encounters are possible for everyone. Commonly, the goal of Islamic mysticism is to mimic Muhammad's ascent. They are also interesting to a variety of scholars of religion. Scholars might analyze features of these two episodes that can be found in other mystical traditions, or might explore what motivated communities to create and transmit stories like this. Scholars interested in cognitive science and neurology are increasingly interested in the role of the brain and brain chemistry in generating out-of-body, or ecstatic experiences such as the possible one described here.

who question the celebration of Hanukkah. At any rate, the objections explain why Mawlid is a national holiday in many places in the Middle East, but not in Saudi Arabia and Qatar, where the Wahhabi/Salafist perspective dominates. Interestingly, in the year 2243 CE, Mawlid will coincide exactly with December 25. It is one of the few Islamic holy days that is celebrated by Sunni and Shi'a, and often in quite similar ways.

Isra/Miraj

Traditions can be found in the Hadiths and subtly echoed in the Qur'an that one night Muhammad was transported in his sleep on a winged horse named Buraq from Mecca to Jerusalem, where he led prayer for a number of past prophets, most prominent among them Abraham, Moses, and Jesus. This story, called *Isra* in Arabic and usually the Night Journey in English, expresses the Islamic belief that Muhammad had the support of all past prophets. A second narrative, called *Miraj*, then commences, in which Muhammad ascends from Jerusalem into the seven levels of heaven. On his way to the highest level of heaven, where he meets God, Muhammad sees the angelic armies of God, the flames of hell, and from there again Jesus and many of the Israelite prophets. Once in the presence of God, Muhammad is given the prayers that comprise the ritual of salat. He then returns to Jerusalem, where Buraq flies him back to Mecca. The al-Aqsa mosque in Jerusalem was built (possibly in the second half of the seventh century) to mark the spot from which it was believed Muhammad ascended into Heaven. This is the reason Muslims commonly consider Jerusalem the third-most holy site in Islam, after Mecca and Medina.

The most common date for celebrating *Isra* and *Miraj* is the twenty-seventh of Rajab, the seventh Islamic month. Practices associated with this celebration include fasting, telling the story of the journey, additional prayer, and poetry performances. As with Mawlid, sweets can be handed out and cities decorated. Similar objections to the celebration of *Isra* and *Miraj* to those concerning Mawlid are commonly founds in certain Muslim groups.

Laylat al-Qadr

The month of Ramadan was chosen for the key Islamic fast because of its association with the month in which Muhammad received his first revelation. The Qur'an does not specify which day of the month it was, so different Islamic communities choose different days. Typically, Sunni Muslims choose one of the odd-numbered days in the last third of the month (e.g., 21st, 23rd, 25th, 27th, or 29th), though the 27th is the most commonly designated night for this observance, while Shi'a communities tend to prefer the 19th, 21st, or 23rd. The celebration is called Laylat al-Qadr, or the Night of Power. It is common for one to stay up through the night in prayer, to hear and reflect on the ninety-nine names of God, and for sermons and songs to be delivered at a mosque. Additionally, some Muslims might retreat to a mosque not merely for Laylat al-Qadr, but for the entire last ten days of Ramadan, a ritual known as *itikaf*. Regardless of which night Laylat al-Qadr falls on, however, it is commonly regarded as the most important night of Ramadan, and the Qur'an claims that piety on this night is worth a thousand months of piety. Sufis commonly choose to retreat into solitude, rather than community, on this night.

Eid al-Fitr

The Ramadan fast lasts for the entirety of the month. On the first day of the following month, called Shawwal, there is a feast, called Eid al-Fitr, that marks the end of the fast. It lasts for one to three days, depending on location. It is one of the few times

Figure 94. A host tending to the needs of his guests, from the *Al Maqamat al Hariri*, an Arabic illuminated manuscript produced in southern Iraq in the first half of the thirteenth century. The manuscript features ninety-nine surviving miniatures highly esteemed for their authentic depiction of real life.

of the year that Islamic law *forbids* fasting. Indeed, quite the opposite: one is expected to show joy, and fireworks might be let off. Where possible, friends and family gather for an extravagant feast in decorated homes or large public spaces. People might wear new (or their best) clothes or give gifts or small amounts of money to children. It is also customary in many places to honors one's elders.

The ideal is for all Muslims to eat festively on Eid al-Fitr, but of course not all Muslims are wealthy enough to do this. It is very common for Muslims to see this time as one particularly requiring generosity. Payment of *zakat* at this time helps to ensure that everyone can celebrate on this day, but there are other customs as well. One might see communal meals put on by Islamic associations to which the poor are also invited. Local organizations frequently try to raise money on this day to help the poor. Alternatively, non-perishable groceries might be purchased and left anonymously at the homes of the needy, and merchants sometimes give Eid gifts to customers.

In many Muslim-majority countries, Eid al-Fitr is a public holiday during which government and many businesses close. Sunni and Shi'a both observe Eid al-Fitr in similar ways.

Eid al-Adha

The Feast of the Sacrifice, or Eid al-Adha, happens on the tenth of Dhul Hijja, the last month of the year, though the festival continues for two to three days, depending on location. Although this happens to be the third day of the Hajj, and is related narratively to the Stoning of the Jamarat, the observance of Eid al-Adha is not limited

to those on the Hajj. Eid al-Adha recalls the story in which Abraham is commanded by God to sacrifice "his son," which the majority of Islamic commentators take to refer to Ishmael. Together, Abraham and his son willingly submit to the will of God, but at the last minute, God provides a ram to be sacrificed instead, showing Abraham that he has passed the test of loyalty. Islamic commentary traditions, or Tafsir (see Chapter Seven), fill out the details of the story: that Abraham was unable to watch, so covered his face, that when he looked up, he saw his son alive and a ram standing nearby to be sacrificed. Ultimately, the story is understood to illustrate total submission to the will of God, no matter the request, and to illustrate God's mercy and love. It is this fuller narrative expansion of the Qur'anic foundation that informs the celebration of Eid al-Adha.

One attends mosque prayers on this day, but the primary ritual is the sacrifice of an animal, most commonly a sheep, but also possibly a goat, cow, or camel, in gratitude to God. Charity is a key component of this ritual: a family sacrificing an animal is allowed to keep one-third of the meat and give one-third to friends or family, but one-third must also be given to the poor. Families who lack access to animals or to a place in which one can perform an animal sacrifice (e.g., those in modern urban apartments) can pay an organization that performs the sacrifice on their behalf, and in this instance, all of the meat goes to the poor.

Nowruz

For thousands of years, the people of Central Asia have celebrated the vernal equinox, which marks the official start of spring in the

Figure 95. A decorated car with a map of Iran on the hood and Haftsin table, an arrangement of seven symbolic items that are traditionally displayed at Nowruz, the Iranian New Year.

This is accomplished in the variety of interpretations unique to Shi'a Muslims that claim that Nowruz is the day the sun first rose over God's creation, the day humanity first agreed there was no God but God (Sura 7.172), the day Muhammad assigned Ali to succeed him, the day Muhammad and Ali cleansed the Kabah, and the day Noah's Ark came to rest after the flood.

Though Nowruz was made Islamic by Shi'a Muslims, many of its rituals retain their pre-Islamic significance, and today Nowruz is a feature of Persian/Iranian culture, celebrated therefore by Persian Zoroastrians, Jews, Christians, and Baha'is, as well as Shi'a and Sunni Muslims in Afghanistan. One particularly colorful ritual of Nowruz is the Haftsin table: a celebratory table set out with seven items that all begin with the "s" sound in Persian, each with symbolic meaning. These seven items usually come from the following list: sumac (signifies the color of sunrise), vinegar (signifies age and patience), dried Persian olive (signifies love, fertility), sweet pudding (signifies sweetness), coins (signifies affluence), something sprouting (signifies rebirth), hyacinth (signifies fragrance), apple (signifies health and beauty), and garlic (signifies medicine). A few other items are commonly added to the seven: a Qur'an, decorated eggs, a goldfish in a bowl, a mirror, candles, or rose water, or the poetry of Hafiz, each with its own symbolism.

Northern Hemisphere. Determining the precise start requires observation by human eye, but this day is always on or around March 21 on the solar calendar. Sasanian Persians (third–seventh century CE) designated this day as the beginning of the new year (*now ruz* means "new day"), hence its current designation as Persian New Year.

The arrival of Muslims, with their lunar calendar, was not enough to supplant the popular celebration of Nowruz. In fact, Nowruz was not only popular with the people, but also with Shi'a rulers, such as the Buyids (see Chapter Four) in the tenth century. Nonetheless, a certain discomfort can be seen in some Islamic sources with the non-Islamic origins of Nowruz. The solution was to keep the festival but reassign its significance, much like Christians did with Saturnalia.

Islamic Culture

Dress

How people dress, and what dress expresses about individuals and their cultures, is a rich area of research. Dress is often coded to articulate something about a culture's values and its social structure. For instance, if purple and gold are colors associated with royalty, the poor would often not be allowed to wear those colors. If a group rejects wealth and signs of conspicuous consumption, then generally that group will discourage its members from wearing jewelry and fine clothing. Clothing says something about one's status in the world, and helps to demarcate the boundaries between groups. Clothing, as we have seen in other chapters, can be a part of people's communal identity. Religious communities can also have expectations concerning dress, and these expectations can often be gendered, that is different for men and women.

Just like in Judaism and Christianity, there exists in Islam the expectation that all people dress "modestly." That sounds simple enough, but how "modesty" is defined, whether by Muslims or non-Muslims, is complex and diverse. How one defines modesty, whether that person is religious or not, depends on two aspects of being human: how one's culture informs one's sense of modesty (e.g., how we learn what the group around us expects), and each individual's personal sense of modesty (e.g., some people simply do not feel comfortable in revealing clothing, regardless of how permissive one's surrounding culture might be).

Modesty is defined in countless different ways, not only in Muslim-majority countries but also in places where Muslims are the minority. There are Muslim women whose definition of modesty is to dress with the majority: in North America or Europe, they may choose not to cover their hair, but in a Muslim-majority country, they do. For these women, modesty means not attracting attention to one's self, and they feel that to wear a hijab in a non-Islamic country is to draw attention. For other Muslim women, dressing modestly requires them to cover their hair and neck, and two options exist for this. The **hijab** is a scarf that covers the hair and neck but leaves the entirety of the face and eyes exposed, while the chador is a loose cloak that covers the hair and falls down to be wrapped around the whole body. Some Muslim women, however, feel that modesty requires them to cover not only their hair and neck, but most of their faces too. The niqab covers the hair and all of the face

Figure 96. A Muslim woman wearing a burka.

Figure 97. Ceiling of Shamsuddin Hafez's tomb in Shiraz, Iran.

Western responses to the burka and niqab range from curious to tolerant to xenophobic. Some people express concern for the freedom of Muslim women to dress as they wish. It is a fact that some Muslim women are forced to wear the burka or niqab by fear of punishment from totalitarian regimes and patriarchal fathers, husbands, or brothers. But it is also the case that some Muslim women themselves choose to wear the burka or niqab: it is simply how they define and experience their own modesty. This fact makes it impossible, therefore, to generalize about, or legislate on, Muslim women's dress based on some examples of oppression.

except the eyes, where a narrow opening is left. And finally, the burka (see Figure 96) offers the most coverage: the entire body, head to foot, with a mesh over the eyes to allow some visibility but no visibility from the outside in.

Whether one chooses no head covering, the hijab, or the burka depends in part on personal choice, but sometimes also on the legal school one (or one's family or group) follows. The practice of wearing a burka or niqab tends to be seen in places where the Salafist approach to *fiqh* is powerful: Saudi Arabia, parts of Pakistan, and Afghanistan under the Taliban. But of course, families around the world can subscribe to Salafist legal interpretations, so the burka and niqab can be seen wherever Muslims live, including North America and Europe.

As a rule, these various dress practices relate to how to dress in places where non-familial men will be, either in public places or when male guests come to one's home. When at home before one's male kin, or in places with only women, the woman need not cover her hair. In part, there are cultural practices at work here: in honor-based cultures, controlling women's dress and behavior is meant to protect family honor. In other words, this cultural gender pattern can be seen much more broadly than in Islam alone. Having said that, it is impossible to discern when exactly veiling became a standard practice and expectation of Muslim women.

Visual Art

"Islamic art" refers to the variety of artistic materials that were produced in Islamic

Figurative Art

"Jahangir Preferring Sufi Shaykh to Kings," a miniature by the Hindu painter Bichitr.

"Despite the prohibition of figurative painting or sculpture in some of Islam's legal schools, Islam has its own venerable tradition of figurative art, generally referred to as 'Persian miniatures,' a tradition that began in the thirteenth century, and came to fruition in the fifteenth and sixteenth centuries, influencing Ottoman, Safavid, and Mughal art. Persian miniatures were paintings in illustrated books of poetry. Although figurative art was prohibited in copies of the Qur'an, this prohibition did not extend to other books, including collections of tales, history and poetry."

(Excerpt from William Rory Dickson and Meena Sharify-Funk, *Unveiling Sufism: From Manhattan to Mecca*. Sheffield: Equinox Publishing, 2017, p. 105)

cultures, but it bears pointing out that only some of this art was informed by Islamic *religion*. For instance, upon entering a mosque, one notices the absence of figural art: there are no paintings, mosaics, or stained-glass windows containing the figures of Muhammad, or the four Rightly Guided Caliphs, or the twelve Imams. This is because Islamic jurists strongly objected to the creation of figural art. Yet their objection was only effective as it pertained to mosque decor and liturgical practice; outside of liturgical settings, Muslims were creating art with human and animal images just like everyone else. On occasion, they even created images of Muhammad and of the Imams. And not surprisingly, it was always permissible to create official portraits of one's rulers (sultans, kings, caliphs, and imams). But one thing is unclear: when Muslims created art with geometric or floral patterns instead of figural images, was it because of the belief that it was wrong to depict living creatures, or was it because geometric patterns were common and attractive.

Muslims were famous for several kinds of art. Finely woven textiles, sometimes with intricate patterns, used for making clothing and furniture, were highly sought after by Muslims and non-Muslims alike and became the hallmark of elite European society in the Middle Ages and early modern period. The prayer rug was a common piece of functional art in Islamic life, and an elaborate and extensive system of factories also produced standard rugs. Calligraphy is another highly recognizable Islamic art form. Calligraphy was used to write the Qur'an, informed by the belief that a consistent and proportional script added to the beauty, harmony, and power of the divine text. But it was also used to create

Figure 98. Jameh Mosque of Isfahan, Iran, known for having four facing *iwans*, or vaulted arched openings.

art, designs, and animal shapes using calligraphic words, the Shahada, and the Arabic word Allah prominent among them. Muslims were also innovative in the creation of glossy ceramics called lusterware, and renowned for metalwork. Much of these different types of art were created in miniature, something Muslims were also known for.

Architecture

Everywhere that Muslims went, they built. And what they built tended to be drawn equally from local pre-Islamic traditions and from transnational Islamic traditions. Thus, for example, early Umayyad buildings drew from Christian styles (which in turn had drawn from Roman styles). But later Muslims looked back to these Umayyad buildings and saw in them a traditional model to

be emulated. Thus, later Abbasid Muslims created buildings that were inspired by Umayyad buildings, which were themselves inspired by Roman-Christian buildings. Likewise, mosques and minarets in China are made of wood, not stone, and strongly resemble the architecture of Chinese temples and palaces. In other instances, however, Islamic buildings resemble non-Islamic buildings not only because of influence and inspiration, but because Muslims took over and repurposed those buildings. Each of these cases can be found in the city of Istanbul: the seventeenth-century Sultan Ahmet Mosque, also known as the Blue Mosque, was modeled on the Christian Basilica known as Hagia Sophia. And the Hagia Sophia itself was converted into a mosque in the fifteenth-century, merely with the addition of minarets on the outside and Qur'anic phrases on the inside, and by covering over Christian iconography. The Hagia Sophia (see Figure 28, p. 61) is now a museum.

In this context, how does one speak about a "Muslim" architecture? In part, this can be done by focusing on artistic styles and architectural forms that, for a variety of aesthetic and theological reasons, Muslims appear to have preferred. Of course, this includes first and foremost minarets. The minaret served several functions: it was a monument; it marked the location of the mosque; it was used for surveillance; and it was sometimes also used to issue the call to prayer. Also included here are pillared halls, especially for prayer spaces, though eventually and where possible, these came to be replaced

Sufism in America

As we saw, Sufism played a significant role in the global expansion of Islam into India and eastward from there. Sufi Islam interacted with the cultures and religions it encountered in those lands. This is no less evident in Sufism's introduction to North America. It began with the arrival of an acclaimed Indian musician and his brother in Manhattan in 1910. The court musician and Sufi master Inayat Khan (d. 1927) traveled for sixteen years throughout North America and Europe, giving talks, concerts, and establishing his Sufi Order in the West. He represented Sufism as a practice little connected with the outward aspects of Islam. When American culture began experiencing a shift away from – and general suspicion about – organized religion, most forcefully in the 1960s, many became interested in mystical traditions that appeared to transcend religious and cultural borders, such as Yoga, Zen Buddhism, and Sufism. This all fed into the development of the New Age movement in North America, arguably led by a convert who was proclaimed both a Sufi and Zen master or guide simultaneously. He was Samuel L. Lewis, also known as "Sufi Sam," and he died in 1971.

Samuel L. Lewis (Sufi Sam)

by high domes that allowed for vast open worship spaces beneath them. Enclosed courtyard gardens and arches, particularly pointed arches, are commonly found in Islamic buildings, as are iwans, especially in Persian/Iranian mosques. An iwan is a rectangular hall with a high ceiling and one end open (see Figure 98).

Several features are consistent in mosque design. First, they face Mecca, and inside have a prominent niche that shows the direction of Mecca, called the *mihrab* (see Figure 90, p. 246). Mosques also need a *minbar*, commonly elevated in order to help the Imam be better heard in large mosques. They also need access to clean water, for the observance of *wudu*. But in addition, in terms of design and structure, mosques also commonly lack figural art and require spaces that allow for gender segregation. While figural art could be found in much Islamic architecture, it is consistently absent from religious architecture. Exquisite art and designs, made with glass mosaics, fresco paintings, and stucco could be found in mosques, but the designs were geometric, floral, or calligraphic (see Figure 97, p. 258). And from the ninth century onwards, women were either excluded from the mosque or were segregated onto a balcony or adjoining room. This practice was influenced by certain approaches to Qur'anic interpretation that became widespread after the ninth-century. The Qur'an itself says nothing explicit about the separation of men and women in the mosque.

Music

Muslims rarely refer to the sounds associated with religious rituals – the call to prayer, Qur'anic recitation, and salat prayer – as "music." This is because Islamic cultures have tended to take the position that voice and percussion alone is not music (music requires stringed instruments). But it is also the case that Islamic cultures had moral concerns with music, because of the tendency for musical gatherings to bring men and women together, to involve alcohol, and to refer to subjects perhaps not in keeping with "religious" values. And yet, despite this, Islamic worship is very musical, in that it is almost always conducted with tonal and melodic variation. Across the Islamicate, the call to prayer, Qur'anic recitation, and salat prayers combine some consistent practices and expectations with some local variations.

Qur'anic recitation is the highest pious art form in Islam. Professional Qur'anic reciters can be extremely popular, and their live and recorded performances highly sought after. But Qur'anic recitation is not only an art, it is also a science called *tajwid*. Recitation of the Qur'an is tightly regulated, with many rules applying to where one must pause, which letters must be pronounced and how they are to be pronounced, and how long certain sounds are to be elongated. As a rule, Saudi Arabian and Egyptian styles of Qur'anic recitation are the models that reciters are expected to follow, though increasingly singers and reciters are expressing themselves musically using some of their own cultural traditions. Traditionally, Qur'anic reciters have been male, but here too breaks from tradition can be seen, as Muslim women are starting to exert their rights and abilities at recitation.

Muslims in Popular Music

Muslims can be found in all aspects of global cultural life, including popular music. Some Muslims make music, and their religion plays no part in it, as with Christians and Jews. Others, however, refer explicitly to their religion in their lyrics, and their religion informs their art. Mos Def raps social justice and human rights, which appear to be the core of Islam for him. Lupe Fiasco, another rapper, explores his identity as a Muslim living in a world in which so much violence is done by Muslims. His song, "Muhammad Walks" opens with a line from the *jumah* prayer and the traditional *adhan*, or call to prayer, before presenting his view of Islam as a religion of peace closely related to Judaism and Christianity. In "The Spark," from their critically acclaimed album *Things Fall Apart*, hip-hop group The Roots refer to their maintenance of the five pillars of action and to their assurance that God hears prayer.

Sami Yusuf is a popular Islamic singer, whose music touches explicitly on Islamic religious values and relies on Persian musical instrumentation. Much more controversial, and less popular than it used to be, is a genre of modern punk-rock called *Taqwacore* – hardcore Islamic punk music. This music, like all punk-rock, is critical of tradition and authority, and thus is intended to offend. Music, films, and books associated with Taqwacore have been banned in some Islamic countries.

Syncretism and Folk Religion

We have already seen many examples of religious syncretism in these three religions – when one religion takes over a feature or practice from a competing religion. We have also seen instances of "folk religion": that is, popular practices that do not enjoy official support. The example of fortune-telling parrots illustrates both of these. This practice is looked down upon by most Muslims because of its non-Islamic origin and resemblance to magic, and though it is less common than it used to be, the practice still persists. In it, parrots select a fortune from a row of envelopes arrayed before prospective clients. In Pakistan, for example they may advertise such services as "Islamic book of oracles/omens" (*Islami fai-nama*). Often contemporary advertisements claim that the oracles are free from any taint of frivolous matters, betraying a certain anxiety and defensiveness concerning the religious orthodoxy of divination. Premium services can entail an oral consultation wherein the fortune teller refers to a "Quranic oracle book" (*Qur'ani fal*) which offers "prophetic" oracles each listed beneath the name of an Islamic prophet.

Fortune-telling parrots, Lahore, Pakistan.

Outside of the mosque, local variants and the addition of musical instrumentation feature more prominently. Across the Islamicate, Muslims are known to incorporate the music of kettledrums, trumpets, oboes, drums, and stringed instruments into the musical celebrations of festivals, such as the start and end of Ramadan, both Eids, departure for and homecoming from Hajj, and Mawlid. Because of the tradition of orthopraxic debate, it should not surprise us that debate is common among Muslims about music. Some feel that the Qur'an allows, at most, vocal beautification of the Qur'an, and claim that the addition of anything that sounds more musical is haram. Their view of *popular* music, naturally, is even more dim. Other Muslims interpret the Qur'an and other Islamic sources differently and find nothing to suggest that they should not create or enjoy music, whether religious or secular.

Muslims in the World

In 2010, the global Islamic population was approximately 1.6 billion, comprising the second-largest religious group in the world.

263

Slightly over 60% of the world's Muslims live in South Asia and South-East Asia (e.g., Indonesia, Pakistan, India, and Bangladesh), about 20% live in the Middle East and North Africa (e.g., Egypt, Iran, Turkey, and Saudi Arabia), and approximately 15% live in sub-Saharan Africa (e.g., Ghana, Nigeria, and Sudan). Finally, about 3% of the world's Muslims live in Europe and North America. Put differently, 80% of Muslims in the world live outside of the Arab Middle East. Not only is it important to register that not all Muslims are Arab (far from it, in fact), but also not all Arabs are Muslim: approximately 10% of the Arab world is Christian, Jewish, or atheist. While Islam began in Arabia, and while Arab culture and theology continue to be very attractive to Muslims around the world, the fact is: Islam is culturally, ethnically, and linguistically diverse.

For Muslims living in Europe and North America, the greatest challenge is likely the draw of assimilation and acculturation: giving up traditional dress and diet in order to fit in more easily. This can be the case not only as a matter of convenience, but also occasionally because of harassment and suspicion. In an age when Islamist terrorism and violence invites suspicion of all Muslims, people can react negatively to traditional Islamic dress, particularly the niqab and the burka. Some Western nations have even attempted legally to ban the niqab from certain spheres of public life, all the while claiming to support religious freedom. Negotiating life in the midst of these tensions is not easy for Muslims.

Of global Muslims, as many as 20% are Shi'a, though as always, precision is very difficult to achieve. The majority of Shi'a are found in Iran and Iraq, which along with Bahrain and Azerbaijan comprise the only four Shi'a-majority nations in the world. In addition, sizable Shi'a minority populations can be found in eastern Saudi Arabia, Lebanon, United Arab Emirates, Kuwait, and Qatar. There is frequently sectarian violence between Shi'a and Sunni Muslims in the Middle East. Radical Islamist groups like al-Qaeda and Daesh target Shi'a (and Sufis for that matter) as often as they target non-Muslims.

Chapter Summary

Islamic practices, like all religious practices, are composed of features that are partially universal and partially local. That is, Islamic practice reflects local culture that is to varying extents consistent with Islamic practice in other locations. Many of the differences in Islamic practices could be called accidents of history, but we would not want to imply by this phrase that there is an original form of any Islamic practice from which variants deviate.

Glossary

Arkan. Refers to the five pillars of action: Shahada (confession), salat (prayer), *zakat* (alms), *sawm* (fasting), and Hajj (pilgrimage). Though these five are found in all forms of Islam, they can sometimes be done differently by Shi'a Muslims, who also consider other practices to be arkan.

Ayatollah. This is the honorary title given to Twelver Shi'a jurists and clerics who attain the highest level of theological learning. The name expresses the belief that humans, because of their learning and wisdom, can be "signs of God." The only higher office than Ayatollah for Shi'a Muslims is Grand Ayatollah, of which there are fewer than a hundred in the world.

Fiqh. Refers to "understanding" required in the human effort to understand and apply divine laws to human living. This naturally allows personal opinion and local traditions to shape legal practice, which is why there are competing Madhhabs: Hanafi, Shafi'i, Hanbali, and Maliki.

Halal/haram. Halal is anything permitted, while haram is anything forbidden. These words are mostly associated with diet (e.g., pork and alcohol are haram, meat that is proper and properly killed is called halal), but also extends to other actions (e.g., stealing, lying) and thoughts (e.g., associating anything else with God, or *shirk*).

Hijab. Modesty is practiced by Muslim women in many different ways. The most common practice is to wear a hijab, which covers hair and neck. Sometimes, however, depending on personal preference, culture, or legal school of thought, modesty involves covering all (burka) or most (niqab) of the face, as well as the hair and neck. One's practice of modesty might also lead one to wear a loose robe, called a chador, which hides the shape of the body.

Ijtihad. Refers to the creative, intellectual effort it takes to participate in *fiqh* in order to develop shariah. Sunni Muslims have tended to be more conservative, declaring with the consolidation of the four legal schools that *ijtihad* should stop. This approach prevailed until the rise of new Sunni radical schools in the eighteenth century onwards. Conversely, it has never prevailed among Shi'a Muslims, who were more comfortable with continual creativity and innovation.

Imam. A simple word with many uses, Imam refers most commonly to the person who leads prayers and delivers the *khutba* (sermon) during *jumah* prayer. An Imam is expected to be male, mature, and educated in the relevant Islamic theological sciences. While Shi'a Muslims also use the term in this way, they also use the term to refer specifically to the descendants of Muhammad, who because of their bloodline relationship to the Prophet had unique access to God's wisdom and direction.

Jumah. The Arabic word for Friday is also the word used to refer to congregational prayer, which happens at mosques at midday on Fridays. The word itself derives from the word for gathering. In Muslim-majority cultures, *jumah* prayers mark a break in market activities, resumed again when the prayers are completed.

Niyya. This word refers to intention, and it is a central component of many Islamic practices. For example, forgetting to eat is not fasting, so every day of Ramadan begins by expressing the intention to fast. Likewise, one converts by repeating the Shahada with the intention of converting.

Shahada. "I testify that there is no god but God and Muhammad is the messenger of God," with "and Ali is the vice-regent [*wali*] of God" added in the Shi'a iteration. It expresses the core of Islamic faith (similar in function and form to the Jewish Shema); it is part of the call to prayer (*adhan*), can be found on the flag of Saudi Arabia (and other flags), coins, buildings, tile panel art, and calligraphic art.

Wahhabism. Muhammad ibn 'Abd al-Wahhab was an eighteenth-century Islamic jurist, preacher, and scholar who initiated a program of purifying Islam of practices he disagreed with, even though they were widely practiced and approved. This approach has come to be associated with extreme, intolerant, and rigid views of proper Islamic practice, and provides the foundation for most modern radical Islamist movements.

Other Important Vocabulary

Adhan	*Isra/Miraj*	*Masjid*	Ramadan
Ashura	*Itikaf*	Mawlid	Salat
Chador	Iwan	*Mihrab*	*Sawm*
Eid al-Adha	Jamarat	Minaret	*Sa'y*
Eid al-Fitr	Jihad	*Minbar*	Shafi'i School
Ghusl	*Jizya*	Muezzin	Shariah
Hajj	Kabah	Muharram	*Tawaf*
Hanafi School	*Khutba*	Nowruz	*Tajwid*
Hanbali School	Laylat al-Qadr	*Qibla*	*Wudu*
Ihram	Madhhab	*Qiyas*	*Wuquf*
Ijma	Maliki School	*Raka*	*Zakat*

Discussion Questions

1. How has the historical spread of Islam shaped its various practices?

2. Considering the variety of Islamic practices associated with religious life and holy days, is it possible to separate religion and culture?

3. How might the term *orthopraxic* be applied to both Islam and Judaism?

4. Consider how the encounter of Muslims with other cultures (e.g., Persian, Turkic, African, European, Mongol, Indian, etc.) both in the past and today complicates any discussion of what constitutes authentically Islamic practice.

5. Considering the evidence presented in this chapter, what role does interpretation play in determining Islamic practice?

6. What is the relationship between ritual and religious identity? How might ritual function as a way for a member to claim membership in a community? How might it function to deny membership to someone? How might it function to remember the past and establish group identity?

Recommended Reading

Ahmed, Leila. 1992. *Women and Gender in Islam: Historical Roots of a Modern Debate.* New Haven, CT: Yale University Press.

Rippin, Andrew, ed. 2008. *The Islamic World.* London: Routledge.

Schimmel, Annemarie. 1985. *And Muhammad is His Messenger: The Veneration of the Prophet in Islamic Piety.* Chapel Hill, NC: University of North Carolina Press.

Recommended Websites

http://www.islamicsupremecouncil.org

- The Islamic Supreme Council of America offers summaries of Islamic spirituality, but also recent legal rulings.

http://www.visual-arts-cork.com/islamic-art.htm

- A website on art and architecture in Islam. Includes thousands of images as well as academic commentary on items.

http://islamicbulletin.org

- Simple summaries and explanations in numerous languages of many Islamic practices.

—Part Four—
The Continuing History of Religions

We tend to think about Judaism, Christianity, and Islam as religions of the past, even though they still exist and continue to develop and change. In fact, these religions have survived where others have died precisely because Jews, Christians, and Muslims have adapted to sometimes rapidly changing and traumatic conditions. These three religions have long histories, but the history of religion is not a thing of the past, wherein *true* religions were revealed a thousand or more years ago while new religions are hoaxes played on gullible people. The history of religion is still happening!

Not only are the religions of Jews, Christians, and Muslims still developing, but new religions are growing from them, like new branches off a large tree. Christianity grew out of Judaism. Islam did not grow out of Judaism and Christianity in quite the same way, but Islam would be impossible without the foundation of its Jewish and Christian precursors. The LDS Church, on the other hand, grew directly from Christianity. Its practitioners believe in Jesus Christ, yet they have unique beliefs that set them apart from other Christians. Baha'ism grew directly out of Shi'a Islam, wherein some of their beliefs and practices clearly reflect those of Muslims,

and sometimes more precisely Shi'a antecedents, even as some of those are altered.

What is fascinating about Latter-day Saints and Baha'is for historians of religion is the realization that "prophets" and revelations are not solely features of the distant past. Prophetic revelation apparently happened most recently less than two hundred years ago. And nor can prophets and revelation be confined to the Ancient Near East or Middle East, to far-off "romantic" lands; it apparently happened too in upstate New York.

One final thing is revealed by the study of the LDS Church and Baha'is: rarely does a generation pass without someone somewhere claiming some religious status, to be a wise teacher, a prophet, or a messiah. But history is littered with the bodies of dead religions. All religions start small, with only a few supporters. Look around and consider current small "fringe" religions, perhaps Raelians, Hare Krishnas, Scientologists, or Heaven's Gate. The study of religion warns us not to assume that these fringe religions will stay minor. The number of Christians and Muslims was once impossibly small. Latter-day Saints and Baha'is survived and their numbers grew. The point is, the survival and growth of new religions is never predictable. They present scholars with many questions and many data: why do some religions survive and others do not?

Earlier in this book, I discussed the theological narratives of earliest Israelite history and of the careers of Jesus and Muhammad in the theology chapters rather than the history chapters for each religion. This was not, as I said then, because there were no Jews, Christians, or Muslims in those earlier years, but because those stories tell us more about the theological interests of Jews, Christians, and Muslims and less about the actual past. Those stories tell us, for instance, that Jews, Christians, and Muslims saw God as profoundly active in history, in their world, and in the establishment and shape of their religion. It is also helpful to recognize that the initial period of each of these religions was one of great flux, in which the charisma of a revered founder was the primary motivation for the existence of the religion and belief and practice were all still highly contested. Although all features of a religion are susceptible to contestation, they do eventually reach a degree of stability that is impossible in the earliest period. The history chapters therefore tended to begin for each religion at the point at which the religion as we know it today (more or less) took shape.

I have replicated that approach for the history of Latter-day Saints and Baha'is in this final chapter. One might think that religions that developed in the nineteenth century might be said to have grown in the full light of history. This might be true in some respects. We do have much more material evidence of their early years than we do for Judaism, Christianity, and Islam. For instance, no one knows for certain when Jesus died, but we know when Joseph Smith and Mirza Husayn Ali died. And yet, when we look closely at the LDS and Baha'i founding narratives, we find

the same tendency to write divine guidance and providence into them. In other words, the origins narratives do not just describe what happened. They also make a case that God had a pivotal role in their foundations. Therefore, the real significance of those narratives, just as for Judaism, Christianity, and Islam, lay outside of the historical realm. Two more caveats are in order here. First: why is there no "new" religion for Judaism in this chapter? The answer is simple: for whatever historical or cultural reasons, a new religion growing out of Judaism has simply not happened yet, and it is impossible to know why. Some readers may be familiar with Jews for Jesus, and wonder if this is not a new development within Judaism. The reason I would argue that Jews for Jesus does not constitute a new religion is that they are indistinguishable from mainstream Evangelical Christianity, particularly in their beliefs about Jesus, about biblical inerrancy, and in their push to evangelize and convert. In other words, Jews who are "for Jesus" are Jewish people who have converted to Christianity, but retained some of their Jewish practices.

Second: what does it signify that I have placed Latter-day Saints and Baha'is in a chapter of their own, and not included them in the various appropriate Christianity and Islam chapters? The significance is strictly a structural one. The theology and practices of both groups are sufficiently unique both to be taken seriously and covered separately. Latter-day Saints self-identify as Christian; many Christians reject that claim. Conversely, Baha'is claim that Baha'i is a new religion, with which Muslims readily agree. The placement of these religions here is not intended to take a position either way; that is a theological dispute among them.

Latter-day Saints and Baha'i Religion

Chapter Overview

In this chapter we survey the histories of the founding and development of the LDS Church and Baha'i religion, as well as the theological innovations, collections of sacred writings, and distinct practices that most commonly characterize each group.

Latter-day Saints

History

In an American period of Christian millenarian fervor and excitement called the **Second Great Awakening**, Joseph Smith Jr. (1805–1844) proclaimed that all forms of Christianity had gone wrong, and that the true form had been revealed to him. In 1830, he introduced a new piece of scripture, which he called the Book of Mormon. People were drawn to this new scripture, and the building of a new religion appears to have been based on it, starting in Palmyra, a village near Rochester, New York. Initially, they called themselves Christians, believing they were the restored, original form of Christianity. Others, however, called them – derisively – Mormonites or Mormons, after their book of scripture. They came to adopt the formal designation the Church of Jesus Christ of Latter-day Saints, abbreviated to Latter-day Saints or LDS, and more popularly to Mormons. Though the term "Mormon" once had a pejorative edge, it no longer does.

What comes next appears to be a steady cycle settling in new places, persecution from people already living there, and then expulsion and exile. The motivation for this was a search for the new City of Zion, and the result was a gradual westward movement of the groups. Whether the cause of the persecution lies in the religious claims, teachings, and practices of Mormons that other Christians were offended by, whether they feared being outnumbered by Mormons, or whether it was questionable Mormon business dealings depends on which sources one consults. But the fact is: wherever Mormons

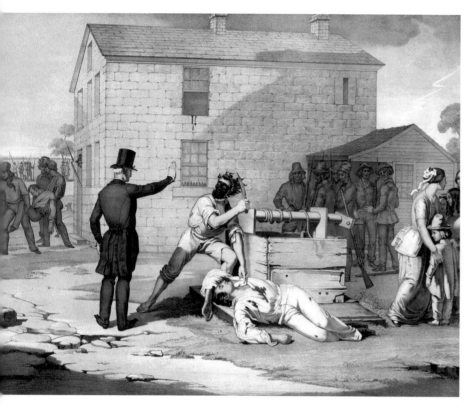

Figure 99. "Martyrdom of Joseph and Hiram Smith in Carthage Jail, June 27th, 1844": lithograph of a painting by G.W. Fasel.

persecution. In 1838, many of the Kirtland Mormons, including Smith, had to flee. They went westward, following in the path of those who had done so seven years earlier.

But the Mormons who had settled in Independence had already been expelled from there. In 1836, they had created their own settlement in a town called Far West, Missouri, north of Independence and what is now Kansas City. Smith and the Kirtland Mormons thus went to Far West, making it the new headquarters of the church. The name Far West might sound at odds with a modern map, but it can be useful to remember that at this time, the western border of Missouri was the western-most edge of the United States of America.

Although Caldwell County, with Far West as its seat, was originally established by the state of Missouri in 1836 precisely to assist Mormon re-settlement, peace there did not last. In 1838, Mormons were forced to leave Missouri entirely – by authority of the Missouri Extermination Order – and Joseph Smith was arrested (for treason) and imprisoned for six months. His people fled north into remote Illinois, purchasing a town and renaming it Nauvoo.

Six months later, Smith escaped his guards, and after arriving in Nauvoo, took over its administration, becoming mayor and head of its militia. In 1843, he publicly endorsed polygamy, and life became difficult again. There was considerable anger and confusion

settled, persecution and prosecution followed. This early persecution surely explains the emphasis many Mormons place on freedom of religion and freedom of conscience.

In 1831, open persecution from Christian clergy forced Mormons from Palmyra. Some went to Kirtland, Ohio, while others carried on westward to Independence, Missouri. The city of Independence was a goal because Smith had predicted that the Second Coming of Christ would occur there soon. However, Kirtland is where Mormons built their first temple, which they completed in 1836, and so the town became the destination for many Mormon converts. As Mormon numbers rose in Kirtland, so did suspicion and

in Nauvoo among his own people, and revulsion against polygamy among non-Mormons. Non-Mormons called for the eradication of Mormons, and in 1844, a group of dissident Mormons (also unhappy with polygamy) published a newspaper called the *Nauvoo Expositor* in which they were critical of Smith and the way he was running the city. He shut down the paper, but the public backlash was immediate. Smith was arrested by state officials on flimsy grounds, and was imprisoned in the Carthage Jail. While in his cell, a mob broke in and assassinated him on June 27, 1844. He was thirty-eight years old.

In the wake of Smith's death, members of his immediate family vied for power with members of the church's leadership bodies. While it was Brigham Young who succeeded Smith, tension over succession as well as over polygamy led to fragmentation. Some Mormons remained in Illinois, while others moved to Iowa, Missouri, Michigan's Upper Peninsula, Pennsylvania, and Texas. Today, several smaller break-away groups of Mormons – those who rejected the authority of Brigham Young – still live in these states. Prominent among these groups is the Reorganized Church of Jesus Christ of Latter-day Saints, originally led by Joseph Smith's eldest son. It is now known as the Community of Christ, with its headquarters in Independence, Missouri.

While some Mormons remained behind after Joseph Smith's death, causing the religion's first schism, a larger number followed Brigham Young. They went west into what is now Utah, but was then isolated territory governed by Mexico. After Smith's 1844 assassination, Young planned for a mass migration from Illinois to the valley of the Great Salt Lake, where he hoped Mormons could be free from the persecution that already had driven them from Ohio, Missouri, and finally Illinois. The main migration began in 1846, but was done over winter and many died along the way. They eventually made it to Utah in 1847 (a trip of about 1300 miles/2200 km) where they settled. About 70,000 joined them over the next twenty-two years.

In 1846–1848, the US went to war against Mexico, winning control of the south-western quadrant of what is now the United

Figure 100. An anti-Mormon political cartoon from the late nineteenth century.

States of America, including Utah, and Mormons fought in that war with the US. This signaled, and perhaps ignited, a Mormon desire to participate in the American political process. Mormons lobbied to make Utah a territory of the USA, which was eventually granted in 1850. A year later, Brigham Young was appointed Utah's first governor. But the goal of creating a Mormon state was impossible, for Mormons were not the only ones drawn west by opportunity. The discovery of gold and silver in the Utah Territory, along with the longer-standing promise of gold in California, ensured a steady flow of non-Mormons to and through Utah. The federal grant of Utah to the Mormons did not decrease mutual suspicion and dislike, and tensions continued to rise.

In 1856, polygamy was as much an item of heated federal electoral rhetoric as was slavery, and the issue of Mormon control of Utah was reopened. In 1857, the federal government sent troops towards Utah, fearing that Mormons were planning a rebellion and wanting to put an end to polygamy there. In response, Mormons prepared to defend what they felt was their land, perhaps remembering Missouri's Extermination Order against them. What resulted is called the Utah War (1857–1858). There were no great battles between the federal government and the Mormons, only small skirmishes with few casualties. It ended diplomatically, with Brigham Young handing over governorship to a non-Mormon in 1858.

There were, however, casualties during the war, but they were entirely civilian at an event known as the Mountain Meadows Massacre (1857). A wagon train carrying emigrants to California stopped in Utah, and became a source of suspicion in a tense time. Mormon and non-Mormon sources differ considerably on apportioning blame, but approximately 120 men, women, and children were slaughtered after being tricked into giving up their weapons.

Distrust and dislike of Mormons likely explains the length of time it took for Utah to be accepted as a state into the Union: this did not happen until 1896. The positive turn was surely directly related to the Mormon decision to abandon the practice of polygamy in 1890, since that was the primary source of American federal and cultural opposition to Mormons. Under continual and mounting political pressure from the federal government, the President of the Mormon Church, who carries the authority of a prophet, proclaimed a revelation setting plural marriages aside. This action was widely accepted, but it did cause another breach in the religion, as some felt that the LDS President did not have the authority to set aside a practice endorsed by Joseph Smith himself. Some groups split off, and even though it is illegal to do so everywhere, a minority of the LDS Church continues to practice polygamy, including in British Columbia, Canada.

Through its popular and rigorous missionary program, the LDS Church has both become more integrated into American culture and grown numerically in international distribution. In the 1960s when American culture started to become more liberal and secular, Mormons and Fundamentalist or Evangelical Christians discovered how much they had in common socially, though the latter were also the most ardent opponents of Mormons theologically. American mainstream acceptance of Mormons, however, received a considerable boost in 2012 when Mitt Romney became the Republican

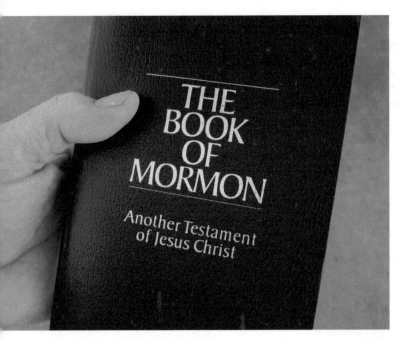

Figure 101. The Book of Mormon.

This story serves as the narrative of origin for the Book of Mormon, a new Christian scripture published in 1830, its theological significance evident in the fact that this date serves as the start date of the LDS Church. Joseph Smith was considered a prophet, whom God had chosen to reveal the true form of worship of Jesus Christ. LDS tradition claims that the Book of Mormon and the work of Joseph Smith represent the restoration of Christianity.

But Smith was not the only one with prophetic status, for Mormon leaders were granted the same status. Thus, Brigham Young was thought to speak with the authority of a prophet, and subsequent presidents of the Mormon Church are titled "seer, prophet, and revelator." They speak with absolute authority, and are thus able to overturn previous beliefs or practices. For instance, when the fourth LDS President overturned the long-defended practice of polygamy, the decision was unchallenged by the vast majority of Mormons. And when the twelfth President proclaimed that men with dark skin could be ordained into the Priesthood, despite the fact that the Book of Mormon describes dark skin as a sign of divine cursing, it too was accepted. Presidents of the Mormon Church thus continue to serve in prophetic roles, even after Joseph Smith.

Party's presidential candidate, though he lost the election to Barack Obama. Indeed, it is noteworthy that Romney was not even the only Mormon competing for Republican leadership that year.

Theology and Scripture

Founders and Foundations

The Mormon theological narrative of origin is set in 1820, when at age fourteen, Joseph Smith received a series of visions that told him that all existing Christian denominations had strayed from the truth. In 1823, an angel named Moroni led Smith to the place where a secret book written in an ancient mysterious script on gold plates was buried. It was not until 1827 that Moroni deemed Smith ready to receive the plates, at which point he set about to translating them with the help of "seeing stones."

Mormon Beliefs

Mormons stand apart from most other Christians in that they are not Trinitarian. They believe in God, in Jesus Christ, and in the Holy Spirit, but they believe these

Mormon Articles of Faith

In 1842, in response to questions about what Latter-day Saints believe, Joseph Smith published this list in a local newspaper, and this is how they appear in most Mormon sources. It is noteworthy how similar they are in some ways to elements of Christian faith, but it is important to note that Mormon theology is complex and distinct from mainstream Christian theology. For instance, the first article sounds Trinitarian, but Mormon theology does not support the Trinity. Rather, though God, Jesus Christ, and Holy Ghost are named, they are conceived as *separate* individuals, together comprising the Godhead.

We believe in God, the Eternal Father, and in His Son, Jesus Christ, and in the Holy Ghost.

We believe that men will be punished for their own sins, and not for Adam's transgression.

We believe that through the Atonement of Christ, all mankind may be saved, by obedience to the laws and ordinances of the Gospel.

We believe that the first principles and ordinances of the Gospel are: first, Faith in the Lord Jesus Christ; second, Repentance; third, Baptism by immersion for the remission of sins; fourth, Laying on of hands for the gift of the Holy Ghost.

We believe that a man must be called of God, by prophecy, and by the laying on of hands by those who are in authority, to preach the Gospel and administer in the ordinances thereof.

We believe in the same organization that existed in the Primitive Church, namely, apostles, prophets, pastors, teachers, evangelists, and so forth.

We believe in the gift of tongues, prophecy, revelation, visions, healing, interpretation of tongues, and so forth.

We believe the Bible to be the word of God as far as it is translated correctly; we also believe the Book of Mormon to be the word of God.

We believe all that God has revealed, all that He does now reveal, and we believe that He will yet reveal many great and important things pertaining to the Kingdom of God.

We believe in the literal gathering of Israel and in the restoration of the Ten Tribes; that Zion (the New Jerusalem) will be built upon the American continent; that Christ will reign personally upon the earth; and, that the earth will be renewed and receive its paradisiacal glory.

We claim the privilege of worshiping Almighty God according to the dictates of our own conscience, and allow all men the same privilege, let them worship how, where, or what they may.

We believe in being subject to kings, presidents, rulers, and magistrates, in obeying, honoring, and sustaining the law.

We believe in being honest, true, chaste, benevolent, virtuous, and in doing good to all men; indeed, we may say that we follow the admonition of Paul – We believe all things, we hope all things, we have endured many things, and hope to be able to endure all things. If there is anything virtuous, lovely, or of good report or praiseworthy, we seek after these things.

to be separate and distinct individuals who together comprise the **Godhead**, a term Mormon theology prefers over Trinity. Also distinct to Latter-day Saints is the belief that humans can become gods, a goal they refer to as **Exaltation**. This exalted state enables Mormon couples to bear children even after death. In addition to Baptism and receipt of the Holy Spirit that are required of all Mormons, Exaltation requires **Ordinances** as well: for men, Priesthood Ordination, and for men and women the Endowment and Celestial Marriage. These will be discussed below among the practices of Latter-day Saints, but it is important to register the way in which, as with all the religions discussed in this book, practice and beliefs intersect so closely they can be difficult to separate.

Mormon theology imagines heaven in three levels, known as the Kingdoms of Glory. The highest level is the Celestial Kingdom, reserved for those who achieve Exaltation, but so too those who were good Mormons who were baptized, received the Holy Spirit, and remained active and committed until death. Below the Celestial Kingdom sits the Terrestrial Kingdom, which is for people who led good lives but rejected the Mormon message, as well as for less committed Latter-day Saints. The lowest realm of glory, but still identified as a realm of glory, the Telestial Kingdom is reserved for liars and the generally bad. Only the Sons of Perdition cannot enter one of these realms of glory, that is those who serve Satan, who are atheists, and who totally reject and work against God.

Mormon Theological Writings

There are four central theological texts for Latter-day Saints: the Bible (Old Testament and New Testament), the Book of Mormon, Doctrine and Covenants, and Pearl of Great Price. LDS tradition maintains that the New Testament provides the foundation of Christian faith, which Latter-day Saints claim to represent exclusively. Thus, considerable attention is paid to studying the New Testament. LDS theology also believes that there are prophecies in the New Testament that anticipate the rise of the LDS Church. In effect, for Latter-day saints, the New Testament accurately records the life of Jesus and his disciples, and the earliest days of Christianity, while the Book of Mormon accurately records Christianity in the latter days.

The Book of Mormon is a collection of fifteen prophetic books in the names of eleven prophets; Mormon tradition maintains that these prophets lived 600 BCE–420 CE, for the account found in the book narrates their departure from Jerusalem before the Babylonian conquest, their arrival in America, and the various difficulties and internal schisms they experienced. The words of these eleven prophets were written down on gold plates in 322 CE by one of them, named Mormon, who then gave the plates to his son Moroni. Moroni is said to have completed the work, hidden the plates, and then to have appeared to Joseph Smith as an angel in 1823 to tell him of their existence. These are the plates Smith claims to have translated, which he published in 1830.

The dramatic pinnacle of the Book of Mormon, the reason why the Church of Jesus Christ of Latter-day Saints can claim to be Christian, comes when Jesus Christ appears in America shortly after his resurrection. It is this event that legitimizes the claims of Mormons to represent an authentic expression of worship of the God of Israel and

Jesus Christ, all revolving around America as the place for the new Zion and the Second Coming. In other words, in Mormonism, America figures prominently in the divine plan of Salvation, a very novel development of an ancient Israelite religion.

The Book of Mormon was instrumental in the founding, development, and spread of Mormonism, but there is little there in it that is conducive to establishing a religious way of life. The work known as Doctrine and Covenants, on the other hand, was far more useful for this need. This work is a collection of revelations and proclamations regarding such topics as the authenticity of the Book of Mormon, setting out Mormon doctrine such as salvation, eternal marriage and family, Baptism, and polygamy, as well as procedures relating to governance and finance of the church. The revelations and proclamations in this work are mainly from Joseph Smith, but because Latter-day Saints believe in the ongoing revelation of God, there are revelations from others as well. The work was first composed in 1835, and has been expanded several times. It also contains non-revelatory material, such as letters and reports.

The Pearl of Great Price is the fourth item of scripture used by Latter-day Saints. This work was first published in 1851, and then contained much overlap with Doctrine and Covenants. Now, the book has a very different form: five sections made up mostly of "inspired" translations Joseph Smith did of parts of Genesis, the narratives of Abraham, the Gospel of Matthew, concluding with excerpts from Smith's historical writings and the thirteen articles of faith (see "Mormon Articles of Faith" text box, p. 274).

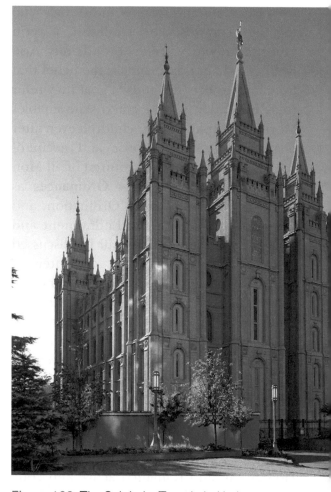

Figure 102. The Salt Lake Temple in Utah.

Practice

The LDS Church has a single leader called a **president**. Joseph Smith was considered the first president, Brigham Young the second, and the LDS Church is currently on its seventeenth President. The more common title for the President of the LDS Church is Prophet. He is considered a seer and revelator, in that he can be the recipient of revelations from God that alter past Church practices. This role and position renders official decrees infallible.

Mormon worship services closely resemble other Christian services. Latter-day Saints meet on Sundays in churches to pray, sing, hear sermons, often delivered by fellow worshippers, and most importantly to participate in the sacrament of Communion, which for Mormons is the consumption of bread and water, representing the body and blood of Jesus Christ. These services are commonly called **Sacrament Meetings**, and they are open to the public, regardless of religion. In contrast, Mormon temples are used not for weekly worship but for the Ordinances, and are open only to Mormons who are in good standing with the Church. In 2019, there were 163 Mormon temples around the world, with an additional thirty-nine planned or under construction, compared with over 30,000 churches.

The key practices of Latter-day Saints are the Ordinances, which are required for the achievement of Exaltation: Priesthood Ordination, the Endowment, and Celestial Marriage. Priesthood Ordination is open to any male above the age of twelve, and assumes only worthiness. In other words, no education is required, and thus it is assumed that all Mormon men can qualify for the Priesthood. There are no paid or professional clergy in the Mormon church. Instead, any member of a congregation who is a holder of the Priesthood and married can be chosen by his community to serve voluntarily for a few years in the role of leader. The term Bishop is used for this office.

Figure 103. A woman sits near the altar in a sealing room in the celestial room of the Salt Lake Temple. She is wearing traditional clothing for the Mormon endowment and sealing ceremony.

The Endowment is a temple ritual that involves a ritual cleansing and anointing, the exchange of promises with God, called covenants, and receipt of a new, secret name and a Temple Garment. Once endowed, Mormons are meant to wear the Temple Garment, which is underclothing worn whether awake or asleep (working out and swimming are common times not to wear the garment). The garment, like many religious garments, is intended to remind the wearer of the commitments she or he made to the temple in the ritual, though it is also said to ward off evil and temptation. The Endowment is available to those who have been Latter-day Saints for at least a year, and who, through interviews with a bishop, are recommended as worthy to enter the temple.

Once one has been endowed in an LDS temple, one may seek out a Celestial Marriage, which is the third ordinance that leads to Exaltation, and like the Endowment, must occur in a temple. Marriages for Mormons happen in two ways. If a couple is married in a church or civil office, the marriage is legal, but it – like other marriages – ends when one person in the couple dies. If a Mormon couple is married in a temple, or by participating in this ritual in addition to their civil or church wedding, they have achieved a Celestial Marriage. This marriage is eternal, in that it carries on into the afterlife. In a Celestial Marriage, the couple is "**sealed**," which means they will be able to find each other and remain married, and even continue to have children, in the Celestial Kingdom. The children of couples who have been sealed through this ritual will also be sealed, and thus the family will exist as a family in the afterlife. When divorce happens to couples who have been sealed, the seal ends, for the seal only applies to people who are legally married. Nonetheless, if a woman wishes to remarry and be re-sealed with a new husband, she must seek formal cancellation of the original seal.

It is worth noting that Priesthood Ordination, the Endowment, Baptism, and even Celestial Marriage can be performed on those who have died; they are called vicarious ordinances. One who was never Mormon can be baptized into the LDS Church vicariously. In this case, a living person of the same sex receives the actual rite, opening the possibility for the deceased to convert; the dead person must decide whether to accept and receive salvation. This ritual has been performed on many historical figures. Mormons understand this ritual as giving a long-dead person who never heard the LDS message the opportunity to convert. The same logic is applied to Priesthood and to Celestial Marriage. In the first instance, a deceased Mormon might be given the opportunity to accept priesthood after death. In the second instance, if one's grandparents were never sealed in marriage, one could perform the sealing ritual vicariously. Thus, the grandparents would be brought together for eternal marriage. Vicarious ordinances can only be performed in a temple.

Many young Mormons also participate in missionary work as part of their religious life. Unmarried men and women between eighteen and twenty-five commonly serve in missions that last twenty-four months for men and eighteen months for women, and typically take place far from home. Missionary work is not required, but it is strongly encouraged and culturally expected. For instance, in 2019, there were 399 active, formal missions and nearly 75,000 full-time Mormon missionaries in the world.

The LDS Church does not have many holy days. They celebrate Christmas and Easter, very similarly to other Christians, but reject the other traditional Christian holy days and periods. Mormon celebration of Easter stresses the resurrection of Jesus over the death, and thus Good Friday is not part of the LDS observance of Easter. Less officially, LDS practice and theology sometimes maintains a traditional Jewish flavor, recalling that Mormon tradition sees the prophets behind the Book of Mormon as Israelites.

In addition, Mormons in Utah celebrate the 24th of July as Pioneer Day, as big a celebration for some American Mormons as the 4th of July. This is the day that Mormons, led by Brigham Young, are said to have arrived in Salt Lake Valley. In Utah, Pioneer Day is a holiday, as well as a church holy day, and is celebrated with parades, fireworks, rodeos, picnics, and where possible, performances by the Mormon Tabernacle Choir. Mormons in the rest of the world remember the pioneers in a variety of unofficial ways (or not at all, in some cases, as this is not a required holy day). Some Mormons also celebrate the 1830 founding of the LDS Church on April 6 annually.

Mormons in the World

There are approximately 15.6 million Latter-day Saints in the world, and they can be found, usually in small numbers, in most countries. In most instances, Mormons comprise less than 1% of a country's population. Despite this, though, sometimes their actual numbers can be quite high: Brazil and Mexico both have well over a million members of the LDS Church, and the Philippines has three-quarters of a million. Though more Mormons live outside of the United States than in it, the US has the most Mormons of any single country: about 6.5 million. Within the United States, ten states have over 100,000 Mormons, and Utah has over 2 million. Utah is not only home to most American Mormons; it is also the most religiously homogenous state, as approximately 68% of Utah is Mormon.

Baha'i Religion

History

Baha'i religion emerged from a collection of creative Shi'a reformers known as Babis. In the "Theology" section that follows, I shall summarize the theological claims and status of the Bab and Baha'u'llah, but here I shall focus on the historical outline of the development and establishment of a new religion. In 1844, in the Iranian city of Shiraz, Sayyid Ali-Muhammad (1819–1850) persuaded a Shi'a cleric that he was a new Bab (see Chapter Seven), and Ali-Muhammad's followers came therefore to be called

Millenarianism

Babis, and therefore Baha'is, claim to have emerged as a distinct religion in 1844 CE, a not very significant-sounding year. But on the Islamic calendar, the timing is both deeply significant and symbolic. The twelfth Imam went into occultation in the Islamic year 260, and 1844 equates to the Islamic year 1260. Thus, Babis could claim that God sent Ali-Muhammad to end one thousand years of occultation and start a new era of light.

The belief that significant events happen in one-thousand-year increments, a common feature of religions, is called millenarianism.

It often manifests in widespread excitement for social change, or the end of an always-corrupt and malevolent present. Often there are expectations concerning the arrival of great figures (e.g., messiahs, prophets, healers) or the inauguration of the end of time (e.g., an eschatological battle, the reversal of the social order). Millenarian beliefs factored very largely not only in the theology of Baha'is but also in the theology of Christians, Mormons, the many Jewish messianic claimants, and the Iranian Revolution. It was even seen socially in the panic surrounding Y2K.

Babis. He eventually claimed to be the *Mahdi*, or messiah. As Babi missionary work expanded, the number of Ali-Muhammad's followers increased and his claims became more widely known. This brought official as well as popular persecution, and when Babis fought back, they were branded as dangerous fanatics. Ali-Muhammad himself was executed in 1850.

Babis might have disappeared entirely at that point, certainly the goal of the authorities at the time, were it not for the emergence of two half-brothers in 1853 to contend for leadership of the Babis: Mirza Yahya and **Mirza Husayn Ali** (1817–1892). The second of these figures would become the more widely respected among Babis, and he soon took on the title *Baha*, or Glory, and from there the full title *Baha'u'llah*, meaning Glory of God. Those who were loyal to him were called followers of Baha, and from there Baha'is.

The reinvigorated Babi movement became the target of persecution again in what is now Iran, but Mirza Husayn Ali found protection and safety in the Ottoman Empire. The situation was complex, because on the one hand, he was being expelled from what is now Iran and summoned by the Ottoman Empire, while on the other hand he appears to have enjoyed quite a warm welcome. The fact is: Husayn Ali's relationship with the Ottomans ranged from generosity and adulation to house arrest. He arrived in 1863 in Istanbul; however, either because he refused to play the role of humble client to his Ottoman patrons, or because of political pressure from Iran, Husayn Ali was soon thereafter removed to a small city called Erdine. From Erdine, he produced many theological writings and directed the travels of his

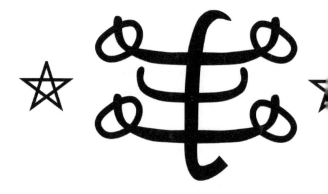

Figure 104. Baha'i symbol.

missionaries. The Ottomans eventually tired of him, and in 1868, Husayn Ali was arrested and exiled to Akka, a city in Ottoman Syria, now called Acre or Akko and since 1948 controlled by Israel.

From Erdine and from Akka, Husayn Ali was able to communicate with his followers in Iran in particular and, as communities arose, around the world. His imprisonment conditions eased in 1870, though he was still confined to the city itself, and in 1877 he was finally free to leave.

From the Akka prison, Husayn Ali wrote some of his more famous "proclamations," which took the form of letters to world leaders. These letters were addressed to the Shah of Iran Nasirud-Din, the British Queen Victoria, the French emperor Napoleon III, the Tsar of Russia Alexander II, Pope Pius IX, and several Shi'a clerics, and were signed with the theological title "Baha'u'llah." In these letters, Husayn Ali pleaded for religious tolerance of Baha'is and the end of war, extolled the end to slavery and the rise of democracy, called for care for the poor, and proclaimed himself variously as the spiritual return of Jesus Christ, the fulfillment of the biblical messiah, and as God's chosen one. He instructed the Pope to sell off all of the lavish property of the Catholic Church, and to live in poverty, and condemned the Iranian Shi'a clerics for corrupting the teachings of Islam. Husayn Ali died in 1892 just outside of Akka on a property called Bahji.

Husayn Ali designated his eldest son, Abbas (1844–1921), to lead the community after his death, at which point Abbas took the title Abdul-Baha, which means "Servant of Glory." This is how most Baha'is know him. That decision was contested by a few family members, led by Abbas's younger half-brother. Baha'is were once again under suspicion from Ottoman officials, yet Abbas was able to oversee the establishment and growth of Baha'i communities in Iran, Russia, Egypt, Turkey, China, Japan, Canada, and the United States by communicating with converts in these locations. The holy sites revered by Baha'is were established under the guidance of Abbas, who secured the remains of Sayyid Ali-Muhammad and had the Shrine of the Bab built in Haifa, Israel.

Revolution in Turkey in 1908 led to the easing of restrictions for many Ottoman prisoners. Now completely free, Abbas traveled extensively throughout Europe and North America in 1911–1913, speaking about Baha'i principles. On this lengthy trip, he addressed not parliaments and leaders but churches, synagogues, and mosques. These visits capitalized on the growing popularity of Baha'i religion, which had already arrived in the West. When Abbas went to Chicago in 1912, he participated in the ground-breaking ceremony for the world's first Baha'i temple in Willamette, Illinois, already many years in the planning.

Figure 105. Baha'i temple and gardens in Haifa, Israel.

In his final will, with the authority of his title Abdul-Baha, Abbas made two requests, with lasting implications. The first was to appoint a successor, the young Shoghi Rabbani (1897–1957). Baha'is know him as Shoghi Effendi (Effendi is a term of respect, like Sir), and the title that Abbas gave him: "Guardian of the Cause of God." The second was to echo and elaborate on Husayn Ali's call for the foundation of an international Baha'i governing body called the **Universal House of Justice**. Shoghi Rabbani extended the international push of Baha'is into Europe and North America, and his thirty-five-year tenure leading Baha'is was largely uneventful; he died of influenza while visiting London.

During Shoghi Rabbani's life, Baha'i religion became more administratively efficient and structured. A growing religion requires administrative support, not only to read and respond to letters seeking guidance, but also to assist in questions of governance. He oversaw the establishment of local councils to govern Baha'is everywhere a Baha'i community could be found. These local councils answered to a National Spiritual Assembly, who then answered to a number of international bodies: the International Baha'i Council, the Hands of the Cause of God, and after 1963, the Universal House of Justice.

A few Baha'is chafed at the degree of organization imposed upon them. Though they came to nothing in the end, the most noteworthy opposition to Effendi came from Ruth White in the 1920s, and Ahmad Sohrab in the 1930s, both Americans. White left the religion of her own accord, while Sohrab was excommunicated for his opposition. As we shall see below, unquestioned acceptance of the divine theological authority of Baha'u'llah, Abdul-Baha, and Shoghi Effendi remains key to Baha'i membership.

Shoghi Rabbani's death in 1957 was sudden and unexpected, and he did not leave a will or indicate who should succeed his guardianship. In the absence of other options, the Hands of the Cause of God set in motion the foundation of the Universal House of Justice. The future founding of this institution was endorsed in the writings of Husayn Ali (as Baha'u'llah) and Abbas (as Abdul-Baha), but Shoghi Rabbani had decided that the world Baha'i community was not quite large or mature enough for

it yet. In the crisis of leadership that followed Shoghi Rabbani's death, however, the Hands moved forward with it, setting up first an interim group called the Custodians, who then gave way to the Universal House of Justice in 1963.

By the 1960s, the long-standing practice of *appointing* members to national councils was replaced by the practice of electing them, Baha'is in each location electing their own national council members. This was carried forward to the Universal House of Justice, which is composed of nine male members democratically elected every five years by all the members of the approximately 180 National Spiritual Assemblies around the world. The Universal House of Justice continues to serve as the supreme governing body for all Baha'i matters.

Core Theological Ideas

Founders and Foundations

The foundational theological claim of Babis, and from there Baha'is, is that Sayyid Ali-Muhammad reinitiated the Shi'a office of the Bab, the figure who acts as an intermediary between God and people. He also claimed to be the *Mahdi*, or messiah, and he assured the arrival of a Promised One, which Mirza Husayn Ali claimed to be when he took on the title Baha'u'llah. As the Baha'u'llah, Husayn Ali then proclaimed that the Bab and himself were each a **Manifestation of God**, the most recent in a long line of Manifestations, which includes but is not limited to Abraham, Moses, Jesus, Muhammad, Zoroaster, Krishna, and the Buddha.

Later Baha'is conceived of Baha'u'llah as the most Mighty Branch, the perfect Exemplar, the unerring interpreter, and the incarnation of every perfect virtue. He was highly revered. Abbas was similarly theologized, not only in the title Abdul-Baha; Husayn Ali gave him the title Guardian of the Cause of God, and Shoghi Rabbani called him a "mystery of God." This was a way of saying that Abdul-Baha was not the equal of the Bab or Baha'u'llah, but was nonetheless without human error. These theological claims and their acceptance form the foundation of Baha'i religion.

Baha'i Beliefs

Baha'i theology is monotheistic, and in it God is described in much the same terms as in Islamic theology: merciful, compassionate, and forgiving, and so on. In fact, Baha'is claim that Baha is the hundredth name of God, completing the ninety-nine given to Muslims. Baha'is also believe that the only way to know anything about God is through the divine messengers sent by God, called Manifestations of God.

One of the key theological concepts upheld by most Baha'is concerns the doctrine of the **Covenant**, which refers to the obligation of loyalty and obedience to the authority of the Bab, who predicted the arrival of Baha'u'llah, who appointed the Abdul-Baha, who appointed Shoghi Effendi. Rejecting that line of divine succession or attempting to insert oneself into it threatens the unity of the religion; people who do so are called Covenant Breakers. Since Shoghi Rabbani died before he could appoint a

Figure 106. This photograph may be of the students of Tarbiyat School for Girls which was established by the Baha'i Community of Tehran in 1911; the school was closed by government decree in 1934.

successor, the Universal House of Justice took over that Covenant.

There is no single version of the principles of Baha'i belief, but ten were especially commonly touched on in the public speeches of Abbas. They are: 1) The oneness of humanity: that humanity is a single tree, the nations its branches, and people its leaves. This truth, properly recognized, would bring permanent peace to the world. 2) One world government: that until people come to accept the first principle, they are to be assisted in peaceful living by submitting to an international court of arbitration to settle their disputes peacefully. 3) Independent investigation of truth: that no single person or group can understand all things perfectly, and that all people must seek the truth out for themselves. 4) Oneness of all religions: there is one religion serving one God, and all religions have worked progressively towards ever-improving expression of that religion. Thus since Baha'u'llah is the most recent such expression, he is the closest to understanding divine reality, but he was not the last. 5) Science and religion do not operate in opposition to each other: religious beliefs that are not consistent with science are nothing more than superstitions; at the same time, science without religion is empty. 6) Equality of men and women: men and women must have the same rights, and the same access to education; only then can there be peace, prosperity, and progress. 7) Elimination of prejudice: all forms of prejudice, whether based on nationality, political affiliation, ethnicity or race, religion, or sex, are destructive. 8) Mandatory education: not only should women have equal access to education, but education should be required of all people. Education is the surest path to mutual understanding, which leads naturally to peace. 9) Reducing the gap between rich and poor: though the rich have the comforts and ease of life that come with wealth, they cannot have happiness until they give up some of that wealth to the poor, such that no one has to struggle to survive. 10) A universal auxiliary language: though all people should be trained in their native language, they should also all be trained in a single universal language, in order to facilitate international communication and stress human unity.

Baha'i Theological Writings

Baha'is give tens of thousands of texts the theological authority of "scripture." These include the writings of Sayyid Ali-Muhammad (as the Bab) and Mirza Husayn Ali (as the Baha'u'llah) as the highest level of scriptural authority, followed by the writings of Abbas (as the Abdul-Baha) and Shoghi Rabbani, and to a lesser extent the written decisions of the Universal House of Justice. The total volume dwarfs the scriptural volume of the Bible or Qur'an, and covers topics such as law, social justice, apologetics, mystical revelation, history, governance and politics, and above all in volume, letters to communities and to individuals called Tablets. Baha'is maintain that Husayn Ali wrote in excess of

---

The Gleanings

The *Gleanings* is a popular compilation of selections from the Tablets that Husayn Ali wrote, translated by Shoghi Rabbani. This passage reflects the stress he put on education, arguing that education leads to peace and freedom for all. Note the deliberate style of English that Rabbani chose, mimicking the English of the famous King James Version of the Christian Bible.

Man is the supreme Talisman. Lack of a proper education hath, however, deprived him of that which he doth inherently possess . . . Education can, alone, cause it to reveal its treasures, and enable mankind to benefit therefrom . . . If the learned and worldly-wise men of this age were to allow mankind to inhale the fragrance of fellowship and love, every understanding heart would apprehend the meaning of true liberty, and discover the secret of undisturbed peace and absolute composure.

Gleanings from the Writings of Baha'u'llah 122.

fifteen thousand Tablets, signed with the authority of the Baha'u'llah.

Though all are authoritative and though all are considered divinely guided, these sources of theological authority can be further distinguished: the writings of the Bab and Baha'u'llah are considered divine revelation; Abdul-Baha and Shoghi Effendi are considered infallible interpreters of the writings of the Bab and Baha'u'llah; and finally, the Universal House of Justice is entrusted to offer legislation and explanation, but not interpretation. The writings of Baha'u'llah (though he preferred dictation over writing himself), Abdul-Baha, and Shoghi Effendi can be used to establish proper belief and practice; the writings of the Bab are inspiring and foundational, but in legal matters they were superseded by Baha'i writings that followed, and the decisions of the Universal House of Justice are binding, but not a source of doctrine.

The vast majority of these writings were composed originally in Persian and Arabic. But Baha'is do not give either Persian or Arabic any exalted scriptural status. They are encouraged to read these writings in their own language, and translation of Baha'i texts is therefore a constant enterprise. To date, less than 10% of Baha'i Arabic and Persian texts have been translated into English. English is also a key language in the theological expression of Baha'is: Shoghi Effendi generally composed his theological writings in English, and he was a deeply respected English translator of many of Husayn Ali's and Abbas's writings. Also, the decisions of the Universal House of Justice are issued in English and translated as quickly as possible, though English is used as the primary language of communication among Baha'i institutions.

Though Husayn Ali wrote a tremendous amount in the name Baha'u'llah, all of which is highly revered, arguably his most important work, and the most foundational book for Baha'is as a religion, is his *Kitab-i-Aqdas*, commonly called *The Most Holy Book*. It is a book of laws, and was originally completed in 1873, while he was imprisoned in Akka. The text was later supplemented by a series of answers he gave to questions posed to him by a secretary. This book set down laws governing prayer, fasting, marriage and divorce, inheritance, and civil/property laws. As we shall see below, these laws strongly echo the predominantly Islamic environment from which Baha'is drew.

Baha'i Practice and Holy Days

The development of Baha'i theology was deeply reliant on Shi'a theological ideas. It was also deeply reliant on Sufism. Baha'i discussions about practice emphasize love of, devotion to, and unity with God. Like Sufism's endorsement of *fana*, or annihilation (see Chapter Seven), Husayn Ali's *Seven Valleys* imagines seven stages that lead to "absolute nothingness," in which the self ceases to exist.

Baha'i life is meant to be embedded in the real world. One must avoid attachment to worldly and material distractions (such as money, career, and prestige), but one is to remain engaged with the world. Prayer, for instance, should not merely be about communing with God, but ought to motivate one to action that improves the world. To the same end, ideal Baha'i personal characteristics emphasize social relationships over individual piety, in that courtesy, truthfulness, and integrity are more critical than perfect piety and adherence to divine law. Lying, slander, gossip, and gloating over the failures or sins of others are strongly discouraged.

While there is no equivalent to the detailed and rigorous science of establishing Islamic law for every aspect of life, Baha'i practices do generally resemble some Islamic practices. For instance, prayer, fasting, and a tax are all obligatory. Husayn Ali composed hundreds of prayers for different occasions. Prayer is mandatory once a day, commonly around noon, for Baha'is over fifteen years old, and there are three versions, varying in length, from which one can choose. The shortest prayer reads: "I bear witness, O my God, that Thou has created me to know Thee and to worship Thee. I testify, at this moment, to my powerlessness and to Thy might, to my poverty and to Thy wealth. There is none other God but Thee, the Help in Peril, the Self-Subsisting." Before the daily prayer, one is to perform a ritual cleansing, and the direction of prayer, or *qibla*, is the tomb of Baha'u'llah at Bahji. Longer prayers also involve prostration, and are spoken in the language of the worshipper; it is not required that the prayers be spoken in the Arabic or Persian of their composition.

Given that there are only ten Houses of Worship, serving (primarily) continents not communities, congregational prayer is not a feature of Baha'i worship (though there are occasions when Baha'is pray together). When prayer happens in community, it is done in homes and rented spaces, but otherwise it tends to be done individually. Sermons and a liturgical structure are absent from Baha'i worship.

Baha'is between fifteen and seventy years old, in good physical health, and not pregnant, nursing, menstruating, traveling, or undertaking harsh manual labor, practice the obligatory Nineteen Day Fast during the nineteen-day month of Alá (generally March 2–20), the last month of the year. The fast happens from dawn to dusk each day of the month, and applies to all food, drink, and to smoking. Baha'is do not consider the fast an act of self-punishment, but rather an invigoration of the soul.

The third main Baha'i practice is a tax called *Huququ'llah*, or **Huquq** for short. The term means the "right of God," and it represents the belief that since all things come from God, they belong to and are therefore owed to God. Baha'is with an annual wealth beyond approximately $3000 are obligated to pay 19% annually of the wealth beyond what they need to survive. Thus, the tax is not applied to value of one's home or business, but only to the excess amount. Today the tax is paid to the Universal House of Justice, and it is policed only by individual conscience. Baha'is share with Muslims the belief that giving up a portion of one's wealth purifies people of their attachment to it. The money is used for missions and outreach, for the maintenance of Baha'i properties, and for care of the poor.

In terms of diet, there are no foods that Baha'is must avoid, though consumption of intoxicants such as alcohol and mind-altering drugs is forbidden. Smoking is explicitly discouraged, but not forbidden, and vegetarianism is explicitly endorsed, but not required.

The Baha'i calendar follows a solar cycle and has nineteen months of nineteen days each. This requires the use of an intercalary period in order to match the length of the solar year: four (sometimes five) days inserted between the last two months of the year. And like Judaism and Islam, Baha'i holy days begin at sundown on the day previous to the dates given below. The intercalary period is treated as a holy period in itself: extra charity and gift-giving are practiced in this period preceding the fast.

Baha'is meet on the first day of each month for one of the Nineteen Day Feasts, offering the opportunity for congregational fellowship, spiritual devotion, and administrative business. Homes but also sometimes community centers are the location for these events, and they are open only to members of the religion. The title "feast" is mostly symbolic, for these meetings need to involve only modest provisions. In some locations, this meal is conducted as a potlatch-style meal, while in other places someone hosts the meal and feeds the guests.

There are six key holy days that Baha'is observe, along with a few of lesser importance. The key holy days require the day off work and school, and they are Naw-Ruz, Ridvan, the Twin Birthdays, the Declaration of the Bab, the Martyrdom of the Bab, and the Ascension of Baha'u'llah.

The year 2015 marked an important change in Baha'i practice: the implementation of the **Badi** calendar, which started on March 20, 2015. The Badi calendar detaches the Baha'i calendar from the solar, or Gregorian calendar. It does so by setting the Iranian city of Tehran (the birthplace of Husayn Ali) as the place for measuring the precise moment of the vernal equinox, and using that to mark the start of the new year for all Baha'is around the world. In addition, they decided to rely on astronomical tables rather than personal sightings, making it more precise and predictable. The irony is

that the Badi calendar introduces fluctuation in the timing of Baha'i holy days where there used to be consistency. For example, Naw-Ruz used to fall on March 21, and now it will be either March 20 or March 21. Likewise, all Baha'i holy days will follow suit.

The Baha'i New Year is celebrated on the holy day of Naw-Ruz, March 20 or 21. The distinct spelling (see Chapter Ten) is deliberate; it represents the Baha'i wish to distinguish their holy day from the competing cultural and religious holy day. While the celebration of Nowruz among Shi'a has sometimes been controversial because of its non-Islamic origins, Ali-Muhammad and Husayn Ali wrote explicitly about the significance of the renewal of time that the holy day represents. Abbas considered the vernal equinox a symbol of the divine Messenger, or Manifestation of God. The fact that the Baha'i fast happens in the last month of the Baha'i year means that in effect, the feast of Naw-Ruz not only begins a new year but also celebrates the end of the fast; the fast thus ends at sundown on March 20 or 21, and the observance of Naw-Ruz for some begins right then with a celebratory dinner. Naw-Ruz is above all for Baha'is a time for spiritual renewal, emblematic of spring renewal, and of reflection on the unity of all the various Messengers whom God has sent.

Ridvan, which Husayn Ali ordained and called the Most Great Festival, lasts for twelve days, during which the first, ninth, and twelfth days (falling on April 20/21, 28/29, and May 1/2) are particularly marked and considered holy days in and of themselves. Ridvan (meaning "paradise") was the name Husayn Ali gave the garden where he stayed on the eve of his departure from Baghdad to Istanbul in 1863. It was there that he revealed to his inner circle of supporters his exalted status as "him whom God shall make manifest" alluded to in the writings of Ali-Muhammad. The first, ninth, and twelfth day represent the day of Husayn Ali's arrival to the garden, the day of his family's arrival there, and finally the day of his departure for Istanbul. During Ridvan, Baha'is hear and reflect on the Tablets of Baha'u'llah, some written about himself during Ridvan and some written for the purpose of its celebration, seeing in this day the inauguration of the most recent Manifestation of God. In addition to spiritual reflection, Baha'is gather on these days for meals and celebratory parties; they are encouraged to celebrate according to their own cultural context.

Interestingly, the first day of Ridvan is also the time designated for the annual election of the nine people who comprise each Local Spiritual Assembly. Elections also happen at the national level for each National Spiritual Assembly, and every five years during Ridvan the members of the Universal House of Justice are elected. Participation in this electoral process is considered by many Baha'is to be a religious obligation.

Baha'i theological tradition sees a very deep connection between the Bab and Baha'u'llah. Both were Manifestations of God, and Baha'u'llah was the fulfillment of predictions of the Bab. Because of this, they are called the Twin Manifestations. The closely integrated theological relationship can be seen in a number of ways. First, Baha'is celebrate the Declaration of the Bab – his announcement that he was a Messenger of God – every May 23/24, and they remember the Martyrdom of the Bab every July 9/10.

The close theological relationship can also be seen in traditions about and celebrations of the birthdays of the Bab and Baha'u'llah. For over a century, their birthdays were celebrated separately on their solar days (October 20 for the Bab; November 12 for Baha'u'llah). However, another feature of the implementation of the Badi calendar involved the pairing of these birthdays into a single two-day celebration called the Twin Birthdays. The timing was set as the first and second day of the eighth new moon after Naw-Ruz. These will now fall in October–November on the solar calendar. The first ever celebration of the Twin Birthdays as a single festival was November 13–14, 2015.

The Ascension of Baha'u'llah is celebrated on the day of his death, May 28/29, ideally at 3 am on the appropriate day, the moment of his death at Bahji. Baha'is reflect on the difficult life of Baha'u'llah and celebrate how he was able to respond peacefully to those who persecuted him, and may read or chant portions of his writings.

Baha'is in the World

Since 1963, the number of National Spiritual Assemblies in the world has tripled, a reflection of the quickly growing numbers of Baha'is internationally. Consistent with that, the global number of Baha'is has reached approximately five million. There are eight continental Houses of Worship in the world – in Australia, Germany, India, Panama, Samoa, Uganda, the United States, and Chile (and two local Houses of Worship). About 25% of the world's Baha'is live in India; the United States has the second-largest number of Baha'is in the world.

Chapter Summary

This chapter has looked at two new religions that have grown out of old religions, their predecessors. The phenomenon is no different than Christianity and Islam growing out of what preceded them. Sometimes the new developments maintain old ideas and practices, and sometimes they develop innovative new ideas, but always they are shaped by the world around them. Thus, this too would apply to Judaism, which though we cannot know whether it "grew" out a predecessor religion was certainly shaped by its encounter with the world around it.

LDS Glossary

Exaltation. By undergoing the Ordinances and living the life of a committed Mormon, one can hope to achieve Exaltation. To be exalted is more than mere eternal life-after-death. Rather, it is to become a god, not God that is, but "like God."

Godhead. Mormons believe in God, Jesus Christ, and Holy Spirit, but they do not agree with the Christian formulation of the Trinity: three persons in one entity. Rather, they believe that God, Jesus Christ, and Holy Spirit are separate individuals, which together comprise the Godhead.

Ordinances. Special services that take place only at an LDS temple, and only in the presence of other Mormons: Priesthood Ordination, the Endowment, and Celestial Marriage. Mormons must undergo these Ordinances in order to achieve Exaltation.

Sacrament Meetings. The name of weekly LDS worship services. These occur in chapels and churches, never at temples, which are reserved for the Ordinances. LDS worship includes the singing of hymns, prayer, sermons, and local church business. These services are open to all people.

Sealing. Sealing is a ritual that married couples and families can undergo, in which through the ritual people are connected beyond death. Married couples in this state can continue to produce children after death. As with all Mormon rituals, this one too can be performed vicariously, that is for a deceased person, in which the deceased is given the opportunity to be sealed if they were unable to while living.

Second Great Awakening. An intense, Protestant revival movement located in the north-east United States in the nineteenth century. This millenarian movement stressed enthusiastic and exuberant experience of the Holy Spirit, populism, individual theological creativity, and rejection of skepticism.

Other Important LDS Vocabulary

Bishop	Endowment	Nauvoo	Telestial Kingdom
Book of Mormon	Missouri Extermination Order	Pearl of Great Price	Temple Garment
Brigham Young		President	Terrestrial Kingdom
Celestial Kingdom	Moroni	Priesthood Ordination	Utah War
Celestial Marriage	Mountain Meadows Massacre	Sons of Perdition	Vicarious ordinances
Doctrine and Covenants			

Baha'i Glossary

Badi. The name of the new Baha'i calendar, inaugurated in November 2015. Development of this calendar marks the deliberate split with the Christian Gregorian calendar. The new year begins on the calculated vernal equinox in Tehran, and all other holy days are timed relative to that date. Thus, Baha'i holy days will always fall on one day or another, instead of the same day annually as before.

Covenant. The acceptance of the Covenant in Baha'i religion means to accept the rightful order and the authority of the theological offices of the Bab, Baha'u'llah, Abdul-Baha, Shoghi Effendi, followed by the Universal House of Justice. Those who challenge, reject, or try to place themselves in that order are called Covenant Breakers.

Huquq. The spiritual obligation to return to God 19% of all wealth and property holdings whose value exceeds about 2.2 oz of gold. It is a voluntary payment, collected and disbursed by the Universal House of Justice.

Manifestation of God. Each great religious founder and figure is, in the estimation of Baha'i religion, a Manifestation of God: Abraham, Moses, Jesus Christ, Muhammad, Krishna, Zoroaster, Buddha, and also Ali-Muhammad and Husayn Ali. These figures all came to particular people in particular times, and therefore manifestations will continue. Husayn Ali, as the Baha'u'llah, is the most recent one; he is not the final one.

Mirza Husayn Ali. Born in Persian Tehran in 1817 into an elite family. At the age of twenty-five he claimed to be the Manifestation of God promised by the Bab, and then eventually to be returned and reincarnated figures of the world's religions. He thus took on the title Glory of God, or as he is more commonly known, Baha'u'llah.

Universal House of Justice. Extolled and described in early Baha'i writings, the Universal House of Justice was established in 1963 because Shoghi Abbas died before he could appoint a successor in the role of Guardian of the Faith.

Other Important Baha'i Vocabulary

Abdul-Baha	Bahji	Martyrdom of the Bab	Shoghi Effendi
Akka	Covenant Breakers	Millenarianism	Tablets
Ascension of Baha'u'llah	Declaration of the Bab	Naw-Ruz	Twin Birthdays
Babism	*Kitab-i-Aqdas*	Nineteen Day Fast	
	Mahdi	Ridvan	

Discussion Questions

1. The foundation and development of what would become the religions of Judaism, Christianity, and Islam happened in very ancient settings. In contrast, the first Mormons and Baha'is lived in a context that was modern and very soon to be characterized by science and secularism. Can you see this difference reflected in those two religions?

2. Geography is often a key component of religious identity. Most Jews, Christians, Muslims, and Baha'is look to Israel and the Middle East for their historical origins. Mormons in contrast tied their religion to the United States from the very beginning. How is this reflected in features of LDS theology and identity?

3. Mormons and Baha'is both grew out of long-standing religions, were persecuted, and survived. What do we learn about the history of religion from this?

4. Two of the persistent questions in the study of religion concern how religions are founded and how they survive, but because Judaism, Christianity, and Islam started so long ago, we lack many of the data that might allow us to answer those questions. Given that the history of Mormons and Baha'is happened so much more recently, does studying them help us to answer questions about more ancient religions?

Recommended Reading

Bushman, Richard Lyman. 2008. *Mormonism: A Very Short Introduction.* Oxford: Oxford University Press.

Davies, Douglas J. 2003. *An Introduction to Mormonism.* Cambridge: Cambridge University Press.

Ostling, Richard N., and Joan K. Ostling. 1999. *Mormon America: The Power and the Promise.* San Francisco, CA: HarperCollins.

Smith, Peter. 2008. *A Concise Encyclopedia of the Bahá'í Faith.* London: Oneworld Publishing (Reprint).

Smith, Peter. 2008. *An Introduction to the Baha'i Faith.* Cambridge: Cambridge University Press.

Stockton, Robert H. 2013. *The Bahá'í Faith: A Guide for the Perplexed.* London: Bloomsbury.

Recommended Websites

http://eom.byu.edu

- The original *Encyclopedia of Mormonism* (New York: Macmillan, 1992) published by Daniel H. Ludlow is now updated and available free at this site.

https://www.lds.org

- Official website of the LDS Church.

http://www.bahai.org/library

- Contains many Baha'i texts in translation.

http://bahaiteachings.org/bahai-faith

- A good summary of Baha'is today, with many discussions of contemporary issues from a Baha'i perspective.

Bibliography

Adair, James R. 2008. *Introducing Christianity*. World Religions Series. London: Routledge.

Ahmad, Aziz. 1960. "Sayyid Aḥmad Khān, Jamāl Al-Dīn Al-Afghānī and Muslim India." *Studia Islamica* 13: 55–78.

Ahmed, Leila. 1992. *Women and Gender in Islam: Historical Roots of a Modern Debate*. New Haven, CT: Yale University Press.

Ali, Kecia. 2014. *The Lives of Muhammad*. Cambridge, MA: Harvard University Press.

Beavis, Mary Ann, and Michael J. Gilmore, eds. 2012. *Dictionary of the Bible and Western Culture*. Sheffield: Sheffield Phoenix Press.

Bell, Catherine. 2008. "Extracting the Paradigm: Ouch!" *Method & Theory in the Study of Religion* 20: 114–24.

Berg, Herbert. 2009. *Elijah Muhammad and Islam*. New York: New York University Press.

Bowden, John, ed. 2005. *Encyclopedia of Christianity*. New York: Oxford University Press.

Braun, Willi, and Russell T. McCutcheon, eds. 2000. *Guide to the Study of Religion*. London: Cassell.

Bushman, Richard Lyman. 2008. *Mormonism: A Very Short Introduction*. Oxford: Oxford University Press.

Campo, Juan E., ed. 2009. *Encyclopedia of Islam*. New York: Facts on File.

Chadwick, Robert. 2005. *First Civilizations: Ancient Mesopotamia and Ancient Egypt*. Sheffield: Equinox Publishing.

Clark, Stephen R.L. 1990. "World Religions and World Orders." *Religious Studies* 26: 43–57.

Cobbing, Felicity, and David Jacobson. 2015. *Distant Views of the Holy Land*. Sheffield: Equinox Publishing.

Davies, J. Douglas. 2003. *An Introduction to Mormonism*. Cambridge: Cambridge University Press.

Davies, Philip R. 2018. *The Bible for the Curious: A Brief Encounter*. Sheffield: Equinox Publishing.

Dickson, William Rory, and Meena Sharify-Funk. 2017. *Unveiling Sufism: From Manhattan to Mecca*. Sheffield: Equinox Publishing.

Dorff, Elliot N., and Louis E. Newman, eds. 1999. *Contemporary Jewish Theology: A Reader*. Oxford: Oxford University Press.

Droge, Arthur J. 2012. *The Qur'ān: A New Annotated Translation*. Sheffield: Equinox Publishing.

Durkheim, Émile. 1915. *The Elementary Forms of the Religious Life*. New York: Macmillan.

Bibliography

Efron, John, Steven Weitzman, Matthias Lehmann, and Joshua Halo. 2009. *The Jews: A History*. Upper Saddle River, NJ: Pearson Education.

Ehrman, Bart D. 2012. *The New Testament: A Historical Introduction to the Early Christian Writings*. Vol. 5. Oxford: Oxford University Press.

Eliade, Mircea. 1957. *The Sacred and the Profane: The Nature of Religion*. Translated by Willard R. Trask. New York: Harcourt, Brace, & World.

Ende, Werner. 1978. "The Flagellations of Muharram and the Shi'ite 'Ulama.'" *Der Islam* 55: 19–36.

Ernst, Carl W. 2011. *How to Read the Qur'an: A New Guide, with Select Translations*. Durham, NC: North Carolina Press.

Fitzgerald, Timothy. 2006. "Bruce Lincoln's 'Theses on Method': Antitheses." *Method & Theory in the Study of Religion* 18: 392–423.

Foley, Michael P. 2005. *Why Do Catholics Eat Fish on Friday? The Catholic Origin to Just About Everything*. New York: Macmillan.

Frazer, J.G. 1929. *The Golden Bough: A Study in Magic and Religion*. New York: Macmillan.

Freud, Sigmund. 1964. *The Standard Edition of the Complete Works of Freud*. Edited by J. Strachey. London: The Hogarth Press.

Gómez-Bravo, Ana M. 2017. *Comida y cultura en el mundo hispánico* [*Food and Culture in the Hispanic World*]. Sheffield: Equinox Publishing.

Gutiérrez, Avelino, and Magdalena Valor. 2014. *The Archaeology of Medieval Spain, 1100–1500*. Sheffield: Equinox Publishing.

Haider, Najam. 2014. *Shi'i Islam: An Introduction*. New York: Cambridge University Press.

Halbertal, Moshe. 2013. *Maimonides: Life and Thought*. Translated by Joel Linsider. Princeton, NJ: Princeton University Press.

Hartman, Tova. 2007. *Feminism Encounters Traditional Judaism: Resistance and Accommodation*. Waltham, MA: Brandeis University Press.

Harvey, Graham, and Jessica Hughes. 2018. *Sensual Religion: Religion and the Five Senses*. Sheffield: Equinox Publishing.

Hodgson, Marshall G.S. 1974. *The Venture of Islam: Conscience and History in a World Civilization*. Chicago: University of Chicago Press.

Hoffman, Lawrence A. 1986. *The Canonization of the Synagogue Service*. Notre Dame, IN: University of Notre Dame Press.

Hughes, Aaron W. 2015. *Islam and the Tyranny of Authenticity: An Inquiry into Disciplinary Apologetics and Self-Deception*. Sheffield: Equinox Publishing.

Johnson, Paul. 1987. *A History of the Jews*. San Francisco: Harper & Row.

Jung, Dietrich. 2011. *Orientalists, Islamists and the Global Public Sphere: A Genealogy of the Modern Essentialist Image of Islam*. Sheffield: Equinox Publishing,.

Keller, Rosemary Skinner, and Rosemary Radford Ruether, eds. 2006. *The Encyclopedia of Women and Religion in North America*. Bloomington, IN: Indiana University Press.

King, Richard, ed. 2017. *Religion, Theory, Critique: Classic and Contemporary Approaches and Methodologies*. New York: Columbia University Press.

Knauf, Ernst Axel, and Philippe Guillaume. 2016. *A History of Biblical Israel: The Fate of the Tribes and Kingdoms from Merenptah to Bar Kochba*. Sheffield: Equinox Publishing.

Koschorke, Klaus, Frieder Ludwig, and Mariano Delgado, eds. 2007. *History of Christianity in Asia, Africa, and Latin America, 1450–1990: A Documentary Sourcebook.* Grand Rapids, MI: Wm. B. Eerdman's Publishing.

Kraemer, David C. 2007. *Jewish Eating and Identity Throughout the Ages.* New York: Routledge.

Küng, Hans. 2007. *Islam: Past, Present and Future.* Oxford: Oneworld Publications.

Leinsle, Ulrich Gottfried. 2010. *Introduction to Scholastic Theology.* Washington, DC: Catholic University of America Press.

Lincoln, Bruce. 2007. "Concessions, Confessions, Clarifications, Ripostes: By Way of Response to Tim Fitzgerald." *Method & Theory in the Study of Religion* 19(1): 163–168.

———. 1996. "Theses on Method." *Method & Theory in the Study of Religion* 8: 225–227.

MacWilliams, Mark, Joanne Punzo Waghorne, Deborah Sommer, Cybelle Shattuck, Kay A. Read, Selva J. Raj, Khaled Keshk, *et al.* 2005. "Religion/s Between Covers: Dilemmas of the World Religions Textbook." *Religious Studies Review* 31: 1–36.

Maffly-Kipp, Laurie F., Leigh E. Schmidt, and Mark Valeri, eds. 2006. *Practicing Protestants: Histories of Christian Life in America, 1630–1965.* Baltimore, MD: Johns Hopkins University Press.

Marx, Karl, and Friedrich Engels. 1964. *Karl Marx and Friedrich Engels on Religion.* Edited by Niebuhr Reinhold. New York: Schocken Books.

Masuzawa, Tomoko. 2005. *The Invention of World Religions: Or, How European Universalism Was Preserved in the Language of Pluralism.* Chicago: University of Chicago Press.

McCutcheon, Russell T. 1997. *Manufacturing Religion: The Discourse on Sui Generis Religion and the Politics of Nostalgia.* New York: Oxford University Press.

———. 1999. *The Insider/Outsider Problem in the Study of Religion: A Reader.* London: Cassell.

McDannell, Colleen. 1995. *Material Christianity: Religion and Popular Culture in America.* New Haven, CT: Yale University Press.

Migeon, Gaston, and Henri Saladin. 2009. *Art of Islam.* London: Parkstone International.

Morgan, Michael L. 2001. *Beyond Auschwitz: Post-Holocaust Jewish Thought in America.* New York: Oxford University Press.

Nasrallah, Nawal. 2013. *Delights from the Garden of Eden: A Cookbook and History of the Iraqi Cuisine.* Second Edition. Sheffield: Equinox Publishing.

Nasr, Seyyed Hossein, ed. 2015. *The Study Quran.* New York: HarperCollins.

Nicholson, Reynold A., ed. 1925–1940. *The Mathnawi of Jalalu'ddin Rumi.* London: Gibb Memorial Trust.

Nongbri, Brent. 2013. *Before Religion: A History of a Modern Concept.* Cambridge, MA: Yale University Press.

Orsi, Robert. 2008. "The 'So-Called History' of the Study of Religion." *Method & Theory in the Study of Religion* 20: 134–138.

Ostling, Richard N., and Joan K. Ostling. 1999. *Mormon America: The Power and the Promise.* San Francisco: HarperCollins.

Pals, Daniel L. 2006. *Eight Theories of Religion.* Second Edition. New York: Oxford University Press.

Rippin, Andrew, ed. 2008. *The Islamic World.* London: Routledge.

Safi, Omid. 2003. *Progressive Muslims: On Justice, Gender, and Pluralism.* London: Oneworld Publications.

Schiffman, Lawrence H. 1991. *From Text to Tradition: A History of Second Temple and Rabbinic Judaism.* Hoboken, NJ: Ktav.

Bibliography

Schimmel, Annemarie. 1985. *And Muhammad Is His Messenger: The Veneration of the Prophet in Islamic Piety*. Chapel Hill, NC: University of North Carolina Press.

———. 1975. *Mystical Dimensions of Islam*. Chapel Hill, NC: University of North Carolina Press.

Segal, Eliezer. 2000. *Holidays, History and Halakhah*. Northvale, NJ: Jason Aronson.

Senn, Frank C. 2012. *Introduction to Christian Liturgy*. Minneapolis, MN: Fortress Press.

Shahab, Ahmed. 2016. *What Is Islam? The Importance of Being Islamic*. Princeton, NJ: Princeton University Press.

Smith, Jonathan Z. 2004. *Relating Religion: Essays in the Study of Religion*. Chicago: University of Chicago Press.

———. 1998. "Religion, Religions, Religious." In *Critical Terms for Religious Studies*, edited by Mark C. Taylor, 269–284. Chicago: University of Chicago Press.

Smith, Peter. 2008. *A Concise Encyclopedia of the Bahá'í Faith*. London: Oneworld Publishing.

———. 2008 *An Introduction to the Baha'i Faith*. Cambridge: Cambridge University Press.

Stausberg, Michael. 2008. *Zarathustra and Zoroastrianism*. Translated by Margret Preisler-Weller. Sheffield: Equinox Publishing.

Stockton, Robert H. 2013. *The Bahá'í Faith: A Guide for the Perplexed*. London: Bloomsbury.

Tylor, Edward Bennett. 1903. *Primitive Culture: Researches into the Development of Mythology, Philosophy, Religion, Language, Art, and Customs*. London: J. Murray.

Watt, Montgomery. 1962. *Islamic Philosophy and Theology*. Edinburgh: Edinburgh University Press.

Weber, Max, and Talcott Parsons. 1958. *The Protestant Ethic and the Spirit of Capitalism*. New York: Charles Scribner's Sons.

Williamson, Beth. 2004. *Christian Art: A Very Short Introduction*. New York: Oxford University Press.

Wolfart, Johannes C. 2003. "If I Were a Lutheran, What Would I Do?" *Religious Studies and Theology* 22: 41–54.

Index

Numbers in *italic* denote pages with figures. Numbers in **bold** are used for pages with box text.

Index